THE COMING
DECLINE

THE COMING
DECLINE

A WORLD WITHOUT ECONOMIC GROWTH

MICHAEL WEIDOKAL

To Kate and Jack

TABLE OF CONTENTS

Chapter One

A World That Expects Growth

THE WORLD APPEARS TO have turned against growth. For the longest time, the level of growth achieved by a national, state or local economy was the ultimate measure of that economy's success or failure, and of its health or sickness. However, growth is no longer in favor for many followers of economics as well for many of those who observe and measure the economy, either as a profession or a hobby. For those that would like to see the focus on growth lessened, growth simply ignores too many other issues. For example, in recent years there have been attempts to shift the focus of measuring economic success away from the generation of growth towards more abstract goals such as the creation of happiness or the improvement of a society's quality of life.

It is unlikely that it is a mere coincidence that these attempts to recalibrate the measurement of economic success away from a focus on growth has come at a time when economic growth has become much less certain.

In fact, it is certainly no coincidence that many of those who are leading the efforts to focus on more abstract measurements of economic success are coming from countries or societies that have found themselves unable to generate much economic growth in recent years. Every few months a new study seems to appear touting a new formula to measure economic success, which titles ranging from "The World's Happiest Countries" to "The World's Most Sustainable Economies", with each of these claiming that the era of growth is over, having given way to the era of "happiness" or the era of "sustainability". It should be no surprise that the authors of these studies are often coming from countries or societies that have failed to generate significant economic growth in recent years but have not given up their ambition to explain to the world why their ways of doing things are superior. In fact, these studies often receive a great deal of media coverage, with reporters fawning over the countries that are declared to be the "happiest", or those that are living the most "sustainable" lifestyles, often without questioning how these rankings were compiled, or the agendas of those who compiled them.

While measurements such as happiness, inclusiveness, sustainability and many others all have their merits, the measurement of economic growth remains the essential measure of an economy's health. No other measure better determines the vitality of an economy or the progress that an economy is making over time.

Think of it like a football (or soccer, depending upon your location) match, where happiness is the fluidity in which a team plays, sustainability is the health of the players and inclusiveness is the teamwork. Well, in this analogy, growth is the actual score of the match. The other factors are nice, but it is the score that decides whether or not the team wins or loses and determines where the team is located on the table (or in the standings, again choose your regional preference). If your team loses too many times, your team will be relegated to a lower division. If your economy fails to generate enough growth, your country could fall into a lower group of economies. In this analogy, China has surged to the top flight of countries thanks to decades of soaring economic growth rates, whereas Greece has been relegated to the middle income group of economies due to its lack of economic growth in the 21st century, Simply put, the ability of a country, a state or a city to generate sustained high levels of economic growth conveys power to that country, state or city, whereas an inability to generate economic growth over the longer-term drains a country, state or city of its power and competitiveness.

Growth is also the measure that takes into account more other factors that any other measurements that has been devised so far. While an economic growth figure may seem extremely straightforward at first, in fact, it encompasses a wide range of factors. For example, an economic growth result (we'll focus on the standard GDP growth rate from now on) includes many factors. The growth of the market is a key factor, including consumer spending, business spending and government spending. Likewise, the production of goods and the provision of services are also major components of growth.

Whereas consumption and production are tangible components of economic output and its growth, there are many other variables that go into determining economic growth over the longer-term. These include technological advancements, which plays a crucial role in positioning an economy to grow over longer periods of time. Wealth levels are another important factor, as strong domestic markets shield an economy from many forms of external risk. Economic policy is obviously another important factor, although strong economies can sometimes overcome unsound policy, at least for a period of time. Having access to consumers, especially those with higher levels of purchasing power, is another crucial factor in an economy's ability to generate growth. A well-developed financial system is yet another factor that plays a role in determining an economy's level of growth, while factors such as commercial development and the ability to attract investment also impact how well, or how poorly, an economy does when it comes to its ability to generate growth.

While growth remains the single leading measure of an economy's health and vitality, many economists believe that the use of GDP growth has seen its time come as the sole leading measure of an economy's success and direction. This has led to numerous other measurements being developed as a means of determining the health and vitality of an economy. For example, something called the Genuine Progress Indicator was created a few years ago in order to account for factors such as environmental health and social well-being. This was just one of many such calculations that were created over the past few years to lessen the perceived dependence upon GDP growth as the sole measure of how well an economy was performing.

Many of these new measurements attempt to focus more on living standards and less on economic output. For example, the physical and mental health of a country's population is quantified in many of these new measurements.

Likewise, well-being, often in the form of social and health security, is another popular component of many of these new measurements. Often these alternative measurements are associated with longer-term growth trends, as changes in public health and happiness rarely manifest themselves over the shorter-term. Supporters of these sorts of new economic measurements like to claim that they are a more accurate representation of an economy's impact on the population than standard GDP growth. However, it is also clear that, without long-term GDP growth, high levels of living standards and popular well-being are difficult to maintain.

For most of the world, measuring relative economic power and success is the easiest method for one country to compare its success against another. This is due, in large part, to the fact that there are so many statistics available that can be used to measure one economy's success or relative power against another's. GDP growth rates are very easy to compare, as are measurements of the size of the economy, its share of exports and many more. Just think back to the early months of the Covid-19 pandemic, when comparing international case numbers and fatality rates became an international obsession. In fact, countries compete with one another all the time, and, to a lesser degree, states and provinces compete with their fellow states and provinces, just as cities compete with other cities. Still, the data is much clearer when it comes to country-against-country competition. This does not just apply to economic competition. For example, countries, at least the largest of them, often compete over which has the greater military power. For others, sporting prowess is an important battlefield, with events such as the Olympics serving as a way for countries to attempt to assert their strength and vigor over their rivals. Even culture is not immune from international competition, with issues such as language, music and popular culture often resulting in competition between countries. While all of these other fields may not be directly related to economics, it is clear that, without long-term economic growth, a country's position in areas such as military power, sporting success or cultural influence will weaken over time.

No matter what sort of calculation, formula or concoction is created to measure a country's economic success, they all, so far, fall short of economic growth. First, many of these new calculations are simply too subjective, reflecting the biases of those that created these calculations. For example, countries with extensive social welfare systems have often attempted to create new measurements of economic success that emphasize the importance of wealth equality, extensive social services and other such facets of their economic systems. Likewise, some poorer countries have attempted to shift the focus to happiness, although it is hard to find a more subjective factor to measure. What we keep coming back to is the fact that, no matter what measurements we use to attempt to determine the success and power of a country, a state or a city, we keep coming back to economic growth. Without long-term and sustained economic growth, no country, state or city has been able to significantly enhance their position in the world, or the long-term well-being of their citizens.

The Modern World Has Known Nothing Else Than Growth

Since the Industrial Revolution, countries that have undergone industrialization and modernization have known little other than growth. In general, all of the world's major economies have enjoyed long-term economic growth over most of their modern histories. Sure, there have been periods of decline, sometimes steep and sometimes lasting multiple years, but in general, the trendline for the output for the world's largest economies has been almost steadily upwards. Once the process of industrialization had transformed an economy, that economy appeared to be immune from long-term decline, or at least that is what the last couple of centuries led us to believe.

Let's go back in time and see how global economic output (measured as always in this book as GDP) has evolved. To do so, we will rely heavily upon the work of Angus Maddison, the famed British economist whose work on the measurement and analysis of historical economic output and growth has become the basis for much of our ability to compare and contrast long-term historical economic data, as well as for much of our economic data before the 20th century. Of course, the accuracy of such historical data, particular when we delve far back into human history, is subject to debate, but in our quest to quantify and compare long-term economic data, we need a basis for our calculations. Therefore, this combination of Maddison's long-term historical data and our range of sources for more modern data will give us at least the opportunity to compare economies across eras.

Using this combination of sources, here is a chart showing the long-term evolution of global economic output:

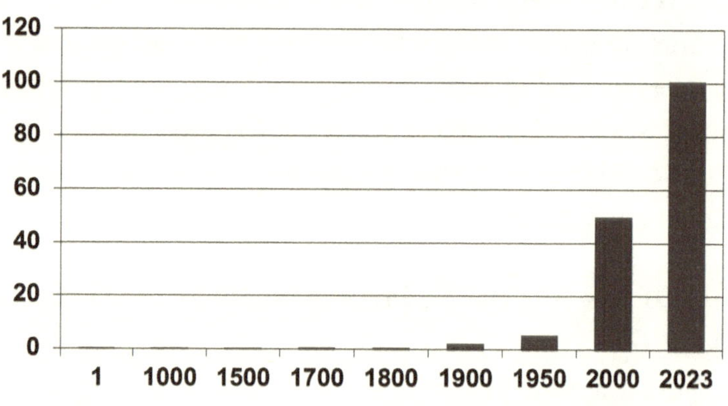

Source: Maddison, World Bank

As this chart shows, the global economy has made incredible strides since the Industrial Revolution. Based on Maddison's historical data, global economic output essentially did not increase at all over the 1000-year period from the year 1CE to the year 1000CE, with global GDP rising from $103 billion in the 1CE to $117 billion in 1000CE. It's no wonder that the post-Roman period in Europe is known as the Dark Ages, for in the centuries after the Roman Empire's peak of its economic power in the 2nd Century CE, economic output in most of Europe fell precipitously and for a very long time. Even during the near-eight centuries that stretched from the year 1000CE to the late 18th century, when the Industrial Revolution emerged in Britain, global economic growth was minimal at best. According to Maddison, and some of my own economic research, global economic output rose from $117 billion in 1000CE to approximately $550 million in the year 1780. That near 400% increase in economic output may sound impressive, but remember, it took 780 years to achieve. To put that in perspective, global economic output has risen by 500% during my lifetime (I was born in 1972). So it took the world economy 780 years to reach the level of economic output that existed at the time of the start of the Industrial Revolution, but it took just the relatively short lifetime (wishful thinking, perhaps) of this author for the global economy to do the same.

Despite this impressive record of remarkably steady growth over the past two-and-a-half centuries, it is the recessions, crashes, depressions and other calamities that often stick in one's mind when considering the history of the world economy during this period. For example, we consider the 19th century the period of great economic expansion for the United States, one that would take that young country from the position of a minor player on the global stage to the world's largest economy by the end of that century. This gives the impression that the US economy enjoyed almost uninterrupted rapid economic growth, perhaps along the lines of what China achieved over the past four decades. In fact, while the US economy did expand dramatically from the beginning to the end of the 19th century, this expansion was constantly interrupted by a series of severe recessions, panics and depressions that occurred at a frequency that is hard to comprehend for a 21st century mind. It is now estimated that the US economy fell into at least 24 recessions over the course of the 19th century, some of which would today be referred to as depressions as their impact on economic output in the US was sometimes nearly as great as that of the Great Depression.

The largest of these downturns in considered to have been the Panic of 1893, which led to a decline in industrial production of more than 15% between 1892 and 1894 and led to a major increase in political instability in the United States. As we know now, despite 24 recessions, panics and depressions, the United States economy expanded rapidly overall during the 19th century and entered the 20th century as the largest and wealthiest economy in the world, showing that despite this extreme volatility, the US economy managed to remain on track for long-term economic growth through the 19th century.

Overall, it is the crises that typically receive the bulk of the attention in the study of economic history, just as it is the wars and upheavals that attract the majority of the attention in general history studies. The mild recessions that led to minor declines in economic output and relatively quick recoveries, and make up the large majority of recessions, are not the ones that attract much attention. Instead, it is major crises that are studied from all angles, crises such as the Great Depression, the 2008-2009 Financial Crisis (sometimes referred to as the Great Recession) and the Covid-19 pandemic. Yet even these crises eventually gave way to renewed economic growth, even if some countries only returned to growth after a great deal of stress and unrest. The fact is that all of the world's economies are many times larger today than they were at the start of the Great Depression, showing that, even amid the tremendous economic dislocations that such an event (and other subsequent events) caused, the overall trend remained one of growth for all economies around the world. This has led the world to believe that, no matter how bad a downturn is, the global economy will always find a way to return to growth.

GROWTH IS TAKEN FOR GRANTED

For most of the world's people, long-term economic growth is taken for granted. If you are a ten-year-old American (sorry Latin Americans, I'm referring to the US sort here), your country's economy is now 30% larger than it was when you were born. If you are 40-year-old American, your country's economy is now 200% larger than when you were born. Finally, if you are a 60-year-old American, the US economy is now 530% larger than in the year of your birth.

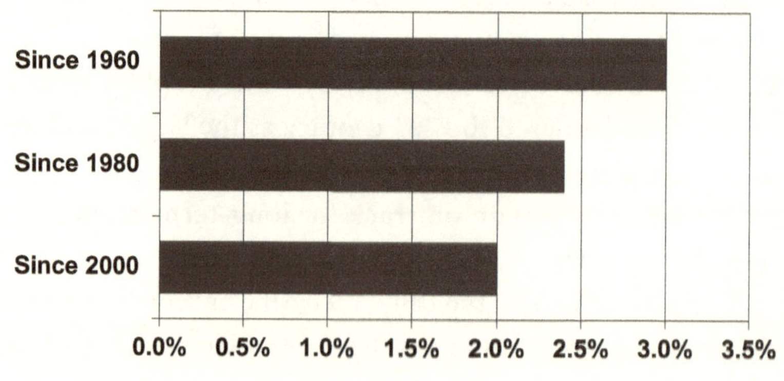

The scale of this growth is even more dramatic if you are Chinese. For a ten-year-old Chinese person, the corresponding figure is 105%, whereas for a 40-year-old in China it is 35,000% and for a 60-year-old it is an astounding 100,000%.

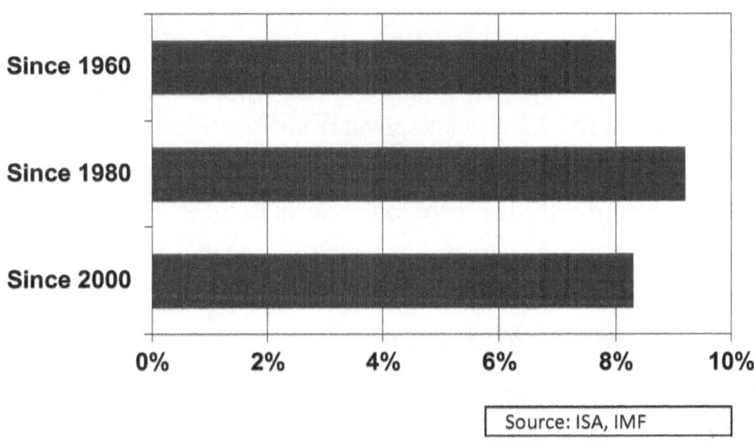

Looking at these figures, it is easy to see why the world assumes that the economy will always grow over the longer-term, for, in modern times, it always has. Such incredible advancements in wealth and development would not be achievable without long-term growth.

While the United States and China have both achieved relatively strong growth rates when compared to their peers, they are not alone. In fact, nearly all economies around the world have been able to generate relatively consistent growth in recent decades, even if their levels of growth may not be as fast as others, or if they have experienced more downturns than others. However, there are some economies that have struggled to generate much growth in recent decades. For a variety of reasons, some economies have found it difficult to generate consistent growth. Of course, we have seen this throughout history, as once powerful economies would find themselves stuck in an inescapable downwards spiral. Sometimes this decline would be dramatic and sudden, but other times, it would be slow and steady. For those that collapsed suddenly, the causes were often wars, natural disasters, plagues or other such dramatic events. For those that declined more gradually, many of the reasons were related to the internal weaknesses of those countries, weaknesses that could be the result of a declining population, a lack of investment in faster-growing sectors of the economy, a lack of competitiveness, or many other factors. Whatever the reason, there have also been losers in terms of economic development, even when most of the world has been winning.

Given the steady growth of most of the global economy, any economy that has struggled to generate significant growth for an extended period of time has been tagged as the "Sick Man" of their respective region, with many economies being forced to wear this label at any given time. The term comes from descriptions of the late Ottoman Empire, whose failure to modernize or generate the levels of economic growth that were to be found in other parts of Europe in the late 19th and early 20th centuries was to result in that country falling far behind its rivals in Europe, leading to various European powers circling the Ottoman state like vultures waiting for a sick animal to die. Today, a few countries are saddled with such an indignity. For example, Greece, since the financial crisis in 2008 and 2009, has found itself jettisoned from many lists of fully-developed economies, as its relative wealth to the rest of the West (of which it is questionably a part) has fallen dramatically during the past decade, even following a strong recovery in the wake of the Covid-19 pandemic.

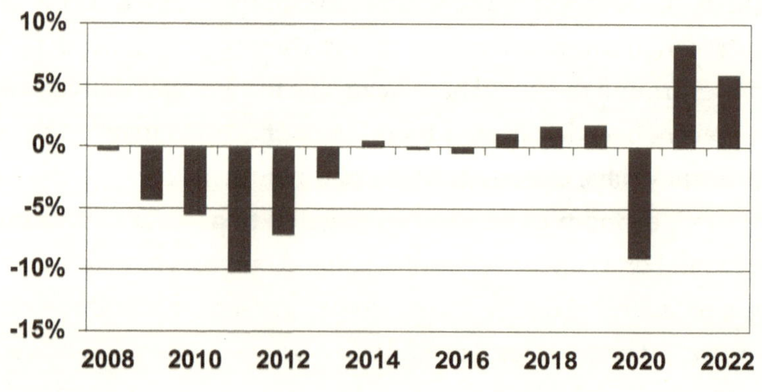

Source: ISA, IMF

Likewise, Italy's 20+ years of stagnation are often viewed from northern Europe as justification for certain prejudices towards Italy from that region. Argentina is another country, that, while once wealthy, has fallen on hard times and is viewed with much skepticism from its wealthier counterparts.

Such disdain is not only reserved for countries. On a grander scale, entire regions that struggle to keep up economically with the world's more dynamic regions are often viewed with a certain disdain. The United States and Canada's ability to grow rapidly in the 19th and 20th centuries stood in stark contrast the economic performance of their neighbors to the south, shaping the North American view of Latin America for the past two centuries. Likewise, many in East Asia today view the slow growth of many Western economies as proof that the 21st century will belong to Asia, and view many of these sluggish Western countries as has-beens that are afraid of the modern world and the technologies and processes that drive it.

This disdain for slower growing economies can also apply to state and local economies. For example, the Rust Belt in the United States (the birthplace of this author) is often looked down upon by those in the US that are fortunate enough to live in faster-growing regions of the country. Likewise, rapidly-growing London is viewed much differently than stagnant areas of northern England as one region continues to grow while the other struggles to meet the challenges of the 21st century. Such disdain differs from the more traditional intra-country differences that arise from wealth disparities such as those between northern and southern Italy, or coastal and interior China. While wealth disparities are often disparaged for being a leading cause of migration between regions or countries, in fact, it should be growth disparities that drive such migration, as this is a relatively efficient allocation of labor.

Struggling economies are often treated as pariahs because of the fact that, in the modern world, steady growth is expected, or even taken for granted. However, as we will see over the course of this book, economic growth in the developed world is slowing. Worse, growth in the developed world has been trending downwards for more than two generations now, and the factors are in place for growth in these countries to continue to slow in the coming decades. Nevertheless, while growth is slowing, recessions and other major crises were often viewed as threats from the past. Now, with two major crises in a span of a little more than a decade, the world is waking up to the fact that severe recessions and disruptions remain a threat to the global economy. Furthermore, this threat from recessions and disruptions has added to the downwards pressure facing developed economies, making it even harder for most developed economies to generate anywhere near the level of growth that they were achieving in previous decades.

Expectations of economic growth in developing countries have also risen significantly in recent decades. This is due in no small part to the remarkable success of East Asian economies during this period. As countries such as South Korea and China have gone from being ranking among the poorest economies in the world to some of the world's most powerful economies, other developing countries in all parts of the world have hoped to be able to emulate this tremendous success and to elevate their populations' living standards, just as East Asia's most dynamic economies have done. As we will see, the rest of the world might be too late, as the ability of poorer countries to lift themselves out of poverty is about to be challenged by many of the same factors that are threatening to lead to much lower levels of global economic growth in developed economies in the years ahead.

Chapter Two

Growth Should Not Be Taken for Granted

CONTRARY TO POPULAR BELIEF, the history of humankind has not been one of constant economic growth and improvements in living standards. Sure, if one takes a very long-term view of human history, it is clear that the overall trend from our emergence in East Africa to our pre-eminence in the modern world is one of remarkable achievements in terms of economic expansion, improved living standards and unimaginable technological advancement. Of course, there have been many periods in which this economic growth has reversed, living standards have fallen and levels of technology have receded. These periods are perceived with such dread that they are typically referred to as "Dark Ages", the most famous of which is the "Dark Ages" period in Europe that stretched from the latter days of the Roman Empire to the early period of the Renaissance. Nevertheless, while these "Dark Ages" are filled with tales of decline and danger, they have all given way to new periods of advancement so that almost all areas of the world are now at their peak of economic output, living standards and technological development. This has reinforced the notion that, no matter how bad things get, the future holds the promise of renewed economic vigor, better living standards and further technological advancements. This notion is furthered by the fact that, since the Industrial Revolution, humanity has generally moved forward in all of these areas.

While the past centuries of growth have given us the impression that the global economy has been moving forwards rather consistently, the fact is that much of our economic history has been filled with volatility. In fact, there have been many periods in which economic output trended downwards for centuries at a time. For example, if one looks at the economic history of Europe from the 3rd century until the 13th century, a period of a 1,000 years, one would see remarkable declines in economic output over the first part of that 1,000-year period, followed by centuries of stagnation, declining living standards and a general lack of technological advancement. It was only when early-Middle-Ages European states chose to relearn the lessons of that region's ancient past that they were able to turn the region's economy in the direction of growth once again. Similar developments have happened over China's long history, most notably during its steady decline between the 15th and early 20th centuries, when China went from having the world's largest economy by a very large margin to one that accounted for less than 10% of total global economic output in 1950. In fact, our studies of pre-Industrial-Revolution economies show us that long-term economic growth was anything but assured and that long-term decline was both possible, but also probable.

Even the first 150-to-175 years after the Industrial Revolution were filled with massive economic upheavals in which double-digit declines in economic output among even the world's most advanced economies were an all-too-frequent occurrence. For example, there have been an estimated 50 recessions in the United States since it gained its independence from the United Kingdom, beginning with the Panic of 1785 that followed the end of the US' War for Independence to the Covid-19 pandemic that was raging as this book was being written. Of these, 38 of them took place during the 160 years between 1785 and 1945, or basically a recession every 4.2 years. Worse, many of these recessions were actually devastating economic events that reduced economic output in the United States along the lines of the contraction recorded during the Great Depression. Since the end of World War Two, there have been 12 recessions in the US, or one every 6.25 years. Moreover, until the Covid-19 pandemic shut down the US economy in early 2020, all of these recessions were relatively mild compared to the severe crises that impacted the US economy all too frequently before 1945.

On a global basis, the picture is the same. Yes, individual countries or regions have suffered great upheavals over the past 75 years, but the overall economic growth trend for the world has been positive. Even when there have been worldwide economic crises, such as the Oil Shocks of the 1970s, the Great Recession of 2008-2009 or the Covid-19 pandemic of 2020, the global economy has quickly bounced back, driven upwards by its more robust economies and its more dynamic industries. In fact, between the end of the Second World War and the Covid-19 pandemic year of 2020, there had been only one year in that 75-year period in which global economic output had actually declined over the course of a year. That year was 2009, when the Global Financial Crisis resulted in a decline in global economic output if just 0.1%. In all other years between the late-1940s and 2020, global economic output increased. This itself is a remarkable achievement that was made possible by a wide variety of factors, including demographic growth, a global trading system that was dominated by a single benevolent power and increases in productivity (at least in the early decades of this period).

As we continue to recover from the impact of the Covid-19 crisis, which itself hit the world economy at a time when growth was slowing, we have to consider whether or not we are in the early stages of another period of long-term economic decline. Sure, this is hard to imagine given the fact that, for 74 of the 75 years prior to the Covid-19 pandemic, global economic output had risen. However, there are many worrying signs that suggest that we are indeed facing the prospects of long-term economic decline such as we have not seen in nearly a century, if not longer. Even more worrying is the fact that many of these signs are coming from what have been some of the world's most-successful economies, those that were the drivers of much of the long-term growth that has characterized the post-war period of the global economy.

Looking back at history, there are many examples of economies that enjoyed very long stretches of growth, only to succumb to even greater long-term declines. A perfect example of this is the Late Roman Empire. In the 1st and 2nd centuries, Rome was the epitome of economic power and success in the ancient world. Not only was Rome the ancient world's most powerful state and its most advanced economy, but it set the standards for all future levels of economic development for the next 1500 years, particularly in Europe and the Mediterranean.

At its peak, Rome was the world's first inter-connected modern economy. This meant that Rome was an economy that was based on trade, investment, productivity improvements and specialization. As Rome controlled the trading routes both within the empire as well as with many of its neighboring states, it was able to guarantee safe passage of goods, labor and resources, bringing together a vast area with diverse industries and resources into a single economy. Moreover, this control of the trading routes within and outside of the empire enabled for specialization to take hold and for productivity to grow at one of its fastest rates in history. For example, farmers in North Africa could sell their wheat and other agricultural products throughout the empire, giving them a vastly larger market than they would have had outside of the empire. Likewise, metalworkers in Spain could sell their products as far afield as the eastern Mediterranean or Britain thanks to the Roman road network and the speed and security that it provided to traders. This enabled Rome to become the largest and wealthiest economy in the ancient world. Furthermore, this wealth spread to a larger share of the Roman population than it had in other contemporary states, where wealth was extremely concentrated in the hands of a very small ruling class.

Unfortunately for Rome's economy, the empire was hit by a series of crises in the late 2nd and early 3rd centuries, crises that would disrupt and dislocate Rome's economy. These crises included plagues that led to a sharp decline in the empire's population, internal conflicts that broke apart Rome's vast single market, and major declines in public revenues which resulted in the state no longer being able to pay for the public services that Rome had become so well-known for during its peak period. Over the next 250 years or so, the Roman empire in western Europe declined, despite the best efforts of Diocletian, Constantine and others, until it eventually fell in 476 CE. Remarkably, western Europe would not return to the levels of economic advancement and the standards of living that were enjoyed by Romans during the peak of their empire until the 18th and 19th centuries.

Another example of an economy that enjoyed long-term growth and prosperity only to fall into just as long of a period of decline and decay as post-Roman Europe is the Chinese economy between the 17th and the 20th centuries. By the 17th century, China had re-emerged as the world's leading economic center as the Qing Dynasty recentralized control of the Chinese economy after the dislocations caused during the late Ming period.

**Share of Global GDP by Region
in 1600**

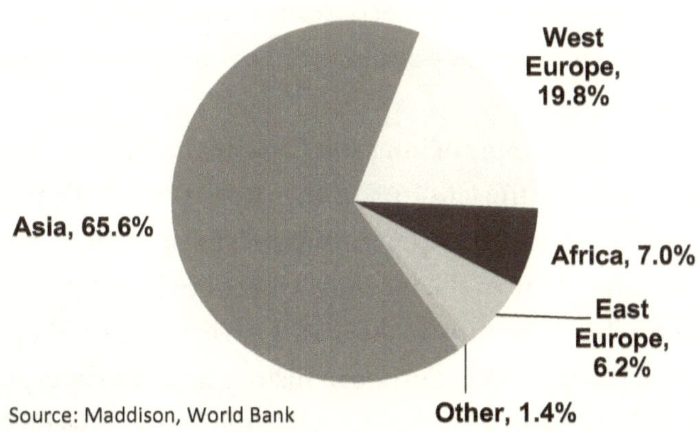

Source: Maddison, World Bank

However, while China's economy was vast in scale and remained technologically advanced, it was soon to fall behind. This was due in no small part to efforts by China to isolate itself at times from the rest of the world and to ignore technological advancements that were being developed outside of its borders. When the Industrial Revolution spread across Europe and North America in the late 18th and early 19th centuries, China was left in the dust, so to speak, as those regions' rates of productivity growth soared past those of China by a dramatic margin. Furthermore, these Western powers amassed vast empires that gave them access to resources and captive markets, while their own demographic growth soared.

By the mid-19th century, China's decline was accelerating. While its vast market was attractive to foreign traders, it also brought Western powers into the country seeking to establish captive markets, much as they had done in their colonies in other parts of the world. As China's economy was not growing, and as China had fallen behind in terms of technology (especially military technology) it found itself unable to prevent these Western powers from carving up China into their own spheres of influence, a humiliating development for a state that had been so powerful not that long before. This decline continued right into the first half of the 20th century, as China again found itself all but powerless to prevent a country with a population seven times smaller than its own at that time (Japan) from invading the country and basically doing what it pleased until Japan over-reached in its imperialist ambitions by declaring war on the United States. By 1949, when the Communist victory brought an end to the Chinese Civil War, the country accounted for less than 4.5% of the world's total economic output, despite accounting for more than 21% of the world's population. Few once-great economies had ever fallen so far.

A third historical example of long and persistent economic downturns can be found in Spain. From the late 15th century until the middle part of the 17th century, imperial Spain was Europe's most powerful state. With an empire that encompassed a large share of the recently "discovered" American continents, as well as imperial possessions in Asia and Africa, Imperial Spain was the closest thing that this period of European history had to a superpower. Spain's rise was both surprising and dramatic. Long a relative backwater for previous empires, the Iberian Peninsula under the Moors became the most advanced civilization in Europe for a period that stretched from the initial Moorish conquests on the peninsula in the 8th century until the gradual collapse of the Umayyad dynasty in the 11th century. Ever thereafter, the Muslim states that resisted what became an ever-greater wave of Christian states advancing southwards on the peninsula retained many advantages in terms of economic, political and technological advancements over their contemporary counterparts in other areas of Europe. Once Spain become a unified Christian state in 1492 (the same year that Christopher Columbus arrived in the Americas), it had inherited both the knowledge and the advancements achieved by Spain's previous Muslim rulers, as well as the scientific and cultural breakthroughs that were spreading out of Renaissance Italy at that same time.

In the 16th century, Spain followed up Christopher Columbus' discoveries in the Americas to establish a vast empire stretching from the Rocky Mountains in what is now the western United States to Tierra del Fuego at the southern tip of the South American continent.

This gave Spain control of territories that were not only many times greater in size than Spain itself, but lands that were rich in gold, silver and other important resources. As a result, Spain suddenly found itself not only possessing the knowledge and skills of the former Muslim rulers of Spain, but also of the vast mineral wealth of the Americas. It could be argued that not since

Rome had a European state been able to combine this access to knowledge and skills (as Rome acquired from Ancient Greece and others) with access to such mineral wealth (much of which, ironically, came from Spain in the form of vast silver mines during the first few centuries of the Roman period).

Unfortunately for Spain, its appetite for territory and power would result in it become dangerously overstretched and constantly at war with many of its European rivals. For example, Spain's possessions in what are now the Benelux countries did give it control of what was then one of the wealthiest parts of Europe, but it also resulted in Spain having to constantly fight costly wars to maintain this control. Likewise, its rivalry at sea with a rapidly-rising England resulted in great losses as the two powers battled for control of key shipping routes in the Atlantic. As a result, by the second half of the 17th century, Spain's power was already being eclipsed by those of rival European states such as England and France. In fact, Spain's decline that began in the 17th century would not come to an end in terms of Spain's relative economic and political position in Europe until the 1990s, a period of more than 300 years.

The eventual declines of Rome, China and Spain all took place during different eras, and each had its own unique causes. Nevertheless, there were also many factors that were common to the declines of each of these entities. Three of them are rather easy to establish, demographic decline, a breakdown in their trading systems and collapses in productivity. In each of these three examples, the state in question had significant demographic advantages that helped to propel their economies forward. In Rome, rapid population growth accompanied the sheer scale of the empire's population, allowing for trade and investment to flourish, and for never-seen-before levels of economies-of-scale to develop. However, the Antonine Plague of the late 2nd century dramatically cut into the empire's population and this, coupled with the disruptions and chaos of the 3rd century, brought an end to many of Rome's demographic advantages. In China, the country's vast population meant that, if a single power could unite the region, it would also enjoy massive demographic advantages that would allow for trade and investment to flourish and for productivity to soar. However, as China turned more-and-more inwards, these advantages were squandered, and when Chinese unity was weakened, these advantages all but disappeared. Finally, Spain itself did not possess anywhere near the demographic, trading or productivity advantages that Rome or China possessed, but by creating a massive global empire, it was able to develop some of these advantages. However, its main rivals in Europe were soon able to emulate Spain's empire building, erasing what was initially a massive competitive advantage for the Spanish state.

RECENT EXAMPLES

In modern times, we have not seen any of the world's largest economies fall into deep long-term declines, at least not until the turmoil of the first part of the 21st century. For example, let's take a look at the United States. Since its independence in 1776, the United States is estimated to have suffered through dozens of recessions, some of which were bad enough to be classified as depressions. However, in the 90 years between the Great Depression and the Covid-19 pandemic, none of the downturns in the United States could be considered to be a major crisis as their impact on economic output was both minimal and short-lasting, at least when compared with the economic crises that bedeviled the US between the 1780s and the 1930s. In fact, if one looks at the overall level of economic growth for developed economies (North America, West Europe and the developed economies of the Asia-Pacific region), they had, as a combined group of countries, managed to record long-term positive economic results for the period stretching from the end of the Second World War until the end of the 2000s. Moreover, while many of the leading economies that comprise the list of the world's developed economies had seen their economies slow over time, none of them had fallen into a terminal collapse, at least not until recent years.

While there may not be any examples of truly large economies experiencing long-term declines, there are some examples among mid- and small-sized economies. Among these mid-sized economies, the best example is probably that of Argentina. It is well known that, in the first part of the 20th century, Argentina was one of the wealthiest countries in the world.

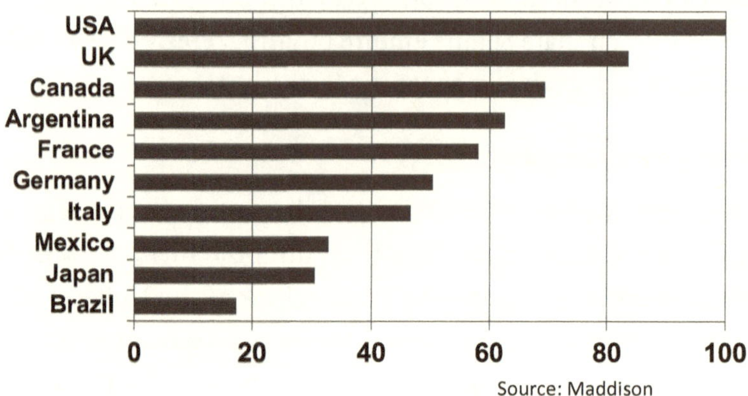

In fact, Argentina possessed many of the same advantages (huge territory, favorable climate, vast resources, growing population) that helped to drive the rapid economic growth and development in other New World countries such as the United States, Canada and Australia. This allowed Argentina's economy to flourish, particularly its agricultural sector thanks to soaring rates of export growth. However, the Great Depression and the loss of key export markets sent Argentina on a downward spiral that it has not been able to pull out of ever since. In fact, over the past few decades, few countries have experienced a higher degree of economic volatility than Argentina, for as the country has proven itself capable of generating high rates of growth for short periods of time, it has proven itself even more capable for falling into some of the world's most devastating economic collapses. Furthermore, its decline continues, as its per capital GDP levels compared with the United States and other major economies have continued to decline on a relative basis.

Among smaller economies, a famous example of a country that has fallen into long-term decline is that of Zimbabwe. Once one of Africa's wealthiest countries, with one of that region's most diverse economies, Zimbabwe is now one of the region's poorest and least-developed economies. In fact, since the 1990s, economic output in Zimbabwe has collapsed, turning the country into one that is now almost-entirely dependent upon international assistance to survive.

In looking at these examples of large-, medium- and small-sized economies that have experienced long-term economic decline, some key factors can be ascertained. For small economies, something as simple as the mismanagement of the economy by the national government or the country's economic policy makers is enough to set that country onto a course of long-term economic decline. For mid-sized economies, this can also be true, but only for those mid-sized economies that lack a degree of diversification. For example, mid-sized economies that are not diversified have been known to fall into long-term decline if there is a combination of economic mismanagement and a collapse of the sector of the economy upon which that country is dependent. In this case, think of Venezuela, a mid-sized economy that has been grossly mismanaged for decades, but has also suffered from the collapse of oil prices in previous years. For truly large economies, simple economic mismanagement or the collapse of a single sector of their economies is not enough to push those countries into a long-term decline from which they cannot escape. Instead, the very fundamentals of their economic power (their demographic situation, their resources, their access to trade and investment, and much more) all have to suffer severe reverses in order to send that economy into a long-term economic downwards spiral. This is what makes it a truly rare experience when one of the world's leading economies faces the prospect of long-term decline.

One such large economy that might just be in terminal decline is Japan. If you went back in a time machine to the late-1980s or early 1990s and suggested

Average Annual GDP Growth by Decade

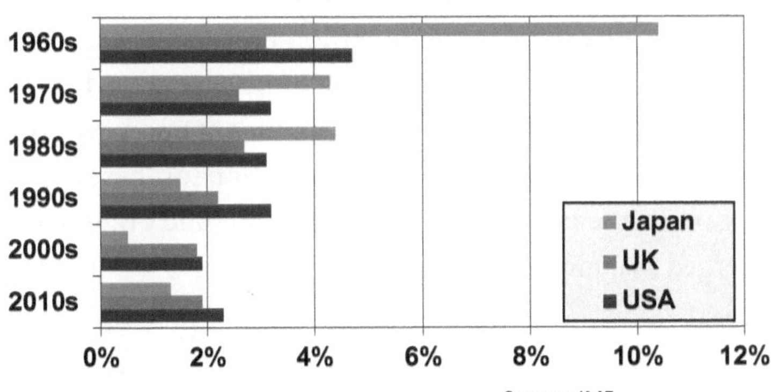

Source: IMF

that Japan more than any other large economy faced a future filled with stagnation, deflation and competitive decline, you would have been judged to have been crazy. In fact, Japan's rate of economic growth in the decades prior to 1992 was higher than that of any other large developed economy in the world, often by a large margin.

If fact, by the early 1990s, Japan's economy was not only growing much faster than that of the country that was most responsible for its defeat in the Second World War, the United States, but it was, by some measures, significantly wealthier than the United States. In fact, the latter achievement is something that no other large developed economy has been able to achieve over the past century, a testament to Japan's economic miracle in the decades after World War Two. However, this growth came to a crashing halt after 1992, and since then, Japan has been one of the world's most stagnant large economies.

So what happened? The most noted cause was the bursting of Japan's real estate and stock market bubbles in late 1991 and early 1992. This resulted in massive damage to Japanese banks, whose excessive lending is often cited as the reason for these bubbles in the first place. Later, the Japanese government and the country's banks attempted to keep afloat companies that were irretrievably weakened by the bursting of these asset bubbles, resulting in investments flowing to the wrong companies and wrong industries at a time when global competition was intensifying dramatically. Meanwhile, Japan's demographic situation had been deteriorating over the previous couple of decades, but this largely went unnoticed until it was too late. In fact, Japan has long had one of the world's lowest birth rates and this, coupled with extremely low levels of immigration, resulted in Japan having by the 1990s one of the world's oldest populations, with a working-age population that was already beginning to shrink. As a result, Japan's domestic market was no longer a driver of growth, leaving the Japanese economy ever-more dependent upon export markets to generate growth. At the same time, the competition for these export markets was growing more intense as China, Southeast Asia and other manufacturing centers emerged as competition for Japan.

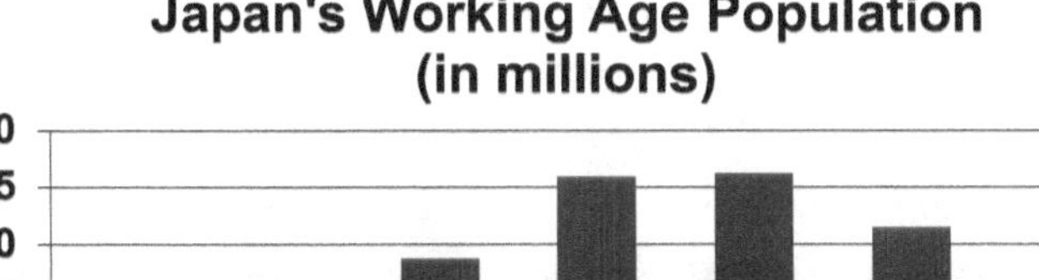

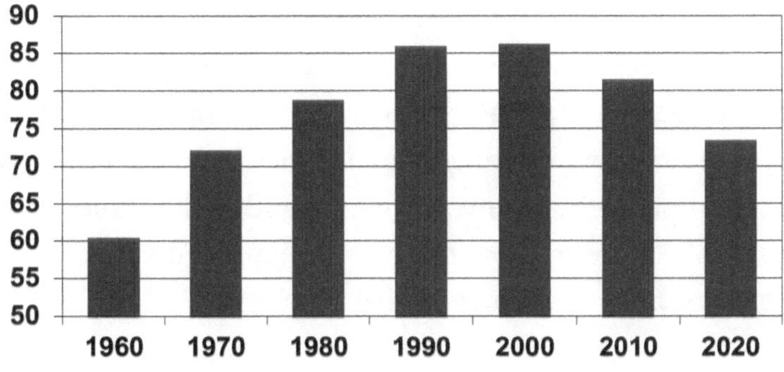

When we look back at the economies that have fallen into long-term stagnation and decline, we find that many of the same factors appear over and over again. For example, an increase in foreign competition within the economy in question's key sector (or sectors) has often served as a catalyst for this decline. A good example of this is again Japan, which by the early 1990s found itself facing severe foreign competition in industries such as electronics and automobiles, two of the industries that were important drivers for Japan's economic miracle after the Second World War. Another factor that appears in many of these countries that have suffered from long-term economic decline is economic mismanagement, often in the form of poor policies or planning. In Greece, an economy whose output today is less than it was in the 1990s, the government's failure to raise tax revenues left it exposed to the threat of a financial crisis, which, once it arrived, left the Greek economy is a precarious position.

One factor that often contributes mightily to long-term economic decline is a deteriorating demographic situation. This can come in the form of a dramatic decline in a country's or a region's working-age population (as in Roman and Byzantine times during and after a plague), or it can come gradually, as falling birth rates and limited immigration result in both the shrinking of the working-age population coupled with the rising in the dependent segment of a country's population (as is happening in places such as Japan and Italy today). Disruptions in trade and investment that prove to be long-lived can also push an economy into a long-term decline that proves impossible to pull out of. This can include the loss of vital markets, both internally (due to unrest or other disruptions) or externally (due to trade barriers). Post-Great-Depression Argentina is a perfect example of this, as the loss of vital export markets in the 1930s resulted in a gradual decline in that country that unfortunately continues to this day. Finally, long-term declines in productivity growth can also result in long-term economic stagnation and decline, and, as we will see later in this book, this is a threat to not only many individual economies in the coming years, but to the entire global economy.

BE PREPARED FOR ANOTHER LENGTHY CRISIS

In the 2020s, it has become apparent that the world needed to prepare itself for the likelihood of another long-term economic downturn. While many individual economies have experienced what could be considered long-term economic crises in recent decades, the global economy has managed to avoid falling into a long-term decline since the Great Depression. In fact, even as the Covid-19 pandemic ravaged the global economy, the widespread expectation was that once the world overcame the initial shock of the pandemic that the global economy would quickly return to growth, something that indeed did occur. This optimism was borne from the fact that the global economy has generally moved forward, with new markets, industries and technologies constantly emerging to create new generators of growth. However, any student of history will know that the potential for a long-term decline in global economic output is not only possible, but also probable at some point in the future. Like a dormant volcano that no one is sure will erupt, but do expect it to one day, so too is the global economy all-but-certain to face periods of long-term decline in the future. As many of the factors that precipitated previous periods of economic decline are once again in place, and as the Covid-19 crisis has exposed the growing weaknesses of many of the world's largest economies, the question we have to ask ourselves is whether or not we are again on the verge of such a long-term decline. Worse, if we are indeed on the verge of a long-term decline in economic output, are we prepared for the potential repercussions of such a development that could change the world as we know it?

Unfortunately, there are many warning signs that point to the possibility that we are not only facing a higher level of risk from long-term stagnation and decline, but that it is entirely possible that we are already in the midst of just such a period. This is particularly true for developed economies, as they have seen their long-term economic performance continuously deteriorate for decades now. At the same time, while it has been emerging markets that have been generating an ever-greater share of growth for the global economy in the 21st century, many emerging markets have struggled to keep up and they too may be facing the prospects of long-term stagnation, or even decline.

One of the key signs pointing to the possibility that we are a world in the midst of a period of long-term stagnation and decline is the fact that global population growth is slowing dramatically, and for some of the world's most important economies, this population growth has already come to an end. At the same time, the trade and investment that played such an important role in generating growth for the global economy in the earlier part of the 21st century has been in decline for more than a decade, and the Covid-19 pandemic led to the greatest decline in global trade and investment since the 1940s. Meanwhile, as has already been mentioned, productivity growth, the third key driver of economic growth, has been almost non-existent for many economies in recent decades. Finally, the world is facing serious threats from climate change and resource depletion, both of which have the potential to severely disrupt the global economy, if not causing an outright collapse of economy as we know it.

If these signs are accurate and are pointing to the fact that we are in the midst of a period of long-term economic stagnation and decline, then we must also admit that we as a modern society are ill-prepared to deal with such a possibility. From an economic standpoint, the world's major economic powers have used most of the ammunition available to them to try and stimulate their economies during and after the Great Recession and the Covid-19 crisis. This has left the global economy with few other resources that are available to its leading actors that can spur their economies forward, leaving them dangerously exposed to the effects of the next crisis that comes down the road. Meanwhile, the world today and all of the intricate social, transport, healthcare and other systems that define the modern world all are based on the notion that economic growth will continue indefinitely, enabling these increasingly expensive systems to be both improved and expanded as we move forward in time. Therefore, it is easy to understand that, if we are indeed unable to return the global economy, or at least some of its leading components, to growth in the coming years, many of these systems will deteriorate and collapse, causing massive disruptions to society.

It is not too hard to imagine what little or no economic growth for a longer period of time will mean for the world. In fact, the risks associated with economic stagnation and decline are too numerous to contemplate. One immediate risk that serves as an example of the threats we are facing is that of debt. In fact, some of the debts that have been accumulated by countries attempting to offset the impact of the Great Recession and the Covid-19 pandemic, are levels of debt that have not been seen since the Second World War. For countries that can generate healthy rates of economic growth, these debts can still be manageable. However, for those countries that can no longer generate such growth, these debts become a burden that could prove to be too great to bear. We've seen how this works in Southern Europe in the first half of the 2010s, when that region's worst-performing economies could no longer afford their rising debt burdens. Likewise, government spending, which soared in the wake of the Covid-19 pandemic, will have to be cut dramatically if economic growth can no longer be generated. Again, we have seen this happen in those countries that have been struggling to record any economic growth in recent years, and the results have not been pretty.

Another risk facing a slower-growing world is the fact that the global population is forecast to continue to age rapidly in the coming decades. If these older segments of the population remain relatively unproductive, as they are today, and yet expensive to maintain due to generous retirement benefits and healthcare costs, it is clear that those countries that are unable to generate sustained rates of higher economic growth will no longer be able to afford the retirement systems that have been enjoyed by the last two or three generations of retired people. If these examples pose a bleak picture of the future, they should, for they are the all-too-real possibilities that are confronting the world as it struggles to generate higher levels of economic growth.

Chapter Three

Do We Need Growth?

IN RECENT YEARS, IT has become more and more common to hear pundits claim that, for the good of our planet, we do not need to generate additional economic growth. For previous generations, economic growth was the be-all and end-all measure of an economy's success and vigor and was the unquestioned leading measurement of economic health and well-being. However, that has begun to change, or at least, to be challenged. This is because two major concerns about the planet's future are calling into question both the need and the desirability of generating economic growth. One of these concerns is the environment, as much of the blame for the current environmental threats facing the planet (climate change, pollution, resource depletion and more) has been placed on the relentless pursuit of economic growth by countries, region, cities, businesses and individuals. The other concern centers around lifestyles and living standards. In that context, many pundits now argue that measures of living standards or of happiness should replace economic growth rates as the true measure of a society's rate of advancement.

In fact, for many countries, there has been a concerted effort to lessen the focus on economic growth, with many countries calling for new measurements to be used or created. In fact, many organizations around the world have done just that in recent years, creating all sorts of new measurements designed to show how countries rank in terms of their environmental footprint, the happiness of their citizens or the levels of inequality within their borders. Of course, it is no surprise that the countries that are pushing the most for these alternatives to economic growth are some of the countries that are recording the lowest rates of economic growth in the world today. Furthermore, many of these countries that champion non-growth measurements are countries that have already reached a certain level of economic development and living standards, ignoring the fact that, for countries with lower levels of economic development or living standards, their aim is to achieve the levels of economic growth needed to raise their level of economic development and living standards. What is happening is that there is now a race to find or create new measurements that could replace economic growth as the leading measurement of a country's economic success and advancement.

As I mentioned, many would-be alternatives to economic growth have already been touted as the next best thing. Some of these are based on measurements of happiness, such as Gallup's World Happiness Report (which ranks Finland as the world's happiest country). Others are based on living standards, such as the United Nations Development Program's Human Development Index (which ranks Norway as the country with the highest level of "human development"). In fact, there are now dozens of such measurements and rankings being compiled by all sorts of organizations, many of which make the claim that their measurements are better at determining the success of a country than that of simple economic growth. In fact, many of these rankings have gained quite a following, particularly in those countries that score well in these rankings, many of which do not score well when it comes to economic growth. However, it needs to be noted that most of these new measurements and rankings are rather dubious, as they use either highly subjective criteria and methodology in compiling their scores and rankings, or often are championed by certain ideologues on the right-wing or the left-wing of the political spectrum. Nevertheless, as we are a society that is obsessed with ranking things, it seems inevitable that more and more of these alternatives to economic growth will be created and that more and more countries will claim success, even if their economies are no longer growing. This is dangerous, for many reasons.

Still, there are many arguments for why the focus on economic growth should be reduced, some of which have a good deal of validity. Of these, the impact on the environment that the quest for economic growth has had probably holds the most water. Given our ability to measure the impact that human activity has on the environment, it is absurd to deny that humans, in our quest for higher levels of economic growth and improved living standards, have caused some significant harm to our planet's health. The evidence for this is all around us. For example, it is clear that the dramatic increase in greenhouse gas emissions over the past two centuries has played a leading role in the increase in global temperatures during that time.

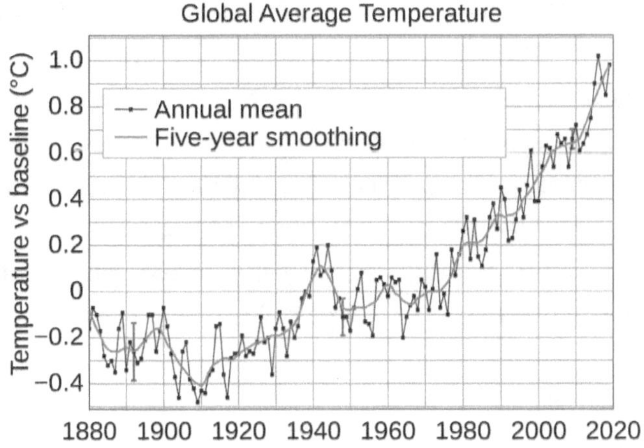

To deny this connection is to deny overwhelming evidence. Likewise, a look to the skies (if it is possible) in many of the world's fastest-growing cities, particularly in places such as China and India, is to see the impact that economic development is having on air quality. At the same time, the deforestation underway in places such as Brazil, Congo and Indonesia is yet another example of how the quest to generate economic growth is proving dangerously harmful for the health of the environment. In fact, perhaps the greatest challenge of the 21st century will be how we can balance the need for economic growth with the increasingly-urgent need to restore the health of our planet. What is important to note is that these two goals are not mutually-exclusive, despite claims to the contrary.

Another issue that has driven the push to find alternative measures to economic growth has been the trend towards the higher degrees of wealth inequality that now exist in many of the world's leading economies. As is well-documented, the economic and technological changes of the past few decades have resulted in a higher share of the world's wealth being concentrated in the hands of a smaller share of the world's inhabitants. At the same time, these changes have reduced the wealth (and the opportunities to acquire wealth) for the world's poorer segments of society, although some gains were made by poorer segments of society in recent years.

As we have witnessed in recent years, this rising level of wealth inequality has played a major role in many of the political changes that have taken place around the world. Whether or not it is the increasing popularity of politicians and political parties that espouse right-wing or left-wing populist platforms, or the proliferation of protest movements around the world, wealth inequality has been one of the leading drivers of the political upheaval that we have seen so far in the 21st century. In the past, when wealth inequality levels had risen to intolerable levels (late 18th century France or the early 20th century United States), the populace demanded policies aimed at reducing wealth inequality. It may well be that we are on the verge of just such an era, but that remains to be seen.

Quality of life is another issue that has become a key driver in the search for alternative measures of economic success. This broad and often hard-to-define issue has generated a great deal of controversy, as how one society measures quality of life might vary dramatically from how another does so. For example, Europeans are rarely hesitant to remind non-Europeans that they work less hours per year (and enjoy more retirement years and benefits) than most other societies. In contrast, many Asian societies are quick to remind others of their hard-working natures, while people in the US are constantly telling others about their individual freedoms. Simply put, measuring quality of life is a thankless task, but that has not stopped countless organizations from attempting to do so. Of course, measuring some variables such as life expectancy, literacy or access to the internet are quantifying measurements, but combining them into something that is designed to measure a society's quality of life often produces results that are far less than satisfactory, and sometimes fail outright to measure current economic success or the economic prospects for a country or region.

Altogether, it is all-but-certain that more and more measurements of economic well-being will be concocted in the coming years. And yes, some of these aforementioned measurements do have their merits. Certainly those that measure the environmental impact of economic activities have a role to play in devising economic policies for the future that will reduce our detrimental impact on the environment. Likewise, wealth inequality, while all-but impossible to remove entirely, is a dangerous factor that needs to be addressed in today's world, so measurements that indicate a country's success in doing so also have their place. Finally, while measuring quality of life might be too subjective and random to do in an accurate manner, it is nonetheless something that most societies and individuals are striving to improve, so again, there is no harm in attempting to measure it. In fact, there is no harm in any of these alternative measurements, so long as they do not overshadow what remains our fundamental need in the modern world, to generate economic growth.

Why We Need to Generate Economic Growth

While the focus on generating economic growth may be anathema to many these days, whether they like it or not, it remains absolutely essential in the modern world. There are simply too many historical examples of what happens to a society when economic growth disappears for a long period of time, and none of these examples should bolster the position of the anti-growth establishment. In fact, many of these examples are quite recent, so their impact can be studied and understood by those that would like to see a lesser focus on economic growth, especially those that would welcome lower growth, or even no growth at all.

Quite simply, our modern world, with all of its conveniences, comforts and advances, has been built on the back of sustained economic growth in nearly all of the world's most important economic centers. The systems that define the modern world, whether it is our healthcare systems, infrastructure, communications, social welfare systems or any other of the many aspects of modern life that we take for granted, were all developed due to this sustained economic growth, for without this growth, the modern world would look much different, and would likely be much poorer and much more violent, than it is today. In fact, growth has become somewhat taken for granted, and is generally expected by most of the world's population. A look at the finances of the modern world and the rising levels of debt show that much of the world lives in the expectation of future growth. Certainly governments, businesses and individuals would not be willing or able to accrue such high levels of debt if they did not expect their economies, revenues or income to grow in the future, would they?

Imagine, for a second, a place where economic growth no longer occurred, where the economy either stagnated or fell into an outright decline. Let's look at one aspect of the outcomes of this decline. In this case, that would be the fact that, without economic growth, major cutbacks in public spending would be necessary. One can imagine the devastating impact that a lack of long-term economic growth would have on a government's financial health. Unfortunately, there are too many recent examples of governments that have had to make draconian cutbacks to government spending as a result of a lack of economic growth. The most notable recent examples have been Italy and Greece, as both of these countries have seen their economic output decline over the past two decades. In both countries, government spending levels have fallen significantly in recent years as government revenues remain well below previous levels. In Italy, the Global Financial Crisis and the subsequent Euro Crisis forced major government spending cuts, including massive cuts in infrastructure spending, something that may have contributed to a series of infrastructure-related disasters in that country in recent years. Another example can be found in those countries that are dependent upon oil exports to generate much of their government revenues. After the price of oil collapsed in 2014 (and again in 2020), these countries have had to make massive reductions in public spending in order to offset the large declines in government revenues that followed this drop in oil prices.

Another result of a long-term decline in economic growth would be quite obvious, and that would be a decline in overall levels of wealth for those countries, states or cities that could no longer generate economic growth. If economic growth stagnated (and if population growth did the same), the result would be stagnant levels of wealth. However, if economic growth turned negative (and population growth was stagnant or positive), wealth levels would actually decline. This would also occur if economic growth levels failed to match the level of population growth in a country, state or region. The former has been witnessed in places such as Japan or Italy, where economic growth and population growth have both been anemic in recent decades. The latter has occurred in recent years in countries such as Nigeria or Brazil, where population growth has actually exceeded economic growth for a number of years, reducing both overall levels of wealth and those countries' relative levels of wealth. This has also been seen in the United States, were varying levels of economic growth among the 50 states that comprise the US have led to major changes in relative wealth levels among the various states that make up the US.

History makes the best case for the argument that the modern world continues to need to generate sufficient levels of economic growth. A look back at history shows us the many examples of the positive impact that economic growth has had on human development, security and social advancement. The Roman Empire and all of its advancements were the result of the ancient world's longest period of sustained economic growth, one that transformed the western world. The Industrial Revolution transformed the West into the world's first modern states, creating never-before seen levels of wealth, scientific advancement, living standards and so much more. In the modern world, China's four decades of rapid economic growth have transformed what was once one of the world's poorest countries into one of its most dynamic, while lifting hundreds of millions of people out of poverty in the process in what might have been the greatest poverty-reduction program in history.

Just as there are many historical examples of how sustained economic growth can improve living standards, society and much more, so too are there many examples of the dangers facing those places that cannot generate sufficient economic growth. The economic collapse of the western Roman Empire resulted in centuries of poverty, strife and general backwardness for much of Europe, with western Europe failing to return to some of the living standards enjoyed by the citizens of the Roman Empire until as late as the 19th century. Imagine that we are currently at our economic peak and that it will take another 17 centuries for people to return to the living standards of today. It seems impossible, but it has happened before. It is not inevitable that we continue to advance socially, technologically, economically or in many other ways. Decline is something we must constantly be vigilant against and always be prepared to prevent.

By promoting policies that support economic growth, governments can help to prevent such a catastrophic outcome. By generating economic growth, we can create high levels of consumption of goods and services, enabling economies to continue to grow and diversify. Likewise, economic growth promotes investment, resulting in wealth being transferred to more regions and to more people. Without growth, businesses, investors and individuals will increasingly hoard their wealth instead of investing it in projects or markets that can further the generation of economic growth. Economic growth also creates jobs, enabling large segments of a country's, a state's, or a city's population to remain productive members of society. Each of these three results (wealth creation, investment promotion and job creation) are vital to the health of a modern economy and all three of them can ensure that an economy continues to generate healthy levels of growth for a sustained period of time. The alternative is too bleak to consider. A long-term decline in wealth, living standards, scientific achievement and much more would be the catalyst for a long-term decline in the state of humanity, something that needs to be avoided at all costs given what we know from history.

SCARY PROSPECTS WITHOUT GROWTH

As we have already touched upon, history shows us the dangers associated with a world without economic growth. There are all too many examples of what could go wrong if the economy stagnates or declines. As we mentioned, Rome's economic decline was so severe and so influential that it took Europe more than 1,500 years to recover from this decline. China's history is filled with extended periods of economic expansion that were followed by extended periods of economic decline, and today's China is still greatly influenced by the insecurity that it feels as it pulls out of a centuries-long economic decline that only ended in the 1980s. Likewise, Argentina in the 20th century showed that it is possible to go from one of the world's wealthiest countries to one of its most-economically-unstable places if economic growth stalls for an extended period of time.

Just as important as the reasons for a long-term decline of an economy are the effects of this decline. Simply put, the disruptions caused by the lack of economic growth can tear apart a community, a country or an entire region. A lack of economic growth leads to a decline in living standards, one that, if it is allowed to continue, can set back decades or even centuries of progress. Security threats also become more prevalent without consistent economic growth. It is no coincidence that many of the world's greatest conflicts and periods of unrest came on the heels of periods of severe economic upheaval and decline. For a city, state or country that cannot generate economic growth, not only is there a decline in its living standards and security, but there is also a decline in its power and influence relative to other cities, states and countries.

These sorts of declines can be seen in many modern examples. One is Japan, whose three decades of economic stagnation have dramatically weakened that country's position in East Asia, particularly as other countries in that region have managed to record some of the highest rates of economic growth in the world during that same time frame. Southern Europe's economic travails are another example in the modern world of the impact of little or no economic growth on a region's living standards and stability. Finally, Venezuela should be the clearest warning of all in the modern world, as its economic collapse has driven what was once Latin America's wealthiest economy into the depths of despair.

For each of these aforementioned examples, there are a number of commonalities. First, governments either mismanaged economic policy in the period leading up to, or during the first phase of, the economic slowdown. In addition, they often botched the response to these economic troubles, or were no longer in a position to adequately respond to these new economic challenges. Second, there was almost always a demographic element to these economic troubles. Sometimes it was a sudden collapse in the working-age population caused by a war, a pandemic or a natural disaster, or its was a longer-term change in a country's demographic situation. Regardless, shifting demographics have proven to be a leading driver of long-term economic change throughout history. A third factor that can be seen in these examples is a severe disruption to trade and investment. Sometimes this can be brought about on purpose, as when a government enacts severe protectionist policies that stifle trade and invest-ment. At other times, this can be the result of conflicts or disasters that disrupt the existing system of trade and investment. Regardless, longer-term declines in trade and investment have always proven to be harmful to the prospects for economic growth and development. Finally, many examples of long-term economic decline and stagnation have been preceded by periods of little or no productivity growth. This can be the result of a dearth of technological advancements or of a lack of investment in technologies or processes that generate productivity growth. Without healthy levels of productivity growth, an economy will find itself dangerously exposed to the threat of longer-term economic stagnation and decline.

THE IMPACT ON LIVING STANDARDS

Despite many claims to the contrary, modern living standards are higher than they have been at any time in human history. There are many facts to support this claim. For example, life expectancy today is higher than it has ever been and has continued to trend upwards in recent years, particularly in poorer parts of the world.

Global Life Expectancy

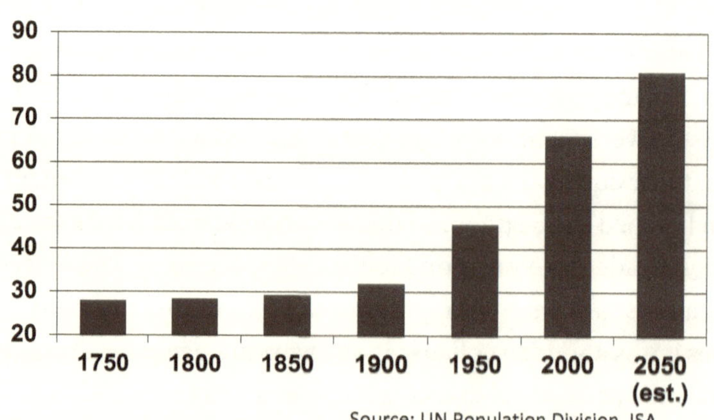

Source: UN Population Division, ISA

Likewise, the world is much wealthier now that it ever was, as not only have incomes increased in much of the world, but many basic goods and services are now much cheaper than they were in the past. Again, the greatest gains in wealth levels in recent decades have come from areas of the world that were quite poor in the past, as an increasing number of people have been lifted out of poverty thanks to decades of economic growth.

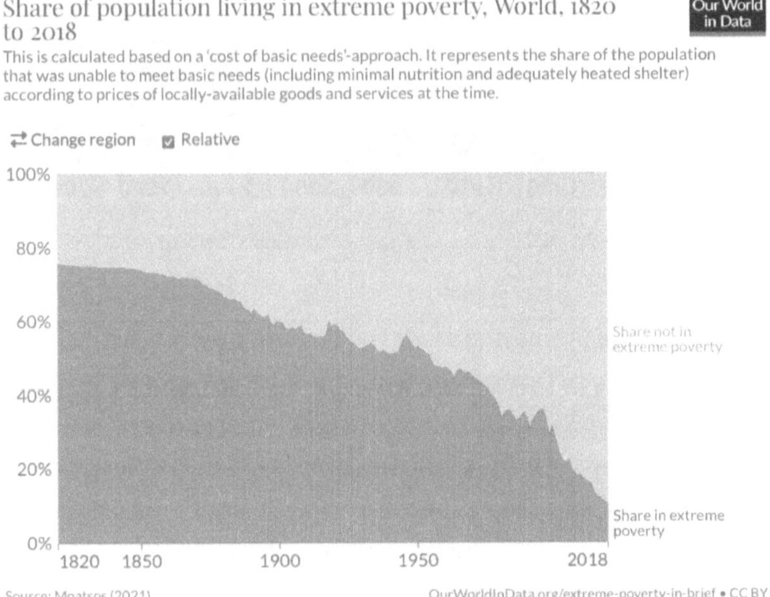

These improved livelihoods and higher levels of wealth have left more time for much of the world to enjoy more leisurely pursuits such as travel and artistic endeavors.

Finally, the world is better educated today than ever before. Not only are people receiving more education over their lifetimes, but today, a person's access to information is greater than it ever was. For example, it has been said that the average person today has more access to information in a single day than Thomas Jefferson or Sir Isaac Newton had in their lifetimes. How people use this access to such vast amounts of information is another topic altogether, but let's just say that there is no reason for a person living in the modern world to lack information and analysis on almost any given topic.

These dramatic improvements in living standards have been made possible as a result of long-term economic growth. In fact, when we look back at the periods of

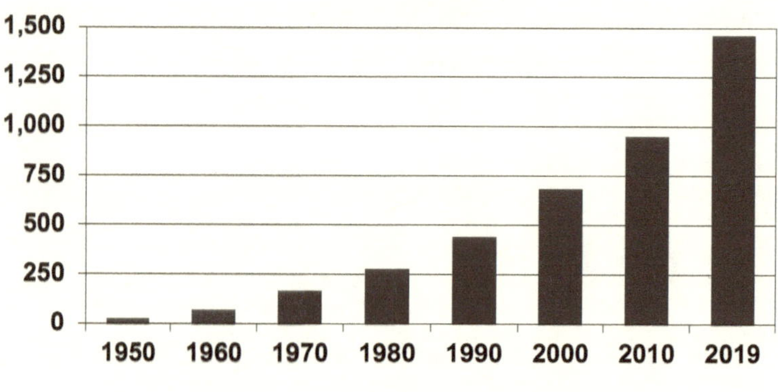

Source: UNWTO

human history when living standards did rise for a prolonged period of time, we can see that these periods were almost always proceeded by a prolonged period of steady economic growth. Rome's Golden Age was proceeded by such a period of economic growth, as the integration of the Mediterranean economy under Roman leadership ushered in the ancient world's most successful economic transformation. In the 19th century, the United Kingdom emerged as the wealthiest country in the world with tremendous advances in living standards only after the Industrial Revolution ushered in decades of strong economic growth in the UK. The same holds true for the United States. It's living standards were also able to rise dramatically in the 19th and 20th centuries thanks to high levels of economic growth that allowed the US to overtake the UK as the world's wealthiest large economy, a position it holds to this day.

As we can see, long periods of economic growth are nearly always followed by significant advancements in living standards. As such, it also stands that long-term economic downturns are among the biggest threats to living standards. Without economic growth, public spending would fall, as we have witnessed in many modern-day examples. So too would wealth generation weaken, something that would impact nearly all aspects of living standards. In fact, without economic growth, the living standards of nearly all segments of the population would be negatively impacted, something that could turn into a long-term decline in living standards if economic growth could not be revived.

Such long-term declines would have an impact across the board, touching nearly all aspects of living standards. For example, health standards would regress, as they did during historical periods of long-term economic decline. Security would be imperiled, as not only would the threat of major conflicts rise, but so too would local security deteriorate as the state would no longer have the funds or the resources to create a stable and capable security system. Leisurely activities would decline, as free time would lessen and as disposable income and economic specialization decline. Finally, education standards and outcomes would deteriorate, leaving people less knowledgeable and less capable of reversing the economic decline that brought about their loss of education and knowledge in the first place.

One area that would be significantly impacted by a loss of long-term economic growth would be security. As we have seen repeatedly throughout history, economic issues, typically those associated with economic decline, or the threat of economic decline, have been a root cause of conflict and instability. There are many examples of this throughout history. Japan went to war with the United States in 1941 because it feared an economic (and military) collapse without access to vital oil and gas imports. Syria's recent civil war started in large part as a result of the economic stagnation of that country, while it fueled popular anger against the Assad regime. When a country is in economic decline, it has little to lose. Furthermore, this economic decline breeds frustration, anger and resentment, which in turn leads to a climate that fosters the spread of extremist ideologies, with right-wing extremism tending to look for scapegoats for a country's economic woes and with left-wing extremism tending to offer solutions that often come at the price of individual liberties. Meanwhile, a general economic decline will often lead to competition for economic resources that can quickly escalate into an all-out conflict.

The internal instability that is either a cause or a symptom of longer-term economic decline can have devastating effects on the economic well-being of a country. Once again, Ancient Rome provides us with a frightening example that can be applied to the modern world. After two centuries of relative peace (the Pax Romana) and a level of prosperity never before seen in the ancient world, Rome descended into internal chaos and strife in the 3rd century CE that resulted in long periods in which the empire was divided into rival statelets. This disrupted the complex economic systems of the Roman Empire by destroying the internal and external trade and investment networks that allowed Rome to achieve such unprecedented prosperity and power, leaving the empire in a sort of proto-feudal state that would come to characterize much of Europe's economy for the next millennium. Chinese history too is littered with examples of periods of internal strife and conflict that brought an end to the proceeding periods of economic expansion and political harmony. In fact, it was only when China's main population centers and trade routes (along the country's rivers and coastline) were controlled by one or two rulers that China was able to achieve its highest levels of economic development and technological advancement. A more modern example is that of the Soviet Union. The rapid economic decline of the Soviet Union in the 1970s and 1980s was a key factor in the internal unrest that led to the dissolution of the USSR in 1991. Furthermore, this dissolution of the USSR into 15 independent countries, some of which faced their own internal divisions, resulted in dramatic economic dislocations in the 1990s that resulted to massive declines in economic output, with some of these new countries still suffering from the effects of the collapse of the Soviet Union fully three decades later.

Economic decline does not just disrupt the internal stability and security of a country, but it can also lead to wars between two or more countries. Again, there are many examples of how this can happen. Looking far back into our history, a good example of this is the near-collapse of the Byzantine (Eastern Roman) Empire in the 7th century. Constant wars and the devastating Plague of Justinian in the 6th century had led to a dramatic decline in the Byzantine economy, leaving it both desperate to recoup lost territories and to revive its economy. However, its weakened state left it vulnerable to a new and surprising enemy, the newly-Islamized Arabs of the Hejaz in the western Arabian Peninsula, who swept north, west and east to conquer much of what had been the remaining territory of the Byzantine Empire (not to mention what was left of the Sasanian Empire in Persia (modern-day Iran). In the 19th century, the Ottoman Empire (based in the same city as the Byzantine Empire) had entered into a long period of economic decline and by the second half of that century, European powers whose economic growth and development had raced ahead of the Ottomans thanks to the Industrial Revolution, were moving in to claim parts of the empire for themselves (or for newly-created vassal states). This led to a series of conflicts in and around the Ottoman Empire that were focused on the Balkans, but also spread to North Africa and the Arabian Peninsula. Finally, many of the reasons for Adolf Hitler's determination to bring Germany into wars with its neighbors in the late 1930s and early 1940s were economic. Some of these economic factors were rather immediate, such as the fact that the German economy was overheating in the late 1930s due to the vast sums spent by the Nazis on German armed forces and infrastructure, as well as Germany's desperate lack of natural resources. Some were more global in spirit, particularly Hitler's realization that Germany would be no match economically with such giant powers such as the United States over the long-term if it were confined to its pre-war borders.

It is hard to dispute the notion that a lack of economic growth has a detrimental impact on issues such as living standards, stability and security. However, it is important to remember that in our quest for economic growth, we need to ensure that future growth is both stable and sustainable. In fact, as we strive to achieve continued economic growth, we must consider the potential negative ramifications of this growth, even as we realize that the need for growth remains firmly in place.

Of these other factors that need to be considered, none is more important to our well-being than our need to protect our planet from the negative impact that our drive for economic growth has had. In fact, we need to do much more to protect the planet as the evidence of our impact on the planet is all around us. Some of this evidence is irrefutable. For example, it is commonly accepted by scientists around the world that the unprecedented increases in global temperatures in recent decades have been driven in no small part by the greenhouse gases that our industrialized economies have released over the past 250 years. Likewise, our quest for land and resources has taken a terrible toll on our planet's flora and fauna, leading some scientists to warn that we are in the midst of the planet's six mass extinction event, with the one underway now being almost entirely the fault of the human race. Meanwhile, while we are warming and depopulating the planet, we are rapidly depleting many of its resources, not only those that drive our economies such as oil or coal, but also those that allow us to live here in the first place, such as water and arable land.

There are also sustainability issues linked to our economies and living standards. One of these is the need to ensure the well-being of as many people as possible, not just a very small percentage of humanity. In fact, one of the foremost goals of our efforts to achieve sustained economic growth is the need to improve living standards for everyone. This is not to say that wealth needs to be forcibly redistributed to poorer segments of society, but rather to suggest that policies need to be enacted that provide opportunities for all people to improve their living standards and levels of wealth. As we have seen in recent years, the rise in the level in wealth inequality in many areas of the world has been one of the most important factors in many of the economic and political problems facing the world today.

For me, it is clear that these goals can be achieved together with the generation of economic growth. In fact, saving the environment and reducing wealth inequality can not only accompany the generation of economic growth, but they can themselves become generators of economic growth by creating new industries and building up a vast new base of consumers. In fact, more and more countries and industries are attempting to do just that, by balancing their need for growth with the opportunities provided by these challenges. While these opportunities are a nice incentive, the biggest incentive remains the fact that we have no alternative, for it we do not do something to improve the health of our environment or to lift more people out of poverty, the very future of our existence on this planet is in severe jeopardy.

Chapter Four

A Century of Growth

IN TODAY'S WORLD, THERE is simply too much focus on near-term results and short-term trends. In fact, much of the world continues to have a short-term mindset when it comes to all types of economic matters. Such a mindset adds to the pressure on economic policy makers, businesses and others involved in making economic-related decisions to find solutions that improve the immediate outlook of an economy's performance, or of a business' balance sheet. Such a short-term focus can allow for long-term risks to build in return for short-term benefits, something that we see happening in economic policy-making more and more in recent decades. Of course, the positive side of this is that such short-termism can allow for quick responses to immediate crises, potentially preventing them from becoming much greater crises. It can be argued that the United States' quick response to the financial crisis in 2008 (after failing to recognize its emergence in the previous years) helped to prevent an even greater economic crisis at that time. In contrast, the European Union's piecemeal efforts to combat the effects of the same financial crisis resulted in a series of lingering problems in Europe the resulted in the region suffering from three separate recessions in the five years that followed the start of this crisis.

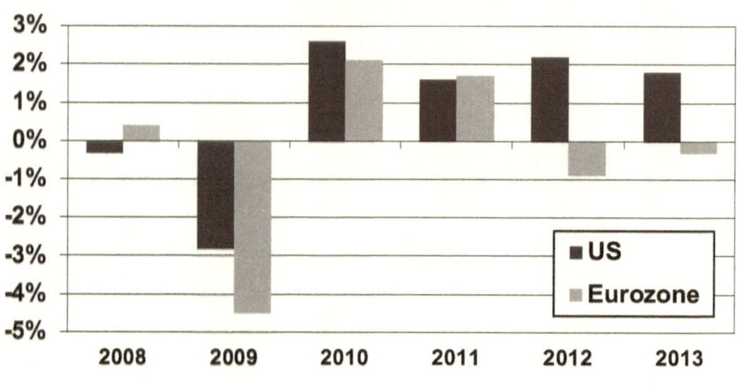

Source: IMF

Perhaps the most watched economic data release these days (apart from stock market indices) is the release of quarterly GDP growth results, particularly those for the world's largest economies such as the United States, China or India. In fact, the release of quarter-on-quarter GDP results is considered to be the most definitive measure of an economy's performance and can lead to great swings in business and investor confidence. Meanwhile, there are two main types of quarter-on-quarter GDP growth figures. One measures simply the growth (or decline) of economic output in the current quarter compared to the previous quarter. This figure is the one focused on by most European economies and a handful of other countries. The other type of quarter-on-quarter GDP growth figure that is often cited is an annualized figure that measures how fast an economy would be growing for an entire year if that quarter's rate persisted throughout the year. This figure is useful as it removes the seasonal effects on the end result. but is used by relatively few economies, although it is the measurement of choice for the world's largest and third-largest economies (the United States and Japan).

While quarter-on-quarter results are the measurement of choice for most developed economies, most emerging markets tend to focus more on year-on-year GDP growth results, which measure an economy's output compared with the same year, quarter or month from the year before. In fact, this figure is probably the one most used to compare economic performances across countries or regions, making it what I would consider to be the most important piece of economic information in the world today. For example, China releases somewhat suspect year-on-year GDP growth results every quarter (and these are almost never revised at later dates, highlighting their questionable nature). Of course, it could be worse. Vietnam often releases its year-on-year GDP growth results a day or two before the quarter ends, and it too almost never revises these figures. For me, I prefer year-on-year GDP growth figures to quarter-on-quarter ones as they take into account the performance of an economy over a 12-month period and reduce some of the short-term variables and one-offs that distort quarter-on-quarter results.

Nevertheless, it can be reasonably argued that both quarterly and year-on-year GDP growth results can either overstate an economy's health or understate its troubles. For example, if a major hurricane strikes the Dominican Republic in August, the third quarter's GDP growth results (quarter-on-quarter) for that country are going to be dramatically impacted, perhaps overstating the downturn faced by the Dominican Republic. Meanwhile, year-on-year GDP growth results will at least take into account the economic performance of that country over the three previous quarters, alleviating some of the impact of the hurricane on the economic results for the Dominican Republic. Still, both measures have their flaws, and these short-term views can cloud the judgement of businesses and economic policy makers. It is clear that a longer-term view needs to be considered.

This focus on near-term economic results leads to many misleading interpretations of an economy's performance, something that can lead to economic policy-making that inadequately assesses the needs of an economy, or to business decisions that are based on faulty interpretations of the ability of a certain market to generate growth for that business. In fact, near-term results often lead to false impressions of the true health of an economy. If an economy records exceptionally strong growth over a quarter or two, this does not mean that the economy in question is necessarily a healthy one, or one that can continue to generate such growth over a longer period of time. Just the same, an economy that falls into a slump for a quarter or two may in fact not be a weak economy, just one that has been impacted adversely by short-term factors. Nevertheless, these short-term results, and the increasing focus on them, do have a major impact on many areas such as business confidence, stock markets and much more. Therefore, while they may not be an accurate representation of the health of an economy, short-term indicators, especially those for economic growth, have an outsized impact on economic decision making in the modern world.

Let's look at a couple of modern-day examples of this, both of which hail from the same region. One example is Germany, Europe's largest economy. Over the past ten to fifteen years, Germany has often been described as one of the world's most successful economies, especially in recent years, as Germany was able to record stronger economic growth rates between 2015 and 2018. However, a longer-term view of the German economy suggests that the relative health and success of the German economy has been overstated. In fact, even with its slightly better-than-average performance in recent years, the fact is that Germany has not outperformed many other European economies over the past 20 years, and in fact, trails behind many of its neighbors in terms of growth during that period.

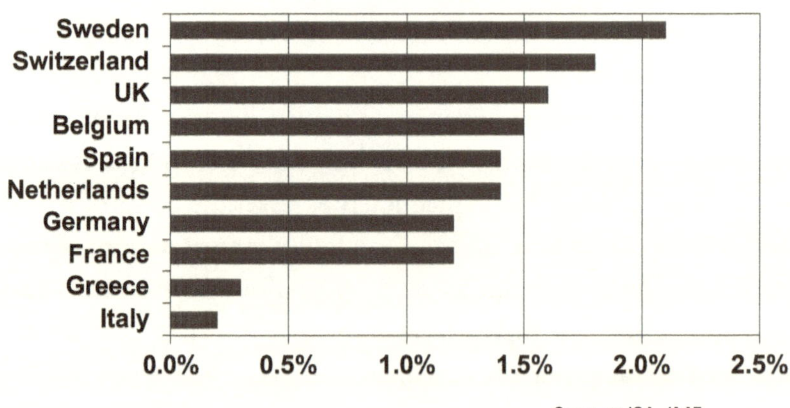

Another example to look at is the United Kingdom, Europe's second-largest economy. Because of the recent chaos surrounding the UK's withdrawal from the European Union and its poor handling of the Covid-19 pandemic, there has been a widespread assumption that the British economy has been severely underperforming its European counterparts. However, the reality has been quite different. Over the past few years, the UK's economic performance has not been as bad as many pundits have led the public to believe. Moreover, when taking a longer-term view, it becomes apparent that the British economy has been, in fact, one of the most successful economies in Europe, generating more economic growth in that region than any other country.

Much of this focus on short-term economic results is being fueled by governments and the media, whose focus on these short-term results has intensified in recent years. For governments, positive short-term results are trumpeted as evidence of the wisdom of their economic policies, while poor short-term results are often blamed on external factors (i.e. factors outside of their control). For the media, short-term economic results can make headlines when they are better or worse than expected. Unfortunately, these short-term results all too often give us a false view of the state of the global economy.

Why the Focus Should be on Long-Term Results

It is clear that the focus on economic results should be on longer-term results, for these results better represent the true health of an economy. For example, an economy that can generate higher rates of growth over a prolonged period of time can more accurately be described as a healthy economy than one that experiences both extreme highs and lows over that same period. Likewise, long-term economic results help us to better identify economies that are in terminal stagnation or decline.

These long-term assessments of an economy's health are useful in enabling businesses and investors to make strategic decisions in terms of investments. On one hand, longer-term economic results can more accurately reflect the impact of investments that may not have many short-term benefits, but do promote growth over the longer-term. Too often investments with long-term benefits are neglected in favor of those that provide short-term bursts of growth, but may be harmful over the longer-term. One example of this long-term type of investment is infrastructure. Clearly, infrastructure investment is costly over the near-term, and the disruptions that it causes can actually reduce economic growth over the near-term. However, investment in infrastructure, when done sensibly, can provide many long-term economic benefits, none of which is more important than expanding an economy's capacity to grow and its ability to raise its longer-term growth ceiling. Likewise, investment in education also brings few immediate benefits for an economy, but unquestionably brings many long-term benefits, particularly with its impact on an economy's ability to develop high-tech, high-growth sectors of its economy.

As we will see, there are many periods in history that can highlight the importance of long-term economic growth on the ability of a society to thrive and prosper over an extended period of time. The post-Industrial-Revolution United Kingdom is a perfect example of this, as it was able to use the long-term economic growth generated by its industrialization to become the world's most powerful country for over a century, a rather remarkable achievement for such a small island nation. The United States too was an economy that was able to transform long-term high rates of economic growth into real power, one that allowed the US to become the most powerful state the world has so far ever seen. Finally, modern-day China enjoyed four decades of rapid economy growth that transformed what had been one of the poorest countries into the world into one that was challenging the United States for global leadership. All of these states owed their tremendous success and their status as the leading powers of the world to their ability to generate economic growth at high rates for an extended period of time.

One topic we should address before we delve too deep into economic figures is the fact that there are a number of issues with regards to the collection of accurate and reliable economic data. This is particularly true when one wishes to go back further in time to compare and contrast economic data from the more distant past. In fact, many economists and historians have attempted to go way back in history to find economic data, or at least to come up with high-level economic estimates, to measure the economic development of ancient states. There are many examples of this, none of which is more famous or well-respected than that of the British economist Angus Maddison, whose work on measuring economic output over the past 2,000 years will be heavily cited in this book. Others, such as Stanford's Ian Morris, have also made giant strides in helping us to understand the economic situation in times long ago and how we can compare economic trends of periods in history with those trends of today's world. Of course, we do not, and cannot, expect pinpoint accuracy with economic output data dating back to the time of the Roman Empire. However, I believe that is very important for historians and economists to try and piece together the puzzles that are historical economies, both to help us understand those periods of history and to allow us to better understand the forces that continue to drive our economies in the modern world.

The closer we come to the present day, the easier it becomes to find accurate and reliable data. It is a welcome development for those of us active in the fields of economics and history that most of the modern world's leading economies have had a fetish for producing extremely detailed and accurate economic data, something that has enabled us to tremendously improve our understanding of economics. In fact, there are many important economies that have a long history of producing accurate and detailed economic data. Many of these economies are in Europe, where we can find surprisingly detailed economic data stretching back to the 19th century (and even longer in a few cases). Furthermore, modern-day Europe is a paradise for bureaucrats, and while this may have many drawbacks for most people, for economists, this presents us with a treasure trove of economic information on the wide variety of economies that comprise 21st century Europe. We are also fortunate that the world's largest economy, the United States, also has a love for detailed statistics, something that can be seen in the incredible wealth of data the accompanies major sports in the US. This holds true for economics as well, as few, if any, countries can match the incredible array of economic data that is being produced by various statistical agencies across the United States, and has been produced for a surprisingly long time. Meanwhile, there are some emerging markets that have also dramatically improved their provision of economic data in recent decades, helping us to gain a better understanding of the underlying issues and trends impacting emerging market economies in the modern world.

During the 20th century, countries that produced accurate and reliable economic data comprised an overwhelming share of the world's economic output, allowing economists to have a relatively clear view of the health of the global economy as a whole. However, in recent decades, emerging markets such as China, India and others have come to comprise a significantly larger share of the global economy and, unfortunately, their economic data is both lacking in terms of historical statistics and in terms of overall reliability. Take China for example. Its quarterly GDP growth results are some of the most anticipated economic data releases in the world, but virtually no one who analyzes these results believe that they are accurate. This can be seen in the simple fact that China's quarterly GDP growth data is released quite early in the quarter and is almost never subsequently revised. In contrast, US or Swedish GDP growth results will often be revised multiple times, sometimes years later as more data is analyzed. Of course, we also have enough off-the-cuff comments from Chinese government officials about the made-up nature of the country's economic data to know that these figures are not accurate. Of course, China is not alone in this, as many emerging markets release highly questionable data, while others (such as many Middle Eastern and African countries) release very little data at all. The problem here is that, as these emerging markets that release too inaccurate, or too late, economic data continue to grow in terms of importance and in terms of their share of global economic output, their lack of accurate and reliable data will make it harder for economists to accurately measure the health and direction of the global economy, and this could lead to the wrong economic policies being put in place in the future.

Undoubtedly, it is difficult, costly and time-consuming for a country in the modern world to compile and release detailed and accurate economic data, hence the lack of such data from many less-developed countries. Despite these difficulties, it is worth the effort for every country to strive to release as much accurate economic data as they can, for this helps businesses and policy makers to formulate the best strategies to generate economic growth in their cities, states or countries. Furthermore, the longer the period that we have accurate economic data for, the more we can learn from the lessons of the past and be able to react to crises when they arise. Furthermore, as we have already discussed, it is extremely important in economics to take the long-term view, and having a strong historical economic record makes this something that is much easier to do. In this book, we will try our best to do just that in order to apply the lessons from our economic history to the modern global economy of the 21st century.

A Look Back at the Century

Let's start our look back at the past century of economic history in the year 1920. For us, life in 1920 is fairly recognizable, with the Industrial Age in full swing, many of the conveniences and standards of the modern world were already in place during this era. Of course, this was a time in which the world was emerging from an earth-shattering period of unrest and upheaval, highlighted by two events which had dramatically changed the world, the First World War and the Spanish Flu pandemic. For Europe, which at this time remained the world's leading economic center (although its grip on this position was weakening significantly), 1920 would have been a year of great uncertainty after the millions of deaths caused by the war and the pandemic, as well as the near-total redrawing of Europe's maps, which saw long-standing powers such as Romanov Russia, the Habsburg Empire and the Ottoman Empire all having disappeared (or about to disappear in the case of the Ottomans). Furthermore, Europe had been dramatically weakened by the First World War, which exposed many of the continent's weaknesses, such as its demographic slowdown, its divided nature and its lack of natural resources. For the rest of the world, life was beginning to return to normal in 1920 as the impact of the First World War outside of Europe was quite minimal and as the Spanish Flu pandemic was in the process of winding down. Nevertheless, massive economic and political changes were underway on a global scale, changes that would forever alter the global balance of economic power.

Much of the world in 1920 was focused on either ensuring that a Second World War could not occur, or in the case of many of the world's newly-created countries, that their territorial holdings were sufficient enough to shield them from revanchist neighbors. Meanwhile, the democratic form of government that was being championed by United States President Woodrow Wilson was spreading faster than ever in 1920, with many new countries adopting this form of government (or a facsimile of it), while more and more people (especially women) were finally gaining the right to fully participate in the democratic process. However, while democracy was making great strides in 1920, the seeds of its destruction were already being sown in many parts of the world, and a new great age of totalitarianism was just around the corner. Nevertheless, 1920 brought a sense of relief to much of the world that had been shattered by war and sickness and there were genuine hopes that a much brighter future lay ahead.

If we look at the state of the global economy in 1920, we must remember that, for much of the world, we are lacking reliable and accurate economic data for this period. As such, we will rely heavily upon Agnus Maddison's work here, as he and his team worked diligently to gather and assess a great deal of the economic data from this era.

In 1920, Europe remained the center of the world economy, accounting for an estimated 30% of total global GDP at that time. However, Europe's economic output had shrunken by an estimated 10% since the beginning of the First World War, with the region's first- and third-largest economies (Germany and France) suffering particularly large declines in economic output during and immediately after the war.

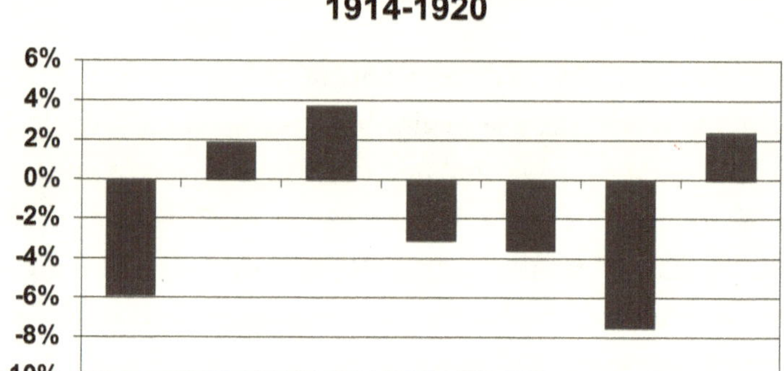

Source: Maddison

Outside of Europe, the United States continued to expand its lead as the world's largest individual economy, as its total economic output in 1920 was now nearly three times larger than the world's second-largest economy. Furthermore, the United States' economic position in the world was dramatically enhanced during the war, as most of its industrialized rivals had suffered great economic losses during the war, with many of these countries finding themselves owing huge debts to the US. This was aided by the fact that, despite the war and the impact of the Spanish Flu pandemic, US economic output was almost 25% larger in 1920 than it was at the beginning of the First World War. Clearly, while the war and the pandemic were a tragedy for the United States in terms of the human costs of these crises, the US was able to emerge from this period with its global role dramatically increased, although the US' soon-to-be return to isolationism would somewhat disguise this fact from the rest of the world for another couple of decades.

In Asia, the economic situation was not greatly altered by the war and the pandemic. The economic weaknesses that had plagued China and India for a long period of time remained firmly in place, with both China's and India's share of global economic output continuing to decline as other areas of the world were returning to industry-driven growth. Only their vast populations kept China and India among the world's larger economies at this time, although China was deeply divided and India was still controlled by the United Kingdom. The one power in Asia that was rising was Japan, as the reforms that were launched during the Meiji Restoration continued to bear fruit for that once backwards and isolated country. In fact, the war proved to be a significant spur for growth in Japan, as economic output in Japan rose by 36% between 1914 and 1920, allowing Japan to maintain the momentum that it had built up in previous decades. With Japan emerging as Asia's only industrialized economy, it was becoming evident that Japan would soon be in a position to make a play at becoming the dominant power in the region, even as it only accounted for a very small share of Asia's population and territory.

Per Capita GDP at PPP in Asia in 1920 (USA = 100)

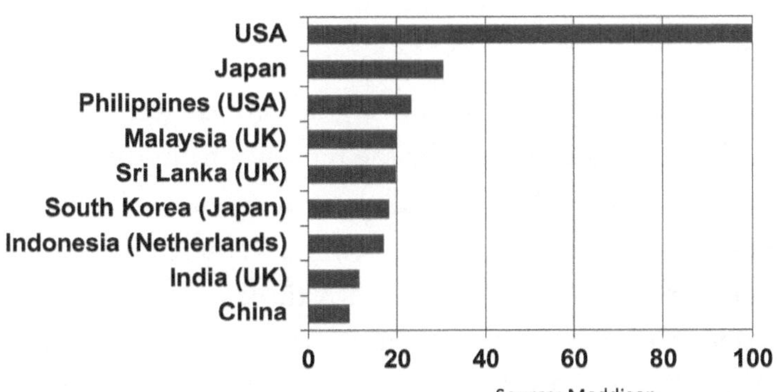

Source: Maddison

Outside of Europe, North America and the Asia-Pacific region, there were few economic success stories in 1920. One region that was performing quite strongly during this period was Latin America, with some countries in that region, most notably Argentina, ranking among the wealthiest countries of the world. In fact, the period leading up to 1920 was one of rapid growth for Argentina, Brazil and many other countries in this region.

Elsewhere, much of the world was mired in severe poverty, with wealth levels that were far below those of the world's advanced countries. Of course, much of Africa and many parts of Asia remained under the control of colonial powers in 1920, as the great decolonialization period lay a few decades in the future. For most colonies, this meant that their economies were geared towards supplying materials and manpower for their colonial masters, while serving as captured markets for goods and services from the colonial power.

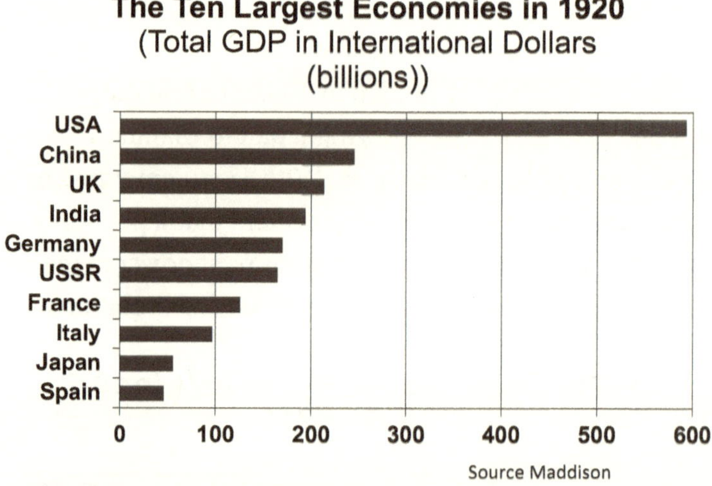

If we look at the chart above showing the world's ten-largest economies in 1920, the list looks surprising like the rankings from the present day. The United States was by 1920 the world's largest economy (having overtaken the United Kingdom in the 1870s and China in the 1880s), and its level of economic output in 1920 was already nearly three times as large as that of the world's second- and third-largest economies (China and the UK). China and India, while quite poor, were the world's second- and fourth-largest economies in 1920 (India was still under UK control at this point), due almost entirely to their giant populations. In 1920, China's population was almost five times larger than that of the United States, while India's was three times larger at that point in time. Meanwhile, Europe remained the region with the largest regional economic output, and despite the impact of the First World War and the Spanish Flu pandemic, European countries were ranked third, fifth, sixth, seventh, eighth and tenth in the rankings of the world's largest economies.

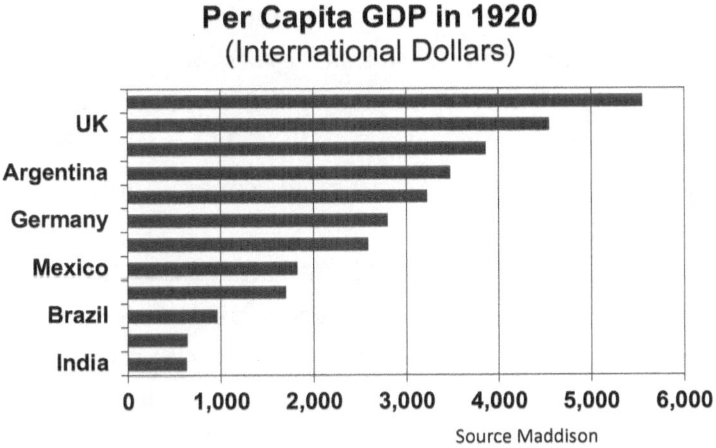

In terms of wealth levels, the New World's leading economies had overtaken war-torn Europe to become the world's wealthiest countries. They were led by the United States, which had overtaken the United Kingdom to become the world's wealthiest country in the early 1900s. As was mentioned, Argentina was also one of the world's wealthiest countries at this point, a painful reminder of how far that country has fallen over the past century. In contrast, Asia's largest economies were among the poorest larger economies in the world, as only Japan had begun to reap the benefits of the Industrial Revolution at this point. Nevertheless, Japan was poorer than Mexico in 1920.

If we take the long view and look at the past 100 years of major events and changes for the global economy, we see that this 100-year period began amid great upheaval and also ended amid comparable levels of unrest and upheaval. No, the conflicts of today do not (fortunately) compare to the carnage of the First World War, and no, the Covid-19 pandemic is not quite the equal of the

Spanish Flu pandemic in terms of its impact on humanity, but nevertheless, the early 1920s and the early 2020s were both times of great change. Furthermore, there were many earth-changing events that took place over this 100-year period. Nevertheless, if we take the period as a whole, we can say that it was one of tremendous economic growth and development, as well as one that resulted in massive improvements in living standards for much of the planet.

The early part of this 100-year period of economic history was a decade that could be described as one of the most up-and-down decades in history. The early part of the 1920s was dominated by the fallout of the First World War and the Spanish Flu pandemic, as well as the reordering of European borders that caused seismic shifts in that region's political and economic landscape. However, this period of uncertainty was followed in much of the world by the "Roaring 20s", a period highlighted by rapid economic growth and a revival in global trade and investment.

Unfortunately, this rapid economic growth in the 1920s was to prove to be unsustainable, as bubbles had proliferated in many major economies, most notably the United States. When the New York Stock Exchange collapsed in October 1929, the end to the Roaring 20s had come and a 16-year period of unimaginable upheaval was about to begin. For the first few years, the scale of the economic decline around the world was like nothing that had been seen since before the Industrial Revolution. In the United States and elsewhere, economic output fell by between 20% and 30%, with some areas experiencing a near total collapse of their economies. Worse, the economic policies that were implemented in the early 1930s often made the situation much worse, particularly those that resulted in massive barriers to trade and investment being put in place, such as the United States' Smoot-Hawley Tariff Act of 1930, which helped to turn what could have been a short, but sharp, downturn into one that lasted for years. At its low point, unemployment rates rose to well above 20%, with some countries recording unemployment rates in excess of 30%. During the height of the Great Depression, international trade fell by more than 60%, while global industrial production declined by about one-third. The modern world had not seen anything like this, and even the older people of the early 1930s, who had lived through made of the economic crises of the latter part of the 19th century, had never seen anything on this scale. Moreover, as we know, the effects of the Great Depression were not limited to astounding economic figures, for this economic catastrophe played a major role in the political upheaval that was to culminate in the largest war in mankind's history on this planet, the Second World War.

While the Second World War was a conflict largely driven by geopolitical issues, there were a number of economic factors that contributed to the outbreak of the largest conflict in human history. In Asia, where the conflict first began, it was Japan's quest to control East Asia and the western Pacific Ocean, and to secure access to much-needed natural resources (especially oil) that led Japan on a path of conquest that began in China and eventually spread throughout the region. In Europe, many of Germany's war aims were also economic, as Adolf Hitler believed that Germany needed much more territory if it would be able to compete economically with the United States and to achieve its geopolitical ambitions in Europe. Eventually, nearly all of the world's leading economic powers would find themselves embroiled in the war, and it would be economic power that would largely decide the outcome of the war as German-Japanese-Italian alliance found itself fighting a US-Soviet-British-led alliance whose economic output was more than four times greater. Simply put, without a quick victory, the Axis had no chance of winning the Second World War.

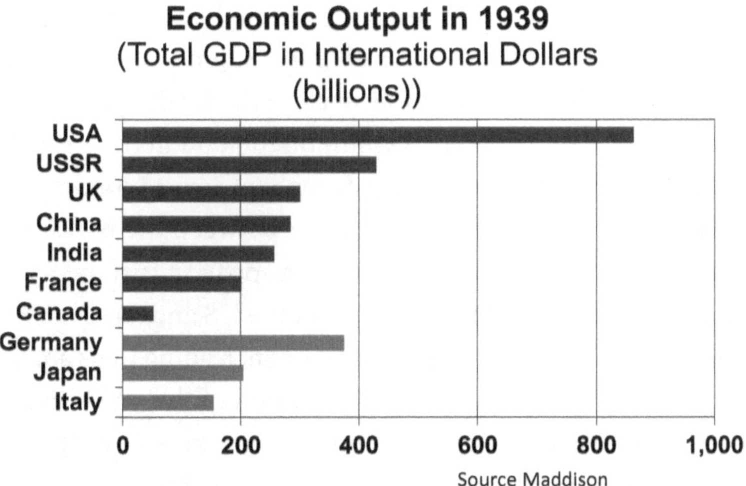

While both Germany and Japan scored great initial successes, their failure to knock out the United Kingdom (and its empire) and the Soviet Union, and their foolish decision to involve the United States in the conflict, ensured that their defeat was inevitable. By the end of the war, many of the world's greatest economies were devastated, even among victorious countries such as the Soviet Union, China and the United Kingdom. Only the United States and smaller allies such as Canada and Australia had come out of the war in the stronger economic position, ushering a period of Pax Americana in which the US would be most dominant economic power the world had ever seen.

In the wake of the Second World War, the world's two leading powers at that time, the United States and the Soviet Union, drifted apart rapidly, with both sides imagining (quite wrongly) that the other intended to do whatever possible to weaken the other and assume sole domination of the world. This quickly led to what became known as the Cold War, with the United States and its allies lining up against the Soviet Union and its allies. Militarily, there was a relatively even balance between the two sides for much of the Cold War, as the Soviet Union's advantages in terms of ground forces were offset by the US' and its allies' advantages in terms of air and naval power. While the military balance was relatively even, the economic balance was not, for the United States and its allies had far more developed economies than the USSR and its allies. In fact, despite a period of rapid economic growth in the USSR over the first couple of decades after the Second World War, the USSR and its allies found themselves unable to close the wealth gap with the West.

In fact, once the Information Revolution took off in the United States in the 1980s, a time when the commodity-dependent Soviet economy was sliding backwards, the balance of economic power between the two superpowers had grown so one-sided that it was becoming apparent that the Soviet Union was no longer a serious rival to the power of the US and its allies. Eventually, this economic weakness did the Soviet Union in, leading to its abandonment by its allies in 1989 and the eventual dissolution of the USSR itself in 1991. Since then, Russia, which was the dominant component of the USSR, has never been able to regain superpower status, again, due mostly to its relative economic weakness.

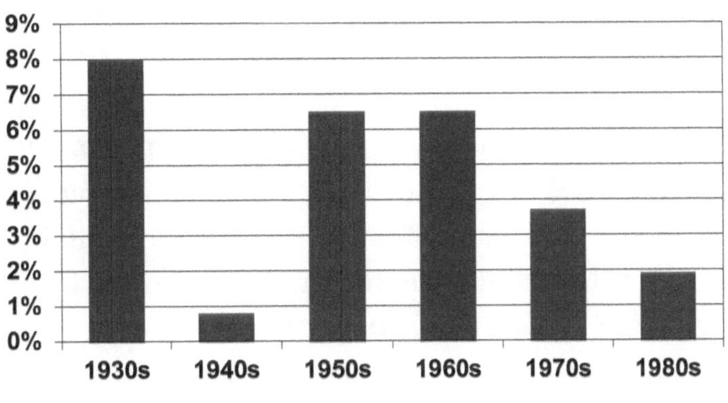

It was this aforementioned Information Revolution that was the next great event in our quick overview of the past 100 years of economic history. While it is a hotly debated topic, the general consensus is that the Information Revolution really took off in the 1980s and was centered in the United States, specifically along the US' West Coast and its high-tech centers in Silicon Valley and Seattle. In fact, to this day, the vast majority of the world's leading information technology companies are based in the US, many in those two hotspots. As we have seen in the decades since the start of the Information Revolution, it has had the effect of allowing some countries, industries and businesses to separate themselves from some of their competitors, as many countries, industries and businesses struggled to adopt to the transformations wrought by this sea-change. In fact, many of those economies that have struggled the most in recent decades have done so because they have failed to adopt the technologies that the Information Revolution unleashed upon the world. However, in another sense, the Information Revolution has been a disappointment, for so far, it has not brought about the great increases in productivity growth that had been expected in the early days of this period.

Over the past three decades, perhaps the most important change to the global economy has been the process of globalization. Prior to the late 1980s and early 1990s, the interconnected parts of the global economy were found only in North America, West Europe and parts of the Asia-Pacific region. However, the dramatic political and economic changes that took place in the late 1980s and early 1990s resulted in much of the rest of the world being "plugged into" the globalized economy. There are many examples of this:

- In Central and East Europe, the fall of Communism in the late 1980s and early 1990s resulted in many countries in that region adopting hyper-liberal economic policies, while attracting large amounts of investment from the West. This resulted in this region becoming a major manufacturing center for exports to wealthier parts of Europe.
- In Latin America, democratic reforms in the 1980s resulted in a major increase in foreign investment into that region, allowing some countries in that region to diversify their economies. Most notably, Mexico joined the United States and Canada in forming NAFTA, resulting in a manufacturing boom south of the Rio Grande.
- East Asia's "Tiger" economies were at the forefront during the early days of globalization, and they were joined by many other countries in that region, including Vietnam, Indonesia, Malaysia and the Philippines. This led to rapid economic growth for most countries in that region.
- India slowly ended its long-standing economic isolation and protectionism in the 1990s, allowing for the world's second-most-populous country to slowly attract more foreign investment and become a major offshore center for a multitude of service industries.
- Most importantly, the economic reforms unleashed in China in the 1980s, resulted in the rapid connection of China to the global economy in the 1990s and the early 2000s. This resulted in huge amounts of foreign investment pouring into China, allowing that country to quickly go from being an economic backwater to the world's unquestioned center of global manufacturing.

Looking back at the long history of the global economy, few events or trends have had a greater impact on the global economy than the recent trend towards globalization. Not only has it connected the global economy like never before, but it has lifted billions of people out of poverty.

Finally, as we will discuss in more detail at later points in this book, there has been a severe backlash against the process of globalization, one that has gained serious momentum in recent years. This has manifested itself in many ways. For example, there has been a major increase in support for protectionist policies on both the political-right and the political-left. At the same time, opposition to many aspects of globalization has led to a dramatic shift in the political landscape, particularly in the world's democracies, with politics becoming both more extreme and more fragmented. These two trends have led to the recent proliferation of trade disputes that have often involved many of the world's leading economic powers, including the United States and China. It's no wonder, given these factors, that global trade and foreign investment has actually declined over the better part of the past decade. Finally, environmental concerns have also played a role in the growing opposition to globalization, and many people now blame globalization for many of the leading environmental threats facing the world today. Altogether, it is fair to ask if whether or not globalization has peaked, if not forever, and least for the foreseeable future.

So what have been the results for the global economy if we take the long-view, in this case the past 100 years. Before we delve deeper into the economic results of the past 100 years, I want to make it clear that I have had to take a few liberties with the data, as comparing global economic data from the 1920s to the data of the 2020s requires a little manipulation and a little smoothing. Nevertheless, the points I am trying to make for this long-term view do not require that the data is 100% exact, but more importantly, that the data between countries and regions can be, with relative certainty, compared and contrasted.

Going back to the year 1920, the size of the global economy was approximately $2.9 trillion, with the world at that time being home to three major economic centers, East Asia, West Europe and North America. This overall level of output represented a 300% increase over the level of economic output in 1820, 100 years earlier. In comparison, the global economy has expanded by anywhere from 800% to 1,200% over the past century, depending upon which figures you use, a much greater increase than over the previous 100 years. This has much to do with the near-total lack of economic growth in Asia between 1820 and 1920, as that region, apart from Japan, was left outside of the Industrial Revolution and its impact on an economy's ability to generate growth. However, since 1920, global economic growth has become much more broad-based, with most regions enjoying higher degrees of economic growth than they did in the period between 1820 and 1920.

Total GDP Growth by 100-Year Period

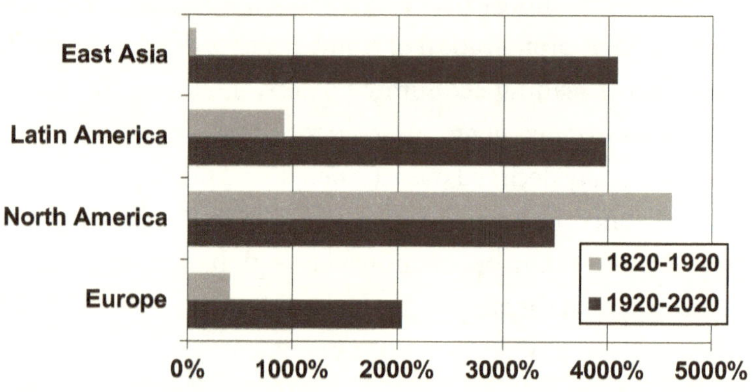

Source: Maddison, IMF

As we can see, Asia, the laggard in the previous century, has become the key driver of growth in the current century. Meanwhile, developed economies that were the dominant drivers of economic growth in the period up to the 1980s and have seen their contribution to global economic growth shrink in recent decades, with some large developed economies such as Japan and Italy generating almost no growth at all. This shift in economic growth generation from the rich world to emerging markets (mostly in Asia) has been a key factor in the recent backlash against globalization in the 21st century.

There are a number of factors that have contributed to what has been one of the most dynamic periods of growth for the global economy over the past 100 years. One of the most obvious factors is demographics. In 1920, the total global population was around 1.9 billion. Today, the total global population stands at just a little below eight billion, or an increase of more than 400% over the past 100 years. This has had the obvious effect of creating more workers and consumers, thus driving economic growth in a most basic manner. Nevertheless, it should be noted that no period in human history witnessed such a dramatic increase in the global population. For much of the past 100 years, this resulted in dramatically-rising working-age populations, although in recent decades, growth in working-age populations has slowed, and in some important economies, it has begun to shrink due to the persistent decline in birth rates around the world. Meanwhile, productivity growth, at least in the first half of the past century, was relatively strong, adding to the demographic benefits enjoyed by many leading economies. Finally, global trade and investment soared in the wake of the Second World War, adding a third driver of growth for the global economy. Of course, back in 1920, global trade and investment had been derailed by the impact of the First World War and the Spanish Flu, and global trade would suffer an even greater setback as a result of the protectionist measures enacted after the Wall Street Crash of 1929 and the impact of the Second World War. However, once the war was over, and the United States took charge of global economic policy, global trade and investment flourished like never before, driving a period of sustained economic growth, one that eventually spread to most corners of the globe.

Deciding who are the winners and losers over the past 100 years can be a challenging task, as few, if any economies, have enjoyed an unbroken century-long run of economic success. The United States is probably the closest to a large-scale winner as there is among the world's leading economies, as it was the world's largest and wealthiest big economy in 1920, and it retains those positions today. The US did give up its position as the world's wealthiest large economy to Japan for a short period in the late 1980s and early 1990s, but today, the US holds a sizeable lead in terms of per capita GDP over the second-ranked large economy (Germany).

In fact, one can consider each of New World economies (the United States, Canada, Australia and New Zealand) all as winners as each of these economies has performed very well over the past 100 years. Meanwhile, Europe's relative position in the global economy has generally waned over the past 100 years, but its ability to recover from the devastation of two world wars to remain one of the wealthier regions in the world also has been quite an accomplishment. Meanwhile, Japan's past 30 years may have been a period of long-term stagnation, but when one considers where Japan was in 1920, the fact that it is now the

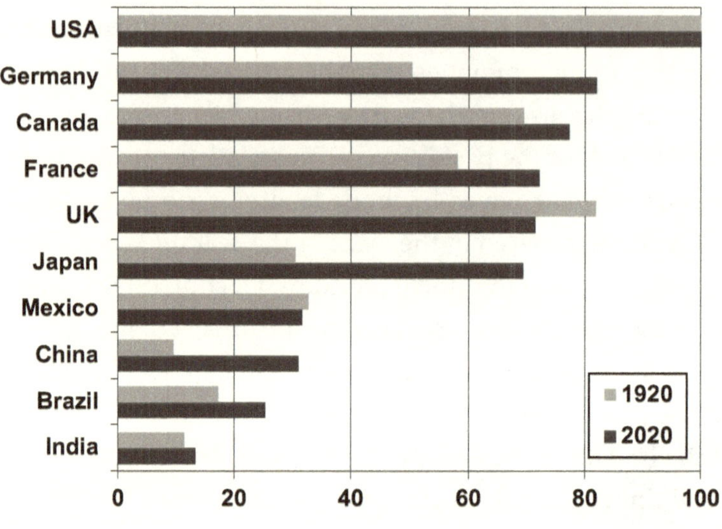

Source: Maddison, IMF

world's third-largest economy should also be viewed as a long-term success. Finally, China's rebirth is perhaps the story of the global economy of the past 100 years, as in 1920, China's economy was among the poorest and least-developed places in the world, while today, China is the world's second-largest economy and the country has lifted itself to middle-income status in a remarkably short period of time given the massive size of the country's population.

So what did these successful economies over the long-term all have in common. For one, they all industrialized, with Europe and the New World economies already being very heavily-industrialized economies for some time and with Japan on the verge of becoming the first such economy in Asia. As for China, it was anything but industrialized for the first 60 years of this past century, but for the past four decades, China's rapid and extensive industrialization was at the heart of its economic success. Meanwhile, each of these successful economies were able to be at the forefront of high-technology, high-growth industries and services, a key factor in these economies' ability to maintain their competitiveness as they became wealthier. Demographically, each of these economies experienced major increases in their working-age populations, at least for a time, although now each of them is facing some degree of demographic decline. At the same time, each of these economies took advantage of opportunities to export goods and services around the world, and to invest in foreign markets. Finally, each of these economies were able, for part of the past 100 years, to achieve higher levels of productivity growth, even if that productivity growth has waned in recent decades.

The global economic growth and development of the past 100 years produced mostly "winners" as the saying that "a rising tide lifts all boats" often applies to the global economy and its individual components. However, there have been some economies that have truly struggled over the past 100 years and have lost ground relative to other economies. For example, some Latin American economies were far wealthier (on a relative basis) 100 years ago than they are today. Meanwhile, some countries and regions that were extremely poor and had relatively low levels of economic development 100 years ago still do today. This can be said of much of Sub-Saharan Africa, which remains the poorest region in the world, just as it was 100 years ago. In fact, those countries and regions that were not located in favorable positions on the map (including positions that were rich in oil and gas), that did not modernize and diversify their economies, and those that failed to take advantage of opportunities to expand their trade and investment, generally performed very poorly over the past 100 years.

Looking back at 100 years of economic trends and developments, there are many lessons that can be learned, and many of these apply to the global economy of the 2020s. Many lessons stem from the Great Depression, the single greatest economic crisis that the world has faced during the entirety of the time following the Industrial Revolution. Among the lessons that can be learned are that a sudden loss of business and investor confidence can cause asset bubbles to burst, that erecting barriers to trade and investment at a time of global economic crisis will make that crisis much worse, and that the political fallout from economic crises can both prolong these crises as well as create new problems for the global economy (and for global security). Another lesson to be learned from the past 100 years comes from the period following the Second World War. Here, many of the world's leading economic powers agreed to create a more inter-connected global economy, one that would allow for trade and investment to flourish. It was fortunate that the United States was the dominant power at the end of the Second World War, for it had shed, for a time, its isolationist bent and used its immense economic power to underpin this new global economic system. It also used its immense military power to control and protect the sea and air lanes that would be used to dramatically expand the level of international trade in the decades following the war. Finally, the third great economic lesson of the past century comes from Asia, where a succession of relatively poor countries showed the world that by industrializing their economies, by protecting local industries and by gaining access to the world's wealthy export markets, a country could lift itself out of poverty in the span of just a generation. In fact, Asia's economic miracle is exactly what many emerging markets today are hoping to emulate, although they may face challenges much greater than those faced by countries such as Japan, South Korea and China.

While the past 100 years of global economics is largely a story of growth, development, expansion and poverty-reduction, there have also been many things that have not developed as well as would have been hoped. For example, the environmental cost of this century of economic growth has been staggering and this factor alone could cause irreparable harm to the global economy in the decades and centuries to come as issues such as climate change, pollution and resource depletion all have the potential to result in dramatic changes to our economy and our living standards. Another factor that we have not been able to resolve, despite long-term economic growth, is wealth inequality. In fact, by some measures, wealth inequality among countries, regions and cities has widened over the course of the past century, while wealth inequality within many of the world's most important economies has also been widening for much of the past 100 years. In fact, while many areas of the world have benefitted tremendously from the economic expansion and modernization of the past century, too many areas of the world have been left behind. Finally, despite all of the evidence to the contrary, too many parts of the world remain enamored with protectionism and barriers to trade and investment. Altogether, these problems that have persisted for the past 100 years remain a serious threat to the global economy and could yet derail many of the achievements of the past century.

What is clear as we look back on the past 100 years is that many of the developments and achievements of this period have outcomes that remain uncertain or unrealized. For example, as the global economy did not experience a dramatic downturn in the 90 years between the Great Depression and the Covid-19 pandemic, many economies had begun to assume that the global economy was "depression-proof". Of course, the dramatic declines in economic output during this latest pandemic squashed many of these hopes. Nevertheless, the fact is that the increasing wealth and diversity of the global economy has put it on firmer ground than it has ever been on, even if it will suffer the occasional crisis or downturn. Another unresolved question involves the role of the United States in the global economy, for it was the US' leadership and power that enabled the modern global economy to take shape after the Second World War. However, the US has a serious isolationist streak, one that has resurfaced in recent years and one that calls into question the willingness of the US to continue to underpin the modern global economy. If the US is no longer willing, is China? And if China is willing, is it able to do so, and would other major economies follow China's lead the way they followed the US for the past 75 years? Finally, it was noted that many parts of the world have yet to benefit from the fruits of the modern globalized economy. Will they ever? Considering that much of the world's population growth will be coming from such regions, it would seem imperative that these areas of the world find a way to modernize their economies and be able to generate consistently high levels of economic growth for a sustained period of time. If not, the outlook for both the global economy and for international stability will gradually deteriorate over the course of the remainder of the 21st century.

Chapter Five

THE WORLD SINCE 1990

AFTER HAVING TAKEN A long-term perspective and looked back at 100 years of global economic history, it is time to shorten our time frame to see how the global economy has grown and developed over the past 30-35 years. While it is safe to assume that most of this book's readers were not alive 100 years ago, it is likely that a sizeable percentage of its readers were around in 1990. While some of them may not remember much about 1990, it still will be a time that is much more familiar to our readers. Just like 1920, 1990 was a time of great economic, geopolitical and social change. Most notably, the long Cold War between the United States and the Soviet Union was coming to an end, with the US and its allies having prevailed due in large part to their tremendous economic advantages over the Soviet Union and its allies. This led to what has been described as the United States' unipolar moment, where there was no other power in the world that was even close to challenging the US' pre-eminence in all areas of power. This was something that has rarely occurred in history and it would last until a new challenger emerged in the 21st century, the challenge from a rising China. Elsewhere, Europe was in the process of further integrating its various economies, a process that would lead to the creation of a major economic player, the European Union. In China, 1990 was a time when that vast country was attempting to recover politically and economically from the protests the year before that culminated in the Tiananmen Massacre. Finally, this era was characterized by the Information Revolution that began for the most part in the United States but quickly spread around the world, connecting the planet like never before and raising hopes that its impact on the global economy would be akin to that of the Industrial Revolution two centuries earlier.

For the global economy, 1990 was a pivotal time. Over the previous 40 years, the global economy had expanded by nearly 700% thanks to a level of sustained economic growth on a global basis that the world has never seen before. However, the rapid global economic growth that had been recorded in the 1950s, 1960s and the early 1970s had already given way to slower, if still relatively strong, levels of growth from the late 1970s through to 1990.

1990 was a time of great dislocations as well. Sure, the United States and Europe will still generating healthy rates of growth, even if they were not as strong as they had been in previous decades. Likewise, East Asian export-ing economies such as Japan, South Korea and Taiwan had been recording remarkable levels of economic growth in the years leading up to 1990 and were taking their place near the top of many economic rankings. Finally, despite the disruptions caused by 1989's unrest, China was now a decade into its great economic transformation that had allowed that country's economy to already make great progress in terms of generating growth and wealth. Outside of these economies, the picture was decidedly more mixed. For example, many economies were in the midst of painful transformations from command economies to more market-driven economies. Likewise, as this was the first phase of the modern world's version of globalization, many economies were being exposed to foreign competition for the first time in recent memory, causing massive hardships for many of these countries.

In 1990, the United States remained the world's largest economy by a comfortable margin. However, it is interesting to note that this period was near the peak of Japanese economic power, and not only was the Japanese economy more than 50% of the size of the US economy, but its per capita GDP level had risen dramatically. In fact, Japan, for a short time, overtook the US in terms of per capita GDP, making this the only time in past 120 years that the United States would not hold the top spot for the highest per capita GDP

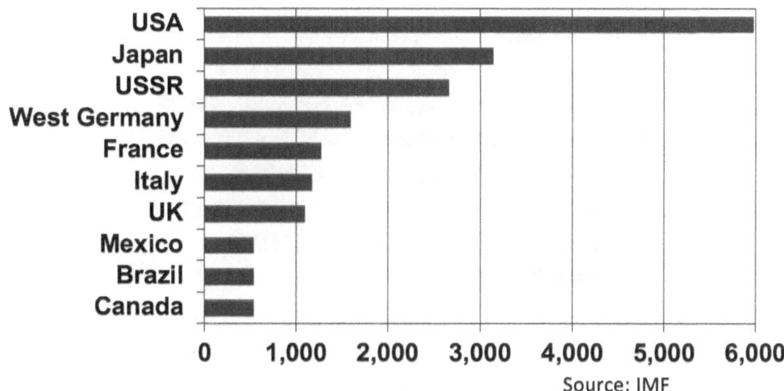

among the world's largest economies. Of course, we know now that Japan in 1990 was on the verge of a great economic slowdown that persists to this day, with that country having lost significant ground to the US both in terms of the size of its economy and its level of wealth.

Another interesting note here is that, in its penultimate year of existence, the Soviet Union was still the world's third-largest economy, with a level of economic output equal to West Germany and the United Kingdom combined. Still, the Soviet economy had lost ground to the United States and many other leading economies in the 1980s, and, as it was about to collapse, it was in a dramatically weakened position. 1990 would also mark the last time that Germany would be split in two, with that country embarking on the process of unification, something that would contribute to Germany's terrible economic performance over the remainder of that decade. Finally, it is interesting to note that China, despite having the world's largest population by a wide margin, is nowhere near to the top of the list of the world's largest economies in 1990, as despite the impressive growth rates recorded by that economy in the 1980s, the China of 1990 remained a desperately poor country, albeit one that was on the verge of becoming a major economic power once again.

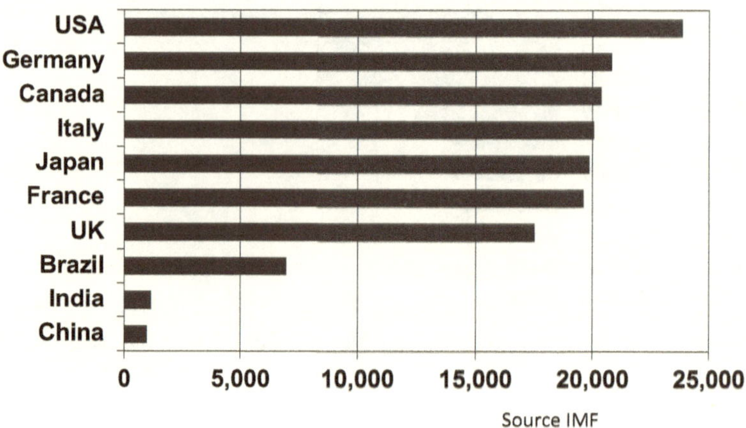

The top section of the ranking of the world's wealthiest countries in 1990 (when measured by per capita GDP at purchasing power parity) looks relatively similar to how it looks today. The United States was the world's wealthiest large economy at that point in history, just like it was for most of the 20th century, and just like it remains to this day. Where the big changes have occurred is at the lower end of these rankings. In 1990, China remained one of the poorest countries in the world, even after the high rates of economic growth recorded over the previous decade. In fact, China in 1990 was still poorer than India, while Brazil's per capita GDP at PPP was seven times higher than that of China. Of course, today, China's per capita GDP at PPP is 17% higher than that of Brazil, and more than 130% higher than that of India. This shows how much the following decades would be dominated by the rise of China and its incredible increase in economic power and influence.

From an economic perspective, the past 30 years have been one of remarkable charge. While much of this change is the result of technological and process developments that have occurred in recent decades, economic and geopolitical events have also served to alter the global economy in many ways. The first of these events was the end of the Cold War, the long-running rivalry between a bloc led by the United States and a rival bloc led by the Soviet Union. In the 1980s, the US-led bloc, which included most of the world's leading developed economies, pulled away from the Soviet-led bloc both in terms of economic growth and technological development. As the Soviet's claim to superpower status relied heavily upon on military power, it suddenly found itself exposed to the impact of its economic weakness, as it could no longer keep up with increases in US military spending.

In fact, the Soviet economy, which once was closing the gap with its rivals in the West, suddenly found itself unable to generate growth, leading to a prolonged period of stagnation and relative decline. As it became more apparent to the Soviet Union and its satellite states that living standards in the West were rapidly pulling away from those in the East, Moscow's grip on power began to weaken. By the late 1980s, those parts of the Soviet bloc that were most exposed to the success of the West (Central Europe, the Balkans and the Baltics) began to break away, eventually ousting their Communist-dominated governments and installing democracies that quickly established deep economic ties with the West. The loss of Central Europe was a particularly bitter blow for the Soviet Union as this region contained most of the advanced economic regions of the Eastern bloc. Once the dissolution of the Soviet bloc had taken place, and a rise in nationalist sentiment similar to that at the end of the First World War had occurred, it was only a matter of time until the multi-ethnic Soviet Union would dissolve as well, which it did in late 1991. What is interesting is that, for all of the power and influence that the Soviet Union had during the height of the Cold War, its collapse in 1991 barely registered among the wider global economy as by that point, the Soviet Union was no longer a major economic power and was not integrated into the wider global economy.

While the Soviet Union and its empire were collapsing, its main rival, the United States, was rebounding from a period of political, social and economic uncertainty. The late 1960s and much of the 1970s were a period of unrest and upheaval unlike anything the United States had experienced since the US Civil War in the 1860s. Politically, the country was torn apart by the Vietnam War and Watergate, events that weakened the trust of US citizens in their government like never before. Socially, ethnic and generational clashes erupted across the US, exposing many of the inherent divisions that continue to impact the United States to this day. Finally, while the US economy had been performing relatively well in the decades following the Second World

War, the Oil Shocks of the 1970s were a major blow for the world's leading economy and exposed the US to the threat posed by its dependence on foreign energy sources.

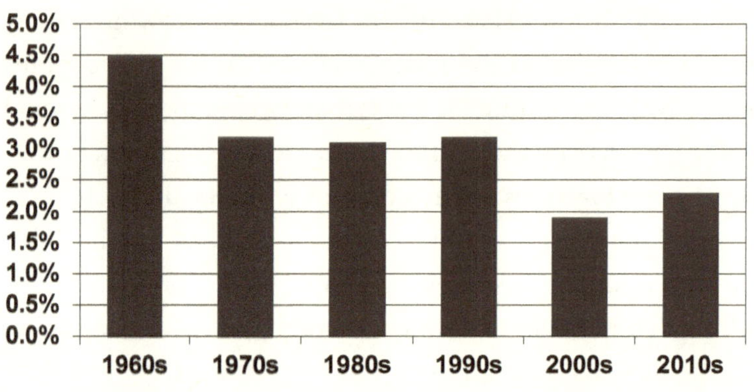

Source: US BEA

After a severe recession in 1981 and 1982, the US economy rebounded strongly over the course of the remainder of the 1980s. One factor in this recovery was the technology boom in the US, with that country at the forefront of the high-tech sectors that would come to dominate much of the global economy in the 21st century. As a result, by 1990, the US had regained much of its confidence and vigor as the collapse of the Soviet Union, and the US' vast lead in terms of economic and military power over all other countries, ushered in a period known as the United States' unipolar moment, or Pax Americana.

While the Soviet Union had collapsed and a single power stood dominant on the world stage in 1990, the wider world was undergoing a massive change. With the US and its allies favoring the spread of their economic model to the rest of the world, and with the Cold War's end leading to dozens of additional economies seeking to be integrated into the US-dominated global economy, the path towards a globally-connected economy now was open. Before this period, those economies that were part of what could be described as a connected global economy consisted largely of North America, West Europe and a handful of countries in the Asia-Pacific region. However, with China,

Southeast Asia, Central Europe, Latin America and South Asia either in the process of being integrated into the global economy in the early 1990s, or about to be integrated, almost the entire world would now be open for trade and investment, one of the most remarkable economic developments in history.

For many economies that were seeking to be integrated into the global economy, the model was East Asia. Here, Japan had showed how a relatively under-developed economy could use investment in manufacturing to dramatically boost exports to wealthy markets in order to drive economic growth at home, with this investment focusing initially on low-cost manufacturing in order to make full use of local labor cost advantages, but later transitioning to higher-cost, higher-tech manufacturing in order to offset the gradual loss of these labor cost advantages. By the 1990s, economies such as Taiwan and South Korea had already followed the Japanese lead and were well on their way towards reaching developed economy status. Now, countries in Central Europe aimed to also follow this model by exporting to West Europe, while Mexico hoped to do the same by exporting to the United States and Canada. Most importantly, China was following this model very closely, and it had an advantage that none of its rivals had, the world's largest potential market. This meant that, while other economies often had to make major concessions to potential foreign investors, China could dictate its terms to these investors, holding out the threat of preventing access to the Chinese market for those investors that refused to play by Beijing's rules. What all of this meant was, that in the span of just a few years, the world went from a global economy that was divided into many blocs that operated quite separately from one another to one that was remarkably integrated. The consequences of this change would be immense.

It was this period of unprecedented globalization that led to the rise of China, or better yet, the return of China, for during much of the past two millennia, China was the world's largest economy, sometimes by a very large margin. When Deng Xiaoping launched China's economic modernization efforts in the early 1980s, it set off an economic revolution that continues to have massive consequences for the global economy today. When these reforms were initiated, China was among the poorest countries in the world, as decades of warfare, isolationism and misguided economic policies had left China among the poorest of the poor, a true economic basket case. Almost immediately, economic growth took off in China as the country underwent one of the fastest industrializations in history. Even the upheaval that culminated in the Tiananmen Square massacre could not prevent China's economy from modernizing, industrializing and globalizing. The opening of China's economy to the outside world, and the promise of the world's largest market, resulted in an incredible surge of foreign investment into the country, much of which went into the country's rapidly-expanding manufacturing industries. This eventually led to China's membership in the World Trade Organization in 2001, the event the ensured China would become the dominant manufacturing center in the world, as its access to lucrative export markets was solidified by its WTO membership, giving investors more confidence in the future of the Chinese economy and its role in global manufacturing. This led to another incredible surge in economic growth in the mid-2000s, with Chinese economic growth eventually peaking at an astounding 14.2% in 2007.

China: Average Annual GDP Growth Rate by Decade

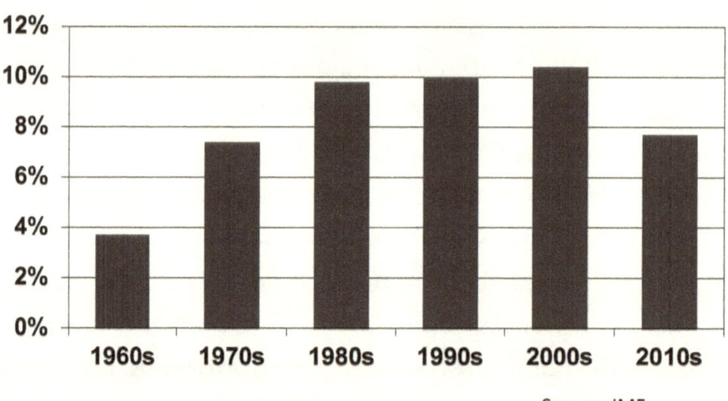

Source: IMF

Since then, economic growth in China has moderated as the country has reached middle-income status. Moreover, China has faced a series of crises in recent years, including a stock market crisis in 2015, a devastating trade war with the United States and finally the Covid-19 pandemic, which brought economic growth in China to a temporary halt in the early 2020s. Meanwhile, China's success has meant that it was losing competitiveness in terms of low-cost manufactured exports, forcing the country to move its manufacturing upmarket. At the same time, China has been transitioning from an economy that is driven by manufactured exports to one that is driven by domestic consumer spending. As China looks to the future, this trend is likely to continue, but many challenges await, including growing resistance to China's rising economic influence and its soon-to-be falling working-age population. As China is expected to generate around one-third of all of the extra economic output in the world in the coming decade, any troubles in China in the coming years will have worldwide ramifications.

The period from the early 1990s until the late 2000s was one of growth for most of the world's leading economies. Furthermore, some economies that suffered significant losses during that period did so as they were transitioning from former command economies to ones that were more market-driven. However, this growth masked the rise of dangerous bubbles in many key parts of the global economy, bubbles that would suddenly burst in 2008. None was more famous than the housing bubble in the United States, which acted as the catalyst for the most significant global economic downturn since the Great Depression. This "Great Recession" had a major impact on nearly all economies around the world and forced governments to take dramatic steps (and make massive spending pledges) to keep entire segments of the global economy afloat.

GDP Growth Rates in 2009

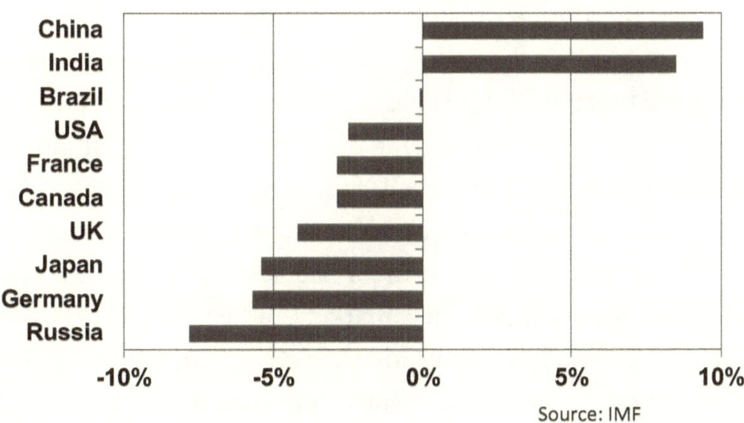

Source: IMF

While most of our focus in this section has been on the global economy of the past 30 years, this period has also witnessed some dramatic political changes. Following the fall of Communism in Eastern Europe, a new degree of centrism took hold in many areas of the world with the radical right and the radical left losing support to political parties and leaders that espoused more centrist economic and political policies. This resulted in elections being dominated by centrist candidates for much of the 1990s and early 2000s, while at the same time, many authoritarian states sought to present a softer image to the world.

However, a number of factors emerged that led to a gradual weakening of this centrist trend in the early 21st century. These included the 9/11 terrorist attacks in the United States, rising levels of wealth inequality, and the impact of the internet and social media on the dissemination and consumption of news and information. As we will see, these factors will continue to play a major role in the following decades and have led to a dangerous increase in support for far-right and far-left policies in recent years.

So what have been the results for the global economy over the past 30 years. First, unlike our trip back in time to 1920, we actually have a great deal of reliable and useful economic data from 1990. For much of the data we will use for this period, we will utilize a number of sources, most notably the International Monetary Fund, the World Bank and national statistical offices. This will give us the ability to make much more in-depth comparisons and analysis of the global economy and its individual components during this period.

In 1990, total global economic output was a little more than $23.5 billion dollars, far less than the estimated $84.5 billion global economy today, but substantially more than the $11.2 billion economy just ten years earlier in 1980. Amid the turmoil of the 1980s, the global economy managed to grow by an average of 3.1% per year during that decade, with most of this growth coming during the second half of the 1980s. In fact, it was this growth, coupled with the rapid progress towards globalization that resulted in 1990 being a period of near-unmatched optimism for the state of the global economy and for international security. With new markets and production locations being connected to the already wealthy countries that comprised the lion's share of the global economy in 1990, the stage appeared set for an unprecedented period of growth and prosperity for billions of people around the world. What is interesting to note in hindsight is that the late 1980s would be the last time (at least until now) that developed economies grew at a faster pace than emerging markets. In fact, prior to 1990, the wealth gap between the world's wealthy countries and its poorer ones had actually been widening, something that globalization was expected to change.

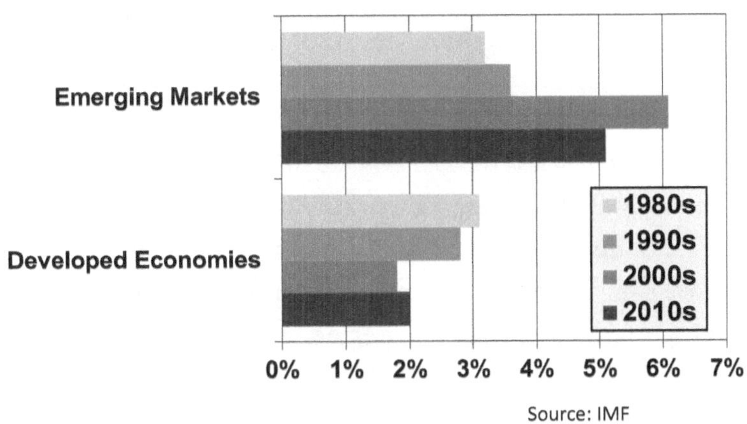

Average Annual GDP Growth by Type of Economy

Source: IMF

When looking back at the last 30 years, this period is likely to go down in history as the period of globalization, as well as the return of Asia as a major economic center, something made possible by the process of globalization. For the first half of this 30-year period, it was the rise of nearly all emerging markets that drove economic growth upwards, sometimes at the expense of less competitive developed economies. However, in recent years, many emerging markets have also slumped, with their growth rates falling substantially of late.

A few things stand out when looking back at the performance of the global economy over the past three decades. First, developed economies have slowed significantly over the past two decades. This is due to a variety of factors, including the demographic decline of Europe and Japan, the shift in manufacturing to lower-cost production locations in China, Mexico and Central Europe, and a dangerous decline in productivity growth.

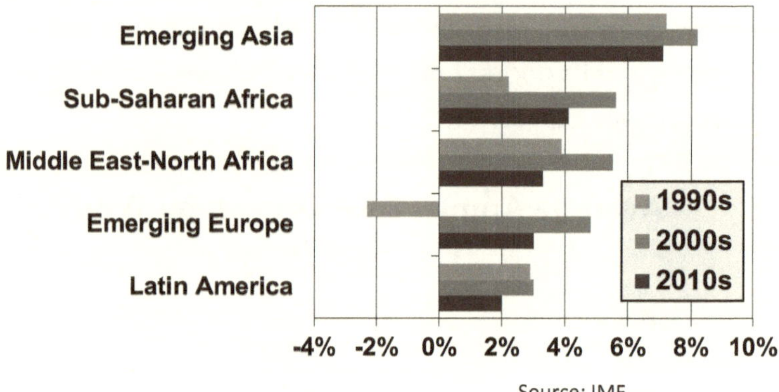

Another interesting result is the fact that, during the height of the globalization period in the early 2000s, emerging markets were growing by more than three times the rate of developed economies, a never-before seen gap in growth between those two groups of economies. This reflects the surge in investment into emerging markets during that period, a surge that transformed many important countries around the world.

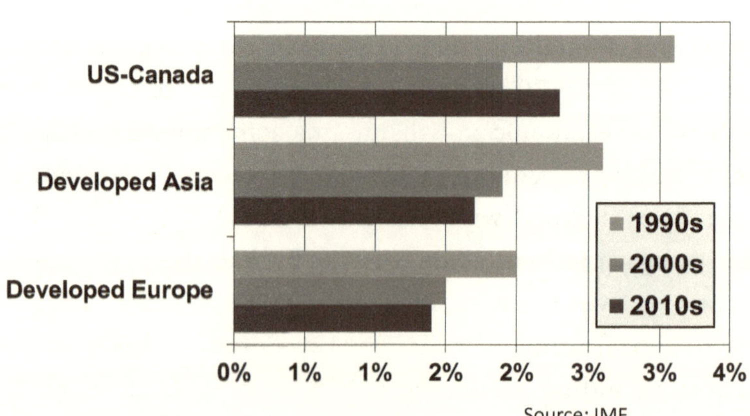

Finally, over time, the focus of the world's economic growth shifted to Asia. In the years before and after the Global Financial Crisis, many emerging regions were able to record relatively healthy levels of growth. In fact, in the years directly following this crisis, it was emerging markets around the world that took the lead from developed economies and became the key drivers of global growth. During these years, this growth was not confined to only Asia, as Africa, Latin America and the Middle East all recorded some of their highest-ever rates of economic growth during this period.

Two factors were important in driving this emerging market growth. First, money flowed into these regions thanks to monetary policies enacted in the United States and elsewhere that were designed to counter the effects of the financial crisis. Second, commodity prices soared during this period, due in large part to the insatiable demand in China for oil, iron, soybeans and a host of other commodities, many of which were sourced from emerging markets outside of Asia. However, as monetary policy shifted again in the mid-2010s and as commodity prices collapsed as well, non-Asian emerging markets suddenly found it much harder to generate growth. For emerging markets around the world, the past few years have been their most challenging period since globalization took hold in the 1990s. Not only is the process of globalization being challenged in North America, Europe and elsewhere, but many of the same constraints that have held down growth in developed economies (shrinking working-age populations, increasing barriers to trade and investment, and lower productivity growth) are now present in many emerging markets as well. Unfortunately for them, the series of recent crises that have befallen the global economy have left them with relatively little ammunition to fight back against these new threats.

So, can we determine who have been the big winners and losers from the last 30 years of economic history? I believe we can, to a point. Clearly Asia has been the big winner of this period, as its remarkable economic growth over the past 30 years has been one of the great transformative events in economic history. Of Asia's main players, it is China that has emerged as the world's next great economic power.

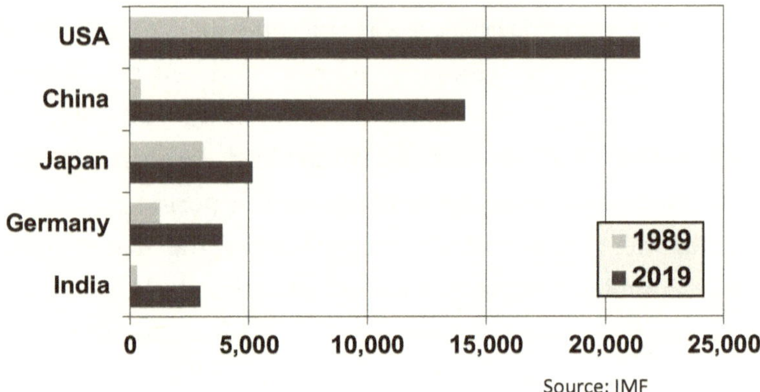

Not only has China become the dominant player in many of the world's leading industries, but its success has lifted more people out of poverty in a shorter period of time than any other country in world history. Likewise, other Asian economies, if not having achieved the level of growth and poverty-reduction as China has done in recent decades, have nevertheless emerged as beneficiaries of the economic trends of the past three decades. Southeast Asia, home to more than 660 million people, has become one of the world's most dynamic regions and is home to what are today some of the world's fastest-growing economies. India, while facing more hurdles in its economic development than China, has also emerged in fits and spurts to become a major economic player in the 21st century.

Outside of Asia, picking winners becomes a little more challenging. Certainly those economies that are home to large-scale high-tech industries or centers (such as the United States' Silicon Valley or China's Shenzhen) have benefitted from the strong growth that these industries have provided. Meanwhile, major economic hubs have thwarted their naysayers and continue to play a massive role in the global economy, attracting both investment and talent in droves, allowing them to outpace their less competitive rivals in the process, even if they suffered more from the Covid-19 pandemic than most other areas. Finally, those countries, regions and cities that took the steps necessary to improve their competitiveness have had their efforts vindicated over the past 30 years, as growth has become increasingly concentrated in those countries, regions and cities that have distinct competitive advantages over their rivals. These competitive advantages can be favorable tax regimes, well-developed infrastructures, highly-skilled labor pools or large amounts of available financing. Regardless, those economies that invested in these areas, or enacted policies that fostered their development, have been the biggest winners of the past 30 years.

On the flip side, there have been many economies that have found the going very difficult over the past 30 years. I have already mentioned the poor levels of economic growth in most developed countries so far in the 21st century. For countries such as Italy and Japan, their struggles during this period have given rise to fears of long-term decline. Worse, the factors that caused their struggles are present in many other developed economies. Another group of economies that have struggled over the past thirty years are those that have failed to invest in high-tech and high-growth industries. A dearth of such industries can be witnessed in many emerging markets, but some developed economies have also failed to develop such industries within their borders.

As well looking back at the past 30 years of economic history, there are many trends and developments that not only have factored into the performance of individual economies and industries, but there are also many issues that remain pertinent today and are continuing to influence the direction of the global economy in the 2020s. As globalization has been the dominant theme of the past 30 years, many of these lessons apply to this trend. Simply put, the transformation of the global economy from one that was divided into blocs into one that was more connected globally than ever before has challenged economies, industries and businesses to improve their competitiveness and responsiveness like never before. Another over-arching theme of the past 30 years has been the rise of the Information Revolution. While this transformation may not have delivered the productivity increases that were expected (so far), it has been the catalyst for so many other dramatic changes around the world, economically, politically and socially. Furthermore, for those countries and businesses that failed to adopt to these changes, the past 30 years have proven to be very challenging indeed. Finally, the two major global economic crises of the first part of the 21st century, the Global Financial Crisis and the

Covid-19 pandemic, have shaken the global economy to its core and resulted in many leading economies, industries and businesses being pushed to the brink of collapse. Furthermore, these crises have shaken many of the core beliefs about the global economy and its future, raising doubts about whether or not economic growth and improving living standards can be maintained in a changing world.

So what went right over the past 30 years. Given the fact that, for much of the world's population, the past 30 years saw their highest levels of economic growth and their biggest improvements in living standards, much must have gone right. One thing that went quite right was the fact that, when faced with major economic and financial crises, the world's leading economies reacted swiftly and with all of their available resources, a sign that the lessons of the Great Depression were not lost on the economic and monetary policy makers of the 21st century. Meanwhile, it is clear that many emerging markets learned the lessons taught by Japan and South Korea and were able to develop export-oriented manufacturing industries that would allow investment and wealth to flow into their countries. For those that learned this lesson, the past years have been relatively prosperous and their outlook for the future is certainly stronger than it would have been had they failed to heed these lessons. Finally, the fact that hundreds of millions of people have been lifted out of abject poverty in the span of a single generation is perhaps the single greatest testament to the economic successes of the past 30 years. Prior to 1990, too many poor countries were failing to generate a higher rate of economic growth than of population growth. However, since globalization took off, dozens of countries, including some with massive populations such as China and India, have managed to record rates of economic growth that are many times higher than their rates of population growth.

While the years since 1990 contain many stories of economic success, there are also many failures to account for. For example, for most economists back in 1990, it was assumed that wealth inequality would decline as the Cold War came to an end and as globalization spread. However, the opposite has happened, as wealth inequality has instead widened in most countries in recent years, as technological and workforce trends have driven a wider wedge between the rich and the poor than at any time in modern history.

Another setback has to be the fact that, while Asia has taken off over the few decades, many regions have been left behind. For example, Latin America is a region that was anticipating much higher levels of economic growth and much lower levels of economic volatility only to find that, for the past three decades, economic growth has been disappointing and economic volatility has increased. A third failure of this period of economic history has to be the fact that, despite the widespread benefits of globalization for much of the planet, protectionism and nationalism have returned with a vengeance in recent years, threatening to undermine the process of globalization and to raise political tensions to much higher levels.

Finally, as we look back at the world since 1990, it is clear that much remains uncertain as to how the trends and developments of this period will impact the global economy in the future. In fact, many of the outcomes of these trends and developments have yet to be determined, particularly as the recent crises have upended many of the key tenets that have emerged during this period regarding economics, politics and international relations. For one, it remains to be seen if the global economy is resilient enough to withstand more serious challenges such as the Global Financial Crisis and the Covid-19 pandemic. As you have seen, the global economy had avoided major crises for a very long time, and thus had not been tested in the ways that it has been in recent years. Can it overcome these challenges? It remains to be seen, but there are reasons to fear for the health of the economy in the years ahead, particularly if new crises arise. Another key question that remains unanswered is whether or not the United States will continue to underpin the global economy and the process of globalization. Already, we have seen a major backlash against globalization in the form of rising protectionist sentiment in the US, and if this sentiment does not prove to be short-lived, will the US abandon the role that is has fulfilled since the Second World War? If not, can China or anyone else step up and replace the US in this role? It looks doubtful that any other economy has the resources or the strength to do so. As such, that brings us to our third unanswered question from the past 30 years of the global economy. Is the period of globalization that began around 1990 coming to an end? If so, what will replace it? More importantly, what will this mean for the future of the global economy.

Chapter Six

THE RECENT PAST

OW THAT WE HAVE taken a relatively long-term look at the history of the global economy, as well as a more mid-term view, it is now time to look at what has happened in our immediate past, in this case, the past decade. In the early 2010s, the global economy was just pulling out of the Global Financial Crisis, a recession that some feared could turn into another Great Depression as governments and central banks moved quickly to prevent such a catastrophe. In the end, another depression did not emerge, and the global economy quickly returned to the levels of growth it had recorded prior to the financial crisis.

Global GDP Growth Rates

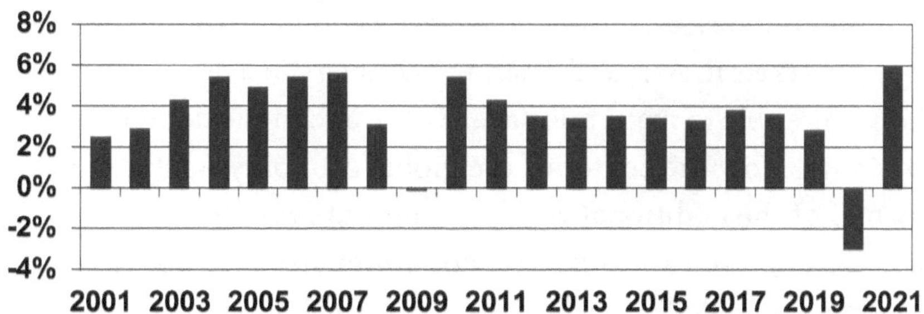

However, the global economy that was emerging from the financial crisis would end up looking much different than the one that had come before. In fact, the changes that occurred in the years following the crisis highlighted the effect that the massive changes that began in the 1980s and 1990s had on the global economy. On one hand, an increasing number of developed economies would find it difficult to compete in the now-globalized economy of the 21st century. This can be seen by the series of crises that wracked the European economy in the years following the financial crisis, as many European countries, especially those in the southern part of that region, had fallen far behind many of their international rivals in terms of competitiveness and growth, and this left them dangerously exposed to the new risks that had emerged as a result of the financial crisis. Meanwhile, other developed economies in North America and the Asia-Pacific region did not suffer the convulsions that took place in Europe, but their rates of growth remained relatively disappointing, at least when compared to what they had achieved in the second half of the 20th century.

While developed economies found it increasingly difficult to generate high levels of growth, the global economy nevertheless continued to grow at a solid pace. In fact, global economic growth between 2012 and 2018 never wavered from between 3.3% and 3.8%, the steadiest long-term growth ever generated by the global economy in recorded history. This was due to the fact that, increasingly, it was emerging markets that were driving this growth. In the first part of the 2010s, nearly all emerging markets were generating high levels of growth, thanks to surging foreign investment and high commodity prices. However, by the second half of that decade, only emerging markets in Asia and a handful of diversified non-Asian emerging markets, were able to main this pace. By the end of the decade, it was clear that Asia was now the center of the global economy, as it accounted for nearly half of the additional economic output recorded each year at that point in history. Even as China's growth slowed from the double-digit GDP growth rates recorded in earlier decades, other Asian emerging markets such as India, Indonesia, Vietnam and the Philippines were there to pick up the slack and continue Asia's leading role as the driver of growth for the 21st century global economy.

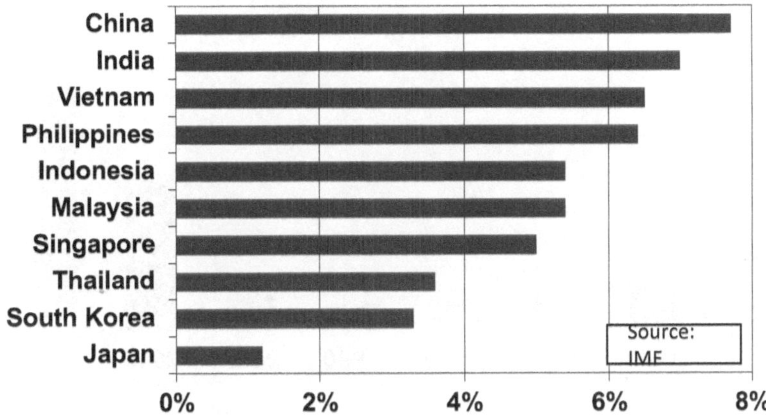

Just before the Covid-19 pandemic drove the global economy into its worst downturn since the Great Depression, total global GDP had risen to more than $87 billion, a dramatic increase in the size of the economy over the other periods we have so far discussed. However, this growth was highly uneven. While some parts of the world were able to record major increases in wealth the coincided with major declines in poverty (such as East Asia and Central Europe), other regions were stagnant, if not receding (such as much of Latin America and the Middle East). Likewise, while living standards continued to improve over the past decade, their improvements were also quite uneven, with dramatic improvements being found in those regions where economic growth relative to population growth was the highest.

An interesting development of the past ten years, and one that will continue to have a massive impact on the world in the coming years, is the fact that, for the first time in a century, the United States had a rival for the position of the world's largest economy. While the US economy expanded at a pace faster than that of most other developed economies, its lead in terms of economic output was being eroded by a faster-growing China. By the end of the 2010s, the US economy was only one-third larger than that of China, with expectations that China would overtake the US in terms of economic output within the next 10-15 years.

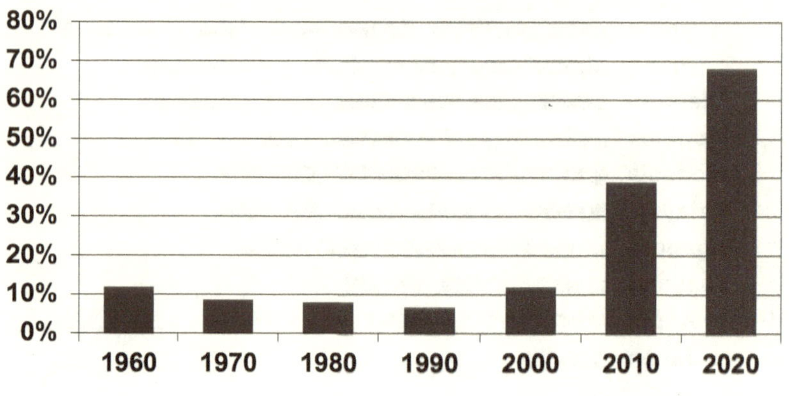

Furthermore, China was no longer just a threat to the United States in slower-growth manufacturing sectors, but it was also emerging as a serious threat to the US' dominant position in many high-tech and fast-growing sectors of the economy. Add to this mix the growing geopolitical rivalry between the world's two-most-powerful countries and it is easy to see why so many analysts view this relationship as a modern-day Cold War, only with the US' rival this time possessing much more economic potential than the Soviet Union could ever muster.

Elsewhere, the past decade has been a challenging time for most of the world's other leading economic centers. Europe, which entered the 21st century with so much hope, found itself bouncing from crisis to crisis, with that region falling into four separate recessions between 2008 and 2020, with the last one dealing a massive blow to an already-fragile European economy. In fact, by the end of 2020, economic output in many European countries was lower than it was 12 years earlier.

Japan too continued to struggle, although efforts to boost domestic demand by the Japanese government allowed for that country to manage to record some growth in recent years. Nevertheless, with a population that was losing hundreds of thousands of people each year, Japan's ability to generate economic growth was continuously limited. Elsewhere, large emerging markets such as

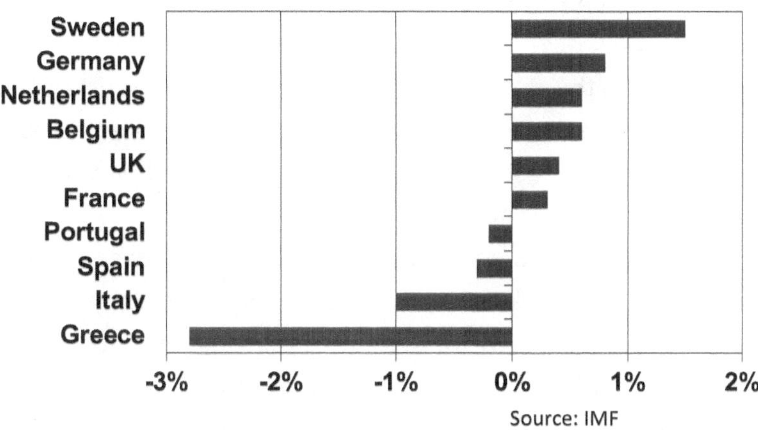

Brazil, Russia and Mexico all suffered through a very disappointing period in recent years, with growth rates falling well below their expected levels. Even India, which for the most part was able to record high rates of growth, saw things take a turn for the worse in recent years.

As growth slowed in many key economies, the distribution of global wealth continued to shift as well. While a great deal of wealth remained concentrated in the world's richest countries, its distribution in these countries continued to shift as many developed economies struggled to generate growth or to attract investment. Meanwhile, more and more wealth continued to be generated in Asia as that region not only had emerged as the dominant exporting region, but its domestic markets were growing extremely fast, thus attracting even more investment to that region. In contrast, many developing regions failed to close the wealth gap with wealthier regions such as North America and West Europe. In fact, many countries in Latin America, Africa and the Middle East actually lost ground in terms of wealth levels over the past decade as they failed to generate sufficient growth or attract enough investment to close this gap. This was one of the catalysts for the political unrest that gripped these regions throughout the 2010s and is likely to remain a key driver of popular anger in these regions in the years ahead, unless countries in these regions can dramatically improve their economic performance.

As we look back at the events over recent years, we can see that it has been a period of momentous change, one that really began with the Financial Crisis in 2008 and continues to this day. The early part of this period was focused on the global recovery from the Financial Crisis, which was the single greatest challenge to the global economy since the Second World War. As you remember, global economic output declined in 2009, and even if the global economy contracted by just 0.1% that year, this was the first such decline in global economic output in decades.

Afterwards, the global economy actually bounced back quite quickly, and growth eventually settled at between 3.3% and 3.8% per year until 2018, which by historical standards was a relatively strong level of growth for the global economy. The big change from previous decades was the fact that this growth was now driven increasingly by emerging markets, especially China and other Asian countries. Only in 2019 did global growth begin to slow significantly, and this was due, in part, to the worsening trade war between the United States and China, as well as the deteriorating health of the European economy. Nevertheless, the 2010s were a relatively successful decade for the global economy, particularly when one considers where the decade started.

Global GDP Growth by Decade

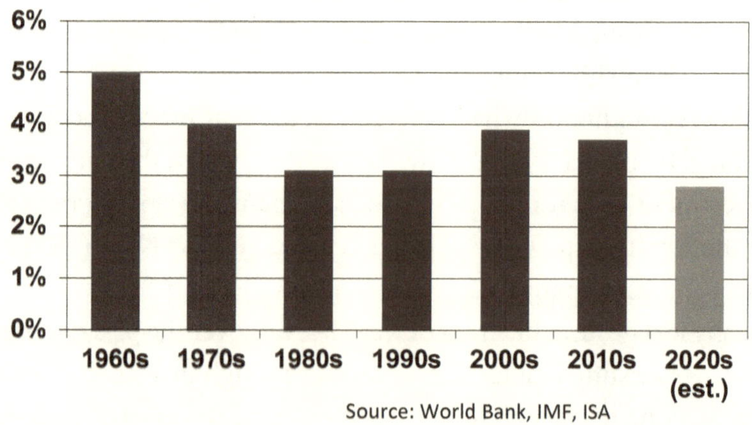

If anything characterized the global economy of the 2010s, it would have to be the growing importance of emerging markets, particularly in

Asia. When the 21ˢᵗ century began, emerging markets accounted for just 21% of global economic output. By the eve of the Financial Crisis, their share of global economic output had risen to 28%, a sizeable increase that was driven by a combination of stronger growth in emerging markets and a period of sluggish growth in developed economies. In 2010, the year when global growth returned, emerging markets' share of global economic output had risen further, reaching nearly 35%, reflecting the fact that developed economies suffered the bulk of the losses during the Financial Crisis. Today, the share of global economic output that is generated by emerging markets has risen to more than 40% as a result of the strong performance by Asian and other emerging markets during the 2010s. The question is now, when will emerging markets generate more economic output than developed economies.

For the world's second-largest developed region, Europe, the recent past has been a time of economic turmoil. First, the financial crisis, while it did not originate in Europe, nevertheless hit that region particularly hard and exposed many of the weaknesses among a number of European economies. In particular, southern European economies such as Italy, Greece, Spain and Portugal had to some degree lost much of their competitiveness in previous years, leaving them dangerously exposed to the impacts of the Financial Crisis. Worse, these countries shared a currency with more competitive countries such as Germany and the Netherlands, preventing them from using currency devaluations as a method of maintaining their level of economic competitiveness. As a result, Europe suffered through three recessions in a short period between 2009 and 2013, with southern European countries suffering particularly severe losses during this period.

Worse, the contradictions within the European Union and the euro itself made it more difficult than it had to be for Europe to combat these crises and to restore the region to growth. In fact, only when the euro depreciated sharply in 2014 did the Eurozone group of countries regain some of their economic competitiveness and they were able to then export their way back to growth. This, combined with low commodity prices, fueled a recovery in most European countries that lasted from 2014 until 2018. Nevertheless, Europe had lost ground during this period to most of its major competitors and had worsened the region's position should a new crisis emerge, which it did in the form of 2020's Covid-19 pandemic.

One of most influential economic trends of recent years was the fall in commodity prices that began in earnest in 2014 and lasted until 2021. Prior to that, commodity prices had soared, fueled by rising demand in China and other emerging markets. This was the catalyst for many countries' recoveries from the Financial Crisis. For example, high oil prices fueled a surge in economic growth in oil producing countries in the Middle East, Africa and elsewhere, and even propelled the United States' rapidly-expanding shale oil sector, a development that has transformed the oil and gas industry dramatically in recent years. Likewise, soaring prices for agricultural goods resulted in a golden age of economic growth for economies such as Brazil, with Asian demand once again driving much of this growth. However, this commodity-fueled boom came to a crashing end in 2014, when the price of oil, gas and dozens of other commodities collapsed over the course of that year.

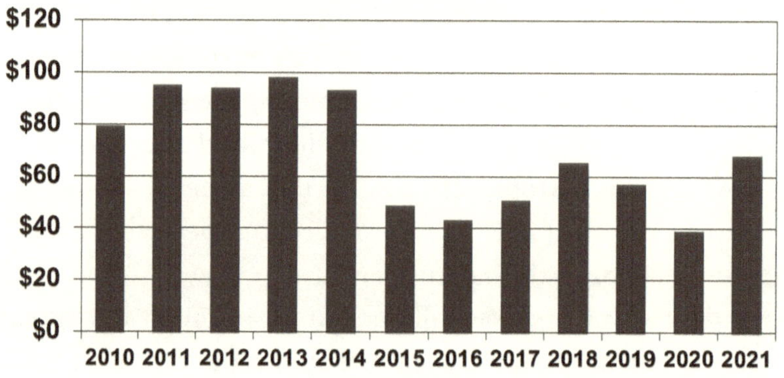

Average Annual Crude Oil Price (WTI US$)

Source: Macrotrends

The reasons for this commodity price collapse were many, with increasing supply levels that were the result of major investments in commodity production being perhaps the most important. Likewise, demand levels did not keep rising as fast as they did in the years immediately after the Financial Crisis, nor as fast as many commodity businesses had hoped for. What resulted was a relatively sudden and dramatic fall in commodity prices, one that brought to a near-immediate end to the high levels of economic growth that had been achieved by commodity-producing countries, particularly those that relied on a single commodity (often oil) for much of their export revenues. This lack of diversification would prove to be a calamity for many countries in the years that followed.

While the early 2010s were a period in which nearly all major emerging markets and regions recorded healthy rates of economic growth, this across-the-board growth for emerging markets would not last. In the early part of that decade, many businesses and investors came to believe that emerging market growth was there to stay and that nearly all important emerging markets would continue providing them with growth opportunities for the foreseeable future. Alas, this was not to be the case. Sure, Asian emerging markets, for the most part, continued to record strong rates of economic growth throughout the decade, but many others faltered.

Still, changes were afoot, even in Asia. In China, 2015's market unrest showed that the once-inevitable rise of the Chinese economy was now vulnerable to a number of threats to its health, as did the impact of the Covid-19 pandemic in 2020 and 2021. Likewise, the changes in monetary policy earlier in the decade that had led to a flood of foreign investment into that region were beginning to be reversed, limiting investment in many Asian emerging markets. India, that great hope for long-term growth, also experienced a higher degree of volatility in the second half of the 2010s and again during the Covid-19 pandemic, and even when it was able to record higher levels of economic growth, these levels were not as high as many had hoped for.

Despite these problems, Asia's recent economic performance has still been much better than that of its emerging market counterparts in other areas of the world. In fact, even as economic growth in Asia has slowed somewhat in recent years, this result has been far better than that of any other region during this period.

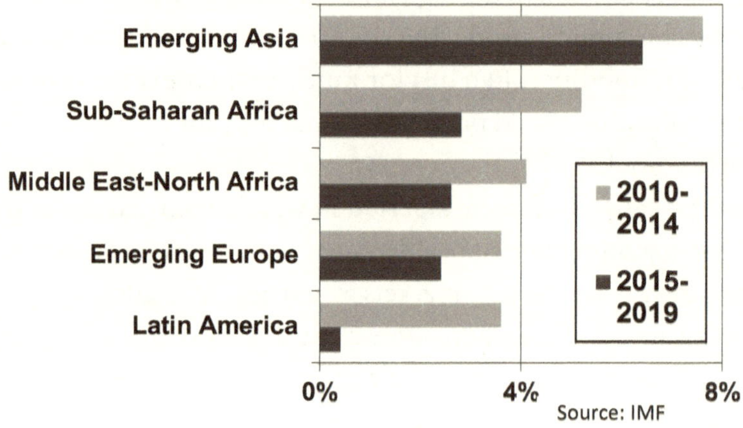

Let's look at the performances of some other emerging regions in recent years. Of all of the regions outside of Asia, the one that has performed better than most others in recent years has been Central and East Europe. Here there are really two distinct regions, with Central European economies that are now closely integrated into the wider European economy performing quite well in the years before the Covid-19 pandemic, but with East European economies, led by Russia, recording very little economic growth during this period. This discrepancy has been due to the fact that while most Central European economies are now quite diversified and have access to wealthier export markets, Russia and most other East European economies have undergone almost no diversification or modernization, while failing to gain access to important export markets for all but the most basic commodities.

One region that was expected to become a key driver of economic growth in the 21st century, but has so far failed to live up to that promise, is Sub-Saharan Africa. This region with a population of nearly 1.2 billion had been expected to record strong growth as its population is rising quickly (it is expected to add another one billion people to its population by the year 2050). However, too many of the region's leading economies remain dependent upon the export of a single commodity (usually oil) and low commodity prices have caused havoc to this region's economies in recent years. The same can be said of the Middle

East and North Africa. Here, the region's more diversified economies (Turkey and Israel) have managed to record relatively solid rates of growth, even if Turkey remains one of the world's most volatile large economies. In contrast, the fall in oil prices in 2014 and their inability to bounce back until the wake of the Covid-19 pandemic has prevented this region's leading oil-producing economies from generating much growth at all in recent years. Finally, the region that has performed the worst in recent years is Latin America. In fact, this region has recorded almost no growth in recent years, due in large part to the fact that the region's largest economies have all faced a series of economic crises during this period.

There are a number of reasons why Asian emerging markets have performed so much better than their counterparts in other areas of the world. One of the most important factors is the fact that Asian emerging markets were able to develop large-scale manufacturing industries while at the same time gaining access to vital export markets, most notable the United States. Only a handful of other emerging markets (Mexico, Central Europe and Turkey) could claim the same. Another factor is that China and other Asian emerging markets invested heavily in their infrastructures, particularly the parts of their infrastructures that were important to manufacturers that were exporting around the world (such as ports, airports, highways and railways). This stands in stark contrast to the infrastructure constraints that remain in place to this day in most other emerging markets, costing them dearly in terms of their export competitiveness. Another important factor is that many emerging markets in Asia have national governments that have steadily supported their manufacturing industries and have sent a consistent message to foreign investors. This has helped to maintain both domestic and foreign investment in these key sectors. Again, compare this to the situation with governments in other parts of the world, and the contrast is quite clear. Finally, Asia's vast scale means that the region's market potential dwarfs that of any other market in the world. This is an incentive for businesses and investors to stick to that region through thick and thin. No matter what type of crisis the region, or an individual country in that region, faces, businesses and investors will remain mesmerized by the opportunities presented by a region that is home to nearly half of the world's population. In contrast, no other region has the current market potential as that of Asia, and this means that, if things become difficult, businesses and investors will be less hesitant to pull up their stakes and leave those markets.

While many emerging markets saw their hopes of long-term economic growth dashed in recent years, developed economies have found themselves facing another threat altogether, that of political upheaval. In the United States in the late 2000s and early 2010s, the Tea Party movement emerged as a significant threat to the status quo in US politics, which had moved to the center in previous decades. While this movement moved the political-right in the US even more to the right, left-wing movements such as Occupy Wall Street did the same on the political-left. This meant that, while the 2008 and 2012 presidential elections in the United States were contested by relatively centrist leaders, there was growing support in the US for more right-wing and left-wing ideologies that were bubbling to the surface during this period. In 2016, this radicalization of US politics burst forth in that year's campaign for the presidential election. On the Democratic side, the more radical left was represented by Vermont Senator Bernie Sanders, who was only prevented from winning the Democratic Party's nomination that year by a concerted effort by the party's leadership to ensure that its centrist presumptive candidate, former First Lady Hillary Clinton, won the nomination. On the Republican side, it was expected that another centrist candidate would win the nomination, just like in 2008 and 2012. However, the fact that there were 17 major candidates seeking the Republican nomination opened the door for businessman and reality TV star Donald Trump, running on a highly right-wing populist platform, to seize the nomination as the centrist vote was split in the early primary contests.

Still, as the presidential election approached in November 2016, it was expected that Clinton would defeat Trump as she was ahead in the polls and as Trump had made a series of missteps during the campaign. However, when the results were announced, Donald Trump, not Hillary Clinton, was the new president of the United States, despite losing the popular vote by a margin of 48.2% to 46.1%. He did this by winning 76 of the 90 electoral college voters in states or districts that were decided by less than two percentage points, including very narrow wins in Florida, Pennsylvania, Michigan and Wisconsin.

Of course, after taking office, President Trump upended politics like few presidents before him. While he alienated many of his key team members, he retained a core of voters among protectionists and social conservatives, enabling him to retain a steady degree of support of around 40% of voters throughout his first term in office. However, after his contentious defeat in 2020's presidential election, he also left a more divided United States, an issue we will come back to again later in this book.

In fact, the rise of right-wing and left-wing populism, as well as the rise in support for more radical positions regarding national sovereignty, wealth redistribution and such, has been one of the most notable aspects of the 21st century thus far. A good example of this is Brexit, the withdrawal of the United Kingdom from the European Union which officially took place in early 2020. When former British Prime Minister David Cameron called for a referendum on whether or not the UK should remain in the EU, he expected British voters to opt for EU membership by a healthy margin. In fact, most people in the UK and in the rest of Europe believed this would be the case, even when, as the referendum day approached, polls consistently showed that the vote would be a very close-run affair. There were many reasons why there was more support for the United Kingdom leaving the European Union than Prime Minister Cameron suspected. Some were reasons that we have discussed already, such as a rise in support for more nationalist and protectionist policies in the UK (as in most other countries). Likewise, the EU's economic struggles in the years before the referendum had cost the EU the right to claim that it would not only boost economic growth in the UK, but across all EU member states. Finally, the United Kingdom was always a rather tepid member of the European Union, as while the rest of Europe had experienced defeat and humiliation in the Second World War, that event was viewed proudly in the UK as perhaps that country's last great moment as a global superpower. Regardless of the reasons, voters in the UK went to the polls in June 2016 and voted by a margin of 51.9% to 48.1% (1.27 million votes) to withdraw from the European Union. Of course, as we know now, the actual withdrawal process was highly convoluted, with much uncertainty on both sides as to what the future relationship between the UK and the EU would be. Nevertheless, this was yet another example of the overarching political trends that were sweeping across Europe and the world in recent years, impacting not only the political direction of the world, but the direction of the global economy as well.

With protectionism and nationalism on the rise in recent years, it is no surprise that the system of open global trade and investment would eventually come under severe strain. What was a surprise to many is that it would be the country that created and maintained this system of global trade and investment, the United States, that would fire the first shots in many of the new trade disputes that have erupted in recent years. Upon taking office in early 2017, United States President Donald Trump moved swiftly to let the rest of the world know that the rules were changing and that the US would now begin to look more after its own economic interests.

His primary focus was on the large trade imbalances that they US had with a number of its leading trading partners, none more important than China. In fact, it appeared that President Trump's eventual aim was for the US not to have a negative trade balance with any trading partner. Given the fact that the United States wields more economic power than any other country, the Trump Administration found itself with a vast array of weapons that it could use to force other countries into line. For example, as the world's largest export market for many other countries, the Trump Administration could threaten a country with tariffs on imports into the US. Alternatively, the United States could use the fact that its financial system and its currency hold dominant positions in international trade and investment in order to easily impose potentially devastating sanctions on any country it chooses, and in recent years, we have seen the US do just that to a number of countries around the world. Together, this desire by President Trump to rebalance US trade and prevent industries from leaving the US, coupled with the immense economic power held by the United States, has led to a series of increasingly dangerous trade wars, highlighted by the trade war between the US and China that began in 2018. With this and other trade wars proliferating in recent years, it is easy to see why the future of global trade and investment is now called into question, as we will discuss in more detail later in this book.

As we try to summarize the global economy of the past ten years, we find that this has been a period of dramatic change. Nevertheless, when looking at the overall performance of the global economy during this period, one would get the impression that, at least until the Covid19 pandemic hit in 2020, the global economy had been enjoying a period of strong growth. In fact, between 2010 and 2019, the global economy expanded by 3.7% per year, which by historical standards is a relatively strong rate of growth for the world as a whole.

Furthermore, when one sees how remarkably steady global growth was between 2012 and 2018, one would be forgiven for believing that many of the utopic dreams of a global economy characterized by steady growth with no more dramatic ups and downs had been realized. Of course, we know that this period of relatively strong and steady growth masked many major changes that were taking place in different parts of the world and in different segments of the global economy, as well as great differences among economies and industries in terms of their performance during the 2010s. Regardless, by the end of the 2010s, global economic output had risen to a remarkable $87 trillion, a number that dwarves the level of economic output at any time in human history and is a testament to the dramatic economic growth that the world has undergone since the dawn of the Industrial Revolution in the late 18th century.

While we can see that the performance of the global economy between the Global Financial Crisis and the Covid-19 pandemic was one of overall steady growth, we have to look deeper at the results to determine which economies were able to recover quicker from that first crisis and which are likely to be in a better position to emerge from the second crisis later in the 2020s. What is clear is that Asia has been the big winner, especially if one views economic competition as a zero-sum game. Sure, the Financial Crisis and the Covid-19 pandemic hit many Asian economies hard, particularly the latter crisis. However, Asia's relative economic performance was much better than that of any other region in the world during this period, and its share of global economic output, manufacturing, exports, investment and on-and-on continued to rise during this period. In fact, if the past few years have confirmed anything, it is that it is not necessarily a shift in global economic power from the developed world to the emerging one, but rather that it is a shift from regions such North America and Europe to Asia.

Apart from Asia, there have been some other economies that can be judged to have emerged with their positions strengthened over the past decade. New

World economies such as the United States, Canada and Australia have again proven that their capacity to generate economic growth is greater than that of their "older" counterparts in places such as Europe and Japan. Likewise, emerging markets that have either a large domestic market or a relatively diversified manufacturing base have generally outperformed other emerging markets amid the turmoil of recent years. Nevertheless, apart from Asia, the period stretching from the Financial Crisis to the Covid-19 pandemic has been one of great challenges and many setbacks, forcing many major economies to face a very uncertain future.

In fact, while it may be difficult to identify too many winners over the past decade or so, it is much simpler to pick out those economies that have lost ground during this period. For example, this period has been a devastating time for Europe. In fact, economic output today in Europe is almost no higher than it was twelve years ago, a testament to the struggles that this region (which accounts for one-fifth of global economic output) has endured. While neither the Financial Crisis nor the Covid-19 pandemic originated in Europe, few regions suffered greater economic losses than Europe during each crisis. As we will see later in this book, many of the factors that have contributed to Europe's dreadful economic performance in recent years will remain in place in the coming years and decades, posing a massive challenge for a region that, just a century ago, was still the heart of the global economy.

Another region that has emerged as a major loser in recent years is Latin America. For the first part of the 2010s, it appeared that Latin America was headed for a golden age, as high commodity prices, driven by soaring demand for metals and agricultural products in Asia, led to that region's highest rates of economic growth in recent memory. However, the collapse of commodity prices in 2014 led to a period of economic stagnation across the region, with major economies such as Brazil, Argentina and Venezuela experiencing very severe economic crises. Then, just as the region thought that the worst was behind it, Covid-19 arrived and brought a swift end to any hopes for a more sustained recovery in that region.

As we look back at the last decade or so of economic history, we can see that that the overall lesson has been that there is a realignment that is underway within the global economy. This realignment is primarily focused on the return of Asia as the center of the global economy, with less competitive economies, such as many European or Latin American economies, struggling to adapt to this changing landscape. Despite these massive shifts, the global economy was still able to generate a strong level of growth in a rather surprisingly-steady manner for a decade-long period spanning the time between the two worst economic crises since the Second World War.

So what went right for the global economy since 2010. First, Asian economies continued to grow at a strong pace, with most economies in the region continuing their rise up the value chain. Some economies, most notably China, moved into middle-income status, while some of the region's poorer countries, such as Vietnam, Indonesia and the Philippines, generated the levels of economic growth needed to lift tens of millions of people out of poverty. Outside of Asia, those countries that were able to expand their presence in high-tech and high-growth industries were able to out-perform those economies that failed to do so. Likewise, those economies that were able to enact reforms aimed at boosting their competitiveness generally outperformed their rivals that failed to enact such reforms.

On the other hand, the past decade or so has been a very challenging period for much of the world. Many non-competitive countries and industries continued to experience a relative decline that was accelerated by the two crises that began and ended this period of time. Inequality in many areas of the world continued to worsen, driving the political changes that threaten to destroy the globalized economy that has brought wealth to so many. In fact, the modern economy has left many countries, industries, businesses and even social classes, behind, threatening to leave us with a world that is increasing one of the haves and the have-nots. As we move ahead, the need to avoid this trap will be one of the most obvious reasons why we need to find ways to generate more economic growth in the future.

Finally, as we conclude our look back at the past 100, 30 and ten years of economic history, we see that we have many questions that are left unanswered as we turn our attention to the future. One of the most obvious questions is that, for much of the world, how will one generate economic growth amid the challenges posed by the modern world. How can we offset the continued demographic decline underway in most key economies? Is automation the answer, and can it help us to achieve the levels of growth that we have achieved in the past? Another key question revolves around globalization. Is the recent shift towards nationalism and protectionism just a phase or is it just beginning? If these trends continue, what will it mean for those countries whose economies are based upon trade and investment? Finally, the last major question that we will be addressing later in this book involves productivity. If demographic decline is inevitable and if trade and investment growth will not return to their previous high levels, is there anything apart from higher levels of productivity growth that can generate higher levels of economic growth in the future? More worryingly, given the recent direction of productivity growth in most parts of the world, how can higher levels of productivity growth be achieved in the years ahead?

Chapter Seven

DEMOGRAPHICS AND ECONOMIC DESTINY

WHEN WE THINK OF Nigeria, we hardly think of a superpower. However, in terms of demographics, it is already a superpower, or it will soon be one. In 1950, Nigeria's population was less than 38 million, or just a little more than half of that of Germany at that time. Today, Nigeria's population is more than 200 million, or two-and-a-half times that of Germany. With one of the highest birth rates in the world, and with an average life expectancy that, while well below the global average, has nevertheless increased substantially in recent decades, Nigeria now has the seventh-largest population in the world. Furthermore, some projections have Nigeria's population doubling once again over the next 30 years, and, if this comes true and other forecasts do as well, Nigeria will overtake the United States to become the third-most-populous country in the world by the year 2050. Of course, this assumes that birth rates in Nigeria will continue to exceed the global average, which is likely, at least in the northern half of the country. Should these projections become reality, Nigeria faces many grave questions, including just how the country will be able to find the resources, land and jobs needed to provide for a population of 400 million people in one of the poorest regions on the planet.

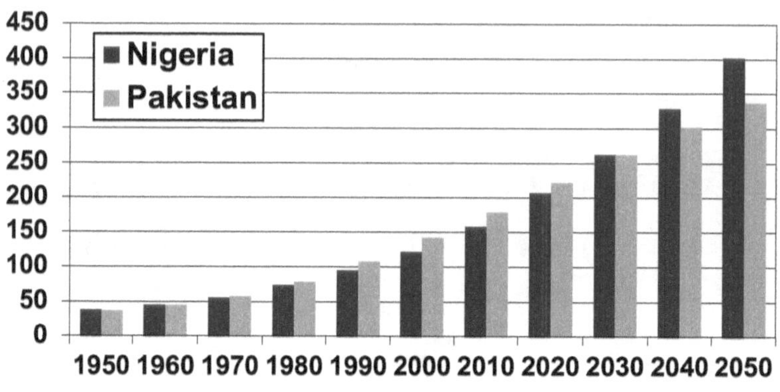

Pakistan is another country that is rarely ever discussed as a great power, but it too has a population that is larger than most people think. Pakistan is currently on the verge of overtaking Brazil to become the fifth-most-populous country in the world, with a population in excess of 215 million. Like Nigeria, Pakistan's population was much smaller in 1950 (40 million), but it too has had one of the world's highest birth rates between then and now, and this has resulted in Pakistan's population increasing by more than 500% in the span of just three generations. Pakistan also faces the challenge of providing jobs, land, water and food for such a massive population, particularly in light of the fact that Pakistan has some of the highest levels of political instability in the world. However, in contrast to Nigeria, Pakistan's birth rate has fallen sharply in recent years and as a result, population growth is forecast to slow in the coming decades. By 2050, Pakistan's population is expected to reach 290 million, well below the estimates for that country's future population from just a few years ago. In fact, if current trends continue, Pakistan's population could end up peaking at around 300 million sometime in the next four or five decades, a positive development considering the strains on Pakistan's resources from the country's huge population.

When we think of Japan, we do tend to think of a rather powerful country. Some of this thinking comes from the country's large population, as Japan has a larger population than any other developed country in the world outside of the

United States. This combination of a wealthy economy and a large population has allowed Japan to have what was for a long time the second-largest economy in the world, and what remains to this day the third-largest economy in the world. However, Japan's demographic situation is increasingly proving to be a drag on the country's economy and its relative power. This is because Japan, since the 1950s, has had one of the lowest birth rates in the world. As a result, population growth in Japan came to a halt in the early 2000s and today, Japan's population is shrinking by more than 500,000 people per year. Worse, the combination of very few babies and one of the world's highest life expectancies has left Japan with one of the world's oldest populations. At the same time, Japan's working-age population has been shrinking precipitously and will continue to do so without massive immigration inflows in the coming years, something that is highly unlikely. As a result, Japan's population is forecast to fall to anywhere between 107 million and 98 million by the year 2050, further weakening its potential to generate economic growth, as well as damaging its strategic position in the Asia-Pacific region.

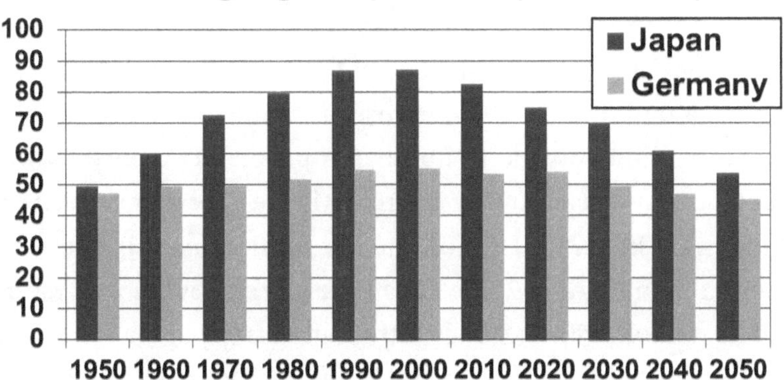

Source: UN

Finally, let's take a look at Germany. Again, this is a country that is in any discussion of the more powerful and influential countries in the world, and few countries have done more to shape the course of the past century, for better or for worse, than Germany. In a European context, Germany is a major demographic power as well, as its population is around a quarter larger than that of the region's other leading powers such as the United Kingdom and France. However, like Japan, Germany has had a very low birth rate for a very long time. As such, Germany's population growth has been very low. In fact, without immigration, Germany's population would have been declining since the 1970s. Only a series of immigration surges, such as the Turkish, East European and most recently, Middle Eastern and African, waves of immigration that have occurred periodically since the 1950s have prevented Germany's population from falling consistently like that of Japan. As we look ahead, Germany's birth rate, while rising slightly in recent years, remains extremely low, so without more waves of immigration in the future, Germany's demographic situation will mirror that of Japan, to the detriment of the German economy and perhaps to the country's power and influence within Europe. On the other hand, Germany is a relatively small country in a geographic sense, so a smaller population would certainly improve Germany's environmental situation in the years ahead.

While population changes have been taking place at the national level, even greater changes can be found at the city or metropolitan area level. Look at Lagos, the largest city in Nigeria and, by some measures, in Africa. While Lagos may not have the global recognition of cities such as New York, Tokyo or London, it has grown to become one of the world's great urban centers in a very short period of time. In 1950, Lagos was home to 325,000 people, which for Africa at that time was a large number of people in one city. However, the city's population has been growing at a remarkable pace ever since, passing the one million mark in the mid-1960s, the five million mark in the early 1990s and the ten million mark in 2010. Today, the city's population is estimated to be around 15 million, with the total metropolitan area population of Lagos and its environs estimated to be more than 22 million. This makes Lagos one of the world's ten largest cities already, and if current growth rates persist, Lagos could find itself as one of the world four- or five-largest cities within a few years. Of course, Lagos has neither the history nor the landmarks that make the world's better-known large cities so famous. However, as the largest city in one of the world's fastest-growing regions, Lagos is sure to play an ever-greater role in the world, and within the global economy, in the years and decades ahead.

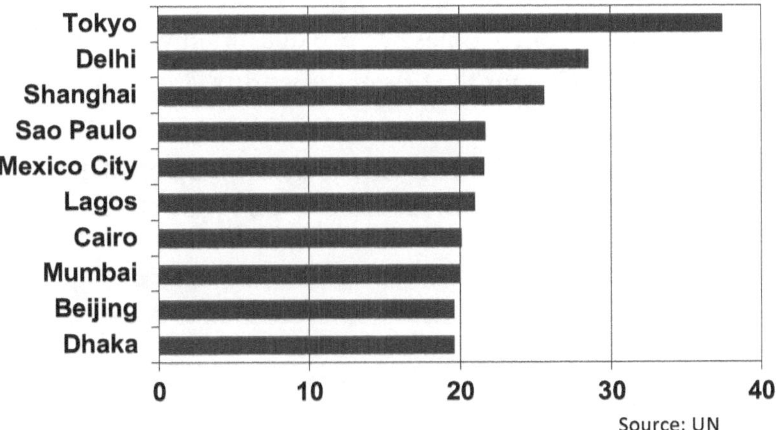

Another giant city that lacks global recognition in the Pakistani port city of Karachi. Prior to the partition of India in 1947, Karachi was a city of around half a million people. However, an influx of Muslims fleeing newly-independent India doubled the city's population almost overnight and Karachi's population has been soaring ever since. Today, the actual population of the city is unknown, but estimates place the population of the Karachi metropolitan area at around 17 million, making it one of the world 15 or 20 largest cities. Like Lagos, Karachi is a rather chaotic coastal city that, while being the largest economic center in its country, has relatively little political power. Nevertheless, the promise of jobs continues to lure more people from rural areas of Pakistan to Karachi, swelling its population. This has already exacerbated tensions within the city, making Karachi one of the world's least stable giant cities.

While the populations of Lagos and Karachi are continuing to grow at a very rapid pace, the population of the world's largest city, Tokyo, is growing much more slowly. This has much to do with the fact that the population of Japan is already in decline, and there are relatively few people left in Japan who are migrating from the countryside to that country's larger cities. In fact, Tokyo has been one of the world's largest cities for centuries now, and in recent decades, its population has been relatively stagnant. Nevertheless, Tokyo and its metropolitan area are now home to a massive 37 million people, far more than any other metropolitan area around the world and nearly four times the number of people living in the metropolitan areas of cities such as Paris or London. This gives Tokyo a massive urban economy, one that contends with that of New York City for the title of the world's largest urban economy.

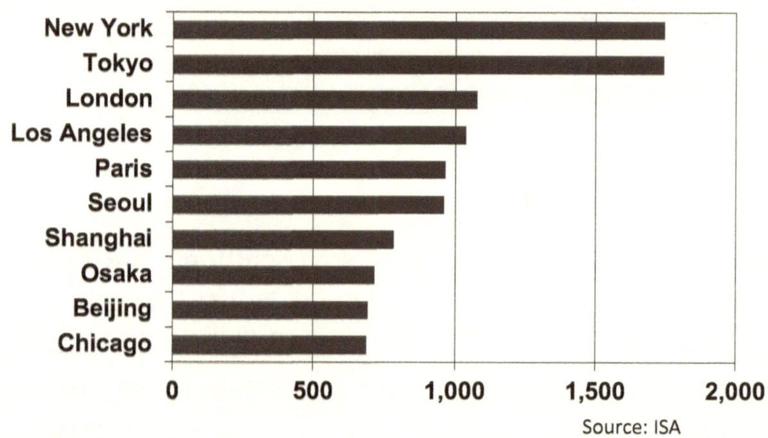

The World's Ten Largest Metropolitan Areas by Economic Output (bil. US$)

However, given Japan's worsening demographic decline and economic stagnation, Tokyo's future is increasingly uncertain. While its vast size and wealth will not diminish, its lead over rival cities will continue to shrink in the years and decades ahead, and unless Japan's demographic situation takes a dramatic turn, its population will inevitably begin to shrink.

One last city to consider here is Berlin, the capital of Germany. While Germany is West Europe's most-populous country, its capital, Berlin, is far overshadowed by the region's larger cities, such as London or Paris. This is because, unlike most European countries, Germany is not dominated by one or two cities. Instead, Germany has a host of cities and regions (Munich, Frankfurt, Hamburg, the Ruhr Valley, etc.) that serve as the heart of various aspects of German life and the German economy. Furthermore, while Berlin underwent a rapid population expansion in the second half of 19th century and the first half of the 20th century, its population has essentially stagnated since the city's division and isolation following the Second World War. Furthermore, the economic dislocations caused by the war devastated Berlin's economy, and the city today continues to be overshadowed economically by other German cities. Now, with Germany's population also forecast to fall significantly in the coming years, Berlin too faces an uncertain future, just like many cities located in countries or regions where population growth is slowing or has already come to an end.

An interesting way to look at the massive demographic changes that have been taking place in the world over the past century or two is to compare two neighboring regions, Europe and the combined Middle East and Africa region, to see how demographic changes have impacted each region, particularly with regards to their economic growth and their power and influence relative to one another. Let's start in 1900. At the beginning of the 20th century, Europe was at the height of its power, having benefitted tremendously from the impact of the Industrial Revolution on the region's economic and military power. In 1900, Europe had a combined population of just a little more than 400 million people, which was nearly 25% of the world's total population at this time. This represented a doubling of Europe's population in just a century, as soaring birth rates and longer life expectancies led to a population boom across much of the region.

In contrast, the Middle East and Africa's combined population in the year 1900 was less than 160 million. This represented just around 10% of the world's total population, and was just 40% of the population of Europe. This is because, unlike Europe, the post-industrial baby boom had yet to reach the Middle East and Africa, and life expectancies were extremely short in most areas of that region at that time. As a result, not only was Europe significantly stronger than the Middle East and Africa in terms of economic, technological and military power, but it also held a large demographic advantage over a region that was many times its geographic size. This is why European powers found it so easy to carve up much of the Middle East and Africa into colonies in the decades before 1900.

Let's fast-forward 60 years to the year 1960. This followed the devastation of Europe in the Second World War, as well as the period of decolonialization in which the remaining European colonies in the Middle East and Africa were granted their independence (although a few would still have to wait a number of years, most notably Portugal's African colonies). Because Europe suffered through two world wars and a series of economic crises, its population growth between 1900 and 1960 was much slower than it was in the 19th century. Even with a baby boom in the 1950s, Europe's total population in 1960 had grown to only 605 million, or 20% of the world's population that year. Meanwhile, the combined population of the Middle East and Africa in 1960 was a little more than 360 million, or just under 12% of the world's total population. So, while Europe's demographic power was already waning by the early 1960s, that of the Middle East and Africa had yet to take off. Given Europe's still massive lead in terms of economic, military and technological power over the Middle East and Africa, the balance of power between Europe on one side and the Middle East and Africa on the other remained tilted completely in the favor of Europe. However, things were about to change.

Europe, Middle East and African Population 1950-2050 (in millions)

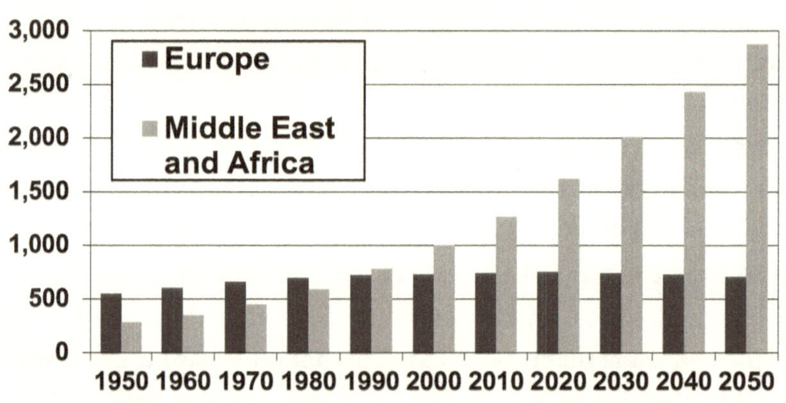

Source: UN

Today, the demographic balance between Europe on one side and the Middle East and Africa on the other has changed dramatically. In recent decades, European birth rates have fallen significantly and are now among the lowest in the world. As a result, population growth in Europe has continued to slow and the region's total population is now just under 740 million.

Furthermore, many European countries have seen their populations already begin to decline, particularly their working-age populations. At the same time, Europe is now home to some of the oldest populations in the world. Altogether, Europe today is home to less than 10% of the world's population, a far cry from its 25% share at the beginning of the 20th century.

In contrast, the populations of most countries in the Middle East and Africa experienced an explosion beginning in the 1960s and continuing, in some cases, to the present-day. This is the result of a combination of some of the world's highest birth rates and a remarkable increase in this region's life expectancies. Today, the Middle East and Africa are home to a combined population of 1.7 billion, an increase of almost 400% since 1960. This gives the region a 22% share of the world's population, again a massive increase over previous levels. In fact, while much of the rest of the world has experienced both a decline in population growth and a stagnation of its overall population level, this region has continued to see rapid population growth, while having one of the world's youngest populations. This gives the Middle East and Africa region a new-found demographic power that it almost never had in its long history due to having a geography and climate that are largely unsuited to support huge populations such as those found along the largest rivers of China or India. Furthermore, it has dramatically altered the balance of demographic power between Europe and the Middle East and Africa, and allowed the latter region to begin eating into the massive lead in terms of economic and military power that Europe once enjoyed over it.

Finally, let's look into the future at the expected demographic situations in Europe and the Middle East and Africa. For Europe, unless there are many massive waves of immigration in the coming decades, this period will be one of population stagnation and eventual decline. By the year 2050, Europe's total population is forecast to decline slightly to around 734 million. By this point, Europe's share of the world's total population will be just 7.5%, perhaps its smallest share since prehistoric times. Not only will this reduce Europe's economic growth potential even further, but it will also further diminish the region's military and political power. In contrast, the combined population of the Middle East and Africa is forecast to rise to an astonishing 3.2 billion, or one-third of the world's total population at that time. This represents a ten-fold increase in the region's population between 1950 and 2050, a level of growth never seen before in any part of the world. On one hand, this will greatly enhance the potential for economic growth in the Middle East and Africa, while increasing the region's global influence. On the other hand, this region already is lacking enough arable land, water and jobs for its current population, so the adding of an additional 1.5 billion people by the middle of this century is a dangerous challenge for an already volatile region.

Let's look at one more shifting demographic relationship before we move on to analyze how demographic changes impact the economy. This one is between China and India, the two countries that each have more than four times as many people as the third-most-populous country in the world, the United States. While we have seen examples of some countries and regions that have recorded sharp increases in their populations in recent decades, or even recent centuries, China and India have had relatively giant populations for thousands of years. In fact, the river valleys of China and India have supported large civilizations for nearly as long as any place on earth and have remained continuously habituated for many millennia. In the year 1700, the Qing Empire, which consists of most of modern-day China apart from the western territories of Xinjiang and Tibet, was home to a population of around 210 million, or 31% of the world's total population. At the same time, the Mughal Empire that consists of what is now most of India and Bangladesh, as well as parts of modern-day Pakistan and Afghanistan, had a population of 158 million, or 23% of the world's population at that time. Therefore, these two empires alone were home to 54% of the world's population before the Industrial Revolution. However, as we have already noted, both the lands of China and India would largely be passed by when the Industrial Revolution swept out of the United Kingdom in the late 18th and early 19th centuries, and this would have a major impact on the demographic situations in both parts of the world.

Let's now jump forward 250 years from 1700 to the year 1950. The Industrial Revolution was now a distant memory for much of the world, but it was only really taking hold in China and India at this time. By the year 1950, China's population had expanded to 563 million, or 22% of the world's total population. Due to the unrest and strife that characterized China in the second half of the 19th century and the first half of the 20th century, population growth was subdued compared with that of most other parts of the globe, resulting in this sharp decline in China's share of the world's population over the previous 250 years. As for India, it had just undergone partition and become an independent state, but this partition meant that heavily-populated areas such as modern-day Pakistan and Bangladesh were no longer within India's borders. Still, the newly-independent India had a population of 370 million in 1950, accounting for 14.5% of the world's total population. Here too, population growth over the previous 250 years had been slower than in other parts of the world, especially in those regions that had industrialized early in this period. Therefore, it can be said that, in 1950, China and India were not only at their low point in terms of economic power, but also in terms of demographic power, as while both China and India had far larger populations than any other countries in the world, their demographic advantage that was so pronounced before the Industrial Revolution had been eroded.

Since 1950, the demographic situations in China and India have changed significantly. China underwent a major increase in population growth in the 1970s, only to have the government put the brakes on population growth in the 1980s via the One-Child Policy that resulted in China's birth rate falling to be one of the lowest in the world. Nevertheless, this has not prevented China's population from rising to more than 1.4 billion today, or 18.5% of the world's total current population. However, it has had the effect of giving China both one of the fastest-aging populations in the world, as well as having a working-age population that is set to shrink dramatically in the decades ahead, as we will discuss in more detail a little later. In India, population growth remained higher for a much longer period of time than in China, and this has resulted in the population gap between China and India narrowing in recent decades. In fact, India's population has surpassed 1.4 billion and has overtaken that of China. Even as India's birth rates continues to fall, this recent period of rapid population growth gives India a much younger population than China, with a working-age population that is forecast to continue growing for a number of decades to come.

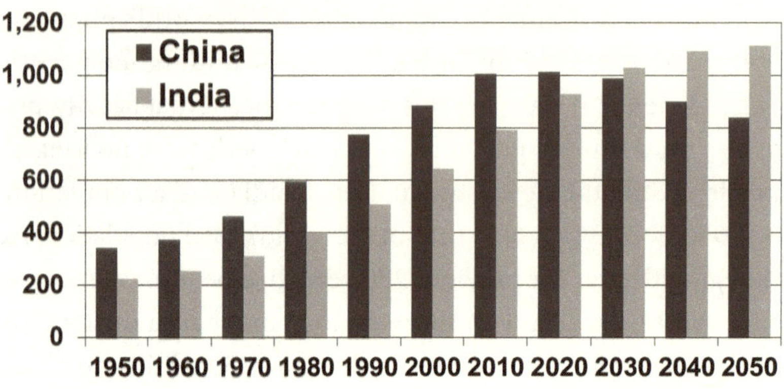

Source: UN

By the year 2050, India's lead atop the rankings of the world's most-populous countries is expected to be solidified, with India's population at that time forecast to be 1.64 billion, or 240 million more than that of China. This is due to the fact that India's birth rate, while falling sharply, is expected to remain much higher than China's. In fact, while Beijing has abandoned the One-Child Policy due to concerns about China's worsening demographic situation, this is not expected to have much, if any, impact on China's birth rate in the years ahead. Still, India is expected to reach its peak population sometime around 2050, and should birth rates fall even further than expected in India in the coming years, that country too could end up facing an uncertain demographic situation such as the one that is developing in China. When we look at the shares of the world's population in 2050 accounted for by India and China, we see that India is forecast to account for less than 17% of the world's population, while China will make up just over 14% of the world's population, its lowest share in recorded history. In fact, whereas China and India accounted for more than 50% of the world's population before the Industrial Revolution, by the middle of this century they will account for just over 30% of the total global population, a remarkable shift in demographic power that will have major implications for China, India and the rest of the world.

DEMOGRAPHY AS A DRIVER OF ECONOMIC GROWTH

Of all of the generators of economic growth, the one the creates the least controversy and is accepted by almost all economists is population growth. The reasons for this are clear. A growing population gives a city, country or region an expanding consumer market, for example. At the same time, a growing working-age population gives a city, country or region a larger pool of labor, enabling it to increase its production of goods or its provision of services. In contrast, a shrinking population reduces the size of a customer base, while imposing limits on production and services.

It is important to note that this generally applies only to economies that are not operating primarily on a subsistence level. In the case of subsistence economies, the rate of economic growth that can be derived from population growth is no greater than the rate of population growth itself, thus not leading to increases in economic growth on a per capita basis. Instead, economies have to have moved beyond the subsistence stage in order for workers to be productive outside of their immediate subsistence activities. This allows for workers to generate production, provide services and create wealth beyond the subsistence level, and this allows an economy to then generate higher rates of economic growth at both the total and the per capita levels. Today, there are almost no subsistence economies left in the world apart from some remote communities in the Arctic or in heavily forested regions in the tropics. However, for much of human history, particularly before the Industrial Revolution, a large share of humanity's economic activities was of a subsistence nature.

If we look way back in time, we can see how this works. For example, prior to the Roman Empire, there were very few cities or states in Europe or the Mediterranean region whose economies were not focused primarily on subsistence activities such as feeding their populations or securing their borders. Sure, some economies did engage in trade with other cities or states, but the scale of this trade was quite limited. Once Rome created a unified economy that encompassed much of Europe, North Africa and the Middle East, it was able to develop unheard of economies of scale in that part of the world, while allowing for regional economic specializations to flourish. This allowed much of the Roman Empire to move beyond having just a mere subsistence economy and instead, it developed an economy that was no longer constrained by the limits of population growth. Instead, it could now combine its population growth, which soared in times when there were no pandemics, with a diversified economy to achieve never-seen-before levels of economic growth in that part of the world. This was the secret to Rome's success and the key reason why it was able to thrive for so long as the foremost political and economic power of its day.

The United States is another example of how demographic growth, when combined with economic specialization, high rates of productivity growth and increasing levels of trade and investment, can generate high rates of economic growth. The United States, like Canada, Australia and New Zealand, is a "New World" country insofar as its population growth has been very high since its "Westernization" (although not for its indigenous peoples) and its population density has been relatively low, allowing for population growth to reach higher levels than other developed economies.

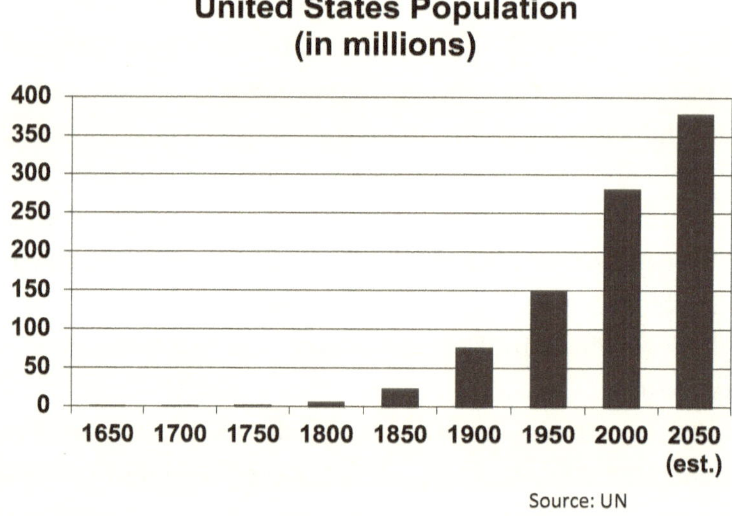

**United States Population
(in millions)**

Source: UN

It is easy to forget that, at the time of its independence from the United Kingdom, the new United States had a population of less than three million people, a population that was about the same size as contemporary Portugal or the territory that would eventually become Belgium. However, unlike these geographically tiny countries (or soon-to-be countries), the United States had a vast amount of land that, while settled by millions of indigenous peoples, was considered "open" to development, a factor that would result in the population of the United States doubling nearly every 25 years from the 1720s (before its independence) until the late 19th century.

Like ancient Rome, this allowed the United States to experience rapid economic growth due in part to its fast-increasing population. Furthermore, as the United Kingdom's North American colonies were almost immediately as developed as the most-developed economies in Europe, the colonies, and later the United States and Canada, were immediately beyond the subsistence stage, enabling for economic specialization and large-scale economies-of-scale to be created, thus generating vast amounts of growth on both a total and a per capita basis. As we have seen, this allowed the United States to overtake the United Kingdom as the world's wealthiest large country (on a per capita GDP basis) in the early 20th century, a position that it has maintained to this day, with only a short brief interruption by Japan prior to that country's economic crisis in 1992. One of the key reasons why the United States has been able to generate higher levels of both total GDP growth and per capita GDP growth than most other developed economies has been the fact that the US has two major demographic advantages over most other developed economies. First, it simply has a much larger population than any other developed economy, giving it a vast labor pool, a massive internal market and the ability to create giant economies-of-scale. Second, the US' working-age population has been growing faster than that of nearly all other developed economies, although the recent decline in the US' birth rate has slowed this growth of late.

A growing population means more consumers, at least when the segments of the population that are growing are among those age-groups that are within the leading consuming age-groups. Furthermore, it helps an economy if a higher percentage of its consumers are earning their money via a job or business rather than using funds transferred from the government to do their consuming. Regardless, consumer spending is the key driver of economic growth for most of the world's leading economies today. As we have moved further away from a subsistence existence, consumer spending has increased in importance. Let's look at some examples of this. In the United States, personal consumption expenditures (PCE) as a share of total GDP hovered around

60% of the US' total GDP in the final decades of the 20th century. Since then, personal consumption has continued to rise at a higher rate than the rest of the US economy as a whole, and now, personal consumption accounts for around 70% of US GDP. Of course, the United States is a more extreme example, as disposable income levels in the US are higher than in nearly all other countries. Likewise, the United States' population is still growing, resulting in the US consumer market continuing to grow. In countries with stagnant or shrinking populations, consumer spending as a share of total economic output has actually begun to fall, and this is proving to be a major drag on economic growth in such countries.

Take Germany for example. In the early 1990s, consumer spending accounted for 59% of that newly-reunified economy's GDP. However, as Germany's demographic situation has deteriorated (and as German exporters have found success selling their manufactured goods outside of Europe), consumer spending as a share of Germany's total economic output has done the opposite of what has happened in the US and has actually fallen. Today, consumer spending accounts for about 52% of Germany's total GDP, a number that continues to fall. Germany's ability to export has prevented Germany's economy from collapsing along with consumer spending in that country, but this growing dependence upon external markets leaves the German economy dangerously exposed to trade barriers or disruptions (such as the Covid-19 pandemic or a trade war). In short, a growing internal market shields an economy from the threats posed by an increasing reliance upon external markets and provides a solid, home-grown engine for economic growth, as long as these increasing numbers of domestic consumers have money to spend.

It is that last factor that I mentioned that prevents many countries that have fast-growing populations from generating the levels of economic growth that one would expect from countries that have high levels of population growth. If the economies are very poor and their economies remain at a subsistence level, then economic growth will be no higher than population growth, Worse, for subsistence economies where the resources needed to maintain per capita levels of food, shelter and the like are being stretched too thinly, than you have the worst-case scenario of a country whose population is growing, but whose capacity to feed and shelter that population is no longer adequate. This situation has led to the humanitarian crises that we have seen repeatedly in recent decades in places such as Ethiopia and Yemen. For the majority of the world's countries that have moved well beyond the subsistence level, disposable income levels have risen sharply in recent decades due to a combination of rising wages and lower living costs. Of course, these increases in disposable income levels have not been uniform, with those of some countries, or those of some income classes, rising much faster than others. Some major economies have even seen disposable income levels stagnate in recent years. In fact, disposable income is a relatively tricky subject, as there are many competing measures of this figure. In my work, I have done a great deal of research into measuring disposable income and have found that, while coming up with reliable data for many countries is a challenging task, it is possible to compare disposable income levels across time or among a group of countries with a fair degree of accuracy.

Disposable Income Per Household in 2021 (in US$)

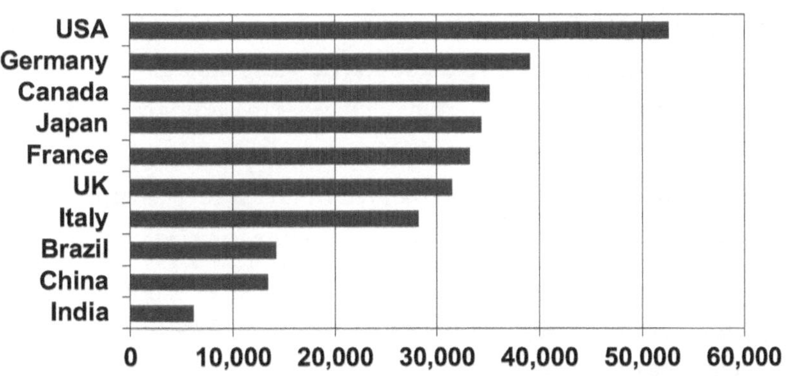

Source: ISA Market Data Report

Through this, we can see how disposable income levels compare across countries and regions. For example, we can see how the very high levels of disposable income in countries such as the United States have fueled their soaring levels of consumer spending in recent decades. Here you have a country that has successfully combined rising populations with higher levels of wealth, thus enabling that country to generate significantly higher levels of economic growth in recent decades than almost all other developed economies. The fact that workers in the United States also face less arduous tax burdens than their counterparts in other developed economies has also helped to drive consumer spending growth. Take for instance high-tax countries such as Belgium and Sweden and here we see that consumer spending growth has been far lower. This is largely due to the combination of lower levels of disposable income and slower population growth. If we look at emerging markets, the situation is even more stark. In some emerging markets such as China, consumer spending growth is becoming an increasingly-important driver of economic growth as wealth levels rise, but nevertheless, consumer spending remains a smaller component of their overall economies due to the dominance of export-oriented manufacturing. In most other emerging markets, particularly those that have much smaller manufacturing bases, consumer spending accounts for a much larger share of a country's economy. For some, increasing wealth levels and the expansion of their upper- and middle-classes is now almost as important a factor in their ability to generate economic growth as is their ability to export to wealthy countries. As such, these emerging markets' domestic demographic situations are now playing a much more important role in the success of these economies, and will continue to do so in the years ahead.

We can see how this combination of changes in demographics, wealth and disposable income can impact the performance of an economy. For example, in the 2010s, consumer spending expanded by an average of more than 4% per year in the United States during that decade, while the US economy expanded by an average of a little more than 2% per year. This meant that consumer spending was an important factor is the US' relative economic success that decade (at least when compared with even slower growing developed economies). On the other end of the spectrum, let's look at a country such as Italy. In the 2010's Italy's economy grew by an anemic 0.2% per year, continuing a run of terrible results for that economy that began in the early 2000s. Worse, consumer spending levels actually declined in Italy in 2010s due to a combination of stagnant levels of disposable income and a worsening demographic situation. As such, whereas rising levels of consumer spending were a key driver of economic growth in the United States, the opposite was true in Italy, where falling or stagnant levels of consumer spending prevented that country's economy from generating much, if any, economic growth.

One last example to look at is China. Here, the consumer sector was, for much of the country's economic miracle, a much smaller component of the country's economy than in other large economies. This was due to the focus on the country's manufacturing sector, which served as the catalyst for China's rapid economic expansion that began in the 1980s. However, while consumer spending in China grew roughly at the same pace as the Chinese economy for much of the 1990s and the early 2000s, in recent years, consumer spending has accelerated, and is now rising faster than the Chinese economy as a whole, meaning that its role as a driver of economic growth in China has been enhanced. However, much of this consumer spending growth has been driven simply by rising disposable income levels, as China's demographic situation is worsening due to decades of extremely low birth rates.

Overall, we can see how demographic changes play a role in influencing consumer spending, and how consumer spending is the most important determinant of the success of many of the world's most important economies. It should also be noted that, while consumerism has also been present, it has never been more important than today, and never before have consumers had the level of influence over an economy as they have in the 21st century. In the world's wealthiest economies, never-before-seen levels of disposable income have transformed their consumer sectors and enabled them to partially offset declines in population growth. However, it remains to be seen for how long this can continue, particularly as many of these countries have bounced from one economic crisis to another in recent years. In emerging markets, consumer spending plays a different role in their earlier stages of economic development. However, as emerging markets move into middle-income status or higher, consumer spending also becomes a more important factor in the success of these emerging markets.

As we look ahead to the future of consumer spending as a driver of economic growth, there are many questions that remain to be answered. For example, we know that population growth will continue to slow in nearly all major economies around the world. If disposable income growth fails to offset these demographic declines, how will consumer spending be able to continue to drive economic growth in the future. These recent economic crises suggest that this is a real problem that could stymie economic development in the coming years, if not longer. Also, there are many societal changes that are taking place that also threaten to slow consumer spending growth in the future. For example, consumer behavior and spending patterns have been undergoing tremendous changes in recent years, particularly as younger consumers shun the type of consumption practiced by their predecessors. This has already caused major disruptions to many transitional consumer goods and services sectors, while giving rise to new sectors in areas such as the sharing economy and online retail. Finally, as environmental awareness continues to rise around the world, many consumers are now taking into account the environmental impact of their consumption patterns and adjusting them accordingly. This is a trend that could continue, or accelerate, in the future, and is one that could have massive ramifications for consumer spending and its impact on economic growth in the years and decades ahead.

While consumer spending is the key driver of economic growth for most of the world's largest economies these days, most of these economies rose to their current levels of wealth on the backs of their manufacturing sectors, while much of their more recent growth and wealth generation has come from their service sectors. Starting with the Industrial Revolution in the United Kingdom, manufacturing was the impetus for a tremendous increase in wealth in those countries that followed in the UK's path. The ability of manufacturing to generate vast new amounts of wealth was best seen in the United States, where the combination of expanding manufacturing industries, new manufacturing processes, seemingly unlimited natural resources and a soaring population combined to make the United States an economy that achieved levels of scale and wealth that had never been seen before. In recent decades, it has been Asia that has emerged as the new manufacturing center of the world, with the region's huge labor force allowing manufacturers to achieve economies of scale that have never been reached before. Nevertheless, manufacturing's share of global economic output has been steadily declining, overtaken by the world's fast-growing service sector. In fact, over the past 50 years, manufacturing's share of global economic output has fallen from 25% to 16%, with even larger declines found in countries such as the United States and Brazil.

In some cases, periods of strong manufacturing growth have coincided, or preceded, periods of rapid population growth. A good example of this is the impact that the Industrial Revolution had on population growth in the United Kingdom. A similar situation occurred in Germany in the late 19th and early 20th centuries, as well as in Japan in the rapid industrialization of the post-war years. Where population growth did follow industrialization, it allowed its growth to continue for a longer period of time, as this population growth dramatically expanded those countries' labor forces. However, in those countries that industrialized at the same time they were recording lower levels of population growth, such as France during the period of Germany's population boom, manufacturing growth was limited by these labor constraints, helping German manufacturing to easily overtake that of France.

While the expansion of the manufacturing sector was the leading factor in the growth of what are today's largest economies, in recent decades, it has been the service sector that has come to comprise the largest share of economic output in nearly all of the world's leading economies. Today, the service sector comprises nearly 80% of the total economic output of the United States, while in China, nearly 55% of that country's total economic output comes from the service sector, a figure that is expected to rise substantially in the years ahead. However, while historical population explosions have been linked with periods of strong growth in the agricultural and manufacturing sectors, the same cannot be said for periods of strong growth in the services sector. In fact, some of the countries that now have some of the lowest rates of population growth in the world also have some of the highest rates of growth in terms of their service sectors. One reason for this is that, unlike in most manufacturing industries, women make up a large share of the labor force in many leading segments of the service sector. This gives women less time to give birth and to raise children, resulting in dramatically lower birth rates.

In some cases, the correlation between population growth and economic growth is declining. A good example of this is China. Much of the Chinese economic miracle of the past four decades occurred during a time when population growth in that country slowed dramatically. In the 1980s and 1990s, China's working-age population was still rising at a strong pace and there was a seemingly unlimited supply of labor for that country's rapidly-expanding economy. However, economic growth in China was able to remain at a high rate for some time after that country's working-age population had begun to expand at a much slower pace. Two other heavily-industrialized economies that were able to grow economically at a pace well above their population growth levels were Germany and South Korea, two countries that have some of the lowest birth rates in the world. In these cases, the impact of significant-ly-worsening demographic situations on these countries' economic results were not has severe as normally would have been expected.

There are two main reasons why economies such as China, Germany and South Korea have managed to continue to grow (at outside of the Covid-19 pandemic) despite worsening demographic situations that include severe declines in their working-age populations. One of these reasons is the prolif-eration of automation in these economies, particularly in their manufacturing sectors, but also increasingly in their service sectors as well. As a result, workers play a smaller role in the production process in more-heavily-automated economies than ever before. The other key factor is that a large share of these countries' economic output is comprised of manufactured exports. By not limiting their markets to just the home markets, which are in any case stagnating or shrinking, countries such as Germany and South Korea can continue to generate rates of economic growth that are well above their rates of population growth.

This weakening correlation between economic growth and population growth is having a number of impacts on society in the 21st century. For example, as the service industry accounts for a greater share of economic output in most leading economies, the impact on birth rates has become quite noticeable. This is due to the fact that the service industry is not conducive to large families for a number of reasons, including the fact that a higher share of the labor force in the service industry consists of women. Another impact of this weakening connection between economic and population growth has been the concentration of wealth in relatively fewer hands, leading to new increases in wealth inequality in many parts of the world. While wealth is concentrated among a smaller percentage of families, poorer families find themselves having to commit more of their time to work, thus reducing birth rates as parents in these families have less time for children. Contrast this with previous generations, when lower- and middle-class families often had a father that worked in manufacturing and a mother that often stayed home and raised large numbers of children. Such families are a rarity in much of the modern world. Because of this, too many people are finding themselves lost in the modern world. The loss of manufacturing jobs in many parts of the world has had a devastating impact on lower-skilled workers, often leading to a sense of hopelessness whose impact on demographics is a dramatic decline in birth rates.

WORLD POPULATION TRENDS

The world's population growth over the past two centuries or so has been nothing short of astounding. After centuries of slow and uneven population growth, the world's population has exploded over the past 200 years, and this had played a very important role in driving economic growth around the world. Now, this population growth is slowing, and in many cases, it is slowing far faster than anyone had predicted. How this will impact the global economy in the coming years is one of the most important questions economists and demographers face today. As we examine this issue in more detail, let's have a look at just how the world's population reached the 7.8 billion, where is stands today.

In the ancient world, population growth was at times extremely rapid, but this had more to do with the low population base in those times. Furthermore, this growth came in fits and spurts, with occasional periods of growth mixed in with periods of population decline, sometimes precipitous, caused by events such as pandemics, conflicts and dramatic shifts in the climate. In fact, the average rate of global population growth between the years 10,000 BCE and 1700 CE was a mere 0.04%. By the time we reached the year 0, when two major historical empires were approaching the heights of their power (Rome in the West and the Han Dynasty in the East), the entire population of the world was just 190 million, or less than the population of Nigeria or the Indian state of Uttar Pradesh today. However, growth began to accelerate in the 1700s, an acceleration that lasted until recent years.

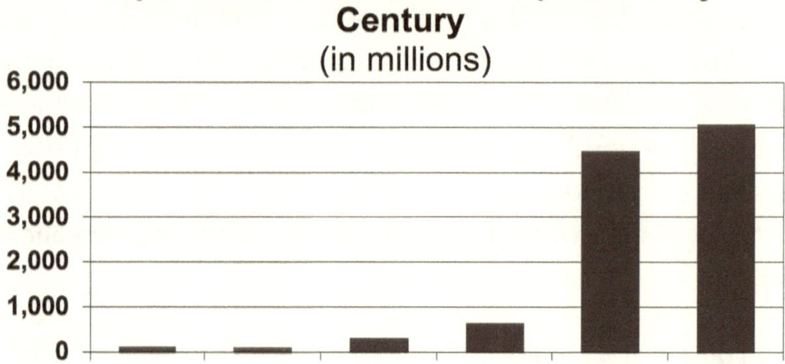

If we go back to the year 1820, the total population of the world had risen to an estimated 1,090,000,000, an increase of a little more than 500% over the previous 1,800 years. Furthermore, as the Industrial Revolution's impact on population growth had only just begun, Asia still accounted for almost 70% of the world's population in 1820, with China's 381 million people and India's 209 million making up the bulk of Asia's population at that time. However, as we know, the Industrial Revolution unleashed a period of massive population growth in Europe and North America. Between the years 1820 and 1950, the population of Europe would grow 151% (from 219 million to 549 million), while the population of North America grow increase nearly 14 times over (from 12 million to 173 million). In contrast, Asia's population, while remaining the largest in the world by a wide margin, would only increase by 88% during this 130-year period.

However, the five decades spanning the second half of the 20th century would witness another period of demographic change in many parts of the world. While the global population grew from 1.65 billion to 2.54 billion between the years 1900 and 1950 (an increase of 890 million), it would grow by a massive 3.6 billion between the years 1950 and 2000, the largest growth spurt in history for the human population of this planet.

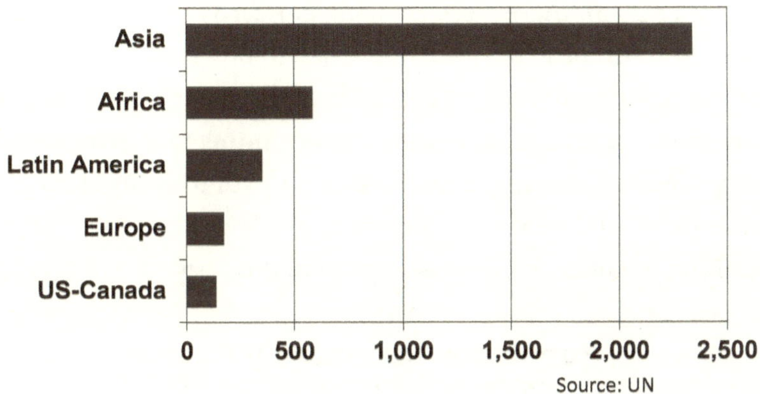

While the post-World-War-Two period in the West is known as the Baby Boom period thanks to the temporary increase in birth rates that occurred in much of the West after the war, the real demographic story in the second half of the 20th century took place in other parts of the world. For example, regions such as East Asia, South Asia, the Middle East, Africa and Latin America all underwent population explosions during this 50-year period, taking what had been many places with relatively-low population densities and turning them into some of the most crowded places on earth. Here are three examples:

- Pakistan: The population of Pakistan rose from 40.3 million in 1950 to 152.4 million between 1950 and 2000, an increase of 278%.
- Mexico: The population of Mexico expanded from 28.5 million in 1950 to 99.8 million in 2000, an increase of 250%,
- Philippines: The population of the Philippines rose from 21.1 million in 1950 to 76.5 million in 2000, an increase of 263%.

In fact, it is hard to find any place in the world that did record relatively high rates of population growth in the second half of the 20th century. This was the one period in human history where the populations of all regions of the world were increasing, some much faster than others. This addition of 3.6 billion people in a span of just 50 years would also prove to be a major boost for the global economy, allowing it to generate growth with a level of consistency never seen before.

By the year 2000, there were growing concerns that global population growth would continue at the pace that it had in previous decades, leading to massive overcrowding and a rapid depletion of the planet's resources. However, there were signs that this rapid growth was beginning to slow, at least in some areas of the world. For example, population growth in many areas of Europe and East Asia, which had already slowed in the later part of the 20th century, was beginning to fall at an even faster pace in the early part of this century.

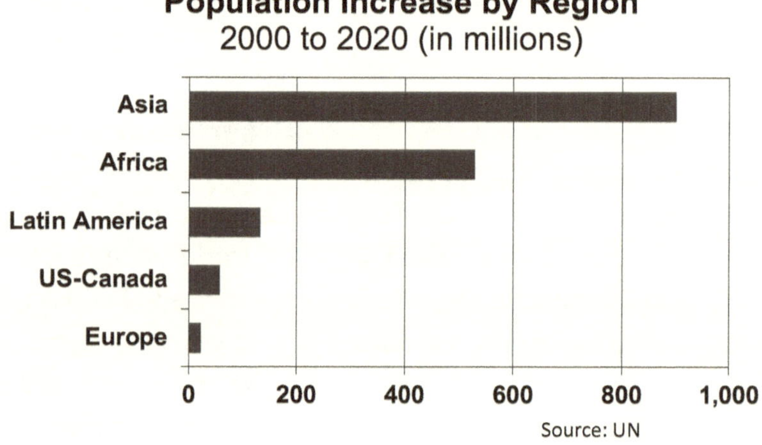

As we will see, this population slowdown that has continued in recent years is having a major impact on the global economy, contributing in a big way to the lower rates of growth that we have seen in many parts of the world. Worse, as this trend looks set to continue, its impact on the global economy is likely to be substantial.

In the past, global population growth spurts were the result of increases in the population of a single region, or perhaps two regions. This is one of the reasons why global population growth had been so uneven until recent centuries. The pattern typically was one where a period of economic and/or scientific advancement in one region led to a subsequent increase in population growth in that region, either through higher birth rates, immigration or longer life expectancies. In the 19th century, the Industrial Revolution led to a population explosion in North America and Europe, while population growth in the rest of the world carried on as it had in previous centuries. Then, for a short period, all areas of the world underwent rapid population growth. However, we appear to be entering a phase where, once again, population growth is concentrated in just a few regions, as we will see later in this book.

Because of their vast size, China and India have always had an outsized influence on global demographics. In China, the country's main river valleys (the Yellow, the Yangtze and the Pearl) have been major population centers since ancient times and remain among the most-heavily-populated areas of the world today. As such, despite periods of war, unrest, famine, flood and other such disruptions, China's population continued to expand at a relatively rapid pace. That was the case, at least, until the One Child Policy was implemented in the 1980s. Since then, population growth in China has fallen dramatically and the country now has one of the lowest birth rates in the world. Meanwhile, India, like China, has long been a major population center, at times having a larger population than its giant neighbor to the east. However, by the year 1995, India's population was smaller than China's by 300 million people. Since then, while China's birth rate has plummeted, India's has remained relatively high and as a result, India's population today trails that of China by a much smaller amount, and as I indicated, India is expected to overtake China to become the world's most-populous country by the end of this decade.

As we have discussed, the Industrial Revolution unleashed a population explosion in the West, first in Europe and later in North America. In fact, it was the combination of the West's technological advances, its industrialized economy and then its fast-growing population that allowed Western states to become the world's dominant powers by the 19th century. In the 19th century alone, Europe's population more than doubled, reaching 421 million by the end of the century. This meant that Europe's population, while still smaller than that of Asia, now dwarfed those of all other regions apart from Asia. This gave Europe as vast work force, consumer base and military manpower, all factors in Europe's ascendance to world domination in the 19th century. In fact, Europe's population by the end of the 19th century was larger than the combined populations of the Americas, Africa and the Middle East. Today, those three region's populations are three-and-a-half times the size of Europe's.

However, while it lasted, Europe's rapid population growth was a major boost for the region's economic power.

The same is true for North America. In 1800, the combined population of the United States and Canada was barely more than five million people, or less than the population of modern Singapore. However, over the course of the 19th century, the population of the United States and Canada would increase by a factor of 15, rising to 81 million. This, coupled with the vast resources of the North American continent and the industrial and technological developments that occurred there, allowed for some of history's most dramatic economic growth. In the 20th century, this growth continued, with the combined population of the US and Canada expanding by nearly 400%, rising to 313 million by the year 2000. Again, while this growth paled in comparison with the population growth rates of the 19th century, it was nevertheless enough to prove to be a major driver of growth. Today, the US and Canada's combined population of 370 million people is still growing, albeit at a much slower pace than in most periods of their shared history. How these countries' economies react to this slower population growth will be a major question facing the region in the years ahead.

While Europe's, and later North America's, rate of population growth eventually slowed, some areas of the world continued to experience rapid population growth until much more recent times. Most of this population growth was concentrated in emerging markets, where industrialization, if it arrived, did so at a much later date than in Europe and North America. In Latin America, the population of that vast region grew by nearly 300% in the 19th century, a much lower rate of growth than in North America as immigration levels were much lower, as were life expectancies. However, population growth in Latin America took off in the 20th century, with the region's population in 2000 being nearly eight-times larger than it was 100 years earlier. In fact, by the early 1950s, Latin America's total population had overtaken that of North America, and today, Latin America is home to nearly 300 million more people than North America. Another region where population growth exploded in the 20th century was the Middle East. In fact, no region of the world recorded faster population growth between the years of 1950 and 2000 than the Middle East, with the region's population increasing from just 100 million in 1950 to 380 million in 2000. So far in the 21ˢᵗ century, population growth in the Middle East has slowed, but in most cases, it remains significantly higher than that found in most other regions of the world.

Finally, Africa is the region where the world's shifting demographic balance of power is most evident. At the beginning of the 19ᵗʰ century, Africa's population was estimated to be around 80 million, or a little more than one-third of that of Europe's population at that time. Over the course of the 19ᵗʰ century, as most of Africa was brutally colonized by the Europeans, its population growth was lower than almost anywhere else in the world, with its population reaching only 141 million by the year 1900. Population growth in Africa remained relatively sluggish in the first half of the 20ᵗʰ century, before soaring birth rates and life expectancies led to unprecedented population growth across much of that region. Between 1950 and 2000, Africa's population nearly quadrupled, rising from 228 million to 811 million in such a short span. Moreover, while population growth has slowed in most other areas of the world over the first two decades of this century, in Africa, it has not. Today, Africa's population has reached 1.3 billion, and, as we will see later in this book, this population growth is forecast to continue in the decades to come.

While the past two centuries have shown us that rapid and sustained population growth can generate high levels of long-term economic growth, we are now confronted with a world in which global population growth is slowing noticeably. This can be seen in the following chart, which shows how the rate of global population growth has changed by decade.

Here we can see the dramatic demographic changes that have been under-way for some time now. From the 1950s until the 1980s, the global population grew at a rate of nearly 20% or more per decade, some of the fastest rates of growth ever recorded. This was due to a combination of the "Baby Boom" in the West and the dramatic population growth that took place in emerging markets during those decades (as well as rising life expectancies in emerging markets). However, since the 1990s, global population growth has been falling at a dramatic pace. During the past three decades, birth rates in most parts of the world have fallen substantially. Even more importantly from an economic perspective, working-age population growth has fallen even further. As a result, what had been a leading driver of global economic growth in the

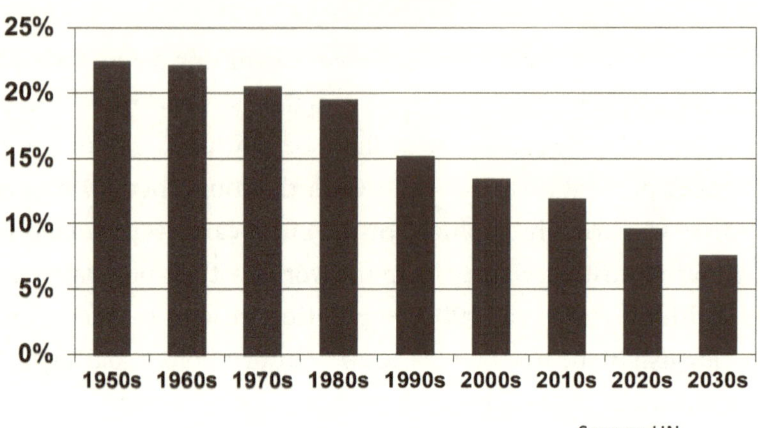

decades after the Second World War was now threatening to become a major drag on growth in the 21st century.

While population growth has slowed in nearly all parts of the world, there are some extreme examples of this. Take Japan, the world's third-largest economy. During its economic heyday, the population of Japan expanded by nearly 50%, rising from 84 million in 1950 to 124 million in 1990. This allowed Japan to not only have a large enough work force to meet the demands of its rapidly-expanding manufacturing sector, but also to develop one of the world's most important consumer markets. However, a major decline in that country's birth rate beginning in the early 1970s, and a near-total lack of immigration, resulted in a sudden slowdown in population growth in Japan. In fact, over the past 30 years, the Japanese population has grown by a measly 2.5 million people, or just 2%. This has led to labor shortages (particularly as the Japanese working-age population is already falling sharply) and a weakening of what was once a leading consumer market.

Another country that has seen its demographic fortunes change for the worse is Russia. In the aftermath of the Second World War and the tremendous loss of life in Russia and other parts of the Soviet Union during the war, Russia's population growth soared, driving the rapid economic growth experienced in Russia and the Soviet Union in the 1950s and 1960s. However, as the Russian birth rate fell sharply, so too did population growth in Russia. When Russia became an independent country upon the dissolution of the Soviet Union in 1991, its population was 148 million, making Russia the world's sixth-most populous country and an attractive market for exporters and investors. However, with one of the lowest birth rates, and with what was, at least until recently, a very low life expectancy for men, Russia's population began to decline not long after its independence. Today, Russia's population is down to 145 million, while its working-age population has fallen even faster. Furthermore, Russia is now just the ninth-most-populous country in the world, having been overtaken by Pakistan, Nigeria and Bangladesh in the 30 years since its independence.

Perhaps the most dramatic example of the population decline that is beginning to take hold in many parts of the world is Bulgaria.

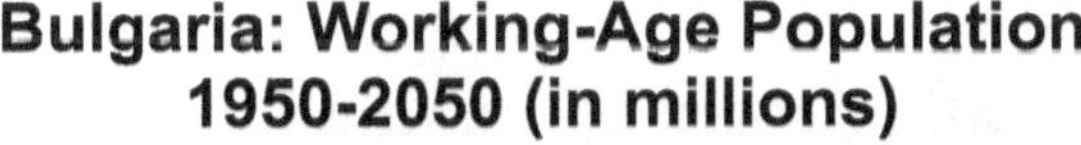
Bulgaria: Working-Age Population
1950-2050 (in millions)

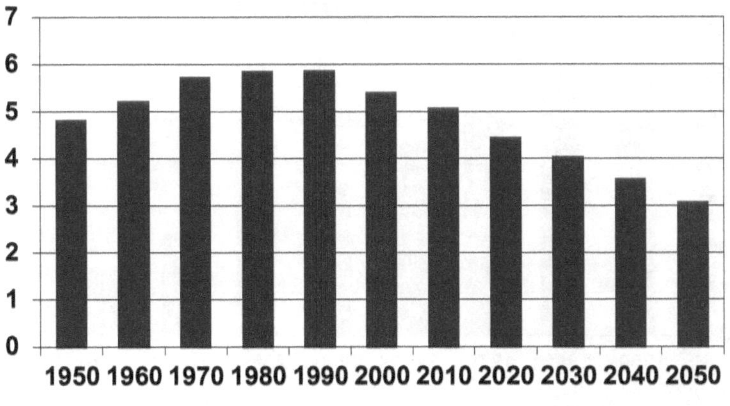

Source: UN

While Bulgaria's impact on the global economy is much smaller than that of Japan or Russia, it nevertheless serves as a warning for how demographic decline can become an irreversible fact. Unlike Japan or Russia, Bulgaria never experienced a post-war population boom. In fact, its birth rate fell below the replacement level already in the 1950s, one of the first countries where this occurred. As this birth rate continued to fall sharply, and as large-scale emigration began in the 1990s, Bulgaria's population has experienced one of the largest declines of that of any country in recent decades. In fact, over the past 30 years, Bulgaria's population has fallen nearly 25%, and its working-age population has fallen even more. Worse, all forecasts for Bulgaria's population in the coming decades indicated that the rate of population decline in Bulgaria will continue to accelerate. This makes it extremely difficult to see how Bulgaria will be able to generate much, if any, economic growth in the future.

While it is well-known that population growth in East Asia and Europe has been falling for decades, it is less commonly known that population growth in many other parts of the world has started to slow substantially as well. Look at Latin America. Not that long ago, the fear in many Latin American countries was that too much population growth would lead to resource depletion and overcrowding in that region. After all, no other region in the world is as urbanized as Latin America.

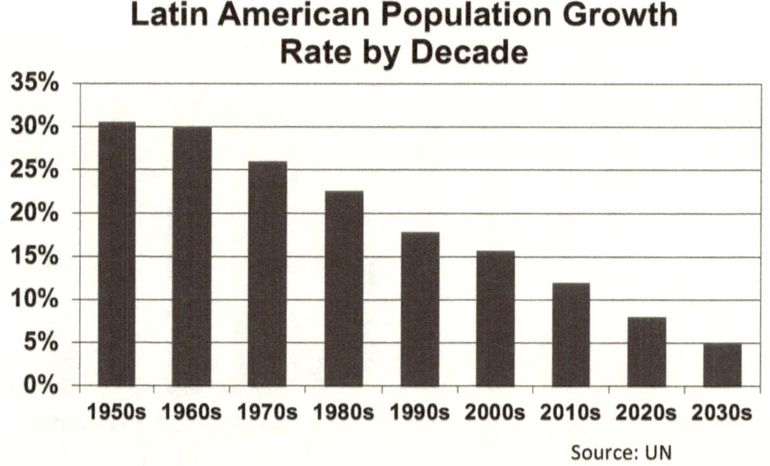

However, as the chart above clearly shows, population growth in Latin America has slowed at a far greater rate than that of the world as a whole. In fact, within a generation, population growth in Latin America could come to a complete halt unless birth rates in the region rebound substantially. As we will see later, this lack of population growth has been one of the reasons why the Latin American economy has been so disappointing in recent years, and why it faces such an uncertain future.

Another place where population growth is slowing to a surprising degree is in the United States. For much of its history, demographics have given the United States a major advantage over most of its rivals. Not only has the United States population grown far-faster than that of nearly all other developed economies, but it has the land and resources available to easily absorb major increases to the country's population, as well as a culture that is more open to large-scale immigration than most other countries. However, in recent years, the United States' birth rate has fallen by a surprising amount. This is surprising because, for the most part in recent decades, the US' birth rate has been higher than that of most other rich countries. However, this situation appears to have changed, and now, the United States' birth rate is following a path tread by many of its counterparts in Europe and Asia. Whether or not this is a short-term aberration or a long-term trend remains to be seen, but if it is the latter, it could have massive consequences for the long-term outlook for the US economy.

Not long ago, forecasts called for the global population to continue rising at a pace similar to that of much of the second half of the 20th century. While this raised major concerns about the impact that this would have on the environment, natural resources, arable land, water and such, it did lead to expectations that the number of potential consumers and workers in the world would continue to rise, allowing the global economy to grow right along with the global population. However, in recent years, these forecasts have been revised downwards in a major way, due largely to the continued decline in birth rates in regions such as East Asia and Europe, the surprising declines in birth rates in the Americas, and the more recent declines in birth rates in parts of Africa, the Middle East and South Asia. Whereas earlier forecasts called for the global population to rise to somewhere between 12 and 14 billion by the end of the 21st century, more recent forecasts call for a significantly smaller number. The most-accepted forecasts at the moment project an increase in the global population between now and the year 2050 of a little less than two billion (half of which will come from Africa), taking the global population to 9.7 billion. In the second half of the 21st century, population growth is forecast to slow even further, with the global population expanding by 1.2 billion to 10.9 billion over the last 50 years of the 21st century.

This means that the rapid population growth that fueled much of the economic growth of the 19th and 20th centuries will no longer be the driving force for the global economy that it once was. For some regions, this demographic dividend has already been lost, with predictable results. It is no coincidence that Japan and southern Europe have generated some of the lowest rates of growth of any economies so far in the 21st century as they both are two places where population growth has slowed the most in recent decades. Likewise, it is no coincidence that Latin America has struggled more than most other emerging regions, as its population growth has slowed dramatically in recent decades. Now, with nearly all of the world's leading economic powers forecast to experience either very little population growth, or outright population decline, the prospects for demographics to boost economic output are worse than ever, for this is not just a temporary shock, but rather, a long-term trend that appears likely to remain in place for the foreseeable future.

Chapter Eight

THE WORLD'S DEMOGRAPHIC DECLINE

BEFORE WE DELVE INTO the demographic decline that threatens to remove one of the key drivers of global economic growth throughout human history, I want to spend a little time looking at what could have been the alternative. This alternative is a world where population growth would continue unhindered until the planet no longer had the space or the resources to adequately provide for its ever-expanding human population. This was the world envisioned by Thomas Malthus, an English cleric whose writings on demographics and economics influenced centuries of study into the impact that demographic change was having on the economy and our planet. As Malthus was writing during the early decades of the Industrial Revolution, he witnessed firsthand the impact that this dramatic change in the economy was having on the British population.

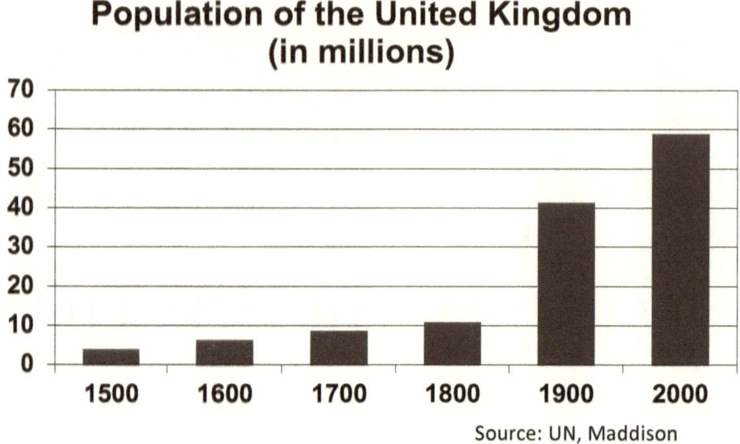

Malthus' most famous and influential work was his *An Essay on the Principle of Population* that he wrote at the age of 32 in 1798. This publication was based on the relationship between economic growth and population growth. However, rather than looking at how population growth drives economic growth, as we are doing in this book, Malthus looked at how economic growth drove population growth. His basic argument was that, when economic growth results in an increase in food production, as it did during that early phase of the Industrial Revolution, population growth would rise accordingly. As a result, the level of food available to the population would rise on an absolute basis, but not on a per capita basis. The most famous result of this coupling of population growth and food output was, in Malthus' view, that eventually there would not be enough food available for the huge population that would one day inhabit the earth and that this would lead to mass starvation. This would, in his view, lead to a world where only the richest and strongest societies would survive, as poorer and weaker societies would starve to death. Given the shocking nature of his forecasts, Malthus would spend much of the next decades of his life updating his seminal work and answering his many critics, who found his outlook for humanity's future much too bleak to contemplate.

While Malthus' views were extremely controversial in his day, they would resonate for a long time come, and influence two centuries of study in the field of demographics and economics. For a long time, it appeared that Malthus' predictions would come true, as population growth and economic growth appeared to rising hand-in-hand for much of the 19ᵗʰ and the 20ᵗʰ centuries. It seemed that, wherever industrialization occurred, rapid population growth soon followed. This was certainly true in Europe and North America, where the rapid pace of industrialization coincided with rapid population growth. In Europe, where industrialization took place unevenly, population growth was generally much higher in those areas of Europe that were in the process of industrialization, while those areas of Europe that were not yet fully industrializing where generally seeing lower rates of population growth. As Europe is geographically quite small, the ability to find land to feed this burgeoning population was limited, resulting in Malthus' predictions looking like they could become reality. Fortunately, there was a safety valve for Europe's rising population in the form of emigration to the Americas or Australia, preventing massive food shortages and helping to drive those regions' rapid population and economic growth in the 19ᵗʰ and early 20ᵗʰ centuries.

Only in the second half of the 20ᵗʰ century, when it became apparent that other factors were also driving population growth, most notably advancements in medicine and healthcare, were Malthus' ideas on the link between population growth and economic growth significantly challenged. However, his apocalyptic view of the impact of population growth stayed with us much longer, and still influences our view of some of the world's poorer regions where population growth rates remain high and where food shortages have become an all-too-frequent reality. Now, as global population growth has slowed dramatically in recent years, many of the fears that had arisen from Malthus' view of the future are being eased, as runaway population growth no longer appears to be the future in store for our species. In fact, it appears that rather than uncontrolled population growth leading to our eventual economic collapse, it could be a dramatic demographic decline that will be one of the greatest threats facing the global economy in the 21ˢᵗ century.

Given the dramatic rate of population growth since the late 18ᵗʰ century, it is little surprise that, until recently, forecasters were predicting that this rate of population growth would continue for the foreseeable future.

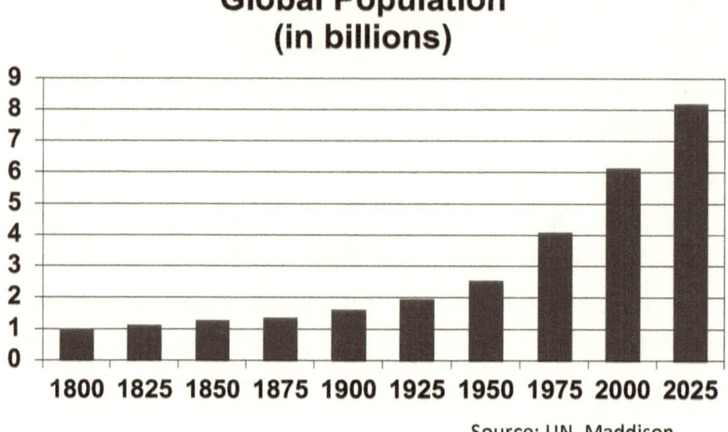

In fact, many forecasters predicted that global population growth will remain high until the late 21st century, with the world's population rising to anywhere from 12 to 14 billion by the end of this century. What these projections failed to predict was that birth rates would fall dramatically in much of the world, particularly in those parts of the world where urbanization was taking place at a rapid pace. As these factors have become apparent and their influence on population growth can be measured with a high degree of certainty, forecasters have been forced to reduce their forecasts for global population growth in the coming years.

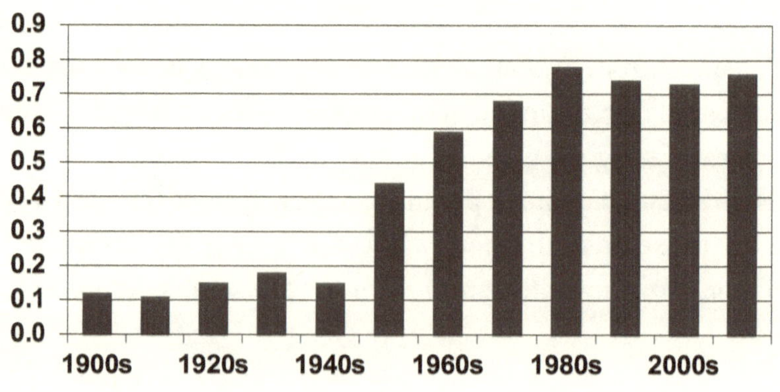

For example, the latest forecasts for the global population from the United Nations Department of Economic and Social Affairs expects the total world population to rise to 9.7 billion by the year 2050 and to 10.9 billion by the year 2100. To compare, the world's population rose by an astounding 271% in the 20th century, but will grow by a more relatively modest 77% in the 21st century according to these projections. In fact, if we look back at population growth by century, it will be the 20th century that stands out as the great outlier, with population growth during that 100 years far outpacing that of any other century for which we have reliable data.

In recent years, many of these population projections have been reduced as the decline in birth rates in many parts of the world has occurred more rapidly than had been expected. Now, should birth rates in those areas of the world (Sub-Saharan Africa, South Asia, etc.) where birth rates remain much higher than the global average also begin to fall as they have done in other parts of the world, it is likely that the current projections for population growth will also prove too optimistic, and that population forecasts will be reduced again. As a result of these demographic changes, our Malthusian fears of a soaring global population and its impact on our planet's resources is actually receding, even as the impact of the rapid population growth of the 20th century is contributing directly to modern-day environmental challenges such as climate change and pollution. Instead, there are growing concerns about the impact that much slower population growth will have on the world, most importantly, how it will impact the global economy. This is because population growth has long been viewed as both an opportunity and a risk for the global economy. It is no secret that, for much of human history, population growth has been one of the most fundamental drivers of economic growth, and it is therefore no surprise that these reduced projections for future population growth have coincided with reduced forecasts for economic growth. In fact, as we are relatively sure that global population growth will continue to slow for the foreseeable future, we can also be sure that it will be other drivers of economic growth, most notably trade, investment and productivity, that will have to serve as the main drivers of growth for the global economy in the years ahead.

CHANGES IN BIRTH RATES

As we discussed earlier in this book, global birth rates have been trending downwards since the 1960s.

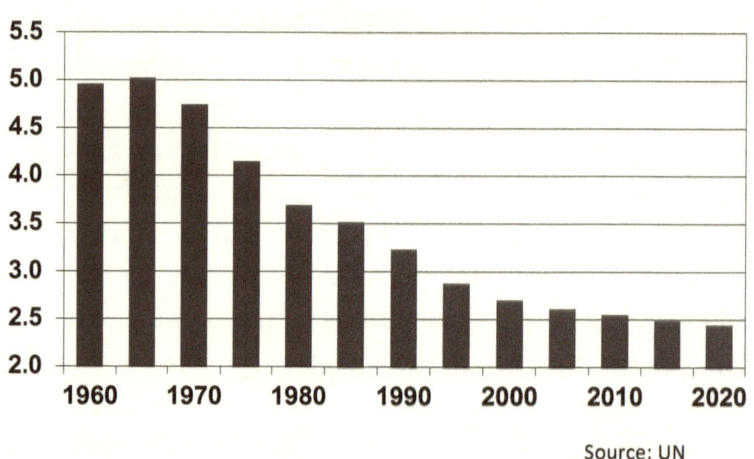

Between 1961 and 1964, the global birth rate (births per women) was slightly more than five, its highest level in the post-war era. However, a number of factors such as contraception, the women's rights movement, urbanization and China's One Child Policy would lead to a dramatic decline in the world's birth rate beginning in the 1960s. Between 1965 and 1980, the global birth rate would fall by a dramatic 26%. For much of the 1980s, the global birth rate would stabilize at around 3.6, but would begin to fall again in the late 1980s. In the ten-year period between 1986 and 1996, the global birth rate would fall again, this time by 20%, falling to just 2.82. Since the mid-1990s, the global birth rate has continued to trend downwards at a very steady pace and is now just 2.4. Keep in mind, the replacement rate (the birth rate at which the global population will neither grow nor shrink) is 2.1. In effect, in the span of just two generations, the global birth rate has fallen by more than half, resulting in what is slower growth for the world's working-age population. Furthermore, many of the world's lowest birth rates are now found among many of the world's most important economic centers, including China, Japan, Germany and Italy.

To see how this has been impacting some of these leading economies, let's take a closer look at how birth rates have changed in some of the world's leading economies, and how this will impact their economic futures.

Birth Rates in 1960

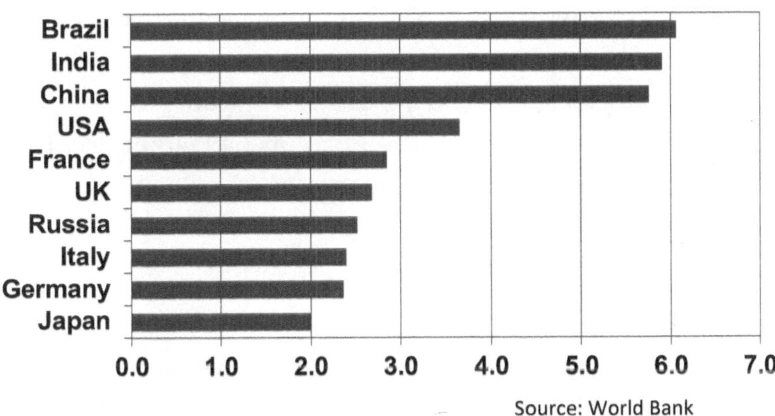

In the 1960's, most of the world's leading economies had birth rates that were significantly higher than they are today. This was a period where birth rates in most of the world's emerging markets were extremely high, in many cases three times higher than the replacement rate. These new births in the 1960s would turn into the new workers that helped to drive the explosion in economic growth that took place in many emerging markets in the 1980s and 1990s. This was particularly true in China, where a massive supply of relatively-cheap labor allowed for that country to generate economic growth rates averaging 10% for a period of nearly four decades. Had China enacted its One-Child Policy in the 1960s, China's economic miracle would have been stunted at birth. Meanwhile, we can see from the chart above that many leading economies such as Russia (then part of the Soviet Union), Italy, Germany and Japan all had birth rates that were falling close to the replacement rate, or in Japan's case, already below the replacement rate. This would play a major role in the economic struggles of each of these four major economies, as their competitiveness would be hit hard by labor shortages and their domestic markets would struggle to generate sufficient growth to boost their overall levels of economic growth. In fact, there would be a clear gap in terms of economic growth in the late 1990s and early 2000s between countries such as the United States, Canada and Australia (all of which had birth rates in excess of 3.3 in the early 1960s) and those developed countries that had much lower birth rates during that period.

Let's now turn our attention to the year 2000, as it is the people born in this period that are now entering, or will soon be entering, the work force. Of course, given the fact that the Covid-19 pandemic has caused so many disruptions for the global economy, these new entrants to the world's work force cannot but help to wish that their parents had either decided to have had children at an earlier, or a later, date.

Birth Rates in 2000

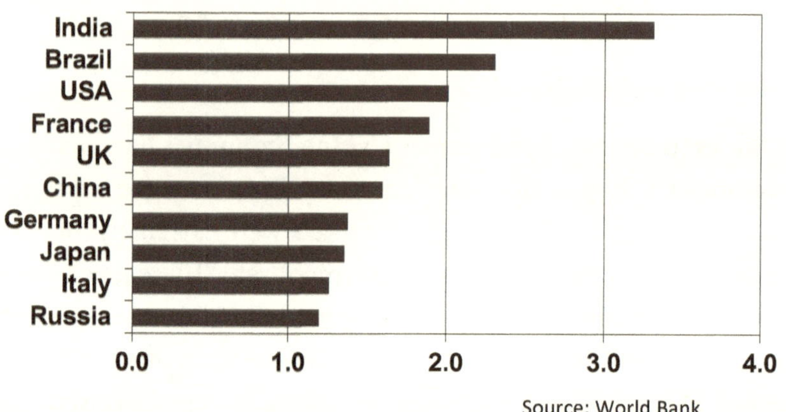

Source: World Bank

As you can see in the chart above, there was a dramatic decline in the birth rates in all of the world's leading economic centers between the years 1960 and 2000. Whereas in 1960, all major economies apart from Japan had birth rates that were well above the replacement rate of 2.1, at the turn of the 21st century, only India and Brazil were above the replacement rate, while the United States was the only large developed economy that had a birth rate that was even near to the replacement rate. In contrast, China's birth rate had collapsed thanks to the combination of the One-Child Policy and that country's rapid urbanization, while birth rates in most of Europe and East

Asia were far below the replacement rate. This dramatic decline in birth rates, which had been taking place since the 1960s, was one of the main reasons why major economies such as the United States, Japan, Germany and others were facing the challenge of worsening labor shortages in the years prior of the Covid-19 pandemic, and why, once the recovery from the effects of this latest economic crisis began, the threat of labor shortages once again proved to be a major challenge for many of the world's leading economies.

While many governments have made significant efforts to raise their country's birth rates in recent years, that fact is that overall birth rates are still trending downwards.

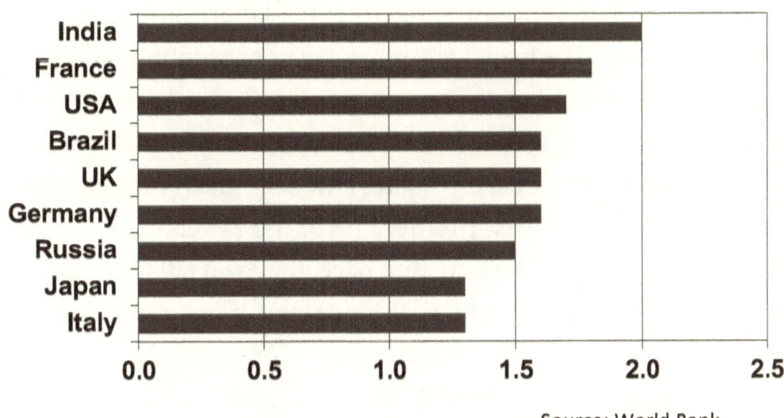

Birth Rates in 2021

As you can see from this chart, birth rates continued to decline over the first two decades of the 21st century, or at least held relatively steady in countries where they were already low. Now, among the world's leading economies, only India has a birth rate that is above the replacement rate, and it is barely above it at that. In fact, the dramatic fall in India's birth rate in recent decades is one of the most important demographic trends of the modern era. Meanwhile, the significant decline in the United States' birth rate in recent years is also a cause for concern, as a higher birth rate in the US in previous decades was one of the reasons why the US economy had been able to consistently outperform its counterparts in Europe and Japan. In contrast, a couple of countries, such as France and Russia, have managed to stabilize their birth rates in recent years, often through large-scale government programs encouraging young French or Russian citizens to have more children.

Nevertheless, the clear-as-day fact is that all of the world's leading economies in the 2020s are having too few children to allow for population growth to continue to be a driver of their economic growth. If birth rates remain at current levels in the world's leading economies, and continue falling in most of its leading emerging markets, the likelihood of labor shortages will continue to worsen, unless automation spreads at a much more rapid pace than it has up to this point in time. We have already seen labor shortages in countries such as Japan and Germany that have not been generating too much economic growth in recent years. Now, as the number of new entrants into the work force declines, even more economies will be exposed to the threat of labor shortages. At the same time, demand levels will be negatively impacted as consumer markets shrink in many areas of the world. An even bigger concern is that birth rates will continue to trend downwards. While they have stabilized (at low levels) in a handful of countries, that fact is that global birth rates have continued to decline at a steady pace over the course of the first two decades of the 21st century. If global birth rates continue to decline at their current pace, they will fall to the replacement rate sometime around the middle of this century, if not sooner. It is obvious that, in such a demographic climate, the impact of demography on the global economy will turn negative, as population decline would become a worsening drag on the global economy. As we have seen, demographics have been one of the key drivers of global economic growth since the onset of the Industrial Revolution, but now, we face a future in which global population trends may start to work against the global economy.

ECONOMIES FACING DEMOGRAPHIC DECLINE

Japan

When we talk about economies facing the threat of long-term demographic decline, the first one that typically comes to mind is Japan. Images of large crowds of elderly Japanese gathered at a city park, or of depopulated villages in rural Japan, is often what comes to mind when one thinks about Japanese demographics. Of course, these images are quite accurate, as Japan is home to one of the oldest populations in the world, as well as being among the country's facing the largest forecasted population declines in the coming years.

It wasn't always this way. In fact, it was rapid population growth that helped to fuel Japan's economic transformation in the late 19th and early 20th centuries. Prior to that, Japan's first real population explosion was believed to have taken place in the 1600s, when its population, by some estimates, more than doubled, reaching around 28 million, already a fairly sizeable population for a country the size of Japan.

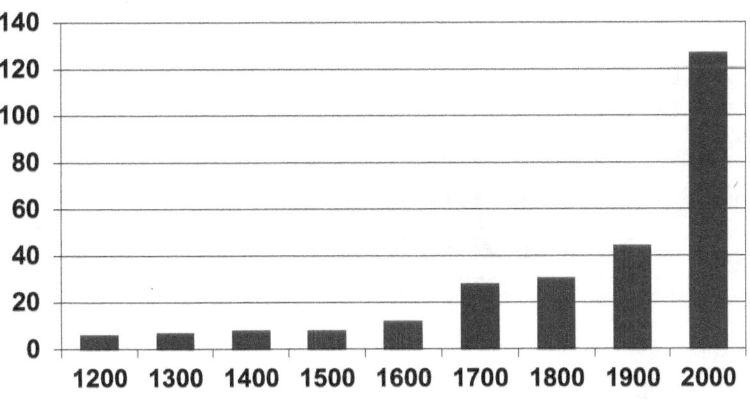

**Population of Japan
(in millions)**

Source: UN, Biraben

However, this population growth would come to an end and for the next 150 years as Japan's population would essentially stagnate during that time frame. Only in the years following the Meiji Restoration did Japanese population growth take off again, with Japan's population doubling from 33 million in the early 1870s to 66 million in the early 1930s. This population growth was temporarily brought to a halt by the Second World War, in which as many as three million Japanese citizens were killed. However, Japanese population growth quickly resumed as a result of a post-war baby boom that resulted in Japan's population rising from 72 million at the end of World War Two in

1945 to 117 million in 1980. This rapid population growth resulted in a major expansion of the country's working-age population, allowing Japan's manufacturing and service sectors to have an ample supply of labor and resulting in Japan having one of the world's fastest-growing consumer markets in the decades following the war.

Unlike in many Western countries, Japan's post-war baby boom was relatively short-lived, lasting only until the early 1950s. In fact, over the course of the 1950's, Japan's birth rate fell dramatically, falling to below the replacement level by the latter part of that decade.

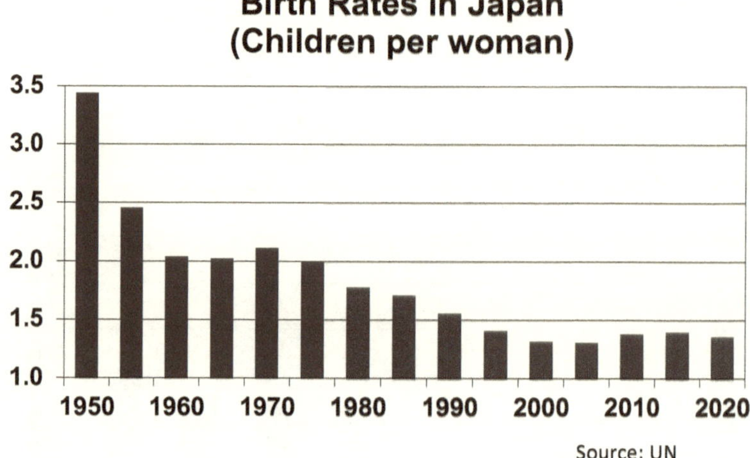

Japan's birth rate would rise to the replacement level again in the late 1960s and early 1970s, but would then trend downwards for the rest of the century, before holding steady in the first two decades of the 21st century at around 1.4, or 33% below the replacement rate. At the same time, the number of births per year in Japan has fallen from more than two million in the early 1970s, to less than 900,000 today, while the number of deaths in Japan now exceeds the number of births by more than 500,000 per year. This is having the expected impact on Japan's working-age population, which is already in decline and will soon find itself declining much faster without an influx of immigration, something that is highly unlikely in a society such as that of Japan.

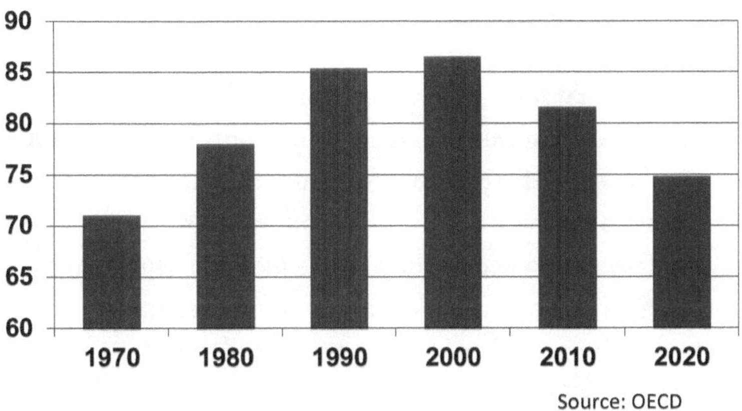

For Japan, its ability to retain its economic competitiveness and to be an attractive market for businesses and investors is jeopardized by these demographic projections. As the country's workforce shrinks, Japan will be forced to turn to automation in a bid to maintain its current levels of economic output, a key factor in Japan's large-scale investments in automation since the late 20th century. At the same time, Japan's dependency ratio (the ratio of the country's working-age population to its non-working-age population) will continue to worsen, particularly as the Japanese have some of the highest life expectancies in the world. The numbers are truly staggering. After peaking at around 87 million in the mid-1990s, Japan's working-age population has already declined by more nearly 25%, falling to 65 million in 2020. No other major economy in the world has witnessed such a massive decline in its working-age population during this period. Worse for Japan, this decline took place while emerging markets such as China and Southeast Asia were connecting to the global economy, giving rise to new competitors for trade and investment at a time when Japan's economic competitiveness was being hit hard by this demographic collapse. Worse, the next 30 years are forecast to result in a continued decline in Japan's working-age population. Between 2020 and 2040, Japan's working-age population is forecast to shrink by another 20%, falling to just above 52 million by the year 2040. At the same time, Japan's over-65 population is forecast to increase dramatically over the near-term, before the impact of Japan's low-birth rates also begins to impact the size of the country's elderly population in the years ahead.

The strains on Japan's finances, its resources and its infrastructure caused by these dramatic demographic shifts are already being realized, and with the country's dependency ratio forecast to worsen dramatically in the decades ahead, Japan will be a test case for many other countries facing similar, if not as immediate, threats of demographic decline. The most notable impact is on Japan's economic performance. In the decades following the Second World War, Japan underwent an economic miracle in which the Japanese economy grew faster than almost any other economy in the world. While Japan's post-war population boom may have been relatively short-lived, its economic boom lasted until the early 1990s. Even with its population boom, the size of the Japanese market alone would not have been enough to drive such high rates of economic growth in Japan. However, thanks to its access to export markets in North America and elsewhere, and thanks to its increasing supply of labor, Japan's economy was able to outperform almost all other large economies for a lengthy period in the second half of the 20th century. However, as Japan was faced with the twin threats of a stagnant, then declining, working-age population and new competition for export markets, its economic miracle came to a sudden end in the early 1990s. Since then, Japan's worsening demographic situation has prevented the country from recording very much growth at all over the past three decades. Worse, without a massive increase in immigration, Japan's demographic situation is forecast to become much more challenging in the decades ahead. This, coupled with many other challenges facing Japan, bodes ill for what was once one of the world's most successful economies.

Europe

As we have discussed earlier in this book, Europe's population growth that had soared during the height of the Roman Empire fell beginning with the Antonine Plague in the late 2nd century CE. While population estimates for Europe for the next 1,500 are highly debated, it is clear that Europe's population stagnated for a long period of time, resulting in Europe's population falling far behind that of more populous regions such as China and India. By the year 1000, Europe's population was estimated to be somewhere between 50 and 60 million, with much of this population concentrated in southern areas of Europe. In fact, Europe's population in the year 1000 was not that much more than it was 1,000 years earlier during the height of the Roman Empire. Furthermore, population growth in Europe over the next 500 years would be relatively slow and intermittent. For example, Europe's population would fall by a significant amount in the first half of the 1300s as first the Great Famine and then the Black Death would kill millions of people across the region. In the 400 or so years between the Black Death and the beginnings of the Industrial Revolution in the United Kingdom, Europe's population would grow, but at a relatively slow pace.

However, once the Industrial Revolution began to spread across the region, those areas that became industrialized realized a massive increase in their rate of population growth. For example, between the years 1700 and 1900, the population of the United Kingdom would increase by nearly 400%, while the population of what would eventually become a united Germany increased by nearly the same amount. In contrast, parts of Europe that industrialized later, or barely industrialized, recorded much lower rates of population growth. For example, in this same 200-year period from the year 1700 to the year 1900, the population of what would become a unified Italy increased by around 250%, while France's population would grow by less than 200%.

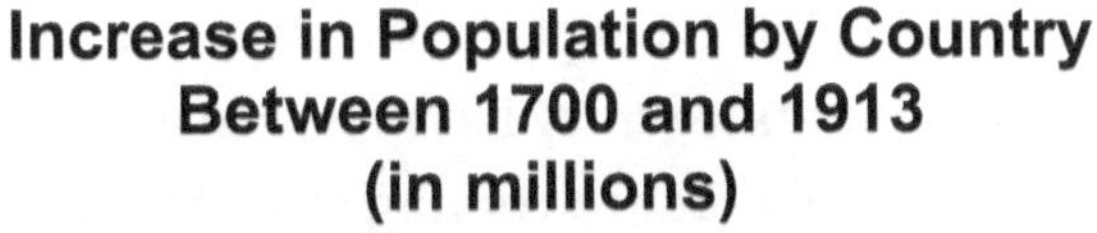

Increase in Population by Country
Between 1700 and 1913
(in millions)

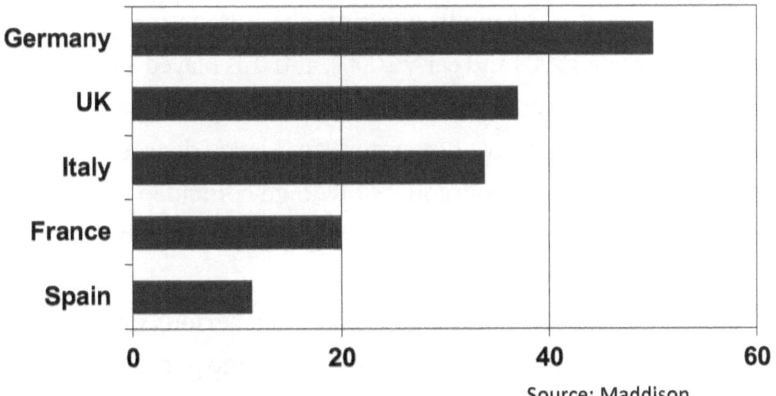

As Europe was the region to industrialize first, it was the first to be impacted by this correlation between industrialization and population expansion. In turn, this combination of rapid population growth and technological leadership over most of the rest of the world was what allowed Europe to be the world's dominant region throughout the 19th century and in the early part of the 20th century. Europe's wasn't just more advanced in terms of economic and military technology, but its population was quite simply exploding.

It was the triple shocks of the First World War, the Great Depression and the Second World War that brought Europe's population explosion to an end. Birth rates fell dramatically in most areas of Europe between 1914 and 1945, while huge numbers of the region's most productive members of society were killed in the bloodbaths of the two world wars. Despite a baby boom in the two decades following the Second World War, Europe's demographic downturn resumed in the 1960s, with birth rates plunging across Europe for the remainder of the 20th century and into the early part of the 21st century. Soon, birth rates across Europe would fall below the replacement rate. West Germany would be the first major European country to see its birth rate fall below the replacement rate, with this occurring in 1970 (it has never returned to the replacement rate in the five decades since then). Surprisingly, the United Kingdom would be the second major European country where the birth rate fell below the replacement rate, with it doing so in 1973. France (1975), Italy (1976) and Spain (1981) would all see their birth rates fall below the replacement rate over the following decade, and since then, no European country has recorded a birth rate above the 2.1 replacement rate, with only France coming close in the early 2010s. Again, this had the impact of resulting in working-age population growth declining significantly in the late 1990s and early 2000s, and this played a not-unsubstantial role in Europe's overall economic slowdown during that period. Like Japan, most European economies are dependent to a large degree upon exports to generate growth, and this demographic slowdown coincided with an increase in competition for export markets and for foreign investment, both from faraway Asia and from nearby Central Europe.

Today, most European countries are facing a serious demographic challenge as their populations age and their working-age populations decline. No country exemplifies this challenge more than Italy.

In Italy, the country's working-age population managed to keep growing for much longer than what we witnessed in Japan, thanks to what had been a relatively high (by European standards) birth rate in Italy until the 1980s. However, Italy's birth rate has collapsed in recent decades and the country now faces a looming decline of the country's working-age population, with some estimates forecasting that, by the year 2050, Italy's working-age population will be 15%-20% lower than it is today. For a country that has been struggling to generate much, if any, economic growth for the past 25 years, this looming demographic crisis could portend even greater travails ahead for what has been the worst performing large economy in the world so far in the 21st century.

Another European country facing a serious demographic crisis is Germany. Whereas Italy has struggled to generate economic growth in the 21st century, much of this has to do with that country's lack of competitiveness and its lack of high-tech, high-growth industries. In Germany, a series of reforms enacted in the early 2000s helped that country to shed its "Sick Man of Europe" title that it had acquired following its economic struggles during the 1990s and to become one of the region's most successful economies. However, very little of this success had to do with Germany's demographic situation. In fact, between 2005 and 2011, Germany's working-age population fell by 5% and then stagnated for a few years, until Europe's Migration Crisis resulted in a large influx of people from the Middle East and Africa, most of whom were working age. Furthermore, while the birth rate of ethnic Germans has remained very low in recent years, these newcomers in Germany have recorded much higher birth rates, resulting in the country's overall birth rate rising slightly. Those shows how immigration can help offset declines in birth rates and working-age populations, and could eventually help to ease many of the labor shortages that were holding down economic growth in Germany in recent years.

While Europe's demographic challenges are not yet as severe as those facing Japan, they are enough to raise many questions about Europe's ability to generate economic growth in the future. For those countries that have combined a worsening demographic situation with lower levels of economic competitiveness (such as Italy and Greece), the impact is already apparent. However, more European countries face such a future if they cannot figure out a way to improve their demographic futures. Even economies such as Germany, Sweden and the

Netherlands that have maintained a higher degree of economic competitiveness in recent years cannot escape the impact that stagnating or falling working-age populations will have on their economies in the future. Whereas Europe's demographic growth allowed it to become the dominant region in the world for an extended period of time, its current demographic decline threatens to further weaken its global position, both economically and politically. While birth rates are unlikely to rise much in the future, immigration is one possibility to help slow the region's demographic decline. However, this is an issue that is highly contentious in Europe, as 2015's Migration Crisis highlighted.

The United States

For the United States, population growth has been one of the key factors in its ability to generate higher rates of economic growth than most other wealthy countries over the past 240 years. What is now the country with the world's third-largest population was, in the year 1800, a country of a little more than five million people, or less than 2% of the population of Qing China or less than 20% of Napoleonic France. However, this already represented a near 500% increase in the population of the US between the years 1750 and 1800, indicating that, thanks to its vast amount of land and its ability to create massive amounts of jobs, the United States would have the capacity to generate amazing amounts of population growth in the coming centuries.

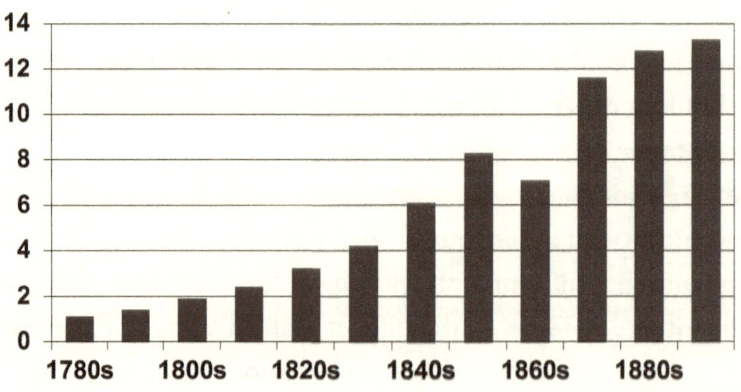

Source: US Census Bureau

In the 19th century, this population growth would be remarkably high and incredibly steady. Between 1800 and 1900, as US cities grew and as the country spread out to take control over a vast landmass between the Atlantic and Pacific oceans, the United States population would rise from 5.3 million to 76.2 million. This population growth was the result of the combination of high birth rates in the 19th century and the large numbers of immigrants that came to the US, mostly from Europe. In turn, this rapid population growth allowed the United States to have a labor force that was usually able to supply the needs of the country's rapidly-expanding economy. Thus, it is easy to see how the United States' population expansion in the 19th century played an important role in the country's simultaneous economic expansion.

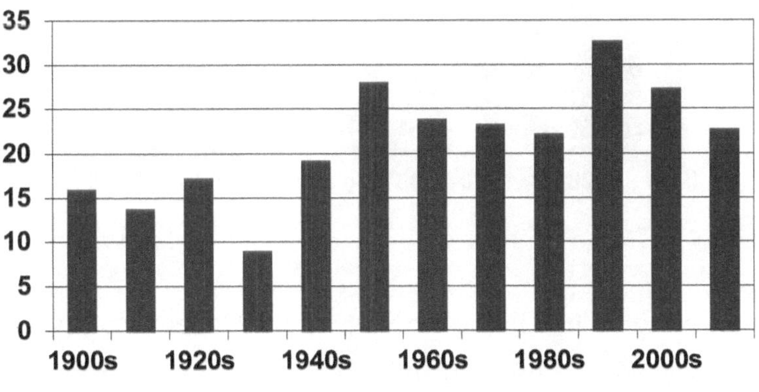

US Population Growth by Decade (in millions)

Source: US Census Bureau

This population growth continued in the 20th century, but its rate of increase slowed, and it was no longer as steady as its had been in the 19th century. This was due largely to the impact of the Great Depression, the Second World War and the fall in birth rates in the US that accompanied the country's urbanization. Nevertheless, the population of the United States expanded from 76.2 million in 1900 to 281.4 million in 2000, a still-impressive increase of 269%, a rate of population growth that only other New World developed economies such as Canada and Australia could compete with. Again, this population growth allowed the US economy to suffer a lower degree of labor shortages than those economies where population growth rates were much lower, or where major wars resulted in temporary declines in manpower. Since the beginning of the 21st century, population growth in the United States has slowed. While it still is expanding faster than almost all other developed economies, its rate of growth has slowed due to a sharper-than-expected decline in the US' birth rate and the recent efforts to reduce the level of immigration into the United States.

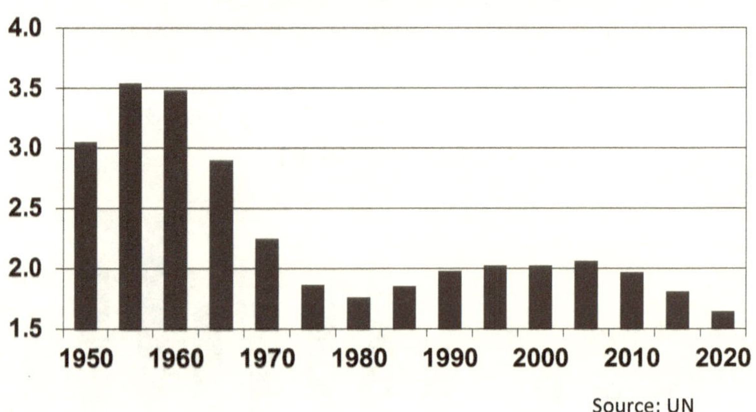

This alarming decline in the birth rate in the United States is the result of many factors, some of which may prove temporary, but some of which, as we have seen in Japan and Europe, may prove long-lasting. Whether or not the United States will see a return of higher birth rates in the future is uncertain, but there is now a real possibility that the United States will realize a long-term decline in birth rates, just like most other developed economies. Of course, the United States has the capacity to absorb more immigrants than just about any other country, and the combination of its long history of assimilating immigrants, its economic system that favors risk-taking, and its vast landmass suggest that the US will continue to be a magnet for both low-skilled and high-skilled immigration in the future. However, as we have seen in recent years, there is a growing opposition to large-scale immigration, and it also remains to be seen if this will prove to be a temporary situation or a long-term trend. This too will have a major impact on the demographic future of the United States, and will impact the US' ability to generate economic growth in the coming years. Remember, in the years before the Covid-19 pandemic led to a massive spike in unemployment, one of the greatest challenges facing the US economy was the worsening labor shortages that were holding back economic growth in many sectors of the economy, shortages that returned not too long after the initial impact of the pandemic on the US' jobs market was felt.

Of course, the demographic situation in the United States is about much more than just birth rates and immigration. Race relations remain a major factor in determining the level of political stability in the United States. Economically, the 13% of the United States that is African-American has faced a high degree of economic marginalization and remains much poorer than other ethnic groups in the US. Meanwhile, the Hispanic and Asian communities in the United States are growing faster than all other ethnic groups in the country, and these communities have enjoyed varying degrees of economic success in recent decades. The fact that the US' Hispanic and Asian communities are growing at such a fast pace, and that the US' African-American community is demanding a greater share of the vast amounts of wealth generated by the US economy, has led to a backlash within the United States' majority white population, as a large segment of that part of the US population has also struggled to adopt to the new realities of the 21st century US economy. Therefore, how the US manages its ethnic relations will likely play almost as important of a role as birth rates and immigration in determining the impact of demographics on the US economy in the years ahead.

China

2,000 years ago, the populations of the Roman Empire in the West and the Han Dynasty in China were estimated to be quite similar. However, whereas the West underwent a massive demographic decline and then long-term stagnation, the population of the lands that make up modern-day China continued to experience rapid population growth. This is why today, China's population is much larger than that of any other place on earth, apart from India.

By the late 1700s China was home to nearly 30% of the world's people, and, as a result, China's economic output for much of the period between the Roman Empire and the Industrial Revolution dwarfed that of all other regions of the world. This should not be a surprise, as economic output in the pre-industrialization era was driven in large part by human and animal power, and these China had in abundance. Even as China's rate of population growth slowed dramatically during the chaos of the second half of the 19th century and the first half of the 20th century, China's population was still much larger than that of any other major economic center in the world. However, as a result of industrialization, demographics and the availability of human and animal labor were no longer the primary drivers of economic growth. The result was China falling dramatically behind in terms of economic growth when compared to the industrialized economies of Europe, North America, and later Japan.

Rapid population growth only returned to China after the Second World War and the Chinese Civil War. Even amid the follies of the Great Leap Forward and the Cultural Revolution, China's population growth in the second half of the 20th century was remarkable.

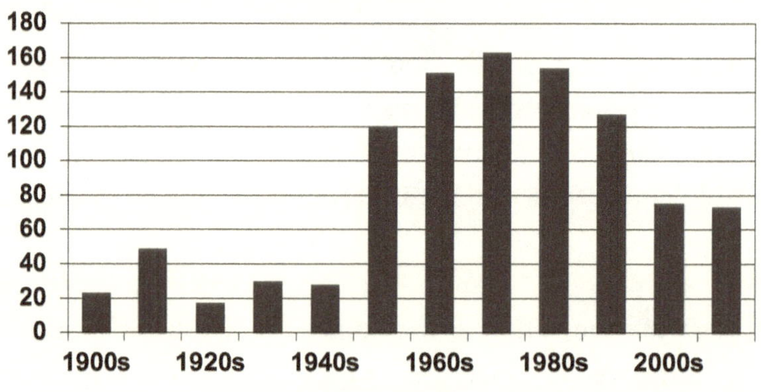

In fact, in the 35 years between 1950 and 1985, China's population doubled from 554 million to 1.08 billion, an increase in the number of people that is greater than today's total population of North America or the European Union. This was one of the reasons why, when China undertook its dramatic economic reforms in the early 1980s, it had a vast labor force that was ready to be utilized to transform China's economy from one of the most unproductive in the world to one that would soon have a massive influence on the rest of the global economy. Of course, China's population is concentrated along the coasts and in the river valleys in the eastern half of the country, making that area one of the most densely populated places on earth. This, coupled with fears about a lack of water and other resources, forced the Chinese government to enact the One-Child Policy in 1979. This led to a dramatic decline in China's birth rate, to the point where today, China has one of the world's lowest birth rates, even after the One-Child Policy was lifted in 2015. Furthermore, overall population growth in China has slowed dramatically, even as the country's total population surpassed the 1.4 billion mark in 2014.

This incredible shift in China's demographic direction could result in what might be the most pressing demographic challenge facing any country in the world over the next couple of decades. This challenge is the combination of China's soon-to-be declining working-age population and what is forecast to be a massive increase in China's elderly population.

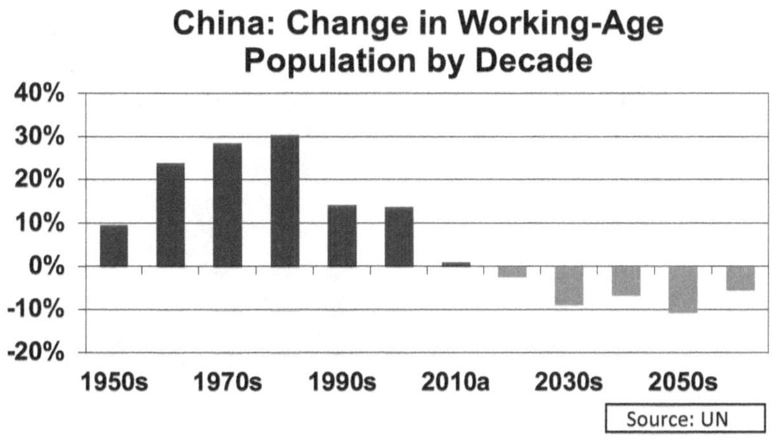

Let's first look at the projections for China's working-age population. Between the years 2020 and 2070, China's working-age population is forecast to decline from just over one billion to 707 million, a decline of nearly 300 million people, or a contraction of 30% from the current level. As you can see from this chart, China's working-age population rose dramatically in the decades before its economic transformation, as well as during the early part of this transformation. Now, China faces one of the most precipitous declines of its working-age population of any country in the world. This means that the labor shortages that had become quite noticeable in many sectors of the Chinese economy during the 2010s are likely to return in the coming years, and will almost certainly worsen in those sectors where large-scale automation is not possible. In those sectors where automation can result in major benefits, China is likely to follow the direction of countries such as Japan and South Korea and introduce widespread automation in a bid to offset the shrinking availability of labor. Nevertheless, these looming labor shortages surely mean that China's ability to generate economic growth of 10% year-after-year is a thing of the past. The fear for China is that they could lead to much lower rates of growth, with there being a real possibility that China's economy will eventually fall into long-term stagnation (much like Japan) if it cannot maintain favorable positions with regards to trade, investment and productivity.

The other fear for China with regards to its rapidly-changing demographic profile is the rapid growth of the country's elderly (in this case over-65) population.

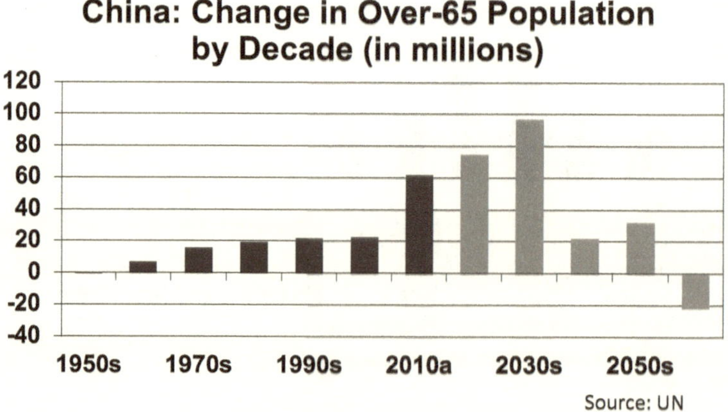

Until the 2010's, China's over-65 population had grown extremely slowly, due in large part to the relatively low birth rates in China in the first half of the 20th century. However, China's soaring birth rates in the 1950s and 1960s, resulted in a surge in the number of people over the age of 65 in China beginning in the 2010s. Furthermore, over the next two decades, China's overall elderly population is forecast to double, rising from 172 million in 2020 to 344 million in 2040. Most countries that face such a dramatic increase in their elderly populations, while at the same time dealing with falling working-age populations, are relatively wealthy countries with well-developed social welfare and pension systems. However, China is a middle-income country that lacks many of these systems that are designed to provide for a country's retired population. How China manages to deal with this looming threat will be one of the most important questions facing that country in the decades ahead. Moreover, it is likely that, as China has to spend more on what will be a relatively unproductive segment of its society, it will find that this is yet another drag on its economy, limiting its ability to continue to generate high rates of economic growth. This is not only a threat for China, but for the entire global economy, as by many measures, China is forecast to generate around one-third of the world's additional global economic output in the coming decade. If China gets this wrong, the whole world will be impacted.

Sub-Saharan Africa

If the world's leading economic centers are all facing demographic crises linked to their falling birth rates and working-age populations, there is one region that continues to have relatively high birth rates and will continue to have an expanding working-age population for decades to come, Sub-Saharan Africa. For much of its history, Sub-Saharan Africa has had a relatively small population given the size of its landmass. In the year 1900, Sub-Saharan Africa's population is estimated to have been around just 90 million people, or just around one-fourth of Europe's total population at that time. However, a population explosion was about to occur. In the second half of the 20th century, Sub-Saharan Africa's population would take off, driven upwards by some of the highest birth rates in the world as well as the introduction of modern medicine, which led to much higher life expectancies for much of the region's population. Today, Sub-Saharan Africa's population is larger than one billion, and many countries in this region continue to have very high birth rates. As a result, while population growth in the world's leading economic centers is either slowing or stagnating, Sub-Saharan Africa's population is continuing to expand at a very fast pace. This can be seen in the dramatic population growth in some of Sub-Saharan Africa's leading countries.

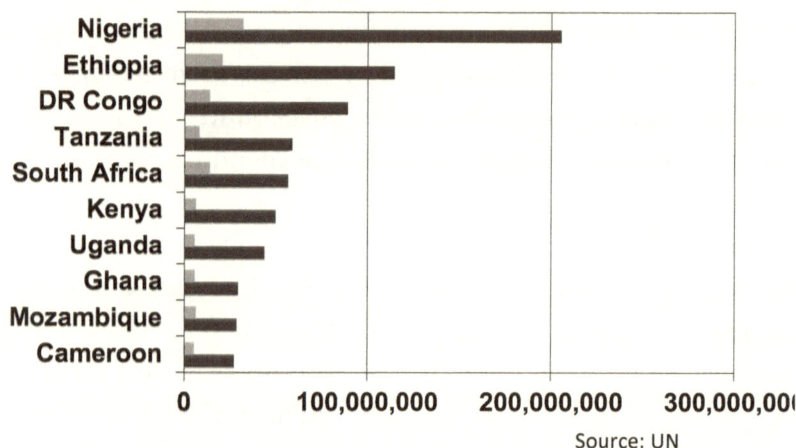

Today, Nigeria's has the world's seventh-largest population, having just passed the 200 million mark in 2019. Ethiopia's population has surpassed the 110 million mark, while the Democratic Republic of Congo is approaching the 100 million mark. Considering where these country's populations were just a few decades ago, the sheer scale of their population increases is staggering.

So far, Sub-Saharan Africa's incredible population growth over this 70-year period has done very little to generate economic growth for what remains the world's poorest region. In fact, for too many countries in that region, economic growth rates have barely exceeded population growth rates, meaning that poverty rates have remained stubbornly high. Only those countries that have been able to export large amounts of oil, gas or other natural resources have been able to generate higher levels of growth, and this has occurred only when the prices for these natural resources are sufficiently high. For example, when the price of oil, gas and other commodities fell in 2014, economic growth rates in most of Sub-Saharan Africa's largest economies were quite disappointing during the years that followed. This has to do with the fact that much of the region's economy remains at a subsistence level, with very little industrialization to speak of. As a result, like pre-Industrial-Revolution era economies, Sub-Saharan African economic growth is driven almost entirely by population growth and little else, and that is not enough to reduce poverty, just as it was not enough to reduce poverty in Europe before the late 18th century.

It is because of this disappointing economic performance in recent years, and the relative lack of industrialization in the region, that Sub-Saharan Africa's economic future remains so uncertain, despite the fact that it will be adding more working-age people to its population in the coming decades than any other region in the world by a wide margin. In fact, Sub-Saharan Africa's population is forecast to expand by a staggering one billion people over the next 30 years, doubling the region's population in the span of a single generation.

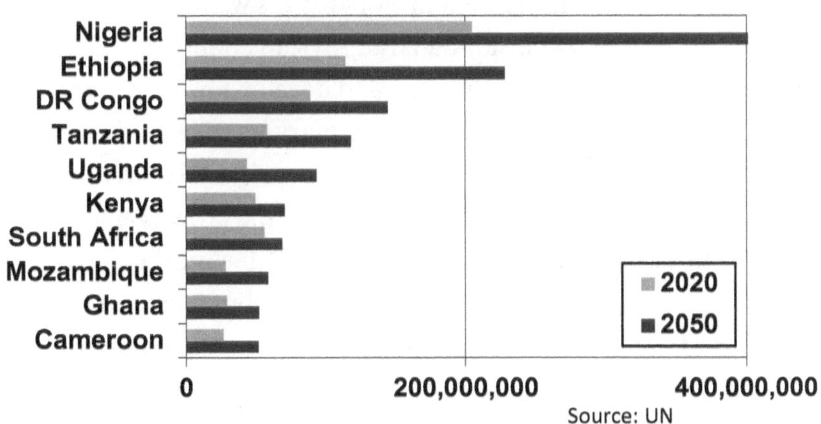

At a country level, some of the numbers are truly staggering. For example, the fact that a country the size of Nigeria already has a population of more than 200 million people catches most people by surprise. However, Nigeria is forecast to add another 200 million people to its population between the years 2020 and 2050, resulting in Nigeria's population totaling a little more than 400 million by the year 2050, roughly the same estimate for the population of the

United States in 2050. However, the United States' total land area is ten times larger than that of Nigeria. How Nigeria finds the land, water and jobs needed to support such a massive population remains to be seen, but at least it has sizeable oil reserves. Other Sub-Saharan African countries without such oil reserves are also forecast to record massive population growth in the coming decades. Between 2020 and 2050, Ethiopia's population is forecast to double to 226 million, while Congo's population will grow to 144 million.

Unless economic growth soars in the coming years and job creation levels take off, the potential for a catastrophe is one of the most serious threats facing this region. Of course, some business and political leaders in the region have attempted to use the promise of a rapidly-expanding (and cheap) labor force to attract foreign investment to the region. However, so far, nearly all of the foreign investment that has flowed into the region in recent decades has gone into the exploitation of the region's natural resources (which create relatively few jobs) and not into major export-oriented manufacturing operations or offshore service centers (which create many jobs).

Now, with trade and investment in jeopardy (as we will discuss in the next chapter), the hopes that some Sub-Saharan African countries could follow the lead of South Korea, China and Vietnam and develop low-cost manufacturing centers focused on exporting to wealthier markets may be dashed forever, jeopardizing the region's long-term economic future, as it is extremely hard for any poor country to manage to generated economic growth at a consistently high rate without being able to export to wealthier markets. In turn, this could lead to mass emigration, as the number of jobs created in the region is insufficient for the numbers of new workers entering the region's labor force each year and as the region's land and water resources are stretched ever more thinly. How Sub-Saharan Africa copes with the challenge of a population that could be rising too fast for its economy and resources to sustain is another sort of demographic challenge that will play out over the course of the 21ˢᵗ century.

Chapter Nine

THE IMPACT OF DECLINING POPULATIONS

HISTORICALLY, THE GROWTH RATE of the labor force of a city, state or country typically had a major impact on its ability to generate economic growth. In fact, the further back in time you go, the more important the size and the growth rate of the labor force is in terms of determining an economy's ability to generate economic growth. Ancient China's great advantage over most other historical empires was its vast population and the fact that, its population growth almost always bounced back following periods of stagnation or decline, resulting in China having such a massive population today. Ancient Rome also had a very large population in comparison to other entities of its day, and this massive population was utilized in very clever ways to allow Ancient Rome to have the most advanced economy of its era, and one that would be more advanced than anything seen in Europe for the next 1,500 years.

Interestingly, while China's population was able to continue to grow, even amid periods of conflict, upheaval and pestilence, most of the territories that comprised the Roman Empire saw their populations decline dramatically in the latter stages of the empire and in the centuries that followed. As such, China was always able to regroup economically as it had both a giant domestic market and a massive work force that would attract investment and serve as an important catalyst for economic expansion. In contrast, most of the territories that had been a part of the Roman Empire became economic backwaters for many centuries, as they lacked both the domestic markets and the labor forces needed to develop an economy as large and as sophisticated as that of Ancient Rome. Interestingly, while other empires would emerge in the period spanning the fall of the Roman Empire and the Industrial Revolution, none outside of China would come anywhere close to replicating the achievements of the Roman economy. This was due, in large part, to the demographic disadvantages faced by much of the world in this long stretch of history. Remember, the total population of the world only expanded from an estimated 250 million around the time of the fall of Rome to 750 million 13 centuries later when the Industrial Revolution began, and most of this population growth was in Asia.

We have already discussed how the rapid population growth that followed the industrialization of regions such as Europe and North American contributed to their economic explosions in the late 18th and the 19th centuries. However, we are now focused on the demographic situation of the 21st century and here, we see that the world is once again facing the prospect of a stagnating population. The impact of this has already been seen in the labor shortages that were hindering the economic growth of many major economies in the years before and after the initial impact of the Covid-19 pandemic. Prior to the cursed year of 2020, unemployment rates in many key economies had fallen to their lowest levels in decades.

This tightness of labor was most evident in countries where birth rates had been low for some time, and where working-age populations were already in serious decline. A good example of this is Japan, where the unemployment rate fell from 5.1% in 2010 (after the Financial Crisis) to just 2.4% in 2019.

Remember, it had been argued that an unemployment rate of between 4% and 6% (depending upon the economy) was considered to represent full employment. However, by the time the Covid-19 pandemic hit, a number of world's largest economies, including five of its six largest economies, had an unemployment rate of below 4%. As a result, labor shortages were becoming more and more evident in many sectors of these countries'

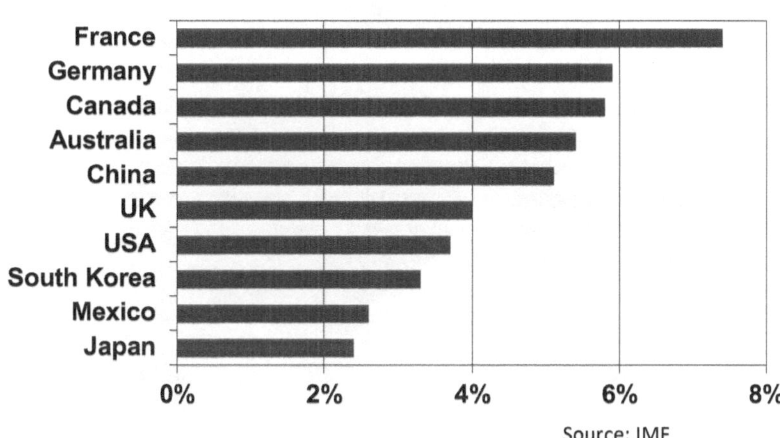

economies, and this was proving to be a real drag on economic growth in these countries. Furthermore, these worsening constraints in the labor sector were contributing to the reduction of the economic growth ceilings for many of these countries. For example, the economic growth ceiling in the United States in the 1990s was considered to be between 4.0% and 4.5%, but today, it is considered to be closer to 3.0% to 3.5%, if not slightly lower. In Europe, the economic growth ceiling in the 1990s was probably closer to 3.5%, but today, it is no more than 2.0% to 2.5%. Finally, Japan's economic growth ceiling is among the lowest in the world, with the Japanese economy likely unable to generate growth of more than 1.5% on a sustained basis. Demographics has much to do with this, as both labor forces are shrinking and domestic market potentials are increasingly limited.

As a result of these growing demographic constraints, some countries today have rates of employment that are extremely high by historical standards. Countries such as the United Kingdom and Germany have their highest employment rates in modern times, with a larger percentage of their population currently engaged in the work force than at any time in recent decades. Furthermore, when you just consider the share of many countries' working-age populations that are currently working, the numbers are even more staggering.

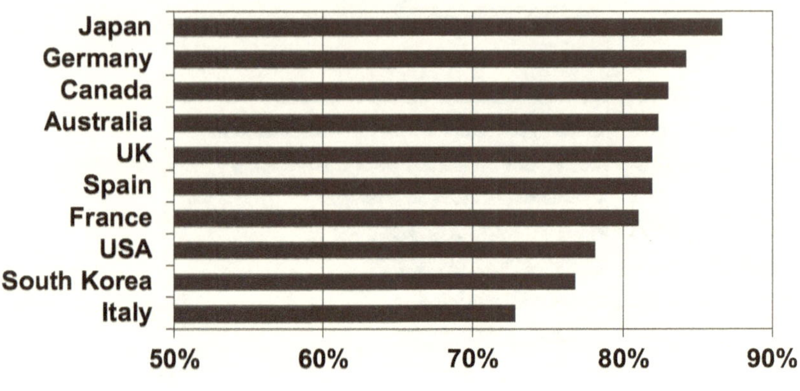

Source: OECD

In most major developed economies, more than 80% of their working-age population is currently employed, suggesting that their labor markets are tighter than ever. Only in countries that have struggled to create jobs in recent years, such as Italy and Brazil, is the share of the working-age population in employment considerably lower.

This dramatic tightening of labor markets masks one problem, however. This problem revolves around the struggles of lower-skilled workers to find their place in the economy of the 2020s. In the past, there were plenty of available jobs in agriculture, and later factories, for unskilled workers, and these unskilled workers could earn a good living in these jobs. Today, the service sector has come to dominate many economies, and unskilled workers have found it difficult to earn enough wages or to gain secure long-term employment in service-related jobs to enjoy a stable life such as those enjoyed by their unskilled predecessors in previous eras. As a result, many unskilled people have dropped out of the workforce completely in recent years, something that could prove to be a major challenge as the need for skills and education increases and as automation and other forms of technology further reduces the need for unskilled labor in many sectors of the economy.

As we have seen, many of the world's leading economies are facing a future in which the size of their labor forces will stagnate and decline. At the same time, the working-age population of a few regions such as South Asia and Sub-Saharan Africa will continue to rise for at least the next few decades. As a result, labor-intensive economic activities that are not taken over by automation could shift to these labor-rich regions. We have already seen this happen in regions such as East Asia and in Europe. In East Asia, as Japan's labor force began to shrink and become quite expensive, labor-intensive manufacturing operations found their way to countries such as South Korea, Thailand, China and now Vietnam. In Europe, shrinking (and expensive) labor forces in countries such as France, Belgium and Italy resulted in many manufacturers deciding to move their operations outside of those countries and transfer them to cheaper locations such as Central Europe or Turkey. However, many of East Asia's and Central Europe's new manufacturing centers are facing demographic declines of their own, and this could result in these places quickly becoming too expensive as labor tightness increases in those regions as well.

As we move ahead, much will depend upon the pace of automation and how quickly some sectors of the economy become less reliant upon human power to generate growth. Should this process take longer than expected, look for labor tightness to once again become a major constraint on global economic growth, and on the growth of those countries where labor shortages are the most acute. This would also provide a major opportunity for those poorest countries that are hoping to attract investment in labor-intensive manufacturing operations that require low-cost work forces with high levels of available labor. However, should the transition to automation accelerate in the coming years, the need for available workers will be reduced for some sectors of the economy, and this could allow these sectors to break free from the labor constraints that have been holding them down so far in the 21st century. This, in turn, could prove to be as revolutionary as the Industrial Revolution itself, for as that revolution freed the economy from the constraints caused by the dependence on human and animal power to generate economic growth, the automation revolution could free the economy from the remaining need for human labor almost completely. The only problem is, there may not be enough consumers in the future to consume the goods and services that will be provided by this newly-automated economy.

If shrinking labor forces are a significant threat to the global economy, at least robots can reasonably be expected to replace humans in many productive and service functions. Unfortunately, robots are unlikely to replace humans as consumers, and this would result in the slowing growth in the number of potential consumers around the world having a greater impact on the future of economic growth than the impact of shrinking work forces today. At the moment, consumer spending accounts for anywhere between 38% (China) and 68% (the United States) of the total GDP of the world's leading economies.

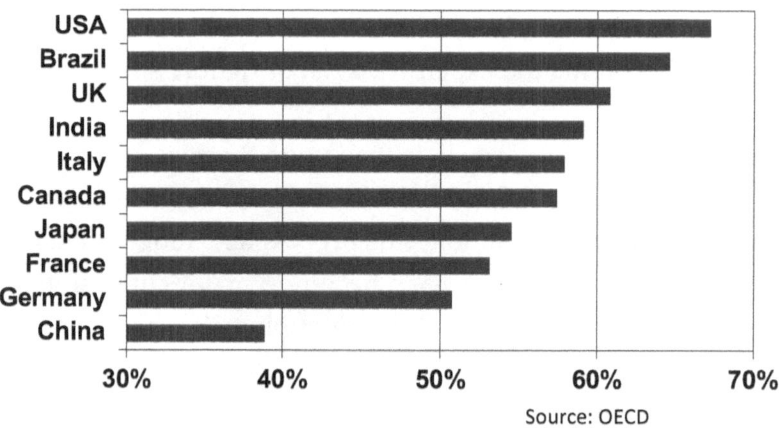

Household Spending as a Share of GDP in 2021

In fact, in many major economies, consumer spending has risen as a share of GDP in recent years, despite the fact that population growth has slowed in all of these economies. In others, the force of population stagnation has resulted in consumer spending playing a slightly lesser role in recent years (such as in many European economies). Nevertheless, consumer spending remains a very important component of every major economy in the world and therefore, the threat of demographic decline weighs heavily on each of these economies' futures. In fact, with population growth slowing in key economies such as the United States, China and the United Kingdom, and with it coming to an end in other key economies such as Japan and Italy, it is highly unlikely that consumer spending will be able to serve as a driver of economic growth as it did in these countries in the past. Add to these demographic influences the changing nature of consumption in the modern world, such as the rise of the "sharing economy", and it is easy to see why so many economists are convinced that consumer spending growth will continue to slow in the coming years, and will even decline in some countries. While it remains to be seen if these shifts in consumption patterns will be short-lived or become a permanent change, these changes have been enough to scare many of the world's most important industries.

One factor that suggests that consumer spending can still continue to grow in the coming years is the fact that per capita disposable income levels have been rising in many of the world's largest countries. In fact, I have done a good deal of research into disposable income in recent years, and for some countries, disposable income levels have risen considerably. However, these rising disposable income levels have developed in a quite uneven manner. For example, in countries such as the United States, there are far more wealthy households than anywhere else in the world, and the upper levels of US households have tremendous purchasing power. However, there is also a larger share of US households that have lower purchasing power levels than in many other wealthy countries, highlighting the widening degree of wealth inequality in the world's largest economy. Elsewhere, the high cost-of-living has held down disposable income levels in many wealthy economies, limiting consumer spending growth. Where there has been a major increase in disposable income levels in recent decades has been in emerging markets, particularly large Asian emerging markets such as China. Here, we have seen the highest levels of consumer spending growth in recent years. However, even as disposable income levels in China and other emerging markets are rising rapidly, the growth in the number of consumers in these countries has been slowing markedly in recent years,

An indirect consequence of these changing demographic patterns is a growing lack of confidence in the ability of the global economy to continue to generate growth in the years ahead. In previous years, while business and investor confidence has wavered, consumer confidence has generally remained high, even amid some of the worst crises of the past few decades. This consumer confidence has played a very important role in the ability of the global economy to continue to generate growth in recent years, with consumers continuing to take risks when businesses and investors would not. However, the threats to consumer confidence are mounting. For example, the Covid-19 pandemic proved to be the single greatest threat to consumer confidence in recent times, forcing consumers to re-evaluate their spending plans at a time when consumer spending was needed more than ever to keep the economy afloat.

Should consumer confidence fail to fully bounce back from this latest crisis, the effect on many economies would be devastating. For example, a long-term decline in consumer confidence would severely depress trade and investment around the world, something we have already witnessed. In turn, this could lead to even lower levels of business and investor confidence, which have been propped up by the knowledge that consumers were continuing to spend, even in times of crisis. If this happens, investment in productivity-boosting technologies and processes could slow, resulting in a further drag on global economic growth. At the same time, lower levels of consumer confidence tend to lead to more support for protectionist measures that would result in more and more economies turning inward, further weakened trade and investment levels. In fact, we have seen this many times in history, including in recent years as rising public anger has threatened to reduce consumer confidence and has led to support for protectionist policies in many countries.

We can already see the impact that falling levels of consumer confidence have had on some of the world's more sluggish economies. For example, consumer confidence levels in Japan have been much lower in recent years than they were during Japan's run of world-beating economic growth. Likewise, consumer confidence levels in Brazil have been depressed for more than a decade, reflecting that country's long-term economic struggles. Unfortunately, for economies that are struggling, persistently low levels of consumer confidence can reinforce these struggles and prevent an economy from returning to growth. In fact, most major economies that have had to pull their way out of a serious downturn in recent decades have done so by attempting to boost exports to other markets, as reviving consumer confidence has proven to be a very difficult task for most countries.

How Likely is a Long-Term Demographic Decline?

Before we assess how likely a long-term demographic decline is, we should first look at whether or not such a decline in population growth provides benefits for mankind and the planet that outweigh the negative impact that such a decline will have on the economy over the coming decades. Indeed, there are a number of benefits that would be derived from a continued slowdown in population growth and there are many experts in the fields of environmental science, politics and others that have made a strong argument that an end to population growth might be the best way to save the planet from the threats of climate change, resource depletion, pollution, over-crowding and many others potential hazards that are jeopardizing our future.

Two areas that deserve mention when we are talking about the benefits of slower population growth are the environment and our planet's natural resources. Without a doubt, the rapid population growth that has taken place around the world over the past 250 years has contributed heavily to many of the environmental problems that we are facing today. For some parts of the world, this dramatic population growth has led to a depletion of resources such as arable land, water, forests and much more. While much of the population growth that took place in the 19th and early 20th centuries occurred in regions that were generally rich in land, water and other resources, much of the population growth that has taken place since the 1950s has done so in regions that are far less well-endowed in such resources. For example, look at the dramatic population growth that has taken place in arid regions such as the Sahel, the Arabian Peninsula, South Asia or the Southwest of the United States.

Another result of the rapid population growth of the past 250 years has been the dramatic increase in the level of air, land and sea pollution around the world. Whereas this pollution led to major crises in cities such London and Paris, today it is the rapidly-expanding cities of Asia and Africa where many of the world's worst pollution problems can be found.

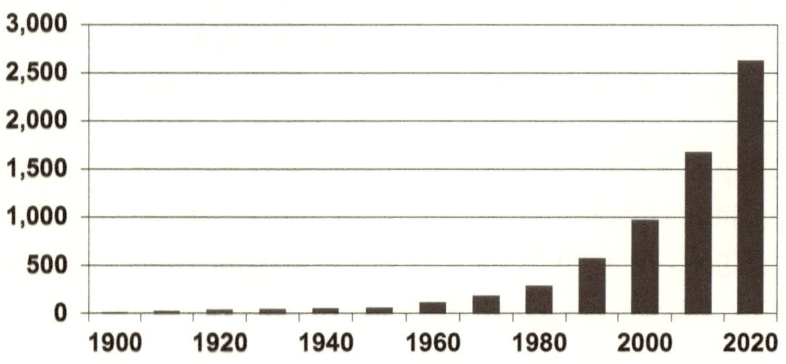

Meanwhile, many parts of the world are today dealing with the worsening problem of overcrowding, particularly as population growth in the modern world goes hand-in-hand with rising levels of urbanization in nearly all corners of the globe. Without a slowdown in population growth, overcrowding will continue to worsen dramatically, making it almost impossible for some areas of the world to function. At the same time, the rapid growth in the number of humans on the planet and coinciding with the even more rapid increase in the number of species of wildlife that are facing extinction, or are becoming critically endangered. As the numbers of humans grow, the available space for other species on this planet continues to shrink. If we hope to save our planet's diverse wildlife, humans will have to set aside more land for this wildlife to exist, and this will only happen if population growth slows dramatically. In fact, when we look at the issue of demographics from a purely environmental aspect, it is hard to argue that slower population growth, or an outright decline in the number of people on the planet, would not be beneficial for the health of the environment, or of the well-being of the other species with which we share this planet.

Another aspect to consider when we look at our looming demographic decline is the impact that population growth has had on stability and security. As we have seen in recent years, rapid population growth has led to increased competition for land and resources in places such as Syria, Libya and many other war-torn parts of the world. If population growth does not abate in the coming years, such resource-driven conflicts are likely to intensify and could end up drawing in the world's major powers, something that could result in a much wider conflict than anything we have seen since the Second World War. At the same time, rapid population growth in regions such as the Middle East, Africa and Central Asia has resulted in an explosion in the number of young-adult males, perhaps the most volatile group of people on the planet. In places where jobs or resources are scarce, these masses of young males could become easily radicalized, something that we have already witnessed in parts of the world where birth rates are particularly high. If population growth slows, these immediate threats to stability and security are likely to ease, something that would go a long way towards increasingly the level of stability and security around the world.

While I certainly agree with those experts who believe that a slowdown in population growth, or even a long-term decline in our planet's population would provide many benefits, the goal of this book is to explain why we are facing the prospect of long-term economic decline, and here, it is clear that these demographic changes are posing some major challenges for the future of our economy. As the growth in the number of workers and consumers continues to fall, particularly in the world's most important economies, the drag on economic growth will be considerable. Furthermore, as population growth slows and our overall population becomes older, the challenge of maintaining the systems that we have created over the past two centuries will be increasingly challenged. For example, how we will be able to maintain our modern pension systems with a lower number of workers (or contributors) and an increasing number of retirees (or beneficiaries)? Surely, we won't be able to tax contributors much more in the future if we hope to maintain economic growth. And what of our extensive educational systems? As the youth segment of the population grows ever smaller, there will likely be a push to cut back on education spending, as an ever-smaller share of the population will actually be utilizing these investments in education. In some cases, we are already witnessing this backlash against education, whether it is in the form of anger at perceived political indoctrination at the university level or the resentment towards teachers and their lengthy vacations. In fact, as we look at our demographic future, it is clear that we are dangerously unprepared for many of the challenges that await us as a result of decades of falling birth rates, and none of these challenges is greater than the negative impact that our demographic decline will have on our ability to generate economic growth.

So, are we destined to suffer from a long-term demographic decline, one that might prove impossible to reverse? Certainly, attempting to change demographic trends from the top down is a rather thankless task and even if governments could convince their populations to have more babies, the change in birth rates would likely be both gradual and limited. Furthermore, demographic changes take a great deal of time, and their impact on an economy would not be realized for many years, if not many decades. This makes costly demographic-boosting programs unattractive to many governments who are more concerned about being re-elected or maintaining their immediate grip on power than about their country's long-term demographic future. Still, some countries have shown that, with a lot of money and a good deal of effort, demographic declines are can at least be arrested, if not fully reversed. For example, Russian President Vladimir Putin, perhaps the world leader of the past 20 years most in tune to the impact of demographics on their country's relative political and economic power, introduced a series of programs in the 2010s and early 2020s aimed at boosting Russia's falling birth rate.

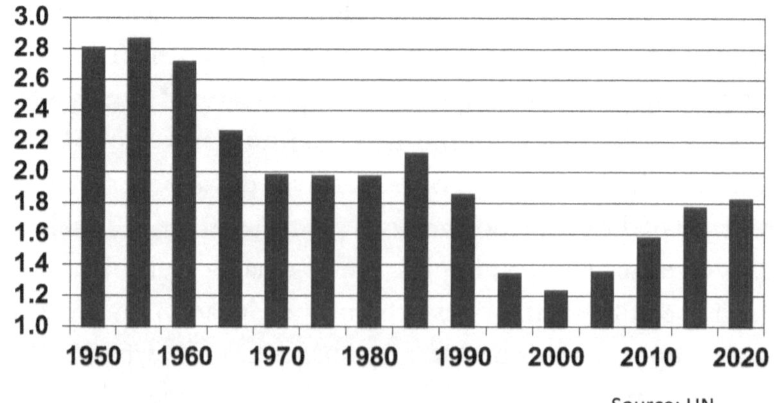

**Birth Rates in Russia
(Children per woman)**

Source: UN

Initial results suggest that these programs are working, for not only has Russia's birth rate stopped falling in recent years, but it has actually risen from 1.5 to 1.7 in a short period of time. Sure, this is still well below the replacement level, but given the dire forecasts predicting a massive population decline in Russia, this has given the country some hope that it will not follow in the demographic footsteps of Japan. At the same time, President Putin's efforts to combat rampant alcoholism among Russian males has resulted in a dramatic increase in life expectancies for men in Russia. Before these programs, Russian men lived an average of 16 years less than the female compatriots, a startling statistic. Today, that gap has declined to ten years. France is another country that has made major efforts to combat the threat of long-term demographic decline. It has done this by using programs such as universal childcare to convince more women to have children, and while this has not prevented France's birth rate from continuing to trend downwards, it is now well above the level of most of its European neighbors.

Despite these examples of how governments can promote childbirth, the fact is that overall birth rates are continuing to trend downwards in almost all areas of the world. In many cases, birth rates have fallen dramatically in recent years, while in others, they fell decades ago, and they remain extremely low to this day. This suggests that the era of domestically-driven population growth, at least in the world's leading economies, is over for now, and may never return. At the same time, migration, that other great driver of population growth, is becoming an increasingly emotive issue, with anti-immigration sentiment rising in those countries and regions that have historically been the leading destinations for the world's migrants. Should this trend continue, another driver of population growth will be lost. As a result, the prospects for continued population growth are now worse than they have been at any point since the Industrial Revolution, and we could be looking at a demographic future that is more closely aligned with that which we witnessed in the centuries before the great industrialization of the planet.

Not only does population growth look likely to continue to slow in the coming years, but the composition of the world's population will also continue to change dramatically. For example, the world's Caucasian, or white, population will begin to fall, first as a share of the world's population than as an absolute number. So too will East Asia's population and its share of the global population. Instead, the global population of the future will be much more dark-skinned, with Sub-Saharan Africans, Arabs and South Asians accounting for a much larger share of the world's population than ever before. At the same time, the world's population will be much older, on the average, than ever before. In fact, as birth rates have fallen and life expectancies have risen, the world's population has already become much older in many parts of the world. In the future, the elderly population will be an ever-greater share of the global population, and this will certainly have a massive impact on society, politics, the environment and much more. Of course, it is the impact that this demographic shift will have on the global economy that we are most concerned about in this book, and here too the impact will be enormous. In fact, if we cannot find ways to make our elderly populations more productive, we are likely to find that this growing segment of the global population is in fact a major drag on the economic growth of the future. That may sound like I am predicting a dystopian future in which the elderly are blamed for the ills of society, but if one sees the situation in places such as Italy and Greece today, one can already see the seeds of resentment building up among young people who will most likely never enjoy the economic benefits enjoyed by their parents and grandparents.

BRING IN THE ROBOTS

For many economists, the answer to reducing the potential impact of demographic decline on the prospects for global economic growth is automation. The belief among many economists is that, once automation becomes widespread, it will solve the challenges posed by shrinking labor forces and allow for humanity to enter into a new era of growth and prosperity. Even better, unlike the economic eras that have come before, this one will require relatively little labor, enabling humans to benefit from rapid economic growth and wealth creation without having to break their backs for most of their adult lives to achieve these goals. Certainly automation appears to be the most straightforward answer to our looming demographic decline. With automation, robots can build (and drive) our cars, and produce (and maybe, but hopefully not, cook) our food. Instead of having to rely upon a shrinking workforce that is prone to going on strike and constantly asking for higher wages, we can employ machines to do most of the work that has been done by humans or animals throughout the history of our species. At the same time, automation will reduce some of the economic problems caused by the fact that our population is aging rapidly. Now, machines can not only reduce the need for the world's elderly population to remain productive members of society, but they could also help to improve the quality of life for a population whose life span is continuing to increase. Considering all of these possibilities, it is easy to see why automation has become the great hope for the global economy as we move forward in the 21st century.

BUCKING THE TREND

While global population growth is certain to continue to decline in the coming years, that does not mean that this decline will be uniform. Nor does it mean that the rates of population growth for individual cities, countries or regions will correspond exactly to their birth rates. This is due to the fact that migration will continue to move people to different parts of the world, particularly those areas that are relatively wealthy and are dealing the threat of labor shortages. In fact, immigration is, at least for the next few decades, an available avenue for many cities, countries and regions for avoiding the full impact of the threat of a demographic decline. One way in which a city, country or region can use immigration to improve their economic outlook is to allow for more skilled immigrants to enter their borders. In fact, skilled migrants typically seek out the most competitive economies, places that can provide them with well-paid jobs or make it easy for them to start their own business. In many cases, skilled immigrants are attracted by strong university systems, with many skilled immigrants arriving at their eventual destination by way of studying at a local university. The benefits of skilled immigrants are clear. Not only do they increase a place's tax-paying base, but they often create companies that become large employers and taxpayers themselves. One need only to look to Silicon Valley to see how skilled immigration has made northern California the most technologically-advanced economic center in the world today.

While there are few people that argue too much against the need to attract skilled migrants, this is not the group that comprises the bulk of migrants in the modern world. Instead, a vast majority of the world's migrants fall into the unskilled category, and it is this category of immigration that generates the bulk of the opposition to immigration in most areas of the world. We have seen how the large flow of mostly unskilled immigrants from Central America into the United States, or from Africa and the Middle East into Europe, has fueled anti-immigration sentiment in those places. However, as we see where population growth is forecast to continue in the coming decades, we quickly see that these regions are places where job creation levels are most likely to be insufficient to meet the demand for jobs in those places, and where resources such as land and water are likely to be stretched dangerously thin in the years ahead. As such, it is hard to see many places becoming more welcoming of large-scale immigration in the future, even as the need for skilled and unskilled workers is likely to grow in many of these would-be destinations for the world's migrants.

While immigration is certain to remain a contentious issue, attempts to raise birth rates are generally supported by most voters, even if these attempts often come to naught. Sure, we have seen how some countries have stabilized what had been falling birth rates, or even managed to boost them a little. However, it seems far-fetched that any country in the coming years will be able to convince their populations to launch their country into a new baby boom. Rather, the downwards pressure on birth rates is likely to continue. In countries where these birth rates are already low, they are likely to remain low, and will almost certainly remain well below the replacement rate for the foreseeable future. At the same time, in countries where birth rates have been relatively higher, but have been trending downwards in recent years, this trend is likely to continue until these countries' birth rates are closer to what we find today in much of East Asia and Europe. Finally, in those countries where birth rates remain well above the global average, we have already witnessed the beginnings of the long-term decline in many of these countries' birth rates, suggesting that these types of countries will also realize a massive decline in their birth rates in the near-future.

As we have seen, demographics do not change overnight. With the exception of major conflicts or particularly severe pandemics, demographic change is a very slow and gradually process. For most of human history, global population growth was a slow affair, broken up by intermittent declines in the global population. However, the Industrial Revolution ushered in an era of unprecedented population growth, and it was this population growth that helped to spur the dramatic economic growth that has taken place around the world since the late 18th century. However, it is now clear that the slowdown in global population growth that has taken place over the first two decades of the 21st century is not a temporary phenomenon, but rather a long-term trend that appears set to continue for much of the remainder of this century. As a result, the world is losing one of its most important drivers of economic growth, one that will not easily be replaced by robots or anything else. Instead, this will place a much greater burden on trade, investment and productivity to drive the global economy forwards in the future.

Chapter Ten

THE IMPACT OF TRADE AND INVESTMENT GROWTH

WE NOW TURN OUR attention to trade and investment as a driver of economic growth. With population growth, it was easy for anyone to understand how an expanding population could directly lead to higher rates of economic growth. However, just because a population grows does not mean that economic growth will exceed population growth unless some other elements come into play. Two of the most important of these elements are trade and investment, which together account for the second main driver of economic growth. To look at how trade and investment drive higher levels of economic growth, we are first going to look back in history to find some examples of how trade and investment impacted various economies at different times in history.

To start, we are going to go back to the impact that trade and investment had on Ancient Rome. However, we first need to understand what the trade and investment climate in Europe, North Africa and the Middle East was before the rise of Rome. What we can see from the pre-Roman era is that while there was a high rate of growth in terms of trade and investment between the various cities and states of this region, the pre-Roman economy primarily consisted of subsistence activities, for without a single power to unify the region, trade and investment flows were relatively limited. For example, while Egypt was the first major power in the eastern Mediterranean, its economy consisted largely of subsistence agriculture. Sure, we have ample evidence that Egypt engaged in trade with its neighbors in Anatolia or Crete, but this trade comprised just a very small part of the economy of Ancient Egypt. It wasn't until the Phoenician city states of the Mediterranean region emerged that trade and investment really began to take off in this region, and still, the Phoenicians were not powerful enough to control the main land and sea trading routes of their ancient world, meaning that they were more intermediaries than actual economies that were trading with one another. Later, the Persian Empire, while a great power in terms of its military capabilities, lacked a sophisticated economy, as again, it was subsistence agriculture that made up the bulk of the Persian economy. Finally, when the Greek city-states emerged as great powers in their own right, they established colonies all throughout the coastal regions of the Mediterranean and Black seas, leading to the most extensive trade and investment network seen to that point in the Western world. Nevertheless, even Ancient Greek lacked the economic scale to truly create a unified infrastructure for trade and investment and this resulted in very uneven economic growth for most of the ancient Greek city-states, even as their level of technological and educational achievements were among the greatest of the pre-Roman world.

In Rome's early centuries, there was little to suggest that the city founded on the banks of the Tiber River would one day emerge to create the most advanced economy ever seen up to that point in history. Over a period of nearly three centuries, Rome gradually took control of the Italian Peninsula, but even when this was complete, it still appeared unlikely that Rome was on the verge of an economic breakthrough of historical significance. However, things would quickly change, beginning with Rome's defeat of Carthage (a descendant of a Phoenician city-state and one of the region's leading economic powers) in 201 BCE, which gave Rome control of much of the Iberian Peninsula and its valuable silver mines. In the following decades, Rome would not only finish off Carthage (giving it control of a large chunk of North Africa), but it would also repeatedly intervene in conflicts in Macedonia and Greece, until much of southeastern Europe was also under Roman control. In the following century,

Rome would gain control of Gaul (modern-day France), the southern half of Britain, Egypt and much of the eastern Mediterranean, bringing this region under the control of a single power for the first time in its history.

With much of Europe, North Africa and the Middle East under its control, Rome was now in command of various territories that had a high degree of economic specialization. For example, the Iberian Peninsula was home to some of the ancient world's most valuable silver mines, while many areas of North Africa provided some of the most bountiful grain crops of this era. Furthermore, Rome put an end to the piracy that had plagued trade in the Mediterranean, while building an extensive road network that connected the various parts of the now giant empire like never before. This elimination of piracy and the construction of a vast road network allowed traders to expand their operations on a massive scale, and the safety and security that Rome brought to the region emboldened investors to begin investing in economic activities throughout the empire. In addition, Roman trade and investment stretched far beyond the empire's borders, with trade between Rome and China in evidence at many points during the height of the Roman Empire. With Rome now enjoying the advantages of high levels of trade and investment, living standards in many parts of the Roman Empire rose to levels that were higher than that of any other ancient society, and were even higher than those experienced by people in the former areas of the Roman Empire until many, many centuries later.

For the Roman economy, the 1st and 2nd centuries CE would prove to be its peak. Beginning in the late 2nd century, Rome would suffer a series of disasters, including pandemics, military rule and eventually a series of civil wars that divided the empire for decades at a time. This would prove devastating to the Roman economy as it would tear apart the extensive trade and investment networks that had allowed the Roman economy to grow so much over the preceding centuries. With these disasters came the collapse of the empire's economic integration, as well as the collapse of the economic specialization that had flourished as long as trade and investment flowed freely throughout the empire. In fact, even as the Roman Empire was able to be reunified in the early 4th century, trade and investment never returned to the levels seen during the 1st and 2nd centuries and instead, the beginnings of European feudalism were evident as subsistence economies returned to the lands of the empire.

If we stay in Europe, we can see the impact of a long-term decline in trade and investment on an economy, for after the decline and fall of the western part of the Roman empire, trade and investment in the region collapsed. This led to subsistence economies dominating the region, and while some trade did go on during this period, it was but a tiny fraction of what it was during the Roman period. In fact, while trade and investment would revive, to an extent, in the east, trade and investment levels in what had been the western half of the Roman Empire would remain depressed for around 1,000 years. It was only in the 13th and 14th centuries that Italian city-states such as Venice and Genoa began to play a role similar to that of the Phoenicians in the pre-Greek Mediterranean and began to revive trade and investment in that region. In terms of trade, their control of vital trade networks between the west and the east allowed them to grow wealthy, and they used this wealth to invest in numerous colonies and trading ports all throughout the Mediterranean and Black Sea regions, much as ancient Greek city-states had done nearly 2,000 years earlier. In the centuries that followed, the wealth and the knowledge that these Italian city-states brought to the West would spread throughout Europe, ushering in a new period of vitality for a region that had been on the back pages for more than a millennium.

When the Ottoman Empire emerged in the 14th and 15th centuries as a major power, it cut off Venice and Genoa from its trading routes to the East. This led to other European powers such as Spain, Portugal, England, France and the Netherlands to seek a western route to the riches of the East. Instead of finding such a route, they found a vast new land whose natural resources were far greater than anything back in these countries' homelands. Eventually, the New World would export much of its mineral wealth to its European colonizers. In turn, the Europeans would invest heavily in their new colonies, building cities, infrastructures and more, while at the same time, decimating the indigenous peoples who had lived in the New World for the previous 14,000 years or more. For a while, the possession of the New World would dramatically enhance the economic power of those states that developed colonies there and would allow Europe to emerge as a center of global economic and military power for the first time since the days of Rome.

Eventually, most European countries would not be able to hold on to their empires, or would squander the benefits they provided. Portugal and the Netherlands possessed homelands that were simply too small to maintain vast empires. France would lose its extensive North American possessions to the English in 1763, but would later have their revenge by helping England's richest North American colonies to win a war for independence against England less than twenty years later. Finally, Spain, the possessor of the largest empire in the Americas, would waste much of the wealth that it gained from its possessions in the Americas on endless wars back in Europe as it attempted to hold on to its possessions in the central Mediterranean and the Low Countries. Altogether, the vast levels of trade and investment that were conducted during the centuries of colonialization in the Americas would prove to be a major boost for those European colonies that held possessions there. Nevertheless, by the time the Industrial Revolution came around and truly revolutionized Europe's economies, most of the region's colonies in the Americas were either independent, or on their way towards independence.

While it can be difficult for someone in today's world to grasp the importance of trade and investment to the success of the Roman Empire or to colonial-era European states, the impact that rising levels of trade and investment has had in East Asia in recent decades is easy to see for everyone. In the wake of the Second World War and the Chinese Civil War, much of East Asia was in ruins, physically, demographically and economically. Not only had the Second World War led to the total devastation of most of the region's most important economic centers, but in its wake were a series of more localized conflicts. Some, like the Chinese Civil War, the Korean War, the Malayan Emergency and the Vietnam War, were devastating to the economies of those countries where the wars were fought. Furthermore, the region (as well as many countries in the region) found themselves on opposite sides of the Cold War between the world's two superpowers, the United States and the Soviet Union. With the region in ruins and much of the region's vast population living in abject poverty, it would have been easy for anyone to dismiss East Asia's economic prospects.

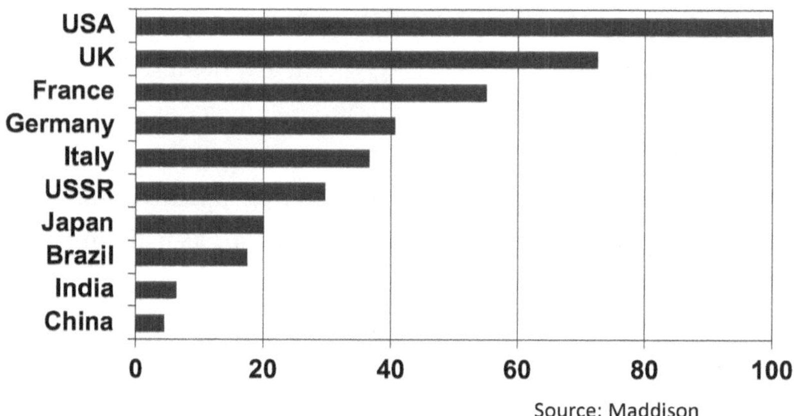

However, as we know now, major economic changes were coming to the region. These began in Japan, which had been the only country in the region to undergo a high degree of industrialization in the period before the Second World War. In fact, it was this industrialization and modernization that allowed Japan to quickly emerge as the dominant local power in East Asia in the latter part of the 19th century and the early part of the 20th century. This allowed Japan to gain control militarily of a vast empire in East Asia that, while proving to be short-lived, was a testament to Japan's economic advantages over its neighbors. In the wake of the Second World War and the demilitarization of Japan, it quickly picked itself up off of its feet and entered into a new period of industrialization and modernization. This time, with the support of the United States, Japan began to invest heavily in export-oriented manufacturing sectors that allowed Japan to begin exporting its manufactured goods to its new allies in the West, most notably the United States. While these manufactured goods were generally cheap and crude in the early days of Japan's export-explosion, they quickly moved up the ladder in terms of sophistication and technology, and within two or three decades, were competing directly, and often successfully, with their Western rivals. This lesson in getting rich via exports to wealthy countries was not lost on other East Asian economies. Beginning in the 1960s and 1970s, relatively poor economies such as South Korea and Taiwan would follow Japan's lead and invest heavily in export-oriented manufacturing sectors, ushering in a period of rapid economic growth across East Asia. At the same time, as investment began to spread across the region, economic centers such as Singapore and Hong Kong would grow to rival the great Western cities of New York and London as centers of trade and investment. East Asia was quickly on its way to realizing its true economic potential.

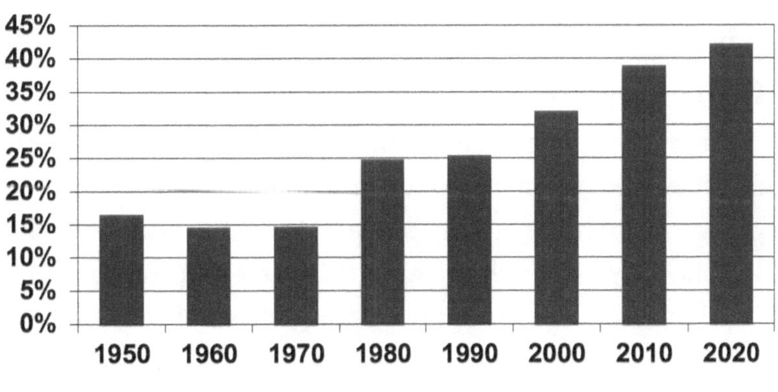

Source: UNCTAD

While East Asia's remarkable economic growth in the decades after the Second World War had a profound impact on the region and its relative prosperity, the combined population of the countries and territories that were part of this economic miracle was only half of that of North America. It was only when China began to adopt the lessons learned from Japan, South Korea and others that the scale of East Asia's economic power began to be felt around the world. Until the 1990s, East Asia's relative economic power compared to other regions was a distant third between North America and Europe. However, with investment pouring into China beginning in the 1980s, and with exports flowing out of China at an accelerating pace at the same time, East Asia's impact on the global economy soon became apparent.

Today, there is little question that East Asia is now the center of the global economy. In recent years, it has accounted for between a third and a half of all additional economic output generated in any given year. At the same time, it is not only a major recipient of foreign investment, but it is now also a leading source of foreign investment, particularly from China. Likewise, East Asia has been the world's leading exporting region for many years, but as wealth has been accumulating in the region thanks to its high levels of economic growth, it is also an increasingly important export market for the rest of the world. In short, it was trade and investment that drove the tremendous success of the East Asian economy in recent years, and it is now in the areas of trade and investment where the region's impact on the global economy is most felt by the rest of the world.

HOW TRADE AND INVESTMENT DRIVES ECONOMIC GROWTH

There continues to be some debate about just how much trade and investment influences the level of economic growth in a city, a state, a country or a region. Some economists continue to point to other factors, such as labor and capital, as having a much greater influence on growth than trade and investment. However, it is my opinion that trade and investment have had, currently have, and will continue to have, one of the largest influences on the economic performance of a city, state, region or country of any of the factors that drive an economy forward. Look at exports, for example. Exports do many positive things for an economy. They bring revenue from other markets. For poorer countries, this allows wealth to flow into the country from places that possess more of it. For countries with small or unconvertable currencies, it brings hard currency into the country, such as US dollars or Japanese yen.

Likewise, exports create jobs. Much of the focus on trade and investment in places such as the United States is that rising levels of trade and investment lead to the evaporation of jobs in sectors such as manufacturing. While this may be true in some cases, in most cases, exports generate jobs, with countries that are successful exporters often having much higher levels of job creation than those that do not. In many cases, such as Mexico or Southeast Asia, the jobs that are created by exports are initially lower-skilled jobs. However, this typically leads to higher-skilled jobs being created later on as these exporting countries move up the value chain over time. Another benefit from exports is that they allow for an economy to specialize in what it does best. We saw this first established on a large scale in the Roman Empire. Today, a good example of this is Germany, whose manufacturing capabilities are boosted by the country's ability to export cars, chemicals and many other manufactured goods all around the world. Finally, exports allow an economy to expand its market. A small country such as Singapore or Ireland would never have had the opportunity to enjoy the level of economic growth that they have done so in recent decades without the ability to export their goods and services far outside of their borders. This is why the biggest champions of free trade remain smaller economies, or those economies that generate the largest share of their economic output from exports.

While the notion that exports are a positive for an economy is widely accepted, at least among economists, it is less widely accepted the imports are also beneficial. Much of this has to do with supply. For example, imports provide much needed supplies for an economy. Sometimes these can be supplies that provide for basic commodities, such as food or energy. For example, countries whose ratio of arable land to population is unfavorable rely upon imported food to ensure that their population has access to a reliable food supply. Likewise, many of the world's largest economies are dependent upon oil and gas imports to provide for their energy supplies. For economies that have benefitted from the modern world's international trading system to specialize in certain sectors of the economy, they are often dependent upon imports to meet their needs in other sectors of the economy in which they do not possess a high degree of specialization or expertise. Germany, for example, is a leading exporter of manufactured goods, but must import nearly all of its energy, IT products and much more. Finally, imports have helped reduce costs for consumers all around the world. Much of this is due to the dramatic expansion of manufactured exports from China and other emerging markets in recent decades that allowed these manufactured goods to be produced at much lower cost levels than they would have been had they been produced in the countries where they were sold.

While the benefits of international trade are clear, there has nevertheless been a downwards trend in international trade growth in recent years, one that pre-dates the US-China trade war and the Covid-19 pandemic.

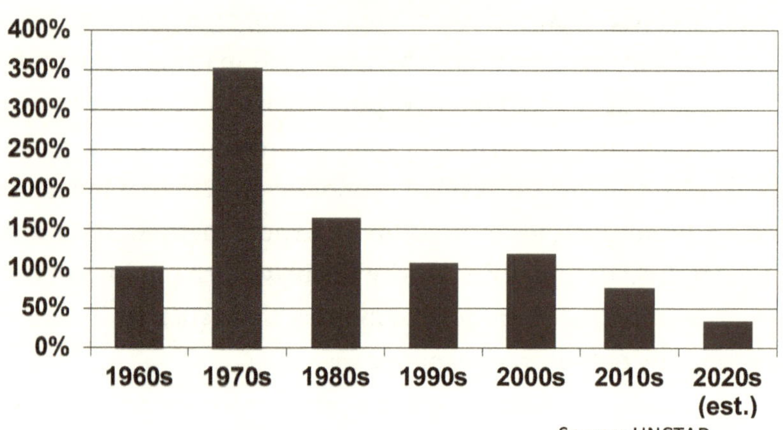

International trade growth peaked in the 1970s (thanks in part to surging energy exports), and remained strong in the 1980s, growing by nearly 17% per year during that decade as the global economy began to open up and the process of globalization took hold. In the following two decades, global trade growth averaged more than 11% per year, providing a major impetus for economic growth in nearly all of the world's leading economies. Keep in mind, it was during the 1990s and the early 2000s that the slowdown in

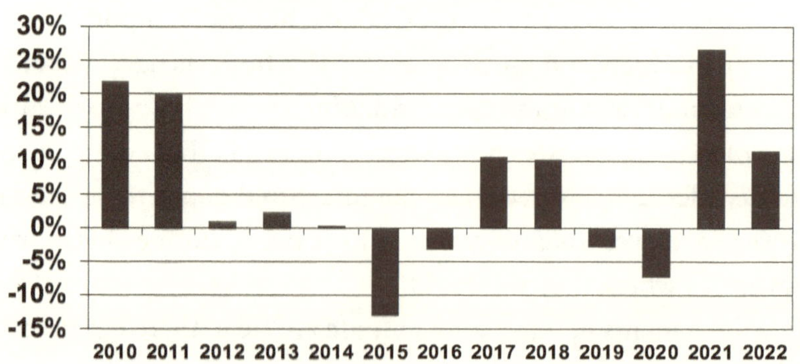

population growth in many of the world's leading economies continued to be felt. Despite this, global economic growth picked up during that period as the impact of rising levels of international trade more than offset this slowdown in population growth. However, over the past decade, we have seen a major decline in international trade growth.

After recovering from the impact of the Financial Crisis in 2010 and 2011, global trade growth stagnated in the following years. In fact, between 2012 and 2019, international trade expanded by a scant 1.6% per year, the lowest rate of international trade growth since the Second World War. Furthermore, this slowdown began well before the Trump Administration took power in Washington and began to implement its "America First" trade policies. During this period, we have seen many of the world's leading exporting countries record declines in their export growth levels.

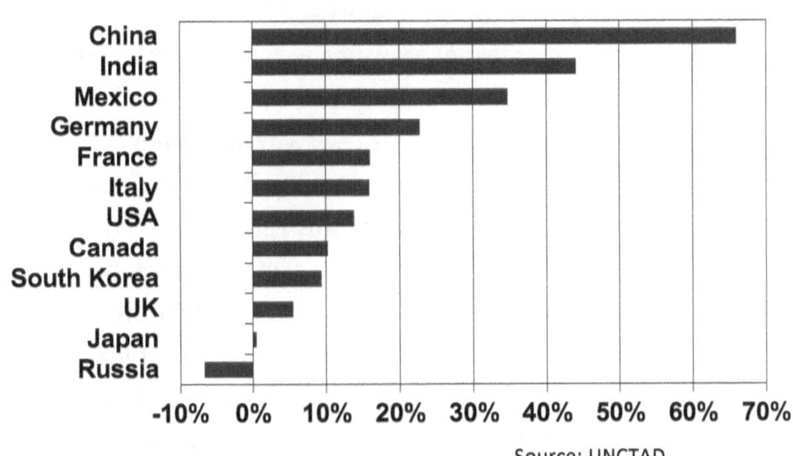

Increase in Goods and Services Exports Between 2011 and 2021

Source: UNCTAD

With population growth slowing, and with (as we will see later) productivity growth also slowing, this fall in international trade growth has proven to be very devastating for many leading economies, and this left them particularly exposed to the impact of the Covid-19 pandemic on their economies in recent years. Worse, it left many economies threatened with a prolonged slowdown, one that will prove very hard to pull out of in a sustainable manner.

There are numerous historical examples of how trade and investment has provided a significant boost to some of the world's most successful economies. We have already seen how trade and investment growth was instrumental in helping the Roman Empire to become the most powerful economy that the world had seen to that point in history. As long as intra-empire trade and investment flowed freely, the Roman economy was able to generate high rates of growth, enabling Rome to establish un-paralleled military power, the ancient world's most advanced infrastructure, and many of the other developments that characterized Ancient Rome and has allowed its legacy to persist to this day. Likewise, Rome's immense market attracted traders from much further abroad, while Rome's vast wealth led it to seek out goods from far outside of its borders. Only when these trade and investment flows were interrupted for a prolonged period of time in the 3rd century CE did the Roman economy turn from growth to a prolonged decline, one that it failed to pull out of, eventually leading to its demise.

Another of history's greatest economies was that of the British Empire. Other European states had overseas empires, but none of these combined Britain's industrialized economy and its overwhelming naval power. These two factors were key in the rapid expansion of the British economy in the 19th century. The Industrial Revolution dramatically raised productivity growth in Britain, and its vast empire gave the country a captive market for its exported goods. The fact that one of the key components of the empire was India, which at the time was the world's second-largest market (at least in terms of population), certainly contributed to the growth of British industry in the decades after the start of the Industrial Revolution. At the same time, Britain's control of the seas in the 19th century enabled the country to maintain control of its key trading routes, something that also benefitted Ancient Rome during its heyday. Eventually, Britain would become not only the leading investor in different parts of its empire, but throughout much of the world. For example, after Spain's and Portugal's Latin American colonies gained their independence in the early 19th century, it was Britain that invested heavily in that region, helping to create one of the greatest economic crises of the 19th century in the form of the Panic of 1825, which was centered on Britain's speculative investments in that region. As long as Britain maintained its empire, it retained much of its ability to trade and invest with large areas of the world. However, Britain's gradual loss of its empire in the 20th century would dramatically change the British economy, resulting in decades of relative stagnation that only ended when a series of painful reforms allowed the British economy to regain much of its lost competitiveness in the 1980s and 1990s.

Two more recent examples of how trade growth has transformed the health of major economies can be found in Asia. The first was Japan. After the devastation of the Second World War, the Japanese economy was transformed into a manufacturing powerhouse, and the basis for much of this growth was Japan's ability to export its manufactured goods to the United States and other major markets around the world.

Source: UNCTAD

To be sure, the Japanese economy had already undergone a dramatic transformation in the decades the spanned the period from the Meiji Restoration in 1868 to the start of the Second World War. During this period, the Japanese economy lost its feudal characteristics and would undergo a rapid period of modernization and industrialization, copying many of the methods and processes that had transformed the economies of Europe and North America in the preceding decades. However, given Japan's lack of access to larger export markets, its economic expansion had just about reached its limits by the 1930s, and this was one of the reasons why Japan sought to create an empire in East Asia, in order to give it captive markets much like the United Kingdom had within its empire. After the Second World War, not only was Japan able to rebuild its industrial base from nearly scratch, but thanks to the new global trading systems championed by its primary World War Two foe, the United States, Japan had, for the first time in its history, access to large export markets that it would use to sell its manufactured goods. As Japan's manufacturing sector became more-and-more competitive, and as the manufacturing bases in markets such as the United States slipped, Japanese exports would fuel a post-war miracle that saw Japan rise to become the world's second-largest economy and, for a short time, the wealthiest large economy in the world. Of course, we know how this story played out. Not only did other Asian economies copy the Japanese model, but they too gained access to large overseas markets, providing cheaper competition for Japanese manufacturers. This, coupled with the demographic decline that has been underway in Japan for a number of decades now, has resulted in the long-term stagnation suffered by Japan since the early 1990s.

The other Asian example of how exports can drive rapid economic growth of course comes from China. Until the 1980s, China was an isolated economy that traded very little with the rest of the world.

However, following the reforms the were launched in the early 1980s, China, like Japan a century earlier, set out on a program of rapid industrialization and modernization, one that would lead to three decades of economic growth that averaged an astounding 10% per year. At the heart of this economic miracle was China's ability to export what were initially low-cost manufactured goods to markets in all parts of the globe. However, as Chinese manufacturing expanded, it began to move upmarket and was soon competing with other major manufacturing centers for export markets around the world. China combined its access to these export markets with its vast, low-cost labor force to create the greatest manufacturing power the world has seen so far. In fact, China's manufacturing sector has been so successful that it now accounts for nearly 30% of global manufacturing, an amazing transformation for a country

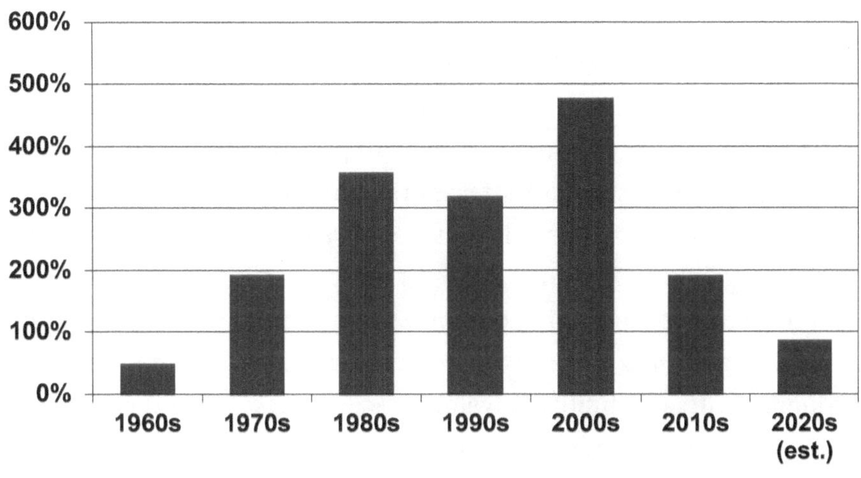

that was so incredibly backwards economically just 40 years earlier. Such a transformation would never have been possible without China's access to export markets, and its ability to export its way to manufacturing dominance. Now, China's decades of rapid growth have resulted in the country's dependence upon export markets having lessened significantly, as more and more of China's current growth is driven by its increasingly-wealthy domestic market. This has happened just in time, as we will see later in the book.

Foreign investment, like trade, is a major driver of economic growth, helping to boost economies all around the world in a number of ways. In fact, for many economies, foreign investment is the catalyst for much of their growth. Think about the success that economies such as Singapore and Ireland have had in recent decades. Clearly, without huge amounts of foreign investment (especially when measured on a per capita basis), these economies would not have enjoyed the success that they did. In fact, foreign investment has not just been a key driver of growth for smaller business hubs, but for the wider global economy. In fact, one can argue that the increase in foreign investment in the late 20th and early 21st centuries was one of the most important factors in the high level of economic growth recorded at the global level during that period. Unfortunately, just like international trade, foreign investment growth has slowed substantially in recent years, and is threatened by a number of factors.

THE NEED FOR FOREIGN INVESTMENT

That foreign investment can boost an economy's performance is undeniable. In fact, foreign investment provides many improvements to an economy. For example, foreign investment increases the amount of capital in a recipient economy. In addition to capital transfers, foreign investment can improve the technological or efficiency levels of a recipient economy. Often, such foreign investment flows into economies that are lacking adequate capital, technological advances or management techniques. At the same time, foreign investment in already-highly-developed economies allows them to further diversify their economies and to bolster their defenses against external shocks. In fact, the biggest contribution that foreign investment makes to the global economy is that it allows wealth, capital and technology to go where it can have the largest impact on global economic growth. Consider the surge of foreign investment into Chinese manufacturing or into Silicon Valley in recent decades.

At the same time, foreign investment can contribute to the development of many long-term drivers of economic growth. A perfect example of this is foreign investment that is used to develop a country's infrastructure. One place where we can see this is in Africa, where investment from China and other major investors has been used, at times, to expand and modernize that region's largely inadequate transport infrastructure. Other such long-term investments can be made in areas such as education and health care, both of which provide significant long-term benefits to the recipients of such investment. For economies that have proven unable to generate long-term and sustainable economic growth on their own, such investment is a tremendous opportunity to establish once-and-for-all an economy that can generate the levels of growth needed to lift large numbers of people out of poverty. Finally, foreign investment is a useful tool to create jobs and generate wealth for its recipients, two of the most basic needs of any economy. Foreign investment can create jobs where they are needed most, such as in regions where the working-age population is continuing to grow rapidly. Likewise, foreign investment can boost wealth levels, allowing for its recipients to develop stronger domestic markets that shield them from the worst impacts of external shocks. When all of these factors are taken together, it can be said that foreign investment is a sign of confidence in the future of an economy. When a city, country or region receives high levels of foreign investment over a long period of time, this is a sign that businesses and investors are confident in that city, country or region and its ability to generate growth in the future.

There are numerous examples of how foreign investment has helped economies to generate higher levels of economic growth. One of these examples we have already touched upon, Latin America in the early 19th century. Here, large-scale investment from the United Kingdom helped to develop that region's infrastructure (especially its railway network), allowing some parts of Latin America to record high levels of economic growth in the decades after their independence from Spain and Portugal. Of course, while this generated growth for many of the recipients of this surge in foreign investment, it didn't end well for many of the investors, who were wiped out by the Panic of 1825. A more recent example can be found in Central Europe, where foreign investment proved to be the catalyst of one of the most notable economic success stories of the past 30 years. When communism fell in this region in 1989, all of the countries of this region had fallen far behind their western neighbors in terms of wealth levels, economic development and living standards. This was due primarily to the economic stagnation of most of central and eastern Europe that began in the 1970s. Once communism fell, Western manufacturers flooded the region with foreign investment, seeking to establish low-cost manufacturing bases that could supply wealthier West European markets with lower-cost products. In particular, the automotive industry invested heavily in countries such as Czechoslovakia (soon to be the Czech Republic and Slovakia).

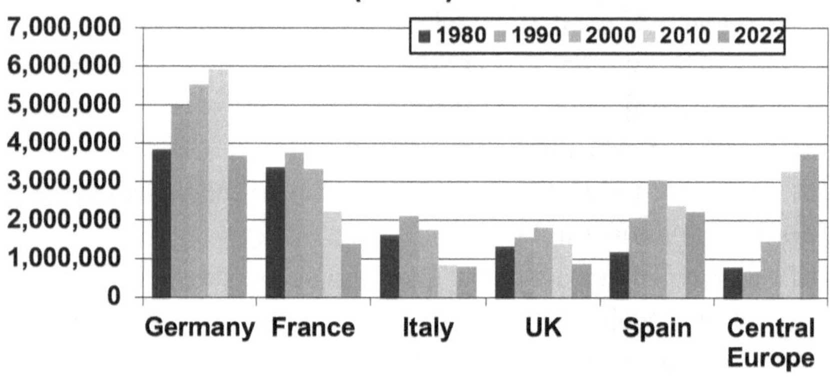

Source: OICA

While this proved to be bad news for less competitive automotive production locations such as Italy, France and Belgium, it resulted in Central Europe becoming one of the world's leading centers of automotive production in a very short period of time. This type of investment helped to propel economic growth throughout the region, and within a generation, some Central European countries had all-but eliminated their once-considerable wealth deficits with West European countries.

One other type of economy that benefitted tremendously from the increase in foreign investment in previous decades has been the economic hub. In fact, in the modern world, a tremendous share of the foreign investment that flows around the world is destined for such hubs. A perfect example of a hub that is the central location for a particular sector of the economy is Silicon Valley in northern California. Here, massive amounts of investment have poured into the region that has come to dominate many information-related sectors of the economy. Another example is London, which, at least until Brexit, was the heart of Europe's financial and professional service sectors, allowing it to attract investment from around the world. Singapore and Hong Kong have developed into two of Asia's leading economic centers on the back of massive inflows of foreign investment into those economies, although Hong Kong's future is clouded by its uncertain relationship with China. At the same time, another type of economic hub, the tax haven, has also seen a huge increase in foreign investment inflows in recent decades, allowing places such as Panama, Luxembourg or the Cayman Islands to accumulate vast amounts of wealth, while providing very little in the way of goods or services that are beneficial for large numbers of people. For many economists, this has become the dark side of foreign investment, as instead of creating jobs or infrastructure, it has allowed businesses and individuals to avoid paying taxes on their profits, creating a dangerous situation that allows issues such as wealth inequality to continue to cause unrest in many parts of the world.

THE DRAMATIC GROWTH OF INTERNATIONAL TRADE AND INVESTMENT

The decades following the Second World War witnessed one of the greatest economic transformations in world history. In this case, it was the establishment of global systems designed to promote and regulate international trade and investment. Those who created these systems were heavily influenced by the fact that global trade and investment had collapsed in the 1930s, a factor that played a key role in the events that led to the outbreak of the Second World War. Determined to prevent such developments from creating a climate conducive to yet another such conflict, the United States and many of its allies were determined to create a system in which international trade and investment could flourish, thus preventing the global economy from falling into another Great Depression. Of course, at the end of the Second World War, the global economy was in tatters, with many of the world's leading trading and investing countries in ruins. In fact, of all of the world's leading economies, only the United States could claim that its economic power had been enhanced during the war. As a result, the US' economic domination at the end of the Second World War was almost unprecedented in world history, with the US' economic output being more than three times larger than that of any other country in the years immediately after the war. Meanwhile, the US' only rival in terms of global power, the Soviet Union, was largely closed off from the rest of the world economically and anyway, had to rebuild a large portion of the country and its economy as a result of the devastation caused by the German invasion.

This left the United States in a position to dictate the shape that the world economy should take after the war. Together with in Western allies, many of whom were struggling to get their economies back on their feet after the war, the US created a host of organizations, treaties and systems designed to connect various parts of the global economy, and by doing so, prevent another world war. For example, the United Nations and its various organizations were initially designed to prevent future great power conflicts, but eventually, also expanded to include the promotion of trade and investment. The best example of this was the creation of the United Nations Conference on Trade and Development (UNCTAD), a body whose main objective is to promote trade and investment in developing countries. Likewise, the United States' Marshall Plan represented a massive US commitment to the economic recovery of Europe via major investments by the US in that region. Finally, the establishment of the General Agreement on Tariffs and Trade (GATT), the predecessor of today's World Trade Organization (WTO), was instrumental in reducing trade barriers between its member states, a major factor in the growth in international trade in the second half of the 20th century.

With the United States economy paramount after the Second World War, it was US foreign investment that played a massive role in helping many countries in Europe and Asia to recover from the devastation of that conflict, including former foes such as Germany and Japan. Between 1946 and 1952, the United States invested $22 billion ($214 billion in 2020 dollars) in helping to revive the economies of 16 European countries. During that same time period, the US invested $2.2 billion ($21.4 billion in 2020 dollars) in helping to rebuild Japan's shattered economy. Such levels of foreign investment had rarely, if ever, been seen at any other point in history. Of course, the United States also offered such aid to countries under the control of the Soviet Union, and some of these countries were very keen to accept such investment, but they were prevented from doing so by Moscow. Altogether, this placed the United States at the center of a new globalized economy, albeit one that was limited to a couple dozen countries in North America, West Europe and the Asia-Pacific region. Thanks to US investment, West Europe and Japan were able to recover economically from the war much faster than anyone had envisioned in 1945. This allowed wealth levels to rise quickly in these areas and for these regions to rebuild many of their key industries, some of which quickly become major exporters in their own right. While these inter-connected economies flourished in the decades after the Second World War, thanks largely to the sharp increase in international trade and investment, most of the world's population remained separated from the benefits derived by this new globalized system, including the large part of the world under the control of Communist regimes, which including China after 1949.

Beginning in the 1980s, many of the countries that were formerly "un-connected" to the group of "connected" countries (North America, West Europe and parts of the Asia-Pacific region) began to enact reforms that were designed to integrate them into the system of trade and investment that had been created by the United States after the Second World War. Sometimes this integration proceeded very slowly (as with India), while sometimes it happened quite suddenly (as with Central Europe). Prior to this reconnection of the global economy taking place, it could be argued that the world's economies fell into three categories:

- The connected West and Asia-Pacific
- The unconnected Communist bloc
- The barely-connected Third World

This meant that the large majority of the world's population lived in countries whose economies were largely isolated from the world's major economies and who had very low levels of trade and investment flows with the rest of the world.

That would soon change. Beginning in the late 1980s, the global economy would go from one that was highly fragmented to one that was deeply inter-connected within the span of less than a generation. Look at some of the examples. China, the most famous example, went from being one of the world's most isolated economies in the late 1970s to becoming one of the world's main trade and investment centers within just 20 years. Latin America, another region whose history of trade and investment with the rest of the world could be characterized as sporadic and inconsistent, suddenly saw its level of trade and investment with the rest of the world soar. Central and East

Europe were isolated from much of the global economy for nearly 45 years after World War Two, but within just a few years, were fully integrated into the wider European economy, with trade and investment growth levels that were among the highest in the world. Even India, the large economy that has perhaps embraced globalization, trade and investment with the most trepidation, is now a fully-fledged member of the global economy.

For those economies that were able to fully integrate into the global economy in recent decades, the rewards have been significant. The more an economy was able to integrate and enact the reforms that improved their economic competitiveness, the more they have benefitted.

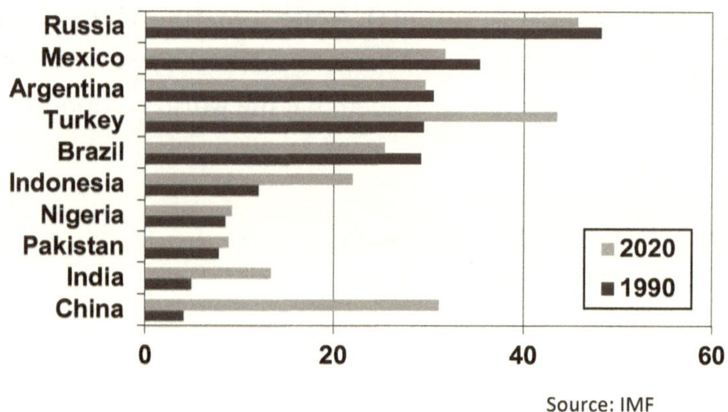

Per Capita GDP at PPP in Emerging Markets (USA=100)

Source: IMF

Nowhere is this more evident than in East Asia, where the ability to attract investment, to develop competitive manufacturing sectors and to gain access to export markets has resulted in hundreds of millions of people being lifted out of poverty over the past few decades. Furthermore, many East Asian countries, led by China, have dramatically closed the wealth-gap between them and the world's developed economies. Central European countries such as Poland and Slovakia are also good examples of how their integration into the global economy and their ability to attract investment and export to wealthier markets has allowed them to significantly improve their economic situations. Finally, even India, with its integration into the world economy having moved slower than many other countries, has been able to use the country's ties to other major economies to boost economic growth and increase wealth levels in that country.

While so much of the world has been integrated into the global economy, and into the systems that were put in place at the end of the Second World War, some parts of the world remain either disconnected from trade and investment, or have very limited access to trade and investment. For example, many areas of Sub-Saharan Africa conduct very little trade with foreign countries and receive very little investment. Furthermore, what trade and investment many countries in that region are involved in consists primarily of exporting commodities to wealthier countries. Latin America is another region where many of its countries have relatively low degrees of trade and investment with the wider world, due in part to the isolation of many parts of the region from the world's leading economic centers. Finally, Russia, the heart of the former Communist bloc, has chosen to carefully control its trade and investment relationships with foreign countries, even as that country is today one of the world's leading exporters of oil and gas. Altogether, while globalization has made remarkable progress in bringing the global economy together in recent decades, there are still many parts of the world that have yet to take advantage of the opportunity to integrate with the rest of the global economy.

While it is evident that trade and investment have been key factors in the generation of much of the world's economic growth in recent decades, it is also evident that the slowdown in trade and investment growth in recent years is not just a short-term aberration, but rather a significant threat that has the potential to upend the global economy. This raises the question whether or not international trade has reached its peak. Recent data certainly would suggest that this is the case, particularly after the Covid-19 pandemic resulted in a large decline in international trade in 2020, albeit one that proved to be surprisingly short-lived.

After growing rapidly for much of the 2000s, international trade was hit hard by the Financial Crisis in 2009. While it rebounded in 2010 and 2011, growth has been hard to come by ever since, and thanks to the pandemic in 2020, global trade levels at the end of that year were lower than they were nearly a decade earlier. Likewise, it is fair to consider the possibility that foreign investment has also reached its peak already. Given the near-decade-long decline in foreign investment that has taken place in the wake of the Financial Crisis, it also appears that this could be a reality.

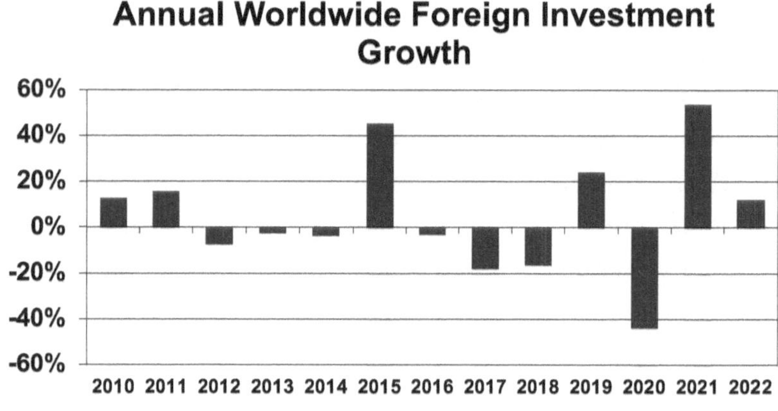

Source: UNCTAD

In fact, foreign investment flows, which had soared in the previous years, have struggled to grow over the past 10-12 years. Interestingly, much of the recent slowdown in foreign investment flows has come from a stagnation in foreign investment in emerging markets, the same markets that had been the catalyst for much of the foreign investment growth of the previous period.

When we analyze long-term foreign trade and investment trends, it is important to remember that, while comparing the data from the past few decades is relatively easy thanks to the breadth and the depth of the data we possess, comparing trade and investment data with earlier periods in history is rather difficult, given the lack of data that we possess from those periods. For example, it has been estimated that global trade fell by 30% to 40% during the Great Depression, but conflicting sets of data mean that we cannot be certain as to the exact scale of the decline. Furthermore, global trade and investment as a share of global economic output was far smaller in the 1930s than it is today, especially when one factors in the share of the exports of services. Likewise, the oil crises of the 1970s only resulted in a relatively small decline in global trade, and then too, the share of international trade to global GDP was much smaller (33%-36%) than it is today

(56%-60%). Based on this evidence, we can draw a tentative conclusion that, the more dependent the global economy is on international trade and investment to drive growth, the greater the scale of the downturns when the global economy runs into trouble. This can be seen in the dramatic impact on global trade and investment that the last two major crises, the Financial Crisis and the Covid-19 pandemic, have had on international trade, foreign investment and global economic growth.

So why has global trade and investment been slowing for much of the past decade? Before the crisis of 2020, international trade had grown by an average of just 1.6% per year between the years 2012 and 2019. In the two decades before this period, global trade had generally grown much faster than the global economy, highlighting its huge impact on the performance of the global economy. However, this has all changed in recent years, and now, global trade is underperforming the global economy, thus proving to be more of a drag on the global economy than a driver of growth.

Increase in Goods and Services Exports Between 2011 and 2021

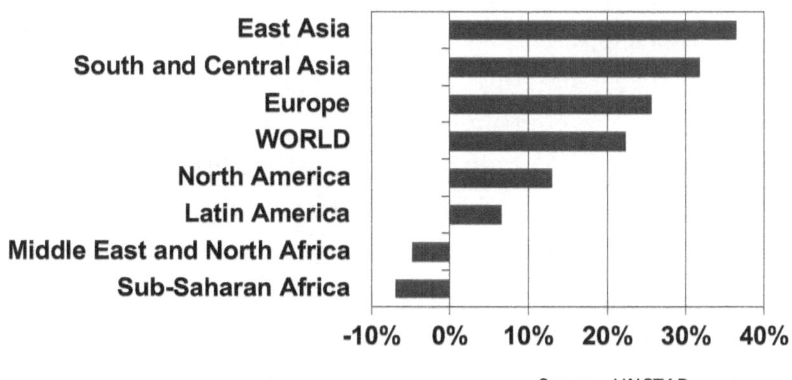

Source: UNCTAD

As we can see, this slower growth in international trade is not just the result of one or two regions underperforming in recent years, but rather, growth being subdued in most regions during this period of sluggish global trade growth. Furthermore, there is very little difference between the growth rates in trade for developed economies and emerging markets, unlike in the previous seven-year period in which trade in emerging markets more than doubled.

If we look at foreign investment growth during this period, the picture is similar. However, as foreign investment levels are far more volatile than international trade levels, trends can be harder to discern. However, the larger picture is one where growth in more developed economies and emerging markets has been relatively similar, and sluggish, in recent years.

There are many reasons why global trade and investment growth rates have been slowing of late. For one, the benefits of globalization may be declining. Of course, international trade and investment growth rates would be higher in the early days of globalization in the 1990s and early 2000s as they were being compared with the low bases of previous periods, when so many of the world's largest countries were engaged in relatively little trade and investment with the rest of the world. Likewise, economic growth in many key centers of international trade and investment has been subdued in recent years, reducing demand for imports and exports and reducing the need for foreign investment. We have also seen a relatively significant decline in business and investor confidence over the past eight-to-ten years, and without higher levels of confidence, businesses and investors will be less keen to take their chances in foreign markets, especially when it is riskier foreign markets that are now often providing the greatest opportunities for growth. The rise of automation is another factor that is contributing to the decline of trade and investment growth. With automation gradually reducing the importance of labor costs in the decision-making process for manufacturers and service providers when it comes to decide where to establish production locations or service centers, an increasing number of these decision makers are choosing to locate these types of operations in the markets of their end-users, thus reducing growth for foreign trade and investment. Finally, the rise in protectionist sentiment in the United States and other important economies has led to an increase in barriers to trade and investment, or the fear that such barriers are imminent. This too has played a major role in the recent slowdown in trade and investment growth.

These recent trends are a very disconcerting development for the future of the global economy. We have seen how in the 1990s and the early 2000s, high levels of international trade and investment growth could be a catalyst for much higher levels of global economic growth. However, as we are now in the midst of the worst period of trade and investment growth since the era spanning the Great Depression and the Second World War, there are mounting concerns that we are in experiencing a similar situation as that devastating period for the global economy. We have seen what the impact of the decline in global trade and investment was during those years and that should be enough to scare policy makers into doing everything in their power to prevent another such period of rampant protectionism from taking hold. However, the fact that we have been hit by two major economic crises in such a short span suggests that public opinion is likely to remain hostile to global trade and investment for some time to come.

Chapter Eleven

TRADE AND INVESTMENT AT RISK

THE PERIOD OF GLOBALIZATION that began in the 1980s led to a massive surge in global trade and investment. Not only did global trade and investment levels rise at a fast pace, but nearly all areas of the world recorded substantial increases in growth rates for imports, exports and foreign investment inflows and outflows. However, recent years have witnessed a major slowdown in trade and investment growth, with both trade and investment essentially stagnant when recent years are taken as a whole. This slowdown in trade and investment growth is generally perceived as being very recent. For many, the policies of the Trump Administration in the United States were the catalyst of this downturn in trade and investment growth, as the US moved to rebalance its trading relationships with many of its leading trade partners. However, if we look more closely at the data, we find that this slowdown in trade and investment growth actually began a number of years before Donald Trump moved into the White House. In fact, while the trade disputes of recent years, such as the dispute between the United States and China, have dominated the headlines, other factors were at work that were leading to a slowdown in international trade and investment and were threatening to bring an end to the golden age of globalization that characterized the global economy for more than three decades.

The first signs that global trade and investment were slowing came as a result of the Financial Crisis in 2008 and 2009. During this time, global trade and investment fell substantially for the first time in decades. At the time, it was assumed that this downturn in global trade and investment was simply to result of the sharp decline in economic growth that occurred in many of the world's leading economies during the financial crisis. In particular, the decline in consumer demand in wealthy economies such as the United States and West Europe was thought to be the main reason why trade growth fell during the crisis, while the loss of business and investor confidence during the crisis was the reason for the decline in foreign investment at the end of the 2000s. These beliefs were reinforced when trade and investment growth returned in 2010 and 2011, and its looked, for a while, as if the trade and investment growth rates of the pre-Financial-Crisis period had returned. However, since 2012, both trade and investment growth were anemic at best. Unlike the Financial Crisis, this was not a temporary setback, for even before the Covid-19 pandemic led to a dramatic fall in global trade and investment levels, neither trade nor investment was able to grow at a sustained pace at any time between 2012 and 2019.

One of the most notable aspects of the situation facing global trade and investment in the past few years has been the proliferation of high-level trade disputes, many involving some of the world's largest economies. In fact, while trade disputes were commonplace throughout the post-war period, the scope and severity of some of the trade disputes of recent years has been unprecedented. Most notably, the worsening trade relationship between the world's two largest economies (the United States and China) has dealt a major blow to the prospects for global trade and investment and is threatening to divide the world into rival economic blocs (a process known as decoupling), something that could bring an end to the period of globalization. Not only do the US and China account for more than 40% of global economic output, but their economic and political power means that they possess a range of weapons that they can use against one another in a trade war. For example, the United States' possession of the world's dominant currency and its control of the global financial system give it formidable tools against any economic rival, even China. On the other hand, the promise of China's vast market, and its huge foreign currency reserves, mean that it too possesses many weapons with which it can fight a major trade war.

It is bad enough that the world's two dominant powers are engaged in a major trade war, one that has outlasted the Trump Administration. However, there are many other serious trade disputes that have emerged in recent years which further threaten to divide the global economy and further reduce the potential for trade and investment growth in the future. For example, the world's two most-populous countries (China and India) have seen their rivalry intensify in recent years, leading to new restrictions on trade and investment between these two giant emerging markets being put in place. At the same time, the United States and the European Union have seen their economic relationship also fluctuate greatly in recent years, a development that could lead to a more permanent break among the leading economic powers of the West. As the current system of global trade and investment is largely a product of the US and European cooperation, a fallout between these two giant economies could spell doom for globalization. Meanwhile, there are too many other major trade disputes to mention here, but should the world's leading economies become more averse to free trade and investment, the likelihood that the number of these trade disputes will increase is obviously very high.

Not that long ago, it was expected that international trade and investment would continue to grow for the foreseeable future and that the process of globalization would continue to the benefit of the global economy. In fact, it was increasingly believed that the continued process of globalization was inevitable as advancements in transportation and communications continued to shrink the planet. However, too many segments of society felt that they were losing out as a result of globalization, and this led to a severe backlash against trade and investment in many of the very powers that championed the modern era of globalization in the first place. This backlash, coupled with the fact that business confidence levels have weakened as a result of the economic turmoil of the past ten-to-twelve years, has resulted in the stagnation and decline of trade and investment growth in recent years. In fact, without higher levels of business and investor confidence, trade and investment cannot grow. Therefore, this confidence needs to be restored, something that could prove to be a very tall order given all of the factors that are now working against trade and investment in today's world.

THE OUTLOOK FOR GLOBAL TRADE

There are many different opinions regarding the outlook for global trade in the coming years. For some experts, there is a strong belief that global trade levels will recover from their recent disappointing levels and return to the growth rates that were seen from the 1980s to the early 2000s. Many of these people believe that the age of globalization is far from over and that the factors that have reduced global trade levels in recent years will prove to be nothing more than a temporary setback to the process of globalization and worldwide economic integration. On the other hand, there are also many experts who believe that the "golden age" of globalization has come to an end and that a retreat to more regional or domestic economic systems is more likely. Often, they argue that the benefits of globalization went to a too few people, and those that did not benefit will continue to lead the calls for an economic retrenchment based on national or local, but not international, interests.

As we look ahead to the remainder of the 2020s, there is still a great deal of uncertainty surrounding the near-term future of the global trading system. I and many other economists believe that economic growth rates in the 2020s could be lower than those of previous decades and this alone suggests that global trade levels will be lower as well.

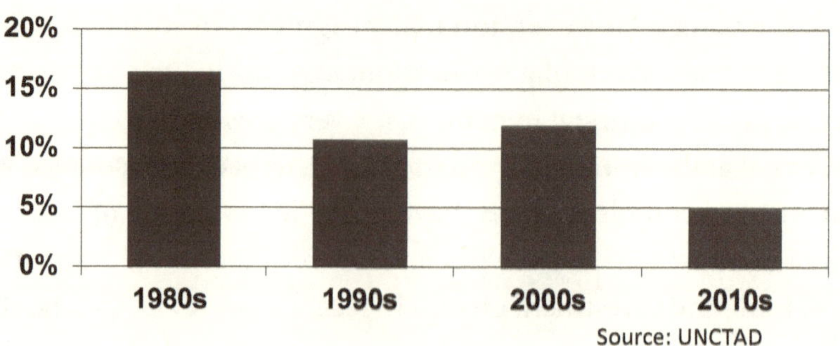

In fact, global trade growth in the 2010s was already much lower than that of preceding decades, a sign that this slowdown is already underway. Furthermore, the Financial Crisis and the Covid-19 pandemic both led to sharp declines in global trade, but in the intervening years, global trade growth was also very disappointing, indicating that these crises were not solely to blame for these poor trade results. With many of the world's leading trading countries either likely to struggle economically or to resist the process of globalization, expectations for a swift recovery for global trade should be tempered.

Meanwhile, the longer-term outlook for global trade is even more uncertain. Clearly, global trade growth has been slowing since the early days of globalization in the 1980s and this trend looks set to continue in the years ahead. With forces such as protectionism, localization, automation and nationalism all working to reduce global trade, and with concerns mounting about trade's impact on the environment, it is easy to envision a future in which support for global trade continues to decline. In fact, we may well have already reached the peak in this era of globalization and economic integration, and we might already be in the downwards phase of this trading era. It has happened before.

There are many variables to consider when we try to ascertain the future of the global trading system. Will consumer and business demand levels rebound from their recent slumps? If so, will consumers and businesses favor goods and services that are imported from outside of their borders, or will they favor locally-sourced goods and services? On top of this, it is uncertain whether or not overall demand levels will rise much in the years ahead, given the uncertain outlook for the global economy in the wake of its recent turmoil. Another factor to consider is whether or not the intricate global supply chains that have been created thanks to this period of extensive globalization can be maintained, or if businesses, consumers and governments wish for them to be contained. The Covid-19 pandemic exposed the dangers facing countries that were dependent upon foreign sources of medical equipment, as an example, while the recent supply chain disruptions have shown just how vulnerable the global economy is to any turmoil within these supply chains. At the same time, the push for localization is likely to continue, with political leaders calling on businesses based in their jurisdictions to "bring home jobs", which in many cases will actually result in factories filled with robots building products to be sold in local markets. Finally, politics will play a major role in determining the future direction of global trade. We have already seen the impact that political changes can have on global trade. For example, the Trump Administration's efforts to rebalance the United States' trading relationships with China, Canada, Mexico and Europe led to a series of trade disputes that significantly altered the flows of imports and exports in the US and many other countries. As we look at the changing demographic and economic situations in many important economies, it is easy to believe that support for protectionist policies will continue to grow in the future, to the detriment of global trade. These and other factors all suggest that global trade growth is likely to be weak at best in the years ahead, and there is a real possibility that global trade levels could actually fall over the long-term, especially if demand levels fail to meet expectations. This would be bad news for major leading economies around the world, particularly those such as Germany, South Korea, Canada and Italy that are dependent upon exports to generate a large share of their economic output.

A Slowdown in Foreign Investment

In the three decades before the Financial Crisis of 2008 and 2009, foreign investment flows had soared, growing by 30% per year between 1980 and 2008. In fact, in the final years before the Financial Crisis, foreign investment flows soared to their highest-ever levels as investment moved around the world at levels never before imagined.

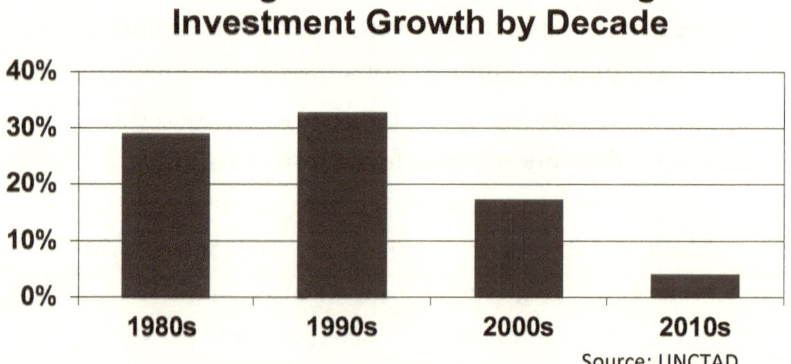

In 2007, foreign investment flows reached a record $1.9 trillion and it seemed that the age of globalization would never end and that as the global economy grew, both in terms of overall output and inter-connectivity, foreign investment would continue to grow as well.

Well, the Financial Crisis brought a halt to the soaring growth in foreign investment flows, with these flows falling from $1.9 trillion in 2007 to just $1.2 trillion in 2009. This spooked businesses and investors, and while foreign investment rebounded in the early 2010s, eventually reaching $2.0 trillion in 2015, the days of soaring foreign investment growth seemed to be over. In fact, since 2012, foreign investment flows have registered very little growth at all, and when one considers the impact of the Covid-19 pandemic, one can see that the level of foreign investment flows in the early 2020s is as low as it was at the height of the Financial Crisis. This decline in foreign investment has played a key role in the struggles of many economies since the late 2000s, as it was rising foreign investment that propelled many of the world's leading economies to growth in previous years. Worse, this downturn in foreign investment has persisted for a long time now, suggesting that it is much more than just a temporary development, but rather, is a trend that could continue for a long time to come.

So why has foreign investment been falling in recent years? Well, there are many reasons for this decline, some of which continue to be disputed by economists today. One important reason is that barriers to investment are rising in many parts of the world, including many of the world's leading recipients and sources of foreign investment. Much like trade, foreign investment is an emotive issue that can be heavily influenced by politics, while heavily influencing the decisions of politicians. A good example of this are the barriers to foreign investment from China that were imposed by the Indian government after a round of clashes between Chinese and Indian armed forces along their disputed border in the Himalayas in 2020. The fact that many of these barriers are often imposed on countries that have powerful economies, and are thus important sources of foreign investment, means that they can be effective means of limiting foreign investment flows. Often, such barriers to foreign investment are erected to protect domestic industries which are usually either in a nascent phase or are in a period of decline often caused by a lack of competitiveness. East Asian economies protected their young automotive and electronics industries from foreign investment until they were ready to compete, and often win, in international markets. At the same time, many emerging markets will protect uncompetitive industries that nevertheless provide large numbers of jobs, fearful that foreign investors will either drive these industries out of business, or will force massive layoffs in a bid to improve their competitiveness. Likewise, barriers to foreign investment are a frequently-used weapon in trade-related disputes, one that is not as directly harmful as a trade barrier, for the benefits of foreign investment are typically not as directly noticeable as those of international trade.

Another factor that drives foreign investment is business and investor confidence. When business and investor confidence levels are high for a prolonged period of time, businesses and investors are usually more willing to take risks. For many businesses and investors, making an investment outside of their home market is a substantial risk, so it takes a certain level of confidence to encourage foreign investment to take place.

Unfortunately, business confidence levels have been relatively tepid in the recent years as economic growth in many key markets has been disappointing and as the risk factors facing many important economies have mounted. Worse, the fact that the global economy has already experienced a number of major crises in the 21st century has prevented business confidence levels from rising too far. As a result, this relative lack of confidence has played a key role in holding down the growth of foreign investment flows in recent years. Likewise, the changes underway, such as localization and automation, that have the potential to reduce the need for such high levels of foreign investment, are also likely to continue. If they continue to gain momentum, foreign investment levels could actually fall in the coming years.

So what is the future for foreign investment and what role will it play in driving economic growth in the years ahead. Certainly foreign investment played a massive role in driving global economic growth from the 1980s to the early 2000s, particularly for many economic centers that have thrived as a result of globalization (such as Singapore or Ireland) as well as for many emerging markets that wisely utilized incoming foreign investment to diversify and modernize their economies (such as China or Malaysia). However, forecasting levels of foreign investment is notoriously hard to do, and as an economist who has been predicting foreign investment levels for more than two decades, I can attest to the challenges that such forecasting can pose. For example, there can be a surge of foreign investment into a particular country for a short period of time, followed by a decade of little or no investment at all. Likewise, a country that has attracted high levels of foreign investment for a very long period of time can suddenly find itself no longer able to attract much investment. Nevertheless, the overall level of global foreign investment can be relatively accurately predicted if one is able to accurately forecast the level of global economic growth and the direction of business and investor confidence in the world's leading economies.

For the current period, the outlook for foreign investment is highly uncertain due to a number of factors. One, economic growth in the 2020s is forecast to be significantly lower than in previous decades, even when one takes the impact of the Covid-19 pandemic out of the equation. Two, business and investor confidence levels have surely been shaken by the major crises that have impacted the global economy in the 21st century, and these confidence levels will continue to be shaken by the many challenges facing the global economy in the post-Covid world. Three, the aforementioned trends of localization and automation are expected to continue, and likely accelerate, in the coming years and decades, further dampening the need for foreign investment. For, the longer period, the outlook for foreign investment is even more uncertain. As we have seen, the era of globalization led to decades of dramatic growth for foreign investment that was only brought to an end by the Financial Crisis at the end of the 2000s. However, we have witnessed a stagnation and decline of foreign investment in the period that followed, raising fears that this decline will continue for the foreseeable future. Given the outlook for most of the factors that drive foreign investment, it is easy to see why many economists are fearful that foreign investment flows will continue to trend downwards for a long time to come. Given just how important foreign investment has been in the generation of economic growth around the world, a long-term decline in foreign investment could have a devastating impact on the ability of many economies to generate consistent economic growth in the future.

PROTECTIONISM RETURNS

Of all of the threats to trade and investment in the modern world, perhaps none is greater than the rising levels of support for protectionist policies in many of the world's leading economic centers. We have seen many times in the past how barriers to trade and investment can lead to a global economic slowdown, or can turn a slowdown into something much worse. China's self-imposed isolation from the rest of the world in the early 15th century turned what was the world's most-advanced economy at that time into one that experienced centuries of decline, until China was so weak economically and militarily that it could not stop the incursions of rival powers in the 19th century, powers who were keen to gain unfettered access to China's vast market. Without this self-imposed isolationism, China may well have been the predatory power in the period that would become known as the era of European imperialism, not Spain, Portugal, England and others. In a more recent time, the decision by the United States and others to impose severe restrictions and tariffs on imports in the wake of the Wall Street Crash turned what was a severe economic downturn into the Great Depression. While the world has largely avoided such comprehensive protectionist policies since the Second World War, those countries that have attempted to isolate their economies from the rest of the world have usually fared much worse in terms of generating wealth and economic growth than their more open counterparts. Maoist China and the Soviet Union are two perfect examples of economies that proactively avoided integrating their economies into the wider global economy, and we know how those economies fared without massive reforms.

Unfortunately, protectionism has returned in a big way in recent years. There is no better example of the resurgence in support for protectionist policies than the election of Donald Trump to the presidency of the United States in 2016, as he ran on what was essentially a protectionist platform. Not only did he campaign on a platform of protecting US industry from foreign competition, but he vowed to use the United States' vast power to force those trading partners that had large-scale trade surpluses with the US to reduce these surpluses, or face the prospect of losing access to the massive US market, or even face sanctions from the US. These policies led to a major trade war between the United States and China, and strained the US' trading relationship with long-time partners such as Canada, Mexico and the European Union. Another example of how protectionism is rising in what had been some of the world's most economically-open countries was the decision by voters in the United Kingdom to withdraw from the European Union. Here too, the promise of protecting local industries and jobs from foreign competition was a deciding factor in the vote, with those regions of the UK that were among the least competitive in terms of their economic position largely voting in favor of leaving the EU. This trend is not only evident in wealthy countries, but even in some leading emerging markets. India is notorious for the degree of protectionism that it affords local industries, while many Latin American countries also have large segments of their electorates that look favorably on protectionist measures. Even a country such as Nigeria has witnessed a surge in protectionism in recent years, with the government there enacting policies that have slowed the pace of economic integration in Sub-Saharan Africa in order to protect industries based in Nigeria.

There are many reasons why this support for protectionism is likely to continue to rise in the coming years. In wealthier economies, the loss of manufacturing jobs to emerging markets or to automation has left a large segment of those countries' populations in a precarious financial state, as the factory jobs that were once so plentiful are now scarce. At the same time, wage growth in many developed countries, including the United States and Germany, often trailed behind the level of economic growth (at least before recent labor shortages), leaving many voters in these countries resentful at what they see as an economic system that is not benefitting them. Meanwhile, the rise of more far-right and far-left political movements has added to the pressure on governments to take a more protective stance with regards to their domestic economies. Even when far-right and far-left leaders and parties are unable to take control of local, regional or national governments, their influence has grown so much that more centrist parties must adopt some of their protectionist policies in order to keep these more ideologically-extreme parties and leaders out of office. At the same time, technological changes are also driving increasing support for protectionist measures, as are demographic changes. As electorates become older, as they are in nearly every democracy in the word, they tend to become more conservative as well as more favorable towards protectionist policies.

Given these trends, and the state of the economy in many of the world's leading economic centers, it appears that support for protectionism will remain high for the foreseeable future. In fact, support for protectionism has been rising in many parts of the world and if this continues, there is a real threat that much more severe restrictions on trade and investment could be enacted in different parts of the world. In fact, recent elections have shown that promises of protecting local jobs, businesses and industries is a big vote-winner, something that will not be lost on politicians and political parties in the elections of the coming years. As a result, there is a real likelihood that the protectionist measures that have led to recent trade disputes are just the tip of the iceberg, and that much more severe and comprehensive trade disputes may be forthcoming, to the detriment of the global economy.

A New Era of Localization

Another threat that has emerged in recent years is localization, or reshoring. This involves the reduction in the use of supply chains, manufacturing facilities and services centers that are located far from the end users of a particular product or service in favor of production and service locations that are located in the home market of the end user. This is not something that is unique to the 2020s. In Ancient Rome, once the chaos of the 3rd century had subsided, Rome underwent a process of localization, in which goods and services were produced and provided from locations much closer to their end users than in the economy golden age of Rome, when goods and services were sourced from all corners of the empire and beyond. 15th century China is another example, as the Ming Dynasty closed China's borders to trade and exploration, resulting in an economy that largely provided for itself. Localization also occurred more recently, as the protectionist policies that were enacted in the wake of the Great Depression resulted in larger economies such as the United States and Germany being forced to produce more goods and services in their home markets.

In recent years, a slow but steady trend towards some degree of localization has returned. Once globalization took off in the 1990s (most notably in Mexico and Central Europe) and the early 2000s (most notably in China), there was a massive amount of investment in production facilities and services centers in those emerging markets that were newly connected to the global economy. This resulted in a dramatic shift in the global manufacturing footprint, with many less competitive economies seeing a dramatic decline in their manufacturing output, while more attractive emerging markets became leading manufacturing centers almost overnight.

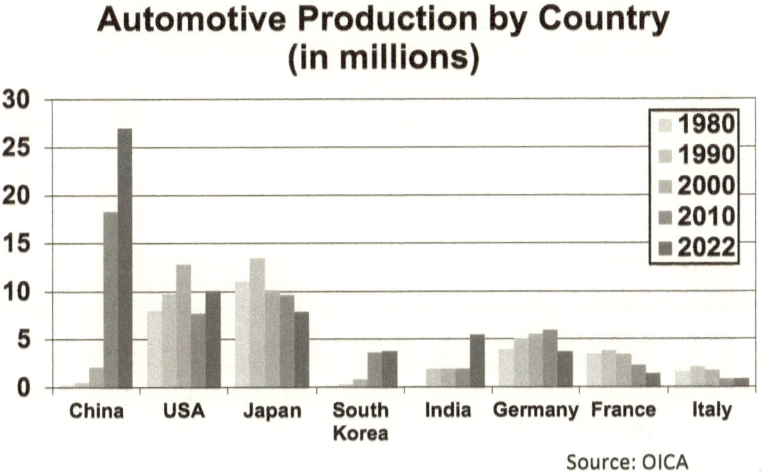

A look at the global footprint of automotive manufacturing shows the impact that globalization had on manufacturing. In 1980, China produced a total of just 509,242 motor vehicles, or just a little more than 1% of the total number of motor vehicles produced in the world that year. In 2022, China produced an astounding 27 million motor vehicles, or nearly one-third of the total number of motor vehicles produced that year. Likewise, emerging markets such as India, Mexico and Brazil also became major centers of automotive production, while smaller emerging markets became major automotive manufacturing locations for vehicles that were largely destined for wealthier markets in North America or Europe. In contrast, the total number of motor vehicles produced in traditional automotive production locations such as the United States and Germany has stagnated over the past four decades, while other long-time, but less-competitive, manufacturing locations such as Japan,

France and Italy have seen their motor vehicle numbers fall dramatically during this period.

The example of the impact of globalization upon automotive manufacturing has been repeated in most of the world's leading industries since the late 20th century. However, in recent years, we have begun to notice a change. In some industries and service sectors, particularly those where the degree of customization is higher, there has been a trend towards more investment going into manufacturing locations and service centers that are located closer to the end-user. For example, in the steel industry, following the dramatic shift to Chinese production, there has been a slow, but increasing, trend towards smaller and more specialized production facilities in markets where there is a high demand for specialized steel products. This hasn't yet shifted the bulk of steel production away from China and other emerging markets, but the seeds have been sown for a major change in the steel industry's manufacturing footprint in the future. The same holds true for many service sectors. Someone in Cleveland or Manchester who has called their computer's helpline on many occasions has certainly been on the phone a long time with workers in India, while someone in Toulouse trying to call for a new internet service has likely spoken with someone in North Africa. This is also a product of the period of globalization, as well as a testament to the incredible advancements in communications that have taken place during the Information Revolution. However, here too there is a growing demand for service centers to be located closer to the end-users of these services. While this issue has not been as emotive as that of manufacturing, it too has the potential to become something that leads to more calls for localized service provision in the future.

There are many reasons why support for localization is growing in many parts of the world. First, local manufacturing facilities and service centers allow companies to be closer to their customers. At the same time, localization can save time (and in some cases money) for businesses that bring their facilities closer to their customers, Likewise, smaller, but closer manufacturing facilities and service centers can be fine-tuned to be more in line with the demands of their customers, allowing for a more flexible product and service offering. Given the threats to trade and investment posed today by rising levels of protectionism, localization is a way to help to mitigate some of the threats of rising barriers to trade and investment. This, for example, was a major factor in the decision by Japanese automakers to move much of their production operations to the United States in recent decades. Environmentally, there has been a backlash against producing goods in far-away manufacturing locations only to ship them halfway across the world to their end markets. Finally, politicians know that bringing home manufacturing or service jobs is a major vote-winner, hence the reason why so many politicians will appear at a newly-constructed manufacturing facility or service center during an election campaign.

Like protectionism, localization appears to be a trend that is likely to stay with us for the foreseeable future. As a result, there is a real possibility that the great shift in manufacturing operations to China may be the last such shift to a single global center for manufacturing that we see in our lifetimes. Instead, it is likely that the trend towards smaller, quicker and more flexible manufacturing facilities and service centers will continue, particularly if the trend towards increasing protectionism also increases. As a result, we could be in the midst of the early days of a dramatic change that will have a major impact on many economies and industries around the world.

A Return to Regionalization?

One of the key drivers of economic growth over the past 40 years has been the increasing level of inter-connectivity among most regions of the world. In fact, the process of the latest wave of globalization began in the 1940s, when the United States used its overwhelming economic and military power to bring together most of the leading economies of that era into a series of binding economic and financial systems that led to an unprecedented surge in global trade and investment. However, this system was limited to those countries that were either under the control of the United States and its allies at the end of the war, or were closely aligned with them. Thus, only a handful of countries were able to truly benefit from this new period of globalization and realize major improvements in terms of economic growth and living standards. Three good examples of this are Japan, South Korea and Italy, none of which was among the wealthier economies of the world prior to the Second World War, but each which utilized their access to wealthier export markets to generate some of the highest long-term rates of economic growth in their history. Until the late 1980s, the globalized economy consisted primarily of North America, West Europe and parts of the Asia-Pacific region, with a large majority of the world's population living in economies that were largely disconnected from the world's other major economic centers.

That all changed with the fall of Communist governments in Central and East Europe, the ending of Communist economic policies in parts of Asia, and the fall of isolationist governments in India and other parts of the world. Soon, these dozens of economies that had been dislocated from the markets of the West and Japan were suddenly integrated into global manufacturing operations and international supply chains, and were connected with global markets. In the space of a single generation, many previously dislocated and uncompetitive economies were suddenly major manufacturing centers and found themselves among the leading growth markets for businesses and investors around the world. The impact on global economic growth was quite noticeable. While economic growth in developed economies slowed during this period of globalization (due in a small part to their loss of manufacturing investment), economic growth in emerging markets soared. In fact, between the years 2000 and 2019, emerging markets as a whole expanded by 5.6% per year, or nearly three times as fast as developed economies during that same period. The peak of globalization may have come in the years immediately after the Financial Crisis, when it was emerging markets that pulled the global economy out of a crisis that was largely started in the developed world.

Alas, economic historians may well look back at the early 2010s as the peak of globalization, as the events of recent years suggest that the pace of globalization is slowing, and this trend towards a globalized economy may even be in the process of being rolled back to some degree. In its place could be something that we have seen many times before in world history, a regional-ized, or fractured, global economy. Regionalization in the context of the global economy is when the world is divided into regional economic blocs. This could take the form of a single economy dominating all of the other economies in its region (such as the United States economy has done at various points in history in the Americas) or when a group of economies in the same region unite to offset potential threats to their region (such as the European Union).

One of the key reasons why many economists believe that we are entering into a new period of regionalization is that the United States' unipolar moment has come to an end. For many, the US' unipolar moment was the period spanning the collapse of the Soviet Union to the rise of China as a major global power, a period of around 20 to 30 years. However, in terms of global economic power, the United States has truly stood alone at the top of the economic mountain since the end of the Second World War, for while the Soviet Union may have been an ideological and military rival to the US, it was never really a threat to the United States' global economic supremacy. Now, with the dramatic increase in China's relative economic power in recent years, the US is facing a serious threat to its economic leadership for the first time in nearly a century. Thus, the US' ability to maintain a globalized economic system is waning, as, apparently, is its willingness to do so. Already, we have seen signs that some of the US' leading economic rivals are seeking to increase their influence and control over smaller economies within their respective regions.

For example, China's economic influence in Asia and adjacent regions is growing tremendously, as evidenced by China's massive investments across Asia, Africa and the Middle East, as well as by its ambitious Belt and Road Initiative. Given Asia's status as the leading center of economic output and growth in the 2020s, China's efforts to dominate the region's economy are a major threat to globalization and to the United States' position atop the global economy. In Eurasia, Russia continues to attempt to exert power and influence in its near-abroad, but Russia's economy power today is but a fraction of that of China, leaving Russia with only its vast energy resources as a means of exerting such economic influence in its region. In Europe, the European Union, if considered a single economy. is the third-largest economy in the world, behind the US and China, and it too is attempting to use its high levels of economic influence to increase its strategic autonomy and to control the economy of Europe and its surrounding regions.

If the United States' ability and willingness to defend the globalized economic system continue to wane, the chances that the global economy will break apart into regional blocs will rise accordingly. In such as system, the United States would remain the dominant economic power in the Americas, while China would increase its control over the vast Asian economy and the European Union would attempt to gain even more economic and strategic autonomy for its home region. In such as world, the United States would no longer be willing or able to guarantee the maintaining of the openness of the world's leading trading lanes, something that could result in sea lanes being closed to rival economic powers in times of conflict or unrest. Meanwhile, those regions that lay outside of these rival blocs, such as Sub-Saharan Africa or the Middle East, could become flashpoints where these rival blocs vie for influence or for access to these regions' resources or markets. Of course, the biggest threat would come from the impact that a move away from globalization and towards regionalization would have on the global economy. As history has shown us, globalization can be a major force for driving economic growth around the world. In a regionalized global economy, the growth potential for most economies, particularly the world's poorer economies, would be severely compromised. This would add to all of the other downwards pressures facing the global economy in the 21st century. However, it is uncertain whether or not most policy makers understand this threat well enough to avoid making decisions that would do lasting harm to the global economy.

The fact that these three factors (rising support for protectionism, the spread of localization and the emergence of regional economic blocs) are all occurring at the same time suggests that the outlook for global trade and investment is very uncertain indeed. In fact, each of these factors appear to be gaining momentum, with political decisions in many of the world's leading economies all driving these trends forward. For example, in the United States, the rise in the support for protectionism has driven calls for increasing localization, both from Democrats and Republicans. In Europe, similar sentiments are pushing a drive to create a strategically-independent economic bloc. In fact, in nearly all major economies, two or three of these trends are now having a major impact on economic policy making, and there is little sign that support for these policies will wane in the coming years.

History tells us that this correlation of factors spells danger for the global economy. If we go back to the example of Ancient Rome, we have seen that trade was curtailed in the empire beginning in the third century. This led to the dissolution of the empire-wide economy into one that was based on local production. At times, the empire even broke into rival regional economies, and even when the empire was reunified under Diocletian and Constantine, it never managed to fully put back the integrated empire-wide economy that made Rome so powerful in the first place. The 1930s are another example of how the coming together of these three factors can cause massive damage to the global economy. Protectionism flourished in the post-Wall-Street-Crash world, especially in the United States, which had been the leading driver of global economic growth in the decades prior to the Great Depression. As a result of the precipitous fall in consumer and business demand in the 1930s and the rise of new trade barriers during that period, global trade collapsed. This led to a new round of localization, as the barriers to trade and the high levels of risk associated with the global economy of the 1930s resulted in many manufacturers choosing to build their products in their home markets. As the 1930s progressed, regional economic blocs were strengthened, with rival blocs emerging around a host of economies, including the British Empire, Germany, the Soviet Union, Japan and others. With global trade and investment severely damaged by the Great Depression and the policies put in place in its wake, the global economy suffered even greater losses than it would have incurred had political and economic leaders reacted in a different manner. Unfortunately, too few of today's political and economic leaders appear to be heeding the lessons of Ancient Rome and the 1930s. Instead, protectionism, localization and regionalization all appear to be gaining momentum.

Chapter Twelve

THE DECLINE OF TRADE AND INVESTMENT

THERE IS LITTLE DOUBT that, in such an inter-connected globalized economy, a long-term decline in trade and investment growth, if not an outright decline its overall trade and investment, will have an impact on all countries, states and cities, although the impact on different types of economies is likely to be quite different from one another. To explain what the impact of such a development would be, I have decided to look at three different types of economies and attempt to explain how each of them will be impacted by such a long-term change. I have divided these different types of economies into three groups:

- Developed economies
- Fast-growing economies
- Low-income emerging markets

DEVELOPED ECONOMIES

Let's start with the world's developed economies. As we have discussed already, the rich world has seen economic growth slow steadily in recent decades, with the average rate of economic growth in developed economies over the past 20 years being less than half of that from the 1950s to the late 1970s. Demographics have played a major role in this decline, as slower population growth has led to labor shortages and a slowdown in domestic consumer demand in most developed economies. With birth rates continuing to trend downwards and with resistance to mass immigration rising in most developed economies, this demographic situation is not going to improve anytime soon. A good example of this is Japan, where decades of low birth rates and little immigration has left what had been the world's most dynamic large economy as one that has become a byword for stagnation and decline.

As a result of these demographic changes, most developed economies today are more dependent upon exports to generate economic growth than ever before. An increasing share of these exports from developed economies are going to either those developed economies that are still generating higher rates of demand growth (such as the United States or Australia) or even more so to fast-growing emerging markets such as China or India. However, in many of these fast-growing emerging markets, population growth is also slowing, such as in China, where the country's working-age population is peaking as I write this book. This is bad news not only for exporters to those markets, but to companies based in those markets, as their own domestic demand growth is set to slow substantially as well. With the growth in the number of consumers in most of the world's leading economies set to slow further in the coming decades, generating growth in domestic markets will become harder and harder, leaving more and more countries, industries and businesses increasingly reliant upon exports to generate growth. Ask business leaders in countries such as Italy or Japan how easy it is to generate growth in their shrinking domestic markets and they will tell you just how crucial access to growing export markets is for their businesses' futures.

While the outlook for domestic markets in the developed world looking increasingly concerning, a decline in international trade and investment would also have a major impact on other aspects of their economies. Take labor, for example. If trade and investment growth remain anemic or turns into long-term decline, it is likely that more production of goods and provision of services will return from outsourcing locations in emerging markets back to developed countries. In some cases, this would result in more jobs returning home. However, with labor shortages looming as a long-term threat to most developed economies, this is more likely to lead to automated factories and service centers springing up across developed countries, particularly those where the outlook for domestic market growth remains a little brighter. As production and service operations return to developed countries, and as labor becomes tighter, labor costs would then rise accordingly. This would lead to rising wages, a positive development, but could fuel inflationary pressures if wages rose too much, as we witnessed in 2021 and 2022. Such a development would likely be welcomed initially, but whether or not it would be enough to offset slower export growth is very uncertain.

FAST-GROWING ECONOMIES

Without a doubt, the biggest winners during the age of globalization have been those emerging markets that have taken advantage of their access to the world's leading export markets. In fact, almost without exception, the fastest-growing economies of the past few decades have been those emerging markets that have been able to develop into export-oriented manufacturing centers. This includes some of the world's most successful countries in recent years, including China, Vietnam, Turkey and others. Another group of countries that have benefitted tremendously from the process of globalization have been those that have become specialized economic centers. This could include financial hubs, tax havens and regional investment centers. Examples of such economies include Singapore, the United Arab Emirates and Ireland. Here, the ability to attract huge amounts of foreign investment on a per capita basis has been the key to their success, as they often combine huge inflows for foreign money with a relatively small domestic population, allowing for these countries to grow very wealthy in the process. Another group of economies that has benefitted tremendously from globalization are those countries that have gained unique access to wealthy export markets, and taken advantage of this access. For example, Central European economies have grown rapidly since they have been able to trade freely with wealthier economies in West Europe. In contrast, Mexico has, to a degree, squandered much of its unique access to the vast North American market. For these economies, an elimination of regional trade barriers has been the key to their economic growth in recent decades.

At the same, those countries that have developed the infrastructure needed to attract investment and to support exporting operations put themselves in a position to take advantage of the opening of global markets during this recent era of globalization. At the same time, those governments that made it easy for businesses and investors to operate in their countries also reaped the benefits of globalization.

For the past few decades, these economies have made great strides in terms of generating higher levels of wealth and improve their populations' living standards by taking advantage of the unique opportunity that globalization presented them. However, for some of them, the rising threats to trade and investment that are becoming more evident is a serious threat to their economic futures, for while many of them have indeed made great strides, they still have a long way to go to becoming fully-developed economies. For example, for many countries in regions such as Southeast Asia or Central Europe, there is a significant threat that the trade and investment that they rely so heavily upon will slow substantially in the coming years, dramatically reducing their ability to generate economic growth. This could leave many countries stuck in a middle-income limbo in which they find it increasingly harder to achieve developed economic status. For their forebears, such as Japan and South Korea, they had access to wealthy export markets to become wealthy themselves. For countries hoping to emulate their success today, there might not be enough time to achieve the status that countries such as Japan and South Korea were able to reach, as access to wealthier markets might be more limited than in previous decades.

If growth prospects for those economies that have been generating much of the world's economic growth in recent years were to evaporate, the consequences would be dire. For example, if the populations of these once-fast-growing economies found themselves unable to achieve their hopes of landing high-paying jobs or of achieving a certain level of wealth or a certain type of lifestyle, popular anger in many of these countries could rise. Just look at where many of the worst protests have taken place around the world in recent years. They have often been in countries or cities where economic growth has been disappointing for a prolonged period of time. At the same time, those countries that were aspiring to further close the wealth gap with their richer counterparts would find that this goal was increasingly difficult to attain. This is something that we have seen in Latin America in recent decades, as that region has actually lost ground in terms of closing the wealth gap with the developed world instead of closing this gap as that region's population had expected. When economic aspirations are not met, popular anger is likely to follow, and this is a major concern for the world as it looks at its economic prospects in the years ahead.

POOR COUNTRIES

While a long-term decline in global trade and investment would have major impacts on the world's wealthiest and fastest-growing economies, not to mention its middle-income economies, it would be the world's poorest countries that would suffer the worst consequences of such a change. Many of these poor countries have some of the world's fastest-growing populations, in contrast to much of the rest of these world, and this raises the stakes on the ability of these countries to generate enough economic growth in the coming years to meet the needs of their expanding populations. There are many examples of poor countries that need trade and investment to improve their long-term economic prospects. For example, in South Asia, poor countries such as Pakistan and Bangladesh, not to mention large areas of India, have huge populations that require economic growth to reduce poverty levels and improve standards of living.

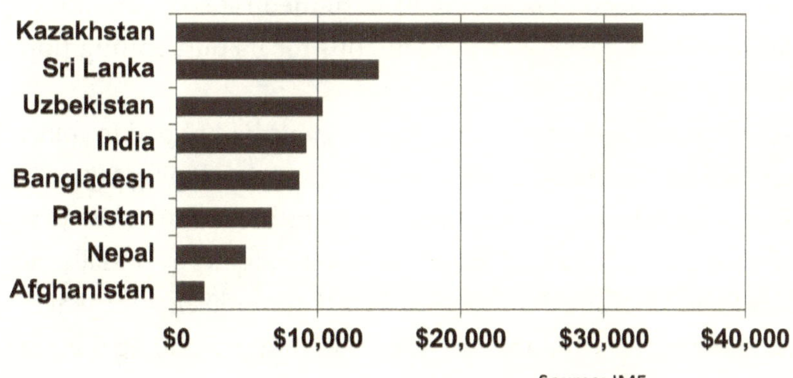

Central America is another region where poverty is widespread and so far, for much of that region, economic growth has not been high enough to significantly reduce poverty in that region. At the same time, this is a region that relies heavily upon exports to North America, as well as investment from that region, to generate much of its economic growth.

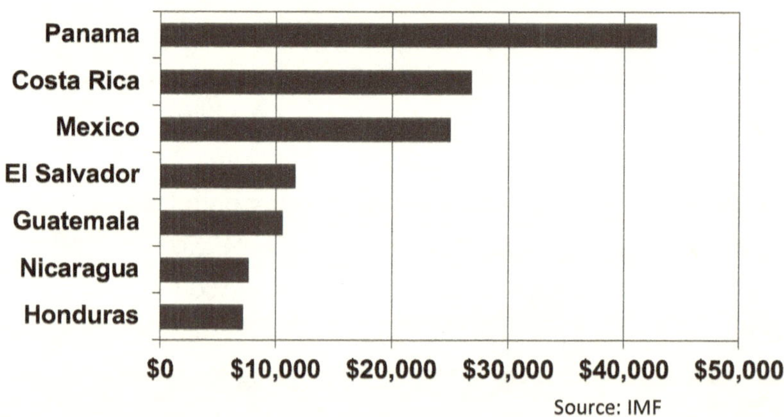

Perhaps the region that best illustrates the developing world's need for trade and investment to help improve its economic prospects is Sub-Saharan Africa. With a population of 1.2 billion that will expand to a whopping 2.2 billion by the middle of the 21st century, no region in the world is more in need of boosting its sustained rates of economic growth in order to reduce poverty and create jobs for its burgeoning population than Sub-Saharan Africa.

Each of these three aforementioned regions had hoped to follow in the footsteps of East Asia and Central Europe by first developing export-oriented manufacturing industries to generate wealth and economic growth, a process that they hoped would raise domestic wealth levels and eventually help these countries to build strong domestic markets that would enable them to reduce their need for exports and foreign investment, thus reducing their exposure to external threats and shocks.

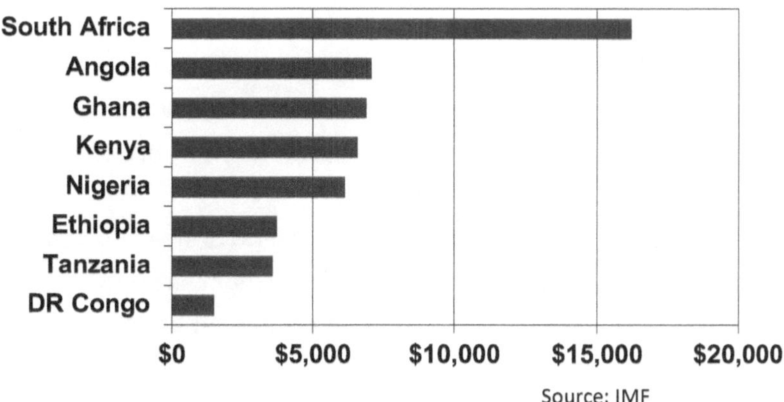

For these countries, globalization is perhaps a once-in-a-lifetime oppor-tunity, as it has allowed those fortunate emerging markets that have benefitted from their unique access to wealthy export markets to develop manufacturing industries or offshore service sectors. As countries such as China and Poland become too expensive for some manufacturing and service operations, poorer countries have been hoping to be next in line for the foreign investment that once went to such countries for these cost-sensitive operations. However, some of the trends that we have discussed, such as protectionism, automation and localization, are jeopardizing the poorest countries' chances of following in the footsteps of South Korea, China, Hungary and others. Instead, should these trends continue to reduce trade and investment levels in the coming years, these aspirations may never be realized.

Without foreign investment or access to key export markets, the outlook for the world's poorest countries is indeed grim. In fact, it is hard to see how many of the world's poorest emerging markets would be able to generate economic growth that is higher than their population growth without these opportunities. For example, foreign investment in manufacturing operations or service centers is often among the leading sources of jobs in emerging mar-kets, so a lack of such investment and trade would jeopardize these countries' ability to create jobs at a time when their working-age populations are soaring.

At the same time, trade and investment is a leading source of wealth creation for many of the world's poorest countries, so the potential for these countries to generate the levels of wealth they need to boost domestic market demand will be reduced if trade and investment levels are disappointing in the coming years. Without a domestic market explosion, as we have seen in East Asia and Central Europe, the world's poorest emerging markets will be exposed to all sorts of economic risks that will lead to higher levels of economic volatility and quite likely, even higher levels of poverty.

If trade and investment levels continue to trend downwards, as they have done for the past decade, there will be very few beneficiaries in any economic segment. Most economies and industries will suffer either declines in growth, or outright declines in output, should trade and investment levels fail to return to growth. In fact, only a handful of countries will be in a position to generate significant growth should the world realize a decline in long-term trade and investment. For example, countries with large, expanding and wealthy domestic markets will be in a better position to generate economic growth than countries with small, declining and poor domestic markets. For example, the United States, thanks to its huge domestic market and high levels of disposable income, is less exposed to the impact of falling trade and investment levels than just about any other economy in the world. At the same time, if the European Union can keep its single market together over the long-term, European countries too will have access to a large and wealthy market. Finally, those countries that have high levels of domestically-generated wealth will also be less exposed to declines in global trade and investment. China is a good example of this, as Chinese firms focusing on the Chinese market have been able to generate immense amounts of wealth in recent years thanks to the incredible increase in wealth levels in that country.

Unfortunately, there will be far more losers than winners if global trade and investment continues to decline over the long-term. In fact, we have already seen just how large of an impact that falling trade and investment levels can have on weaker economies or industries. A good example of this is Latin America, which despite all of the promise of its giant domestic market, remains heavily exposed to rises and falls in global trade and investment.

Overall, it will be countries that are dependent upon exports to generate a large share of their economic growth that will be most exposed to the risk of falling trade and investment levels. Likewise, those countries that cannot generate high levels of investment domestically, or are dominated by industries where the investment decision- making process is outside of their borders, will also find themselves increasingly at risk. As we have seen, there are far too many of these countries around the world, and each of them will find themselves struggling to generate economic growth in the coming years should trade and investment levels continue to fall.

IS A DECLINE IN TRADE AND INVESTMENT INEVITABLE?

Of all of the negative factors that threaten to reduce long-term growth prospects for the global economy, a long-term decline in international trade and investment seems to be the one that is the easiest to avoid, as unlike demographic and productivity changes, this is the one factor that political and economic policy-makers can directly control, or at least greatly influence. The lessons of the past should serve as a warning to those policy-makers that are advocating for a reduction in global trade and investment in favor of protectionist measures aimed at the localization of a country's or a region's economy. The collapse of the Roman Empire's extensive network of trade and investment led directly to that empire's collapse and to more than a thousand years of economic decline and backwardness for much of the remnants of the empire. In more recent times, it is clear to economic historians today that the protectionist measures enacted in the early 1930s were a direct reason why the Great Depression was the greatest economic crisis of the past 100 years. Meanwhile, the decision by the Soviet Union, Maoist China and post-independence India to isolate and protect their economies from foreign trade and investment directly led to these economies falling far behind the integrated economies of North America, West Europe and East Asia in the decades following the Second World War.

These historical long-term declines in trade and investment were driven by a number of factors. For example, protectionism was the dominant theme of those eras, either in the form of governments wanting to shut themselves off from potential threats to their grip on power, or of populations wanting to protect local jobs and industries from perceived threats emanating from beyond their borders. Another factor was the collapse of political and economic stability in these societies. For trade and investment to grow, a good deal of confidence is required, but this confidence is hard to find when there are high degrees of instability and chaos. Political extremism is another factor that has contributed to historical long-term declines in trade and investment. Right-wing nationalism and left-wing protectionism have both played major roles in bringing an end to periods of trade and investment growth. Finally, technological or workplace disruptions have led to major dislocations within job markets in the past, and these disruptions have often led to policies that were damaging to trade and investment.

In most cases, a prolonged downturn in global trade and investment has had terrible consequences for political and economic stability. For Ancient Rome, we've already seen how the collapse of the empire's intricate system of trade and investment led to the long-term economic ruin of much of the former Roman world. For the post-Great-Depression collapse in trade and investment, one of the worst consequences was the dramatic increase in political volatility that led directly to the most devastating war in human history. For those individual countries that experienced long-term declines in trade and investment in recent decades, the result was a lack of economic progress that led to a decline in relative living standards.

Unfortunately, there are many parallels to these times of declining trade and investment that can be found in the modern world. For example, the increasing degree of political fragmentation around the world, both in terms of the world as a whole as well as within individual countries and regions, is something that contributed mightily to the declines in trade and investment in the past and is something that is once again present in much of the world. At the same time, the top-down and bottom-up demands for protectionist policies that we have seen in the past are once again present in many of the leading economic centers of the world today. The threats to the trade and infrastructure that also emerged in times of economic crisis in the past are also becoming more apparent in the modern world, both in terms of the protection of vital trade routes to the regulatory frameworks that govern trade and investment. Finally, massive disruptions to the job markets of many leading economies, such as the switch to service-based jobs in the developed world to the lack of wage growth in many countries, were key factors in boosting support for protectionism in the past and are once again present in many parts of the world.

A WORLD PULLED IN TWO DIRECTIONS

Despite all of the factors that have led to a serious backlash against globalization in many parts of the world, the fact is that globalization remains a very powerful force in the world today. For some economies, globalization has left them dependent upon access to export markets and foreign investment, leaving them with little choice but to continue supporting the maintenance of the globalized economy of the 21st century. For example, countries such as South Korea and the Netherlands are more dependent upon access to larger export markets than ever before and can only maintain economic growth if this access remains in place, while at the same time they are able to maintain their current high levels of export competitiveness. Likewise, many economic centers have thrived thanks for foreign investment, including leading hubs of economic activity such as London and Hong Kong. They too need to be able to continue to attract high levels of foreign investment if they hope to remain within the top tier of global economic centers. In fact, the world today is more connected than it has ever been, and this fact alone means that globalization will remain a potent force in the future. Communications from one corner of the world to another are instantaneous, enabling information, perhaps the most valuable resource in the modern economy, to flow around the world faster than ever. Travel too is faster and more extensive than ever, even after the impact of the Covid-19 pandemic and the growing backlash against the environmental impact of international travel. Supply chains too are spread more widely around the world than ever before, inter-connecting manufacturing and logistics hubs around the world and making any rollback of globalization a costly and painful affair. This has been seen in the supply chain disruptions that caused chaos for many industries in recent years. Finally, most of the world's leading companies are now more dependent upon exporting outside of their home markets to generate growth than they have ever been, making it imperative for most many companies to support the continuation of the globalized marketplace.

The beneficiaries of the process of globalization are many. For example, poor countries have found the opportunity to become rich by exporting to wealthy markets or attracting large amounts of foreign investment. Just look at how exports allowed South Korea to move from the Third World to the First World in the span of just two generations, or how Dubai rose from a backwater port to the leading economic hub in the Middle East in roughly the same period of time. It is not just the poor that have benefitted from globalization. For example, rich countries that have domestic markets that are stagnant or shrinking have been able to remain rich by exporting outside of their borders, or by attracting high levels of foreign investment. Germany's recent economic success has largely been based on its ability to export outside of a stagnant European market, while Singapore's ability to attract incredibly high levels of foreign investment on a per capita basis has made it one of the wealthiest countries in the world. Many businesses and industries have also benefitted from globalization. Small businesses have found it easier to become large businesses thanks to their access to both markets and investment all around the world. Large businesses have been able to extend their global footprint, both in terms of markets as well as production locations. Investors have more opportunities to generate growth than ever before thanks to their access to investment markets in nearly all parts of the world. Consumers have more choice than ever, thanks to goods and services from all around the world now being available to them. Consumers also have been able to save increasing amounts of money as the globalization of production and service locations has generally led to lower prices for most goods and services in recent decades.

While there are many beneficiaries from the globalization of the global economy, there are also some who have been left behind by this process, and it is primarily these segments that have rebelled against the globalized world and have sought to turn back the clock to a time when barriers to trade and investment were far more extensive than today. Sometimes, it has been entire countries that have been left behind. For those countries that have lost out in terms of their ability to export goods and services around the world, or to attract foreign investment, globalization has often resulted in low rates of economic growth, low levels of poverty reduction, and a failure to reduce gaps in wealth and living standards with the world's more competitive economies.

The economic troubles of Southern Europe and Latin America in recent years is directly linked to their relatively low levels of economic competitiveness, a weakness that was largely hidden until globalization forced these regions to compete for export markets and foreign investment with regions that had a higher level of export competitiveness, such as East Asia. It was not just countries or regions that were left behind. Sometimes, it was groups of individuals. For example, lower-skilled or less-flexible workers in developed economies, particularly those with lower degrees of protectionism, have been brutally exposed to the effects of globalization as entire segments of the work force in some countries have seen their operations moved to new locations. The decline of the steel industry in the United States is just one of the many examples around the world of entire sectors of employment that have largely been wiped out by globalization.

In the wake of the impact of the Global Financial Crisis, an increasing number of countries, industries and individuals had found themselves being left behind by the spread of globalization. Since that crisis, opposition to globalization has intensified, driven by rising support from those groups that have suffered the greatest losses. The Tea Party Movement and the election of Donald Trump in the United States in 2016 are examples of this increasing support for policies aimed at rolling back globalization, as are the rise of far-right and far-left parties and the process of Brexit that have taken place in Europe since the Financial Crisis in 2008 and 2009. With another massive economic crisis having recently taken place, this time the result of the Covid-19 pandemic, it is all too likely that opposition to globalization will rise even further in the coming years, as more and more countries, industries and individuals find it harder to find their role in the global economy of the modern world.

THE US AND CHINA WILL DECIDE THE FATE OF GLOBALIZATION

As the two superpowers of the 21st century, the United States and China will decide the fate of this era of globalization. Not only are the United States and China the two superpowers of today, but it appears likely that they will remain the world's two most powerful actors for the foreseeable future thanks to their immense power that is measured in terms of their economic size, the power of their armed forces, their vast populations, their huge landmasses and their leadership in most high-tech industries. The question is, will the two superpowers decide to work together to revive globalization, or will they continue to engage in an escalating trade war, resulting in the world's two dominant powers actively seeking to undermine the other. Should the latter become reality, the likely outcome would be higher levels of protectionism and an increasing fragmentation of the global economy, a process known as decoupling.

It is easy to forget that it was the United States that initially pushed for China's integration into the global economy. Early on, the US' primary interest was turning China against its erstwhile Communist ally, the Soviet Union, in the early 1970s. Eventually, as the Soviet Union faded as a threat to US global leadership, businesses and investors in the US and elsewhere turned their attention to the vast untapped market in China, both in terms of potential consumers as well as potential workers. In fact, US-based manufacturers were among the first major investors in China, helping to plant the seeds of what would become the world's most prolific manufacturing powerhouse. The United States' final push for China's entry into the global economy was the decision by the Clinton and Bush Administrations in 2000 and 2001 to support China's entry into the World Trade Organization (WTO) and to grant China permanent normal trading relations (PNTR) a short time later. Without US support for China's integration into the global economy, China's economic miracle might never have come to fruition.

Now, as China is no longer viewed as just a source of potential consumers and laborers, but as an economic superpower that is challenging US supremacy on many fronts, the United States has turned against the country that it once supported. This about-face is the result of a number of factors, including the hollowing out of the US' manufacturing sector and the loss of manufacturing jobs across the US. In addition, China's membership in the WTO and its favored trading relationship with the United States failed to stop China from bending many of the rules concerning intellectual property and a host of other subjects that have bedeviled US-Chinese relations ever since. Furthermore, one of the key strengths of the United States' economy has been its dominant position in many of the fastest-growing sectors of the global economy, such as information technology and online retail. However, competitors to the US firms that dominate these industries have emerged from China in recent years, threatening to reduce one of the United States' most important competitive advantages vis-à-vis other major economies. In fact, there is a full-blown technological Cold War that is brewing between the United States and China, one that threatens to bring an end to the era of globalization that was championed by the US, and allowed China to become the economic superpower that it is today.

The relationship between the United States and China will go a long way towards defining the shape of the world in the 21ˢᵗ century. While other powers have ambitions of their own, it appears likely that the overall power possessed by the US and China will continue to far outstrip that of any other potential rival. As a result, a duopoly, sometimes referred to as the G2, is emerging. However, will this duopoly cooperate in the fields of economics, trade and investment, or will they divide the world into rival economic blocs. At the same time, will the emerging political and security rivalry between the United States and China lead to a more dangerous breakdown in international cooperation, one that leads to a more dangerous form of Cold War. Whichever future emerges, it is clear that the relationship between the United States and China will be the key issue facing the world economy and the geopolitical balance of power in the 21ˢᵗ century.

HIGH STAKES FOR THE GLOBAL ECONOMY

So much is at stake for the global economy with regards to the decisions of economic policy-makers in the coming years. As we have seen, international trade and investment can be a major driver of economic growth and has played a key role in what we now consider to be many of the economic "golden ages" that are scattered throughout history. Moreover, it is clear that trade and investment is a much-needed component for generating additional economic growth in the future. A look back at our recent history confirms this. While population and productivity growth has continued to slow in most of the world's leading economic centers in the first part of the 21ˢᵗ century, the global economy has managed to record higher rates of economic growth than in most previous decades. This was due, in large part, to the increase in trade and investment that occurred during this period, particularly in the early years of the 21st century.

As this book is attempting to show, so many of the systems that we take for granted in the modern world are dependent upon continuous long-term economic growth to keep them functioning. A range of government spending programs, from the armed forces to social security, are dependent upon ever-rising government revenues that can only be generated if the global economy continues to grow. Therefore, any policies that threaten to reduce long-term economic growth are highly dangerous to the future of the global economy and to the stability of the world. Protectionism, in many cases, is just such a policy. We have seen how protectionist policies in the past have either triggered an economic crisis or made a crisis much worse. These examples should serve as a warning to the economic policy-makers of today that pandering to the public's demands for protection against perceived external threats is bad news for both the economy as a whole as well as the livelihoods of many of those who are calling for these protectionist measures to be enacted in the first place. Unfortunately, it appears that many of these lessons have been forgotten, as the world potentially stumbles towards a new round of widespread protectionism.

Chapter Thirteen

THE NEED FOR PRODUCTIVITY GROWTH

WE ARE NOW GOING to turn our attention to the impact that productivity growth has on the performance of an economy and, as always, we are going to begin by looking at the history of productivity growth and how it has impacted some of the most successful economies in world history. Productivity is important, because as the American economist Robert Solow and others have discovered in their research, there is a strong case for the argument that no single factor has had a greater role in improving living standards than productivity growth. Of course, we are going to start by looking at productivity growth in Ancient Rome. You are probably assuming by now that I have a particular affinity for Ancient Rome and, if you did, you would be right. In fact, much of my research has been focused on the decline and fall of the Roman Empire and the factors that played a role in the eventual collapse of what was the ancient world's most powerful state, attempting to determine if and when some of these factors are applicable to the modern world.

If we try to look back at the world before Roman times, it is safe to say that accurately measuring productivity is an extremely difficult task. Of course, there were some obvious advancements that certainly led to dramatic improvements in productivity at different points in pre-Roman history. For example, the invention of the wheel led to dramatic advancements in productivity in much of the world (although not in the Western Hemisphere as the wheel in that part of the world was not used for transportation until the arrival of the Europeans at the end of the 15th century). However, these major advancements were generally spread out over a long period of time and, as states and other collective units in the pre-Roman era were generally fragile and unstable, hardly the environment conducive for a long period of sustained productivity growth. As a result, in the centuries before the rise of Rome, productivity growth, when measured on a yearly basis, would have been remarkable slow, with many periods in which productivity declined. For most of the world, subsistence economies were the norm, and these types of economies rarely generate high levels of productivity growth.

The emergence of the vast Roman Empire was a game-changer when it comes to fostering a prolonged period of relatively high levels of productivity growth. In fact, it was the nature of the Roman Empire, including its size, its centralization and its diversity, that led to the productivity explosion that took place during this era. For example, the expansive transport infrastructure that was developed over the course of Roman history was one of the most important reasons why productivity growth was able to rise so high for so long in the empire. The ability to transport goods, labor and resources throughout the empire safely and swiftly was something the world had not experienced up to that point and this allowed Roman productivity to rise to much higher levels than that of any other major state in the world up to that point. Another unique factor that allowed Roman productivity levels to rise so high was the fact that the empire fostered economic specialization, with different regions specializing in different aspects of the Roman economy. In this way, those regions with the highest agricultural productivity could specialize on agriculture, while those regions that were specialized in metal working could do the same. This reduced the need to focus much of a region's productive efforts on subsistence activities. Finally, the massive size of the Roman Empire (it had a population of around 60 million people at its peak in the 2nd century) allowed for significant economies-of-scale to be created, with mass production taking place at a scale never seen before in the western world. For many regions of the empire, productivity growth levels would remain high until the late 2nd

Century CE, when Rome began to be hit by a series of setbacks from which it would never fully recover. However, while stability reigned across much of the Roman Empire, it was able to achieve levels of productivity that had not been seen up to that point anywhere in the world, with the possible exception of during the Han Dynasty in China.

As we have discussed, the stability of the Roman Empire began to lessen towards the end of the 2nd Century CE, and this led to the near-collapse of the empire on a number of occasions in the 3rd Century CE. The demographic decline of the empire that followed the Antonine Plague that raged from 165 CE to 180 CE led to major disruptions to the empire's work force, while reducing the size of the Roman internal market (as well as that of many of Rome's external trading partners). Later, as the empire began to be split into rival statelets, the infrastructure network that was so instrumental in boosting Roman productivity levels began to crumble and become dislocated. This resulted in a collapse in internal and external trade, bringing an end to the benefits provided by economic specialization and mass production, with subsistence economies taking their place for much of the rest of the empire's existence. In the end, all of these developments made Rome dramatically poorer, and even when the empire was reunited in the late 3rd Century and the early 4th Century, its economic power was but a mere shadow of what it had once been, replaced by a highly militaristic society riven by religious conflict and threatened by increasingly emboldened forces from outside of the empire's borders. However, while its stability lasted, Rome was able to achieve levels of economic productivity that had not been seen before, and would not be seen again in the West for 1,500 years.

Of course, perhaps the most important period of productivity increases took place during the Industrial Revolution. To understand just how great the productivity increases were during this period, particularly during its early decades, it is instructive to look back at the state of the economy of England and the United Kingdom in the period before the Industrial Revolution. Prior to the Industrial Revolution, England's economy was dominated by agriculture, and while agriculture's share of the English economy was declining in the 1600s and 1700s, it was the service sector, not the industrial sector, that was making most of the gains, with the service sector estimated to be nearly as large as the industrial sector in England at the onset of the Industrial Revolution. In fact, most industrial activities in England and the rest of the United Kingdom were on a very small scale in the 1600s and 1700s, as the UK lacked a large domestic market. However, things were about to undergo a dramatic change.

There are many theories as to why the Industrial Revolution began in the United Kingdom and not in other places such as China or France. One good reason is that the rule of law was strengthened dramatically in England and the United Kingdom over the preceding centuries, and by the second half of the 18th century, the rule of law was firmly established in that country. This led to a greater share of the UK's population being involved in economic and technological decision-making than almost anywhere else in the world at that point in time, while confidence was fostered among the wider population due to strong property rights and the lack of concern over the arbitrary rule of the ruling classes of that period. This led to higher levels of risk-taking, something that we see time and again as a major factor in successful economies. In contrast, the lack of risk-taking too often leads to stagnation and decline for those economies where confidence levels are too low. In Britain, the combination of the rule of law, property rights, dispersed decision-making and what would become a legally-binding patent system all combined to provide fertile ground for technological and process-related breakthroughs, in this case, the Industrial Revolution. These lessons are applicable today, for it is those countries that have systems and norms in place that foster confidence among economic and technological decision-makers that are the ones that are making the technological and process breakthroughs in the modern world.

Over several decades, Britain would go from being a relatively unremarkable economy among many European economies, to becoming the most dynamic and wealthy economy in the world.

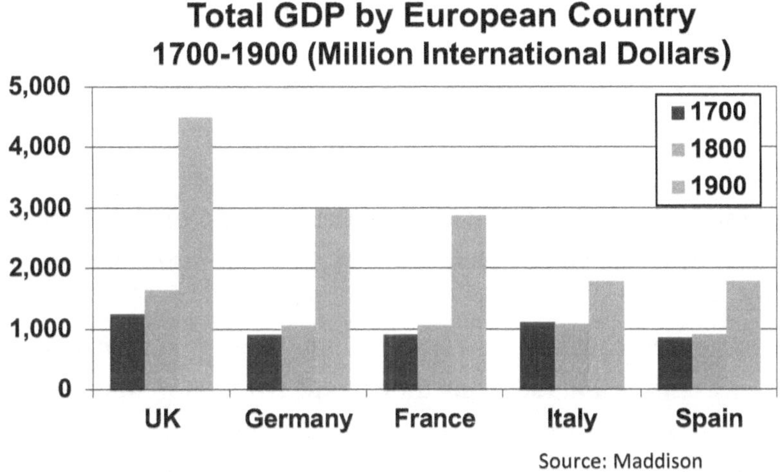

As the United Kingdom industrialized, productivity levels soared to rare heights as the country's economy was no longer constrained by the limitations of human-, animal- or water-generated power. As the UK was the first country in the world to industrialize, it enjoyed a significant first-mover advantage that would persist for a few decades until rivals such as the United States and parts of Germany rose to rival the UK as fully-industrialized economies. The results were clear. Despite its relatively small population, the United Kingdom's total economic output was higher than all other countries or territories apart from China and India for much of the 1800s, at least until the United States overtook it in terms of economic output in the 1870s. At the same time, the United Kingdom's level of per capita GDP was the highest in the world for much of the 19th century, as once industrialization took hold, GDP growth began to outstrip what was at the time a rather high rate of population growth in the UK, allowing per capita GDP levels to really begin to take off in the second half of the century.

Of course, the Industrial Revolution, like all such advancements, did not remain confined to the United Kingdom. In the first decades of the 19th century, industrial production spread to northwestern Europe, and a little later, to North America. In the following decades, major European rivals such as France and what is now Germany also industrialized at a rapid pace, while industrialization was eventually proven not to be just a western phenomenon when Japan industrialized in the second half of the 19th century in the wake of the Meiji Restoration. Over the past century, industrialization has spread to many other areas of the world, most notably East Asia, which is now the hub of many the world's industrial sectors. Wherever it went, industrialization led to an initial burst of productivity growth as economies were unshackled from the restraints that had held them back for as long as anyone could remember, and it was all thanks to a relatively small island off of the northwestern coast of Europe.

Another period that saw tremendous productivity growth in many parts of the world was the period following the Second World War. Many economists have alleged that it was the war itself that led to these higher rates of productivity growth, but the evidence for this is not entirely there. We know that, during the early 1930s, as the Great Depression ravaged the global economy, productivity rates plummeted.

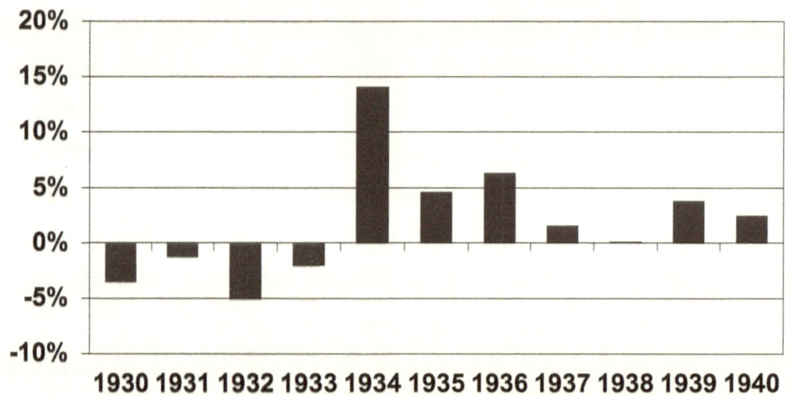

Source: Kendrick, 1961

However, productivity growth returned in a big way in the mid-1930s, and this growth continued right up until the Second World War. However, during the war years, and in the years immediately after the war, productivity growth in the United States and most other major economies stagnated. In the US, productivity growth between 1941 and 1948 averaged just 1.8% per year, hardly a war-time boom. The situation was even worse in countries that suffered massive materiel and manpower devastation during the war, and the dislocations caused by the damage to these countries' economic infrastructure and their labor forces led to dramatic declines in productivity.

However, the period from 1948 until the oil shock of 1973 would see some of the highest rates of productivity growth in the modern world. In Europe and Japan, two regions whose economies were devastated by the conflict, it was a surge in productivity growth that took hold in the 1950s that led to what became known as economic miracles in both regions. It is important to remember just how costly the Second World War was to countries such as Germany and Japan. Both countries' labor forces had been shrunken dramatically by the massive number of lives lost during the war, particularly among young men who normally would have just been entering the work force during the early 1940s. At the same time, the devastation wrought upon nearly all of the leading economic centers of Germany and Japan was on a scale that the world had never seen before. The entire economic and transport infrastructure of regions, cities and towns had been completely obliterated, and the clean-up and rebuilding operations would often last more than a decade in some of the worst-impacted areas of those countries. However, once the labor force started to grow again, and once a new economic infrastructure was established, productivity growth would soar even higher in countries such as Germany and Japan than in many of the countries that had been impacted far less by the devastation of World War Two.

There are many theories as to why productivity growth soared in the decades between the Second World War and the oil shocks of the 1970s. One idea is that the complete devastation caused by the war to many leading economic hubs allowed for a much more modern and productive economic infrastructure to be built from the ground up. This allowed countries that were in a position to build an entirely new economic infrastructure to gain a major strategic advantage over countries such as the United States and the United Kingdom, where much of the pre-war economic infrastructure remained in place. Another theory is that the incredible scale of the capital investments that were made in the post-war period was the leading driver of this productivity growth, with such capital investments having rarely been seen since. This is supported by the fact that much of China's growth in recent decades has also been the result of massive capital expenditures, along the lines of what many leading economies did in the post-war era. Finally, another school of thought is that many of the world's leading economic powers were forced to turn their attention away from their geopolitical ambitions due to their defeat (or their relative weakness compared to the US and the USSR) and to focus almost all of their energies on their economic ambitions, Certainly countries such as Germany and Japan were forced to dramatically reduce their military expenditures by the victorious powers in the Second World War, and these countries transferred this spending from their country's armed forces to areas that were designed to benefit their countries' economies, such as capital investments, transport infrastructure and education.

This post-war productivity boom lasted for around 25 years in the West, a relatively long time by the standards of productivity trends. In Europe, the end of the productivity boom in the 1970s would leave the region exposed to its worsening demographic situation, its lack of natural resources and to foreign competition that would emerge in the following decades. Japan's productivity boom would continue a little while longer, stretching into the 1980s, but it too would end, with productivity growth rates remaining relatively low in Japan ever since. Of course, this post-war productivity boom did not happen in a bubble. In was aided and abetted by the opening of key export markets, most notably the United States, as well as by a "baby boom" that took place in the years after the Second World War. Nevertheless, without the significant increase in productivity growth in the West and in Japan during this period, the high rates of economic growth that were recorded during this period would not have been possible.

These three historical examples of societies whose economies benefitted greatly from lengthy periods of productivity growth all had a number of traits in common that influenced their productivity levels. Perhaps most importantly, each of these three examples were societies where significant technological advancements were either made, or where earlier technological advancements were harnessed so that they could drive economic growth. For example, Ancient Rome was able to develop a series of technological advancements related to construction and engineering that allowed for the creation of the Roman Empire's famous road system, its vast building projects and its lengthy system of aqueducts. In Industrial Revolution-era Britain, massive technological advancements were made, including the use of steam power and the development of new types of metallurgy. Again, these technological advancements were directly responsible for driving productivity growth in the United Kingdom and later for more areas of Europe, as well as North America. Finally, the period directly after the Second World War was also one of great technological advancements, including the use of computers, changes in communications and many more, most of which also had a hand in driving the productivity growth that was recorded in the decades after the Second World War.

While these technological advancements played a massive role in driving productivity growth during their eras, there were many other factors that were found in each of these periods. One such factor was specialization. During the Roman period, the Industrial Revolution and in post-war Europe and Japan, economic specialization was allowed to spread and flourish. This allowed for cities, regions or countries that had particular economic strengths to focus on these strengths, and to have a much larger market ready to absorb their goods or services in which they were specialized. By focusing on their strengths, and by having a market available, these economies were able to record significant improvements in productivity levels that would have been otherwise impossible without the ability to focus on their specialties. In Roman times, manufacturers had the entire empire as a market, and sometimes markets much further afield. During the Industrial Revolution, manufacturers based in England or Wales had the entire British Empire as a captive market, as well as many other markets around the world, with the British Navy ensuring that the shipping lanes needed to get these manufactured goods to these far-flung markets were safe and secure. Finally, thanks to the US-led international trading systems set up after the Second World War, European and Japanese manufacturers could overcome the disadvantage of having domestic markets that were devastated by the war by exporting their goods to the United States and other markets around the world. Having such large markets available to them is a very strong incentive for manufacturers or service providers to improve their levels of productivity.

Another important, but often overlooked factor, is that each of these examples that we have looked at in this chapter had strong education systems. For its time, Rome's population was relatively well-educated, with a relatively large share of Rome's population having access to education or specialized training. The same was true in Industrial Revolution Britain, where an increasing number of people had access to education or vocational training, something that had been sorely lacking across much of Europe in the period between the Roman Empire and the 1700s. Europe and Japan also made major investments in their educational systems after the Second World War, something that was to prove vital in their ability to economically recover from the impact of the war. In each of these three examples, not only was education in general valued, but economically-important fields of education became an important focus of their educational systems. This allowed for much better educated work forces, something that undoubtedly played a role in each of their abilities to increase productivity growth. In fact, their successes in the fields of education meant that rivals would often copy their education systems in the hopes of reaping the same productivity-related benefits.

One other commonality that I would like to touch upon with regards to its influence on productivity growth in these three successful economies is infrastructure. In each of these three cases, investment in the expansion and modernization of these societies' infrastructures would be a crucial role in leading to higher levels of productivity growth. Rome, of course, was famous for its infrastructure, which was more modern and more extensive than anything seen in the world up to that point. Britain too built an expansive infrastructure, particularly with regards to its ports, as most of its trade was sea-borne. Finally, Europe and Japan invested heavily in their infrastructures in the years after the Second World War, giving those two economies a major boost once those new infrastructures were in place. As we will see later in the book, the importance of infrastructure on these economies' successes has not been lost on many countries today, most notably China, whose infrastructure development in recent decades has been among the most impressive in world history.

THE PRODUCTIVITY CHALLENGE

Efforts to determine how productivity growth impacts economic growth inevitably are challenged by the fact that there are so many different approaches to the measurement of productivity. What is agreed upon is that productivity itself is a ratio of a measure of output to a measure of input. However, while this is agreed upon, the actual measurement of productivity has taken on many different forms over the years. For example, there are a number of different types of inputs that go into this measurement. Most important are labor and capital, with the former still being used more than any other input in order to determine productivity levels. Some measurements combine these two inputs. Others take both of these inputs and add to them other types of inputs such as raw materials, energy, services and others. As for output, most productivity measures focus simply on gross output, but others will use value added as the means of deriving a measurement of productivity. With all of these variables, it is inevitable that multiple forms of productivity measures have arisen over the years, and this has resulted in a large number of different measurements being used. Furthermore, there are a number of other factors that have caused problems for those who measure productivity. For example, there is a general lack of reliable statistics for capital input, hence the desirability of using labor productivity data instead. Measuring hours worked can also be a challenge, as can the use of price indices in many sectors of the economy. As a result, this has muddied the waters when it comes to comparing productivity levels between eras or countries and has led to a great deal of confusion among those of us who study economics for a living.

Despite these challenges in measuring productivity growth, it is clearly one of the most important factors determining the ability of an economy to generate long-term high rates of growth. However, as we have seen in recent decades, some economies have managed to generate decent rates of economic growth even in the face of slowing productivity growth. This has largely been due to other factors, such as high commodity prices, high levels of trade and investment, or simply a fast-growing domestic market. For example, Germany has managed to record higher rates of economic growth than most of its European neighbors in recent years, despite recording some of the lowest rates of productivity growth during that period. However, now that these other factors are being challenged, it is clear the productivity growth will be needed more than ever if an economy is to generate long-term growth.

For most of the world's leading developed economies, we have a great deal of productivity data that can allow us to determine how productivity levels have been trending for a longer period of time. Using data from the OECD and Focus Economics, we can see that for most of the world's leading developed economies, the past 50 years have been a period of declining productivity growth. In fact, not only has productivity growth been trending downwards in most major developed economies, but it has also fallen to nearly zero in many of them.

THE UNITED STATES

Unlike most other developed economies, the past 50 years have not been one of a continuous downwards trend in productivity growth. In fact, after falling to less than 1.5% per year throughout the 1980s, US productivity growth rates actually rose to above 2% per year in the late 1990s and early 2000s, thanks in large part to the Information Revolution that was based in the United States, and which gave rise to new industries that were dominated by firms that had many of their operations in the US.

United States Productivity Growth

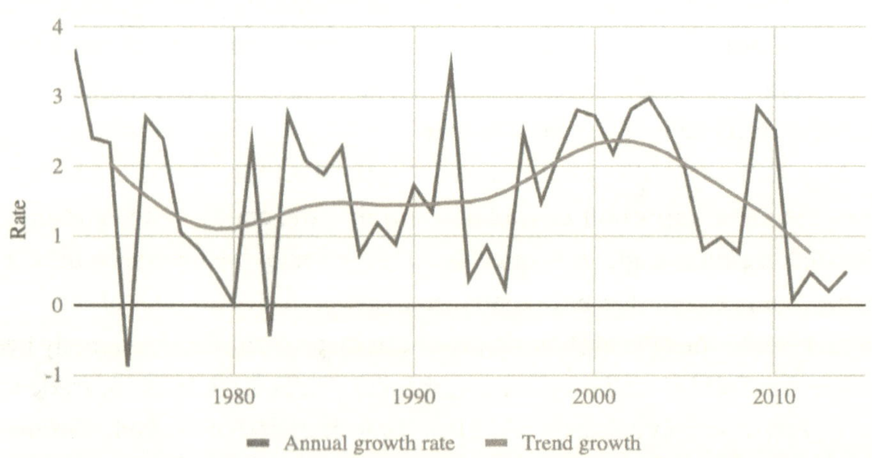

Source: OECD

JAPAN

No developed economy was able to record higher rates of productivity growth than Japan in the 1970s and 1980s, with productivity growth rates during that period being more than twice as high as those of the United States. It is no wonder than that Japan's manufacturing and management processes were being emulated around the world at that point. Since then, productivity growth in Japan has fallen sharply, a trend that has continued now for nearly 30 years. Given Japan's myriad of other problems, including its worsening demographic situation, it will take a major rebound in productivity growth for the Japanese economy to record higher rates of economic growth in the future.

Japan Productivity Growth

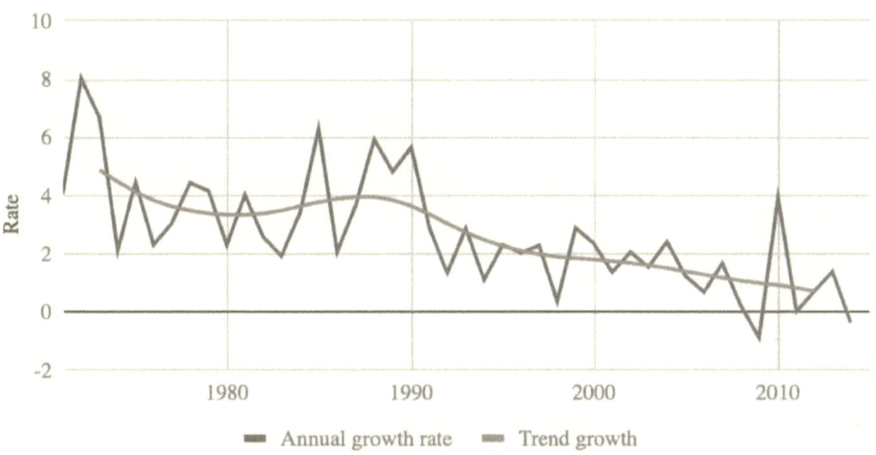

Source: OECD

GERMANY

Like Japan, 1970s Germany saw productivity growth rates that were in excess of 4%. However, these growth rates fell much earlier than those in Japan, but even then, production growth in Germany averaged more than 2% per year into the second half of the 1990s. Since then, productivity growth in Germany has fallen by more than half, a worrying sign for an economy that it dependent upon its degree of export competitiveness in order to generate economic growth. Furthermore, Germany is increasingly reliant upon a number of slower-growth traditional industries (such as the automotive industry) to generate growth, leaving it devoid of many of the faster-growing new industries that are driving productivity growth in other countries.

Germany Productivity Growth

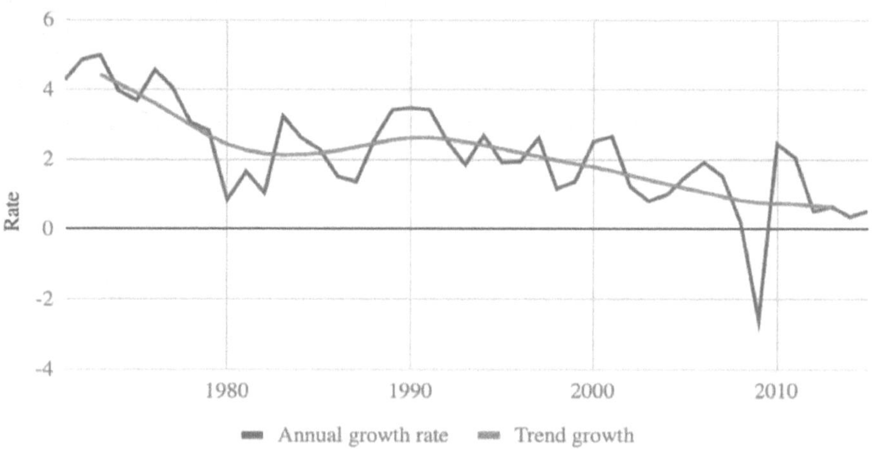

Source: OECD

If we look at other developed economies such as the United Kingdom, France or Canada, the picture looks more or less the same, with productivity growth rates trending steadily downwards over the past two or three decades. As all of these economies are facing uncertain demographic, trade and investment futures, their need for higher levels of productivity growth will become all the more acute in the years and decades ahead.

The same is true for emerging markets. While some emerging markets, especially those in East Asia and Central Europe, have managed to record higher levels of productivity growth in recent years, most emerging markets have not. In fact, if one looks at the productivity growth rates of most emerging markets in regions such as South Asia, Latin America or the Middle East, one will see that productivity growth rates in these countries have generally been lower than their overall rates of economic growth, This shows that these emerging markets have been reliant upon the growth of their domestic markets, as well as trade and investment with foreign markets for much of their economic growth, It is therefore no surprise that, when demographic growth slowed and trade and investment was disrupted, these economies were among those that suffered the greatest declines in economic growth.

One of the great questions of modern economics revolves around why all of the technological advancements of the past few decades have failed to produce the expected dividends in terms of higher levels of productivity. In fact, many of the modern technologies that we take for granted now were once believed to have very limited uses and would not have much impact on the performance of the global economy. For example, it is alleged that, in the 1940s, Thomas Watson, the president of IBM, remarked that he believed that the total worldwide market for computers was probably no more than five machines. Of course, in subsequent decades such technology went from having a peripheral role in the economy to taking center stage, and as other drivers of global economic growth began to falter, suddenly this technology was assigned the role of becoming not just a component of economic growth, but its leading driver. Unfortunately, recent productivity results have been so poor that many are now questioning whether or not many of our modern technologies are actually reducing productivity, rather than driving it to new heights. There are two ways of looking at this view. On one hand, overall productivity growth levels have indeed been very disappointing so far in the 21st century. However, much of this has to do with the fact that a large number of older industries have been holding down overall productivity growth by recording little or no productivity growth themselves. In fact, modern high-tech industries generally have had significantly higher rates of productivity growth than their older and more staid counterparts.

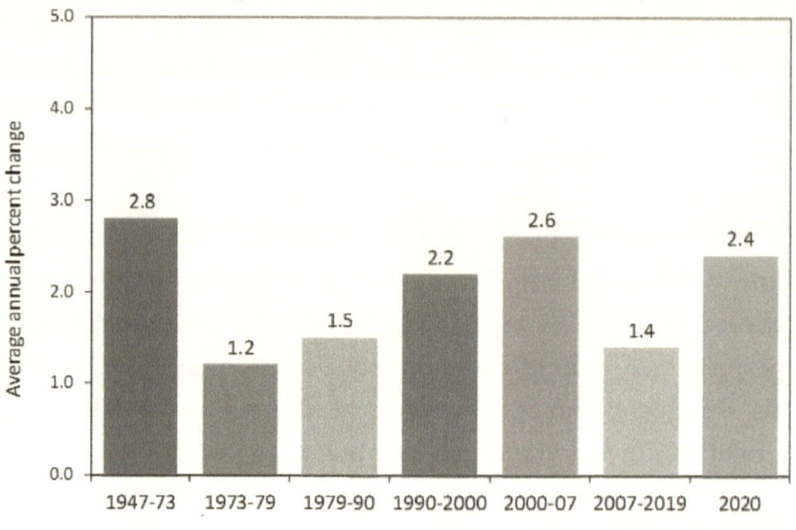

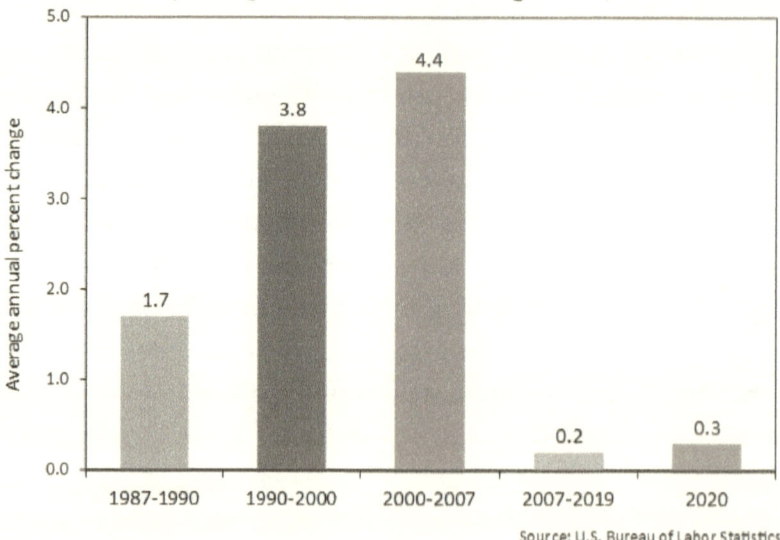

This can be seen in the comparisons of productivity growth in recent decades among countries where high-tech industries play a larger role in their economies and those countries that have relatively small high-tech sectors.

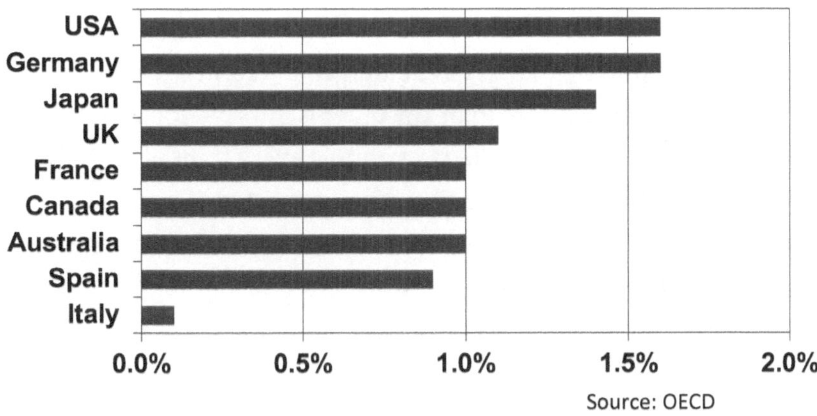

Of course, while there are differences between the more high-tech US economy and the lower-tech Italian economy, the fact is that productivity growth rates over the past decade have been very disappointing for nearly all developed economies. This goes a long way toward explaining why economic growth in the developed world has been trending downwards in recent decades. Sure, much of the blame goes to the rise of emerging markets and the loss of manufacturing operations to these poorer countries, but productivity struggles at home have also played a major role in the slowdown in wealthy countries in the 21st century. The same holds true for most emerging markets. In these economies, productivity growth has also been very disappointing, apart from the aforementioned examples in East Asia and Central Europe. This has exposed most emerging markets to external threats such as declines in commodity prices and falling levels of demand in wealthier export markets. Without higher levels of productivity, emerging markets are not in a position to withstand these external pressures, as we have seen in recent years in places such as Brazil, Russia and South Africa.

As productivity growth rates have not accelerated as had been expected at the dawn of the Information Revolution, and have indeed continued to trend downwards for nearly all of the world's largest economies, questions are beginning to be asked about the impact that the highly-touted technological breakthroughs of recent years will have on the global economy and whether or not they will ever begin to revive productivity growth. Let's look at some of the technologies that hold the promise to revive productivity and drive economic growth upwards in the coming decades.

Of all of the technologies that have emerged in recent decades, the one that defines the modern world more than any other is information technology, for it is everywhere these days and influences almost every facet of life in the 2020s. Furthermore, no other technology has been expected to contribute more to productivity growth than information technology. For a while in the 1990s and the early 2000s, it appeared that information technology would fulfill its promise and lead to a new world of higher levels of productivity growth. In the country at the heart of the Information Revolution, information technology led to significantly higher rates of productivity growth in the late 1990s and early 2000s. This was due largely to soaring productivity rates within IT sectors in the United States during this period. However, since then, productivity rates in the United States and in nearly all other large economies have fallen steadily. For IT apologists, the reason for this downturn in productivity growth is not the lack of a contribution to productivity growth from the information sector, but rather, an inability to accurately measure the effects of these technologies on productivity and economic output. As the technology has moved increasingly away from hardware and more towards software, these measurement challenges have been magnified. Others will argue that this lack of an impact on productivity growth is just temporary, and that in the years ahead, the promise that information technology would allow productivity levels to take over will be realized.

However, there is a growing school of thought that argues that the recent advancements in the information technology sector simply do not have the impact on productivity that the earlier advancements in this sector had in the 1990s and early 2000s. This argument claims that, in the early days of this period, the technologies that were developed brought a wide range of benefits to most sectors of the economy. There are even some experts in this field that will claim that the recent advancements in the information technology sector, rather than boosting productivity, are actually acting as a drag on productivity as they are distracting workers from their jobs. Whereas once it was solitaire on the computer that may have kept workers from doing their jobs, today it is an incredibly diverse array of apps, games, platforms and much more. Regardless, it is clear that, for the past two decades, overall productivity levels around the world have been in decline at the same time that the information technology sector has emerged as the most powerful force in the global economy. Whether or not there is a correlation remains to be seen.

Another technology that has begun to have an impact on productivity levels is automation. For many, automation goes hand-in-hand with job losses, hence its controversial nature in many parts of the world. However, for countries such as Japan, South Korea and Germany where the working-age population is shrinking rapidly, automation holds the promise of allowing certain sectors of the economy to remain in those countries even as their pool of available workers shrinks.

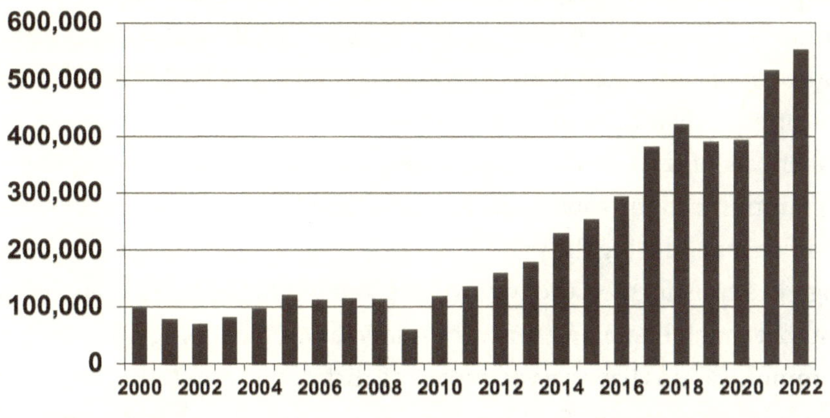

Source: IFR

In many ways, automation is a demographic issue as many of the world's leading economies face imminent demographic decline as low birth rates and aging populations have resulted in both shrinking labor forces and rising retirement-age populations. This has been made apparent by the worsening of labor shortages in many parts of the world in the wake of the Covid-19 pandemic. However, automation's greatest potential comes from its ability to raise productivity levels in a dramatic fashion. For example, automation can eliminate the need for people to undertake repetitive tasks, allowing these tasks to be done more efficiently and at greater speed. At the same time, more dangerous tasks can also be automated, improving workplace safety and reducing the need to invest so much in safety-related programs. In recent years, there have been a number of high-profile studies that suggest that 10% to 15% of all jobs in existence right now could be replaced by automation over the next decade. Of course, automation will lead to the creation of new types of jobs, but the result will be less jobs available for people. However, if automation can help to finally lift productivity levels out of their doldrums, this will be a price that will have to be paid, for without higher levels of productivity growth, economic growth levels are likely to be very disappointing in the years ahead.

Another technology that has failed to bring about the expected benefits to productivity growth has been communications. Few sectors have seen the level of technological advancement that the communications industry has witnessed in recent decades and yet, during this period of dramatic improvements in communications, productivity growth has been falling steadily. Today, the world is more connected than ever, and one can argue that it was these communications advancements that allowed the global economy to survive the worst effects of the Covid-19 pandemic, as remote work became the norm and communications tools such as Zoom and Microsoft Teams became the new office space during the pandemic. However, while communications technology has transformed the way we live and work, there are many who will claim that much like many forms of information technology, advancements in communications have served more as a distractor from rather than a driver of productivity growth. Furthermore, as we look ahead, many experts are beginning to question just how many more advancements in communications technology there will be in the future, and whether or not we have already realized most of the gains in terms of productivity that this sector has to offer.

LITTLE EVIDENCE OF A REBOUND IN PRODUCTIVITY

The fact that productivity growth rates have been falling so far for so long in nearly all of the world's leading economies is an extremely worrying development. If productivity growth rates were fluctuating, or if there had been a period of sustained high levels of productivity growth in the not-so-distant future, there would be less of a concern regarding the impact that productivity was having on the global economy. However, as these downturns have been in place in many cases for three or four decades, there are legitimate fears that not only is this downturn here to stay, but that productivity growth rates could keep falling in the years ahead once the dislocations caused by the Covid-19 pandemic fade away. For many economies, if current trends continue, productivity levels will actually start to decline in the near-future, or will be unable to fall from the lows caused by the dislocations stemming from the Covid-19 pandemic. As we saw in the decade after the Financial Crisis, productivity growth levels did not rebound, even as economic growth did. Furthermore, the fact that all of the great technological advancements of the past few decades failed to reverse this decline in productivity growth is a very worrying fact for as we look to the future, we are increasingly counting on new technologies and processes to drive productivity growth upwards. There are many types of technologies that are being counted on to drive productivity growth, including artificial intelligence, biotechnology and many more. However, the rollouts of these technologies are likely to take many decades and if productivity growth does not rise before then, the global economy is going to suffer many losses as economic growth continues to slow.

This lack of productivity growth is already being seen in one very important component of productivity, business confidence. In recent decades, we have seen a very noticeable decline in the confidence of many sectors of the economy in the ability of technological and process developments to boost productivity growth. As a result, this has led to an overall lack of business investment in capital, labor and other inputs of productivity. In fact, if there is one area where most economists agree with regards to the recent slump in productivity growth, it is the fact that business investment levels have been highly disappointing. Given the events of recent years, including the Financial Crisis and the Covid-19 pandemic, it is easy to see how businesses could remain wary of making major investments in productivity-improving technologies and processes, to the detriment of future productivity growth.

This decline in productivity growth in recent days has been a worrying development for most economists, for not only was it not expected, but it was becoming more apparent that without improvements in our productivity levels, sustaining economic growth will become harder than ever. As productivity levels were trending downwards in the final 20-30 years of the 20th century, the impact of this decline was masked by rapidly-expanding workforces and a global economy that was entering into a phase of rapid globalization, thus boosting international trade and investment levels.

As a result, while productivity levels fell sharply, economic growth did not, as economic output was propped up by expanding working-age and consuming-age populations, as well as by the opening of new markets and new, low-cost manufacturing centers. Furthermore, the slight rebound in productivity growth that occurred in the United States and other more high-tech economies provided hope that the expected return to long-term productivity growth had arrived, driven forwards by the surging information technology sector. At the same time, former command economies where productivity levels had collapsed in previous decades were brought online as part of the global economy and received massive amounts of investment in their production facilities, infrastructure and the like, leading to a surge in productivity growth in many of these emerging markets.

Still, neither the dawning of the information era or the rise of emerging markets could prevent overall global productivity growth for continuing to decline, as it has done for the first two decades of the 21st century. As a result, the global economy is now faced with a massive dilemma as it looks to what is increasingly an uncertain future. On one hand, it is clear that, for most of the world's leading economies, a demographic decline is already taking place, or will soon take place in the years ahead. This will eliminate what has been one of the great drivers of economic growth since the dawn of the Industrial Revolution 250 years ago. Only some of the poorest countries on the planet will continue to see a demographic dividend in terms of population-driven economic growth, and very few of these countries are currently connected to the wider global economy. At the same time, the surge in international trade and investment that played such a key role in driving global economic growth in the latter part of the 20th century and the early years of the 21st century also appears to be in severe jeopardy. Not only has international trade and investment stagnated over the past decade, but popular opinion in many parts of the world has turned against globalization. While there is still time that the moribund global trade and investment system can be revived, it can no longer be counted upon to be an automatic driver of economic growth in the years ahead.

That leaves productivity improvements as the key variable when it comes to the outlook for the global economy in the coming years and decades. If productivity growth trends continue, along with the demographic decline and the threats to global trade and investment, there is almost no way that the global economy will be able to generate much growth in the coming years. Some economies may be able to do better than others, particularly those with a high degree of self-sustainability, but most of the world's economies will suffer if all three of these key drivers of economic growth falter for a prolonged period of time. This places on incredible burden on productivity, for without major improvements in productivity, our economic future will be increasingly uncertain. Unfortunately, if the past few decades are a guide for our future, generating the levels of productivity growth that we will need to allow for long-term and sustainable high level of economic growth will be very difficult to achieve.

Chapter Fourteen

CAN PRODUCTIVITY BE REVIVED?

IN CHAPTER FIVE, WE explored some of the history of productivity, and how growth in productivity levels was an important catalyst for many of humanity's most successful periods of advancement in terms of generating economic growth and improving living standards. One such period was the post-war period that stretched from the 1950s to the 1970s, a period that was characterized by high rates of productivity growth in many of the world's leading economies, including the United States, Europe and Japan. However, beginning in the early 1980s, productivity growth rates in most major economies trended downwards, falling far from their levels of the previous decades. In some economies, there was a renewed increase in productivity growth in the late 1990s and early 2000s, one that was brought on by the Information Revolution. However, this recovery in productivity growth proved to be short-lived, and nearly all leading economies have seen productivity growth rates fall even further over the past 10-15 years. In fact, some major economies now are recording little or no productivity growth at all.

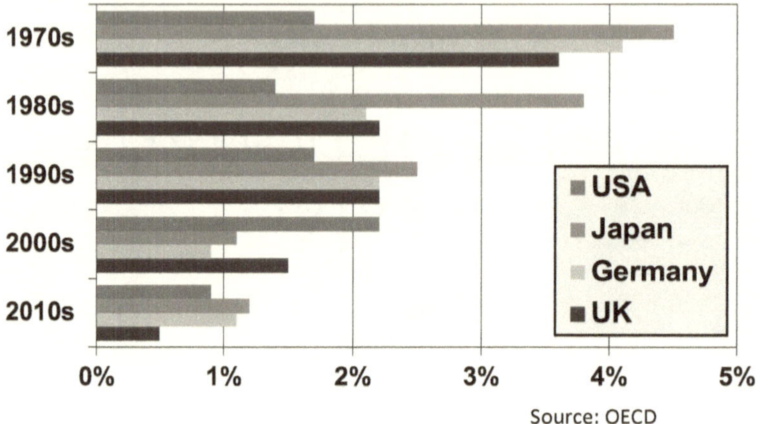

There are a number of reasons that have been given for this long-term decline in productivity growth and for the very low rates of productivity growth in recent years. For example, a lack of business confidence has resulted in relatively little investment going into technologies and processes that could help to boost a company's level of productivity. In fact, businesses in many sectors of the economy are re-investing less of their profits into research and development than at any time in recent history, hindering their ability to improve their levels of productivity. Likewise, governments in most of the world's leading economies have reduced their investments in research and development in recent years, meaning that not only is this a bottom-up problem, but also a top-down one. Meanwhile, the investment that has been made has largely gone into technologies and processes that, for the most part, have failed to generate the level of productivity growth that had been hoped for when these technologies were first introduced. Finally, weaker levels of consumer and business demand, prompted by the recent economic troubles caused by a series of global and regional economic crises, has also played a role in the overall lack of productivity growth in most economies and in most sectors of the economy so far in the 21st century.

Of course, it has not been all bad news in recent years on the productivity front. Some countries, though not many, have managed to continue to record relatively decent rates of productivity growth, even as the overall global level of productivity growth around the world continues to trend downwards. For example, while productivity growth in the developed world has been anemic in developed economies, it has remained relatively strong in many emerging markets, particularly emerging markets in East Asia.

In fact, since 2008, the average rate of growth for productivity in developed economies has been just 0.7% per year, whereas in emerging markets, it has been a much more respectable 3.7% per year. This reflects not only the low productivity base from which many emerging markets are rising out of, but also the relatively higher levels of investment growth, as well as research and development growth, in many key emerging markets, particularly China. In fact, nearly all of this productivity growth has been concentrated in Asian emerging markets, as emerging markets in all other areas of the world have recorded just as low rates of productivity growth as developed economies.

This has played a very important role in the ability of most Asian emerging markets to generate much higher rates of growth than other areas of the world in recent years, particularly as that region's demographic situation is also worsening and as it has faced many of the same external threats as other parts of the world.

While Asian emerging markets and a handful of countries and industries have managed to buck the trend of falling levels of productivity growth, the fact is that most countries and most industries have seen a significant downwards shift in productivity growth levels over a prolonged period of time. This is a very worrying trend for the global economy, for these lower levels of productivity are not just the by-product of the major crises that have befallen the global economy so far in the 21st century, but they are also a result of many other factors that have combined to reduce productivity growth. Furthermore, as we have discussed, demographics, together with trade and investment, are unlikely to be major drivers of growth in the years ahead, leaving productivity as the one area that we can focus on to generate much of the world's economic growth in the years ahead. If we are unable to solve this problem quickly, we face a continued decline in overall rates of economic growth and the potential for more economic crises as our ability to generate the levels of growth to needed to recover from various shocks and calamities in the future will be severely compromised.

It is not all bad news in terms of productivity growth in recent years as there are a few examples of higher rates of productivity growth during this period. For example, South Korea has managed to continue to record higher rates of productivity growth than nearly any other developed economy over the past decade or two. In fact, South Korean productivity growth levels have been higher than just about any other developed economy since the 1990s, helping to explain how a country facing one of the world's most pressing demographic declines can regularly record rates of economic growth than are well ahead of those of most other developed economies. It helps, of course, that South Korea has such a strong position in so many high-tech and high-growth industries. In fact, if we look at productivity growth rates by industry, rather than by country, we can see that it is high-tech sectors such as information technology, telecommunications and consumer electronics that are recording many of the highest rates of productivity growth of any sectors of the global economy.

Unfortunately, there are too few countries today that are like South Korea and can continue to generate high levels of productivity growth in the face of daunting challenges such as a shrinking labor force and intensifying competition from emerging markets. Likewise, there are too many sectors of the economy that are not making any progress when it comes to improving their levels of productivity growth, and there are too many countries whose economies are still dominated by such sectors. Meanwhile, some economists will point to the series of crises that have befallen the global economy in recent years as the main culprit for the weak productivity growth results of this period. However, it is clear that productivity growth had slowed in most major economies well before these crises hit the global economy, indicating that the problems are much more structural in nature, and not simply the product of a weak economy or of the impact of a single crisis. In fact, low levels of productivity growth are one of the main reasons why economic growth has been so anemic in many important economies so far in the 21st century. As we have seen, this is a trend that needs to be reversed, as the other major drivers of economic growth such as rising working-age populations and higher levels of trade and investment are no longer there to boost economic growth as they had been for most of the two centuries following the Industrial Revolution. This makes it imperative that more countries, industries and businesses focus a much greater amount of their attention on increasing productivity for their long-term well-being.

THE OUTLOOK FOR PRODUCTIVITY

While the overall direction of productivity growth in recent decades is clear to all, the outlook for productivity in the coming decades remains highly uncertain. In fact, few economists agree on the outlook for productivity in the future, with some finding themselves in the camp of those who believe that technological and process changes will lead to a productivity renaissance, while others are in the camp of those who believe that the long-term downwards trend in productivity will persist for the foreseeable future, resulting in further productivity declines in many countries and industries. Meanwhile, the disruptions caused by the series of economic crises in recent years are expected by many experts to eventually lead to major changes and disruptions that will change the course of productivity in the future, although so far, there is relatively little evidence to support this belief.

There are some reasons to believe that long-term productivity growth can yet be revived in order to provide a much-needed basis for solid economic growth in the future. Of these, faith in the promise of new technologies and more advanced processes to generate higher rates of productivity growth in the future remains at the forefront on most economists' expectations for productivity advancements. Just because the most recent technological and process advancements have not generated the expected increases in productivity growth does not mean that the advancements of the future will have the same impact on productivity and the economy. The promise of artificial intelligence, automation and 3D-printing, for example, could transform many sectors of the economy that, in recent decades, have generated very little productivity growth into high-productivity-growth components of the economy. If governments would do more to promote these technological and process advancements, it is highly likely that productivity growth would be given a sizeable boost.

At the same time, productivity levels in emerging markets remain extremely low when compared with more advanced economies, indicating that there is also much room for higher levels of productivity growth in emerging markets in the future. As a result, even if productivity growth in advanced economies continues to decline, the rising importance of emerging markets means that overall global productivity growth is not condemned to follow in such a decline. This also holds true at a sector level. While a few sectors of the economy have accounted for the bulk of the world's productivity growth in recent decades, too many important sectors of the economy have struggled to generate much, if any, productivity growth at all. Worse, sectoral reallocation, the shift in labor and other resources from less-productive to more-productive sectors of the economy have not been generating the same levels of productivity gains in recent years as it had done in the past. Nevertheless, it is possible that sectoral reallocation can once again return as a key driver of productivity growth, particularly in the wake of the recent economic crises that have devastated many of the sectors of the global economy that had already been suffering from low levels of productivity growth.

While there are reasons to hope that productivity growth can finally rebound, there are also many reasons that support the argument that productivity growth's long-term slowdown will continue for the foreseeable future. Of these, the most consequential might be the fact that many of the drivers of productivity growth in the past are simply no longer able to generate the levels of increases in productivity that they once did. For example, education, urbanization and institutional development were all major factors in the high rates of productivity growth that were achieved in various parts of the world in the 19th and 20th centuries. However, the ability of each of these factors to generate productivity growth in most economies has now either slowed or has completely stagnated, indicating that their ability to generate productivity growth has been all but exhausted. Another factor to consider is the trend that is seeing governments attempting to prevent job losses during times of economic crisis, thus preventing, or at least slowing, the reallocation of labor from sectors of the economy that generate little or no growth to those sectors that have a much higher capacity to generate growth in the future. This has allowed too many labor resources to remain committed to weaker sectors of the economy and this has hampered the expansion of sectors of the economy that hold more promise for growth in the future. Unfortunately, many governments followed this path during the recent Covid-19 pandemic, and this could prevent those countries from turning around their productivity levels in the coming years.

To try and improve our understanding of the future of productivity growth, let's take a closer look at a few of the key drivers of productivity growth to try and determine how they will impact productivity in the coming years and decades.

LABOR

As we have discussed, the growth of the global labor force that was such an important driver of productivity growth in the past has all but come to an end in many of the world's leading economies. In fact, for most major economies, the availability of labor is becoming a significant drag on growth in many sectors of their economies as their working-age populations stagnate and decline. This trend will not change any time soon as birth rates remain well below the replacement level in most leading economies. Only a significantly re-allocation of labor away from those areas where labor remains abundant to those areas suffering from labor shortages, or a re-allocation of economic activities away from labor-scarce to labor-abundant areas, could help to re-invigorate labor's contribution to productivity growth.

CAPITAL

Capital's contribution to productivity growth has also been disappointing in recent years, contributing to the disappointing productivity growth levels recorded so far in the current century. This is due in large part to the reluctance of many businesses to invest in capital, as business investment levels over the past ten-to-fifteen years have been much lower than had been expected. Worse, what was once viewed as a temporary slowdown in investment in capital now looks more like a long-term trend, one that is having a major impact on productivity. If this does not turn around, and there is little reason at the moment to suggest that it will, it will be difficult for productivity growth to return to the higher levels that it achieved in the past.

TECHNOLOGY

Technological breakthroughs have long been lauded as the great hope for productivity growth. This included the technologies associated with the Information Revolution, which many economists assumed would lead to dramatic increases in productivity levels for many different sectors of the global economy. Unfortunately, as we know now, this was not the case, and despite a short stint of higher productivity growth in some economies with large information technology sectors in the late 1990s and early 2000s, productivity growth has continued to slow, even as the ability to compile and disseminate information has grown exponentially. Of course, there are still hopes that technology can rescue the global economy from its productivity conundrum, with new technologies such as artificial intelligence and faster communications holding great promise. However, the recent struggle to generate higher productivity growth has left many economists with a great deal of skepticism regarding the impact of these new technologies.

ORGANIZATION AND PROCESSES

There are numerous other factors the influence productivity that offer some hope for the future. Among these are the development of new organizational methods and process improvements. Some economists believe that more streamlined organizations can return many sectors of the economy to higher levels of productivity growth. At the same time, it is believed that a greater focus on the development of more advanced processes to create, distribute and market goods and services could also help to boost productivity over the long-term. However, these are areas that have already received a great deal of attention in recent decades, and so far, there is little to show for any of this attention when reviewing the productivity data of the past few decades. In fact, it seems far-fetched to believe that these factors can have a major impact on productivity growth in the coming decades, especially when considering the direction of other factors that have a major influence on productivity growth.

Unfortunately, when we look back at the last few decades of declining productivity growth, it becomes quite apparent that the challenge of reversing this trend is one that will prove extremely difficult to overcome. In fact, without significant technological breakthroughs, it is hard to see how we will be able to reverse this trend at all, given the outlook for the other leading drivers of productivity growth, such as labor and capital. In fact, most of these drivers of productivity growth appear set to continue to weaken, leaving technology, and to a lesser degree organization and process management, as the last great hopes for productivity growth in the 21st century.

OUTLOOK FOR KEY PRODUCTIVITY INPUTS

Current trends suggest that many of the leading inputs that go into productivity (labor, capital, technology and organization) are contributing less to productivity growth than in previous decades, as evidenced by the simple fact that productivity growth has been so poor in so many leading economies for so long. Look at labor, or more accurately labor hours, the input that has had a very significant impact on productivity throughout history. For much of human history, people spent most of their time producing something, either agricultural products, tools or some other basic necessity. However, in the wake of the Industrial Revolution, labor input began to slowly, but inexorably, start to lose some of its influence on productivity levels. This was not an overnight development, and labor remains to this day an extremely important component of productivity, and is likely to be so for the foreseeable future. Nevertheless, there is a seemingly inexorable drive around the world for working hours to be reduced.

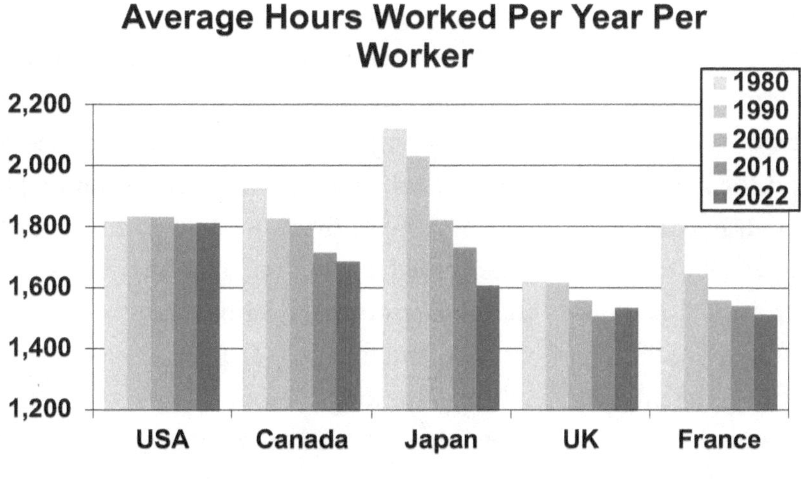

Source: OECD

While this trend is not having the same impact on all parts of the world, it is generally accepted that working hours are falling in all different types of economies. In particular, countries with strong unions and extensive social welfare systems have seen their average working hours fall dramatically in recent decades. This is interesting because most of these countries are also among those that have some of the lowest birth rates and the largest declines in their working-age populations in the world.

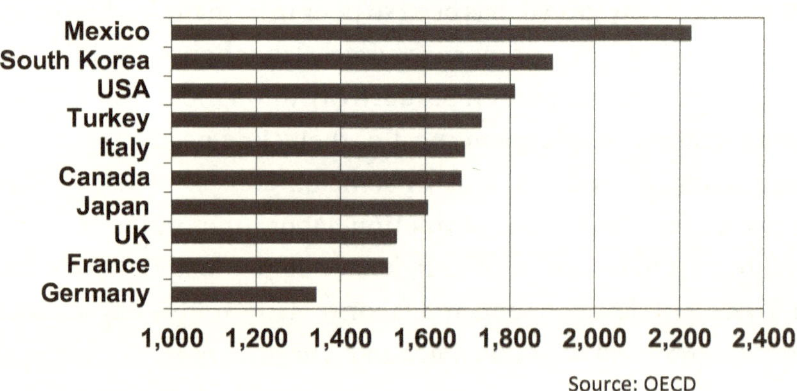

As you can see, this trend towards lower working hours is being recorded in some of the world's leading economic centers. However, many of these same countries are among those that have been recording some of the lowest rates of economic growth in the world in recent years, leading to the question of whether or not working hours are falling because there simply is not enough demand for labor in these low-growth economies, or if economic growth is being dragged down by this decline in overall working hours for those economies' labor forces. It can be argued that both of these answers are correct. Furthermore, it is unlikely that these countries' labor forces are going to be increasing more than they are now, and for those that are already in decline, this decline is likely to accelerate over the longer-term. At the same time, trends such as sluggish economic growth and the spread of automation mean that demand for labor in most of these countries is unlikely to rise significantly in the future. Altogether, working hours are unlikely to increase in most of the world's leading economies for the foreseeable future. Continuing a trend that has been in place for a long time now.

Another productivity input that has been disappointing in recent years has been capital. As we have discussed, businesses have been very reluctant to invest in increased capital expenditure in the 21st century, and this too has had a negative impact on productivity growth during this period.

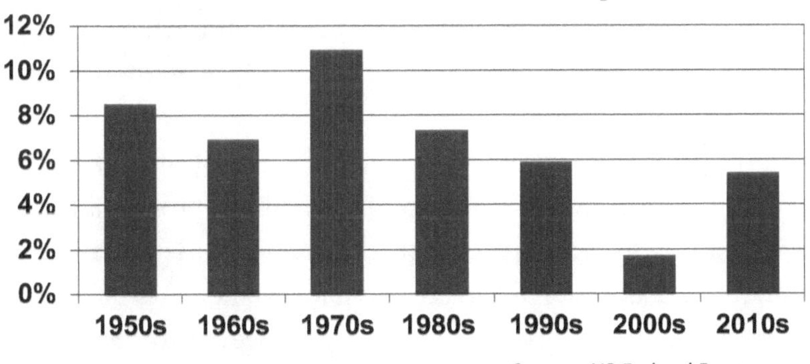

In fact, what was once believed to be simply a temporary downturn in business investment has turned into a long-term trend, raising fears that these lower levels of capital expenditure could be here to stay for some time to come. Given the economic and political turmoil that has taken place in recent years, it is easy to see why businesses have been reluctant to invest in capital, and should this turmoil and uncertainty continue, it is unlikely that business investment levels will rise significantly in the years ahead.

With labor and capital proving unable to drive productivity growth in the manner that they had done in the past, it has been left to technology to solve all of the world's productivity problems. In fact, it was widely known that labor and capital were susceptible to a long-term decline, but there was a widespread assumption that technological advancements would more than offset these weaknesses. Instead, technology has had but a middling impact on productivity growth levels in most industries, raising questions as to whether or not the technological advancements of the past couple of decades have had much, in any, impact in raising the level of productivity growth.

So far, the evidence points to it having relatively little positive impact. Still, there are many economists that continue to insist that the technological breakthroughs that will transform productivity are right around the corner and will be the answer to all of our productivity problems in the future. From artificial intelligence to advanced communications, some economists believe that we are on the cusp of a productivity revolution that will further reduce the impact of labor, and to a lesser degree capital, on productivity growth. However, the lessons of the recent past suggest that we need to temper our expectations for these new technologies, at least until they can prove that they can drive a sustained increase in productivity growth for a prolonged period of time.

In addition to technological advances, there are many organizations that are devoted to finding and developing organizational and process advancements that can boost the productivity of a business, an industry or even an entire country. In fact, organizational and process improvements do offer the modern world some hope for improved productivity. However, this area of research has been in focus for many decades now, and it can be argued that for all of the investment that has been made by businesses and industries to streamline their organizational structures and improve their business processes, there has been relatively little impact on their overall levels of productivity growth, One would think that, with all of the money that has been spent by businesses on outsourcing organizational and process improvements to management consulting firms, there would have been some noticeable improvement in productivity levels in recent years. Unfortunately, this appears to be an area where most of the productivity gains have already been uncovered.

This overview of the outlook for the inputs that go into productivity growth suggest that most of them are in the process of weakening and that they will struggle to generate higher levels of productivity growth in the coming years, The impact of demographics on the productivity levels of most countries and industries is likely to be negative in the coming decades, at least in most areas of the world. At the same time, business investment levels are unlikely to rise substantially in the years ahead, weakening the important capital input.

Meanwhile, most of the productivity gains derived from organizational and process improvements appear to have been exhausted already. This leaves technology as the sole input of productivity that has the capacity to fundamentally change the downwards trend in productivity growth and to restore this all-important driver of economic growth, Unfortunately, here too we have seen relatively little positive impact in recent years as, for all of our recent technological breakthroughs, productivity growth rates continue to trend downwards in most major economies and industries.

So far, most of the worst declines in productivity growth rates have been found among the world's developed economies. This is to be expected, as not only are many developed economies among those places where working hours and available labor are declining the most, but they too have been losing out on business investment to cheaper, and faster-growing emerging markets. Should these trends continue, productivity growth rates in most developed economies are likely to fall even further in the coming years, and in some cases, productivity levels might start to decline over the longer-term. This would be devastating for the economic futures of these wealthier economies. At the same time, while productivity growth rates are somewhat higher in some emerging markets, here too they have begun to decline in a number of cases. In some emerging markets, a lack of economic reform, a lack of investment, or a combination of other factors have led to declines in productivity growth that mirror, and in some cases exceed, those seen in recent decades in more developed economies. As a result, while it might have been assumed that some countries' productivity losses would be other countries' productivity gains, in this case it appears that productivity losses are being recorded across the board, to the detriment of the global economy as a whole. This poses a major challenge for the long-term health of the global economy.

HOW WILL THIS IMPACT FUTURE ECONOMIC GROWTH?

As we have seen, without an increase in productivity growth for the world as a whole, there will be little chance of generating higher rates of global economic growth over the longer-term. Demographics are increasingly becoming a drag on economic growth, as the number of productive people in the world is declining, either as a result of shrinking working-age populations or due to policies or trends that have prevented an increasing number of people from being productive members of society. In fact, if current demographic and policy trends continue, demographic factors will likely become the single greatest drag on growth for the global economy in the decades to come. There seems to be no way around this. At the same time, opposition to international trade and investment is continuing to rise in many areas of the world, for a wide variety of reasons. This trend too appears likely to continue for the foreseeable future, threatening to further reduce global trade and investment growth in the coming years. In fact, it appears increasingly likely that trade and investment growth peaked in the early phase of the era of globalization, and the slowdown in trade and investment that has lasted for more than a decade now is likely to continue. With the environmental impact of international trade and investment also coming into question, there is a growing potential for trade and investment, the leading factor in driving economic growth in the latter part of the 20th century and the early part of the 21st century, to increasingly become a drag on growth for many important economies in the years to come.

The demographic changes underway around the world appear to be irreversible, at least over the near-to-mid-term, and while the trade and investment trends of recent years are reversible, the will to reverse them appears not to be in place at this time. This leaves productivity as the last great hope for global economic growth over the remainder of the 21st century. This is what makes the decline in productivity growth around the world in recent decades so alarming. Moreover, while it was not a big surprise that productivity growth in most developed economies has slumped in recent years, that fact that productivity growth has fallen significantly in many important emerging markets in recent years has come as somewhat of a surprise for many economies. This is a very worrying sign, for most emerging markets are increasingly facing the same demographic, trade and investment pressures as their developed economy counterparts.

What is also worrying is the fact that this long-term decline in productivity growth is not receiving the attention that it deserves, both from the media and from most economists, for it is the factor that is likely to have the greatest impact on the performance of the global economy in the future. Instead, coverage of the global economy has focused largely on trade, investment and changes to the labor market, given that these factors are both tangible and relatively easy to measure and to understand. It is not only in the news or among economists where the issue of productivity decline is not receiving enough attention, for both economic policy makers and business decision makers are also not devoting enough of their attention to this most serious issue. Again, the difficulty in understanding and measuring productivity is largely to blame for this lack of coverage and attention. It is easy for most anyone to understand how economic growth is measured, or how many jobs have been created in any particular month. Even more so, the direction of stock markets is something that is easy for most policy makers, as well as the wider public, to understand and to quantify. This is not the case with productivity. Even many of the most seasoned economic policy makers in some of the world's most important economies struggle to measure and interpret productivity data, making it all the more difficult to formulate policies aimed at boosting productivity. Unfortunately, while job creation levels and share prices have their role to play in the global economy, it is productivity and its future direction that is likely to play the leading role in determining the health of the global economy in the years and decades ahead.

So, can we solve the issue involving the difficulty in measuring and interpreting productivity growth? The signs aren't positive. Rarely is productivity growth the focus of best-selling business or economic publications. Even more rare is when two or more of these publications agree upon just how to measure productively in a sensible way. Therefore, the first task is going to have to be a major international effort to come up with a way to measure productivity more clearly and more consistently across a large number of economies. For the moment, too few economies have reliable productivity data that can easily be compared across countries, and this makes it difficult to increase the focus on this most important issue. This needs to change, for it is in the field of productivity where the future of the global economy will most likely be determined, for better or worse.

Chapter Fifteen

IMPLICATIONS FOR THE FUTURE

WHAT THIS BOOK HAS shown is that there are grave long-term threats to the global economy, threats that have the potential to usher in a new era of sluggish growth, to result in little wealth creation and to usher in a period of long-term decline. As we have seen, there are three main threats to the long-term health of the economy.

First, the demographic changes that have been underway for much of the 21ˢᵗ century (and for some parts of the world much longer) are already having a major impact on many of the world's leading economies and some of the world's most important industries and service sectors. Worse, the impact on these economies and sectors of the economy will continue, and will likely accelerate, in the years ahead. Meanwhile, significant demographic changes are also underway in many parts of the world that had, at least until recently, rather favorable demographic characteristics. Unfortunately, little can be done to avoid these demographic shifts. As a result, working-age populations in most areas of the world, including in most of its largest economies, will either stagnate or decline in the decades ahead, reducing the amount of available labor as well as the number of consumers in these markets. At the same time, the weight of the global population will continue to shift from more productive parts of the world that generally have higher levels of wealth-generation capacity, to areas of the world where productivity levels are extremely low and where wealth is generally scarce and in the hands of a very small sector of the population. It is hoped that such a shift will help to redistribute wealth and jobs to areas of the world where they are scarce. However, there is ample evidence to suggest that this will not have the desired effect in all areas of the world. Therefore, it cannot be taken for granted that today's poorest regions will follow in the economic footsteps of China or Central Europe, and if they don't, these demographic changes will be made worse, with dangerous imbalances causing severe disruptions to the global economy and raising the number of threats to global security.

Unfortunately history has shown us the impact of demographic shifts on the health of the economy. For example, when plagues hit the ancient world, or the world of the Middle Ages, their impact on the demographic situation of a particular region was profound, often leading to a dramatic decline in the size of the overall population. This in turn led to massive economic dislocations that often laid low once-powerful economies, or delayed the economic development of less-developed economies. Conflicts are another example of how a sudden population decline or dislocation can have a devastating impact on an economy. Another is mass emigration, often involving either the most highly-skilled or the least risk-averse segments of a region's society. All of these factors have led to severe demographic declines in the past, sometimes sudden declines and sometimes much slower developing declines. Either way, negative demographic changes, especially those that impact the most productive segments of society, have proven time-after-time that they can reduce the wealthiest economies to poverty and transform the most developed economies to a subsistence level existence.

For many, there is the hope that, while we may not be able to change the direction of global demographics, we can mitigate its impact on the economy and global living standards. This hope is largely derived from the technological advances that continue to be made in many fields, advances that promise to offset the impact of slower population growth as well as the impact of the aging of the population in most leading economies. However, technology will not be able to affect the slowdown in the growth for the number of consumers, particularly in those areas of the world where much of the world's wealth is concentrated. In fact, while this demographic decline is likely to have a positive impact on the environment and some other aspects of our quality of life, it is almost certainly going to be a major drag on our ability to generate economic growth and to create wealth and employment, The fact is that we are staring into the face of a future with less workers and less consumers, depriving the global economy of its most basic driver of growth. As the demographic dividend that has been in place since the Industrial Revolution in the West, and since the 20th century in many other parts of the world, disappears, the global economy will face perhaps its greatest challenge in recent centuries.

As we have also discussed at length in this book, global trade and investment is also facing a very uncertain future. Unlike demographics, this is one factor that can impacted by human decisions in a relatively short period of time, meaning that the decline in trade and investment that has taken place for more than a decade can still be reversed. For example, the direction and growth of international trade is largely controlled by the decisions of policy makers in the world's leading economic powers. The same is true for investment, which has suffered an even greater decline than trade over the past decade. For both to be revived, the world's leading economies will have to abandon their recent protectionist tendencies, for in the past, it has been the decision of the world's leading economic power, or powers, to decide whether or not global trade and investment will be promoted or discouraged. For more than a century, this power has been the United States, and it has been decisions taken in Washington that have ushered in periods of both massive expansions for trade and investment as well as for periods of significant declines in trade and investment.

Unfortunately, economic policy makers are either not well-versed in the lessons of the past, or they have simply forgotten them. This raises the risk that protectionism will be seen as a necessary response to economic or societal challenges, something that we have already witnessed in recent years. We have the data and analysis to show us just how big of an impact that protectionism can have on the economy and yet, there are still persistent calls for trade barriers to be erected and for global trade and investment to be reduced in time of crisis. At this point in time, as we face the threat of declining demographic growth and stagnating productivity levels, there is much harm that can be done through the enacting of protectionist measures that will almost inevitable only serve to protect a very small segment of an individual country's population, its workforce or its economy.

The third main driver of economic growth, productivity improvements, are also uncertain to provide for the level of growth that they have done many times in our past, particularly during those periods where economic growth was at its fastest. Still, there are hopes that the technological breakthroughs needed to boost long-term productivity growth are just around the corner, or may have already begun to emerge. Likewise, process improvements such as those that played a major role in the success of the Japanese economy in the 1970s and 1980s, could also be forthcoming, helping to offset the drags on the global economy coming from other factors. Look at 5G. This latest (at the time of the writing of this book) technology standard for broadband communications began to be rolled out in 2019 and is leading to many advancements in terms of communications and data dissemination. Of course, the four generations of broadband technology that proceeded 5G did little to boost overall productivity levels, but there is always hope that this one, as well as future breakthroughs in communications technology, will have a larger impact on productivity. Artificial intelligence is another technology that many economists hope will play a pivotal role in reversing the decline in productivity growth that has so bedeviled most of the world's leading economies. In particular, artificial intelligence, much like automation, has the potential to offset to impact of demographic decline on the global economy. Of course, we are just in the nascent stages of the development of artificial intelligence, so its exact impact on productivity is hard to know at this point in time.

Historically, there have been periods where productivity growth has slowed, only to rise again thanks to any number of changes in technology, process management or other factors that influence the direction of productivity growth. For example, the turmoil of the Second World War led to technological and process breakthroughs that played a major role in the productivity booms of the post-war decades. Likewise, many of the early technological and process breakthroughs during the early stages of the Information Revolution also helped to boost productivity growth rates, for a time, in the late 1990s and early

2000s, at least in those countries and industries that embraced these break-throughs. Unfortunately, the most recent increases in productivity growth have proven to be short-lived, and the clear trend for productivity growth in most major economies has been downwards in recent decades. Worse, the 21st century has so far seen productivity growth that has continued to slow, and in some extreme cases, has come to a near-end. This suggests that not only is the decline in productivity growth a long-term trend, but that it is also across the board, covering most regions, countries and economic sectors. This is a most worrying development.

THE THREAT OF A BLEAK ECONOMIC FUTURE

In this book, I have focused largely on what I consider to be the three main drivers of economic growth (demographics, trade and investment, and pro-ductivity). This doesn't mean that there are no other factors that can also drive growth. For example, discoveries of natural resources do not fall entirely into one of these three categories, but have proven over time to be a major driver of economic growth for those countries or regions fortunate enough to find such natural resources on their territory. Think about how Spain's gold and silver discoveries in the Americas transformed its power in the 16th century, or how the oil wealth of the Arabian Peninsula turned what had been some of the poorest areas in the world into some of the richest. In recent years, North Dakota's economic fortunes were transformed by the shale boom in the United States, dramatically increasing wealth levels in that US state.

Another factor in determining the level of growth in a country or region is its environment. So far, we have not touched too much on this issue, but my plans are to write an entire book on the subject, focusing on how this most pressing issue will impact the global economy and how we will need to both expand the economy while reducing the harm that we do to the environment. Unfortunately, the threat to the global economy posed by a changing climate and threats to the planet's environmental health are very real. At the same time, it is unlikely that we are going to make new discoveries of natural resources that will be of the magnitude that will enable them to boost the global economy as a whole. Sure, some individual countries or regions could still benefit from such discoveries (as the United States has done with its shale oil and gas industry), but a global economic transformation from such discoveries seems highly unlikely at this point. Add to this the already considerable evidence that the three main drivers of economic growth are unlikely to provide the spark needed to boost the global economy's outlook in the coming decades, and it is clear that we face the real threat of long-term sluggishness for the global economy, or worse, a no-growth future.

This threat from a world with slower economic growth cannot be understated. The world in which we live, the world upon which all of our modern way of life is based, depends on an ever-expanding global economy. Since the Industrial Revolution, this has largely been the case for countries and regions that have undergone the process of industrialization.

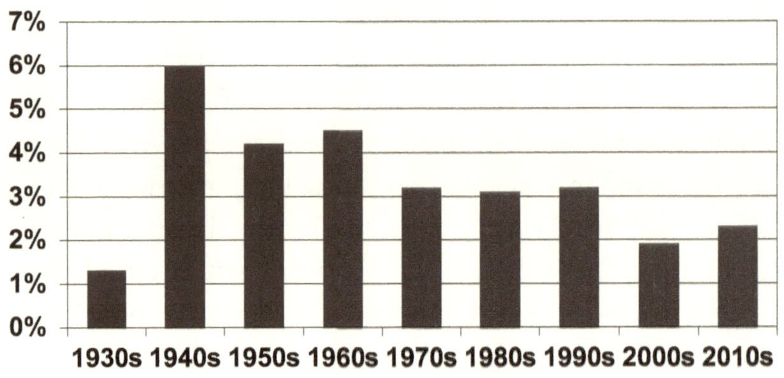

Source: US Bureau of Economic Analysis

Sure, there have been interruptions caused by economic downturns and conflicts, but growth has always returned. For some regions, such as northern Europe or North America, this means that nearly continuous long-term economic growth stretches back all the way to the late 18th and early 19th centuries. For most other parts of the world, this means that the second half of the 20th century and the first two decades of the 21st century have been largely periods where economic growth has continuously trended upwards, even if there has been a great deal of volatility in many of these later-industrialized economies. This promise of an ever-expanding economy has fueled confidence among consumers, businesses and investors that, no matter how bleak the situation may be over the near-term, were confident that long-term growth would be sure to return. This, in turn, has allowed policy-makers and business leaders to make far-reaching decisions based on the assumption that long-term growth was all but guaranteed. This has helped the world to achieve many of its greatest achievements in terms of technological developments, creating a robust infrastructure for the modern world, and creating systems designed to improve living standards for an ever-increasing number of people.

This assumption of growth is important to consider. Before the Industrial Revolution, this was something that was rarely, if ever, seen in human history. For much of human history, life and prosperity were fragile and could be taken away at any time by any number of potential catastrophes. Sure, some societies such as Ancient Rome and Han China were able to achieve periods of growth that spanned centuries, but their existence was far more precarious than that of the modern world, and each proved susceptible to major external and internal shocks that eventually led to their downfall. In today's world, long-term growth and prosperity no longer seems so precarious, at least in those parts of the world where growth has been in place for a long-time and where wealth levels and living standards are relatively high.

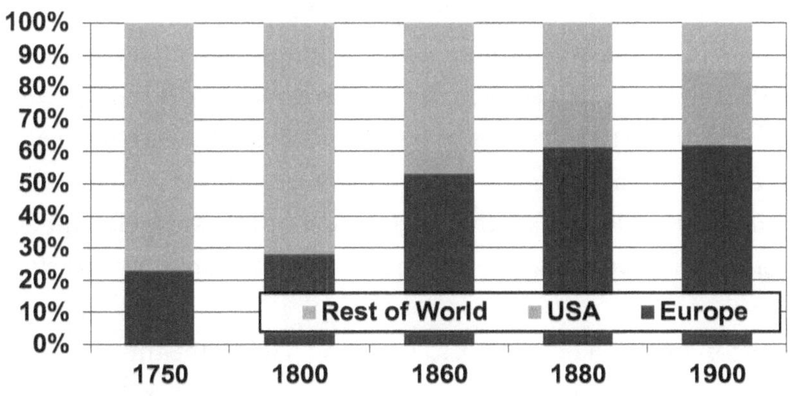

Source: Paul Kennedy

In these parts of the world, it has long been assumed that each new generation would enjoy higher living standards and opportunities to generate wealth than the generation that came before it. However, as we have seen, this assumption is now being challenged, even in the world's wealthiest economies. Not only has economic growth slowed in many of these parts of the world, but there are now significant fears that future generations, at least for some segments of society, will not enjoy the level of wealth nor the high living standards that their forbearers did. As economic growth has continued to slow in many of the world's leading economies, these fears of a bleak future have intensified and for some, a future of prosperity and growth no longer appears as assured as it once did.

It may sound far-fetched, but there is ample evidence throughout history of how a prolonged period of economic decline can result in the collapse of an entire political system, economic system, or way of life. Ancient Rome's eventual collapse was the result of, more than anything else, its inability to restore its complex trade and investment system following the chaos of the 3rd century CE. Sure, it hung on for many generations thereafter, but as a shadow of its former self. China's most successful dynasties also succumbed to economic decline, most notably Ming China's fatal decision to entirely close off its economy from the outside world, turning what had been the world's most technologically- and economically-advanced society into one of the most backwards societies within the span of a few centuries. In a smaller, and more modern context. Argentina had been one of the world's wealthiest countries in the early 20th century, but it was ill-prepared for the external shocks of the 1930s and has been losing ground over the long-term, on a relative basis, to many other similar-sized economies. In the early part of the 21st century, it is southern Europe that appears to be in the midst of a long-term economic decline that is threatening the living standards and futures of that region's population, for no longer do that region's economic struggles appear to be a temporary phenomenon, but rather, a long-term trend towards stagnation and decline.

Unfortunately, too little attention is being paid to the threat of long-term economic decline and what it would mean for the world's living standards. Too much focus remains on the near-term, leading many to believe that the problems currently facing the global economy are of a near-term variety and will inevitably give way to future economic growth, as they have done for much of the world for most of the past century or two, depending where in the world you are. Worse, an increasing number of policy-makers and well-read thinkers are now questioning the need for economic growth, claiming that it has been the drive to generate economic growth that is the cause for many of the modern world's problems. While this may be true, in part, on the environmental front, the fact is that our entire way of living is based upon long-term economic growth, and without it, these systems would collapse, causing untold misery for billions of people around the world. That is why this issue needs to receive far more attention than it has done so far.

Another factor to consider is the fact that the long period of more-or-less consistent economic growth that for some parts of the world stretches back more than two centuries has resulted in the generation of massive amounts of wealth. Consider the fact that, in those areas of the world that do not have a long history of stable and consistent economic growth, the wealth that is generated by the state, by companies or by individuals is often squandered, or taken quickly out of that country. For example, many African countries are home to large reserves of natural resources, such as oil or diamonds, that have generated wealth over a long period of time. However, as few, in any, African countries have industrialized to the point where they have been able to generate long-term sustainable economic growth, much of this natural resource wealth has been squandered. In some cases, this wealth has gone to a country's political and business elites, with little wealth going to the population at-large. Often, this wealth is quickly taken out of the country to more secure locations (such as low-tax centers like Switzerland or Luxembourg) where not only has the economy been growing for a long time, but few questions are asked regarding where the wealth comes from. In contrast, the United States not only has been generating relatively consistent economic growth since its inception, but its giant market has allowed the state, businesses and individuals based there to generate unfathomable amounts of wealth and to keep much of this wealth within the borders of the US. This combination of long-term growth and a vast domestic market is something that China is seeking to emulate, and now, after more than four decades of strong economic growth, we can see the impact that this is having on the ability of China to generate wealth and keep into within that country's borders.

For the most part, much of the world's wealth today is concentrated in just a few areas. For example, it can be argued that nearly all of the world's wealth in concentrated in what amounts to just a handful of the world's countries, nearly all of which either have been generating economic growth for a prolonged period of time, or have giant domestic markets that allow start-up businesses to blossom in giant multinationals, sometimes within a very short period of time.

Wealth is also concentrated in a handful of major economic centers. In the United States, New York may be the country's financial capital and center of more wealth than anywhere else in the world, but there are also huge concentrations of wealth in places such as Northern California and Chicago. In the Middle East, Dubai has emerged as a massive center of wealth for a region that has long not had an economic hub that could be considered among the most important economic centers in the world.

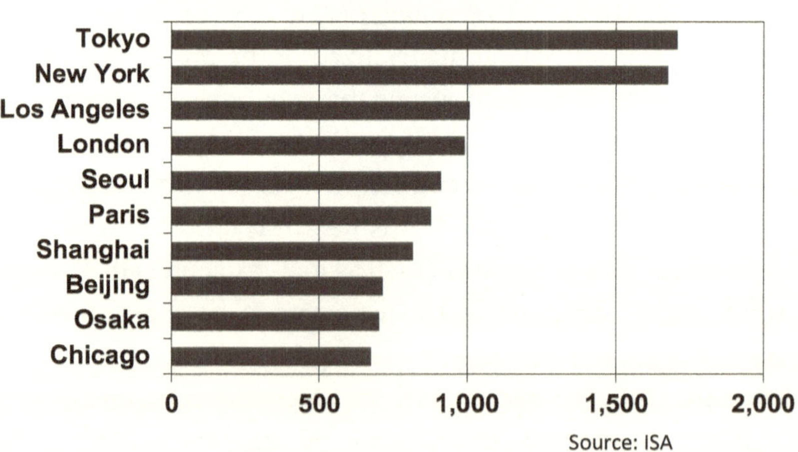

Wealth can also be concentrated within certain industries, or even within individual companies. For example, think about how much wealth today in concentrated in the information technology industry, or in the past, was concentrated in industries such as mining or oil. For that matter, just look at the remarkable market capitalizations of some of the world's leading tech firms today, not to mention the immense wealth of their founders.

It is important to remember that, in some cases, wealth has been spread from richer countries to poorer countries, or from wealthier industries to poorer industries. For example, look at how the wealth generated in China's largest cities and its coastal areas in the 1980s and 1990s began to spread to poorer interior regions of that vast country in the following decades, or how wealth generated in the United States has powered northern Mexico's industrial boom. Among industries, there are also many examples of wealth spreading from more successful industries to those that have had lesser degrees of success. For example, the information technology industry has generated wealth for a whole host of other industries that have either emerged to provide manufacturing support for the industry or have benefitted from the wide range of services created by the information technology industry.

In these days of rising levels of wealth inequality and the backlash that this has engendered against wealth, it is important to remember that, without ever-higher levels of wealth generation, it will be almost impossible to reduce poverty levels around the world. Hundreds of millions of Chinese would not have been lifted out of absolute poverty over the past 40 years if that country had not been able to find a way to initially generate wealth within a relatively small section of that country. In fact, we face a desperate need to generate wealth as the prospects for long-term economic growth are deteriorating. There are all too many examples around the world of countries, regions or cities that were no longer able to generate gains in wealth, and in nearly every case, those countries, regions or cities saw poverty levels rise and living standards fall, sometimes gradually and sometimes dramatically. Furthermore, there are still billions of people around the world living in poverty, including many in what are considered to be some of the world's wealthiest countries, regions or cities. If we do not continue to find new ways of generating wealth, the chances of lifting more people out of poverty will be significantly reduced.

THE IMPACT ON PUBLIC SPENDING

Today, we take many public services for granted. In fact, government-provided services are one of the hallmarks of the modern world. For example, clean drinking water is an essential government-provided service that is enjoyed by an ever-larger share of the global population. Likewise, the roads that we drive on, at least in most of the world, are also provided by the government. The postal service is yet another public service that we take for granted. In fact, there are hundreds of such public services that we utilize in our daily lives that are provided for by our national, state and local governments, funded, of course, by the taxes that we pay as individuals, or which our employers pay as corporate taxes.

While public services are ubiquitous in the modern world, not that long ago, the level of government services that were available to a country's population were far scarcer. Take for example the United States. In 1900, government spending in the United States was but a fraction of what it is today. Here are some examples:

- Public healthcare spending in the United States has risen from just 0.3% of the US' GDP in 1900 to 7.8% today.
- Government pension spending in the United States in 1900 was almost non-existent, but today, it equals 6.7% of US GDP
- Public education spending in the United States in 1900 amounted to just 1.0% of its GDP at that time, while today it is 5.3% of GDP.
- Defense spending in the United States in 1900 (when the US was just coming out of a war with Spain) was only 1.1% of that country's GDP, while today, it is 4.2% of US GDP.
- In 1900, government welfare spending was just 0.1% of the United States' GDP, while today it equals 2.2% of GDP.

Keep in mind, this data is for the United States. There are many countries where public spending today accounts for a much higher share of the country's GDP than that of the US.

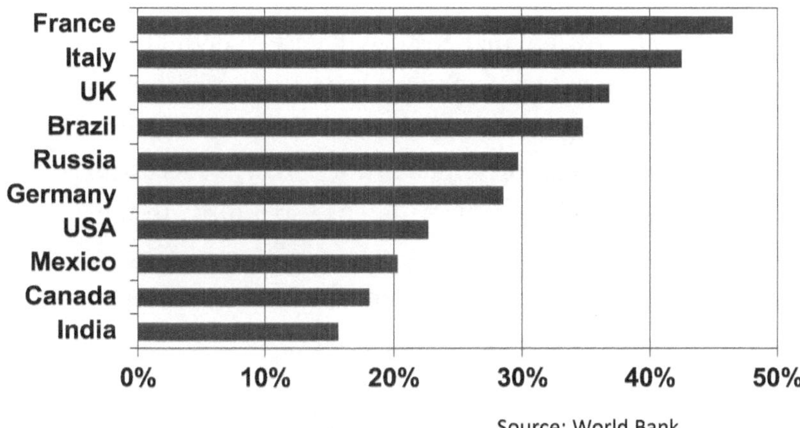

The point is that such high levels of public spending are indeed a relatively new development in the economic history of the world. In the past, most government spending focused on defense, and little on such areas as education, retirement benefits and healthcare.

This growth in public spending is really a development of the post-war era. In much of the world, public spending levels as a share of economic output were very low until the three major catastrophes that befell the world between 1914 and 1945 (the First World War, the Great Depression and the Second World War). In the wake of these crises, voters demanded that the government take a major stake in the welfare and well-being of their citizens. This was done via retirement programs, public healthcare and education, as well as the expansion of infrastructure such as communication and transportation networks. With many of the world's leading economic powers devastated by these three crises, their citizens demanded that their basic needs be met by the government, and this led to an across-the-board increase in public spending that continues to this day.

Let's look at some of the main types of public spending and how they have evolved over the past century.

Defense: At many times in human history, defense spending accounted for the lion's share of government expenditures. Forming, arming and maintaining a military force was an expensive endeavor, particularly in times of war, which were frequent in earlier eras of human history. Many a successful government was laid low financially by runaway defense spending. In the 20th century, defense spending peaked during the two world wars. Since then, defense spending as a share of GDP has trended slowly downwards, particularly in the decades following the Second World War.

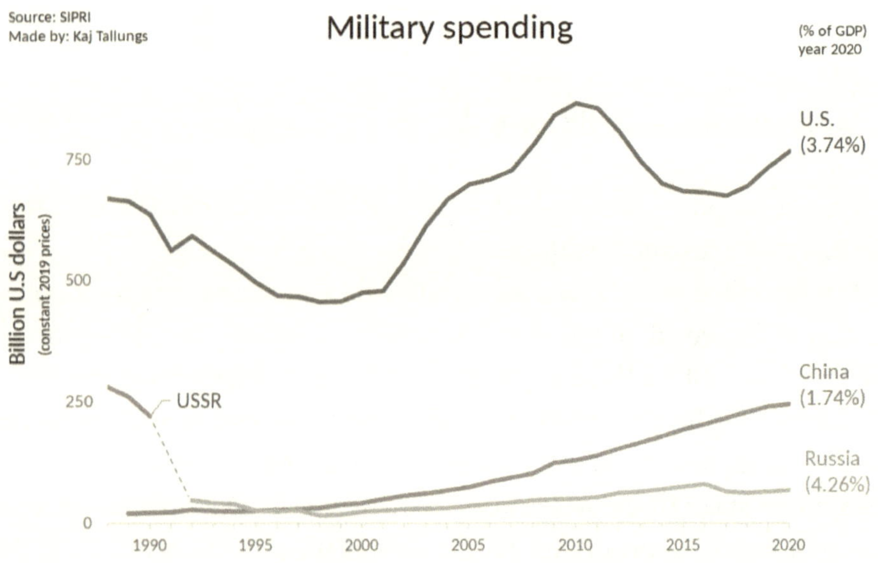

Education: At the state and local level, education spending became one of the leading areas of government spending in the 19th century. In the United States, education spending remained almost entirely in the hands of state governments until after the Second World War. Overall, this was the area in which government spending in most of today's developed economies grew the fastest between the 19th century and the 1970s. Of course, the growth in the student-age populations of developed countries has stagnated since the 1970s, reducing the need for this sector to take a higher share of public spending.

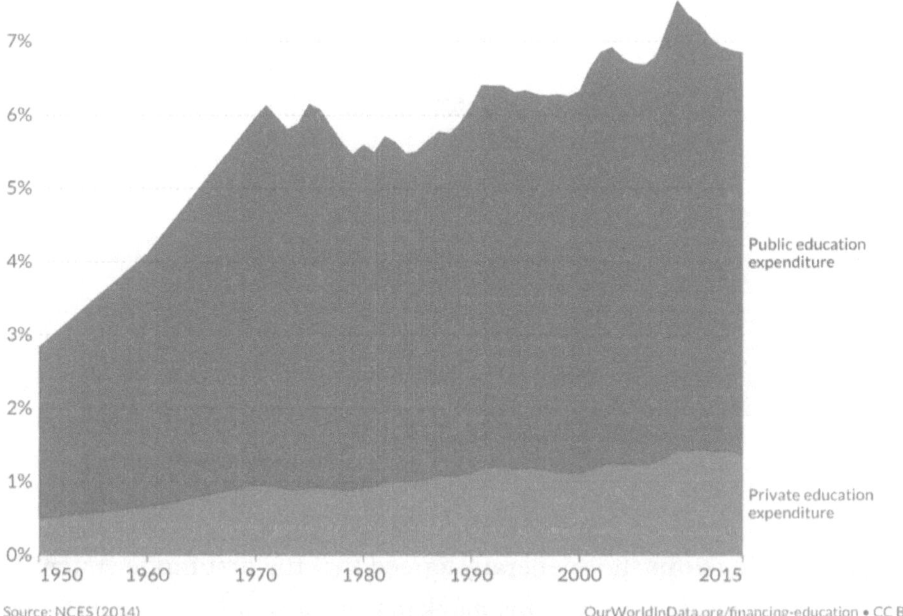

Healthcare: While public spending on defense and education has been relatively high for a longer period of time, that is not the case for healthcare spending. In fact, for most of the world, public spending on healthcare only really took off in the 1960s and 1970s. However, since that time, it has grown remarkably fast. In fact, in the United States, government spending on healthcare has risen from just 1% of GDP in the 1960s to nearly 8% today. Given the fact that populations are aging, and thus facing greater healthcare costs, it is easy to see why public healthcare spending has risen so dramatically in a relatively short period of time.

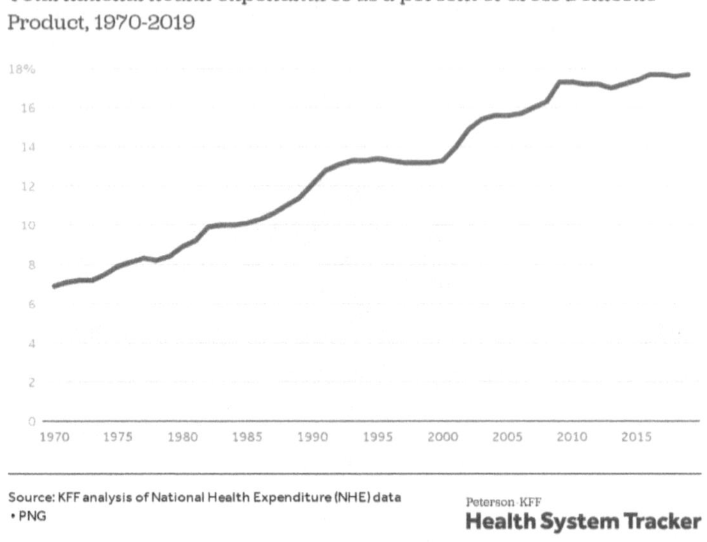

Source: KFF analysis of National Health Expenditure (NHE) data
• PNG

Peterson-KFF
Health System Tracker

Retirement/Pensions: It is generally agreed that the first modern pension system was created by Otto von Bismarck in Germany in 1889. In most cases, more extensive pension systems were implemented in the first half of the 20th century, at a time when life expectancies were barely higher than official retirement ages. Today, most countries have extensive pension systems, and while retirement ages that were set in the early 20th century are more-or-less the same today, life expectancies have risen substantially. Therefore, it is no surprise that public spending on pension programs has risen dramatically in recent decades, and will continue to rise without major reforms.

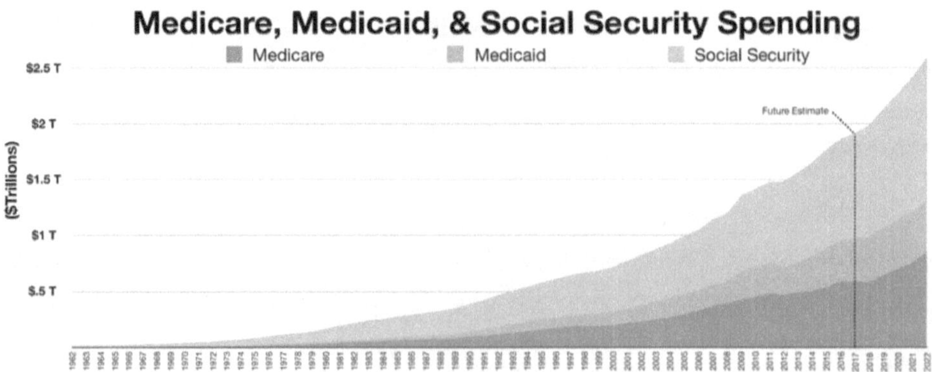

There is little debate that each of these categories of government spending are important and essential in the context of living in the 21st century. In addition, there are many other types of government spending, including spending on infrastructure, the environment and much more that also merit a strong focus from governments around the world. However, as economic growth rates have trended downwards in many parts of the world, and as government spending in many of these categories has risen dramatically, it is clear that we are approaching some type of breaking point in terms of the ability of governments to maintain such rising levels of public spending. Without higher levels of economic growth, we are facing the likelihood of an end to public spending growth, with some types of public spending likely facing major reductions in the years ahead, particularly in slower-growing economies.

We don't have to look too far back in history to find occasions when government were forced to make dramatic cuts in government spending. In fact, the overall low levels of economic growth in many parts of the world in the 21st century have yielded numerous examples of governments that were forced to make painful reductions in spending on a variety of publicly-financed programs. Some of these forced spending cuts were brought about by economic crises. Others were the result of slow, but steady, economic stagnation or decline. Others yet were the result of government mismanagement of the economy and of the public's finances. Finally, some were the result of a dramatic decline in government revenues which often resulted from a country being too dependent upon a single source of public income, such as oil exports.

Here are four countries that have had to make substantial cuts in government spending for one of the four aforementioned reasons.

Greece: Most readers will be familiar with the economic crisis the befell Greece in the late 2000s and early 2010s. This crisis was so severe that Greece's economic output declined by nearly 30% between 2008 and 2016. Worse, Greece's level of economic output today is still smaller than it was in 1999, a worse performance than that of all but a very small number of countries over this period.

This collapse in economic output, coupled with the austerity measures that were imposed on Greece by its international lenders, had the predictable impact on Greek government spending. In 2009, Greek government spending peaked at €128 billion ($178 billion in 2009 US dollars). A decade later, Greek government spending had declined by fully one-third, falling to just €87 billion ($97 billion in 2019 US dollars). This resulted in massive cuts in spending across a range of public sectors, including infrastructure and education. With the outlook for long-term growth in Greece looking relatively poor, it is unlikely that government spending will return to pre-crisis levels anytime in the near-future.

Japan: Unlike Greece, Japan has not been forced to make dramatic reductions in its public expenditures. In fact, public spending in Japan has continued to trend slowly upwards throughout most of the 21st century, despite relatively anemic economic growth in Japan during that period. In fact, in the years between the Global Financial Crisis and the Covid-19 pandemic, government spending in Japan rose by 7.9%.

While overall government spending in Japan has slowly risen in recent years, the Japanese government is facing a great deal of financial pressure, much of which is brought upon it by the country's rapidly-expanding pension costs. With the country's working-age population set to continue its dramatic decline, and with the country's elderly population set to continue to grow for a couple of more decades, Japan's government faces the threat of having to either reduce per capita spending on pensions, or to divert public funds from other sectors to pay for Japan's increasing pension burden. Fortunately, Japan has done a better job than most countries in terms of keeping a sizeable share of its elderly population in productive activities, or else the financial health of that country would be even worse.

Venezuela: No country over the past few decades has suffered a more comprehensive economic collapse than Venezuela. As we discussed, Venezuela, with all of its vast oil wealth, was once Latin America's wealthiest country, something that allowed the government to significantly raise public spending levels in the 1960s and 1970s. However, the collapse of that country's economy in the 21st century has led to what are, by some measures, the greatest cuts in government spending of any country in the world.

Of course, Venezuela is no longer publishing reliable economic or financial data, so the total extent of the government's spending cuts is not known. However, the evidence of these draconian cuts is all around, from the country's crumbling infrastructure to the remarkable decline in living standards of ordinary Venezuelans. This is the most extreme example of what can happen when a country's economy fails to generate growth for a prolonged period of time, and no one is suggesting that this is the fate of the world's leading economies. Nevertheless, Venezuela is a cautious tale of how a once prosperous country can descend into an economic void that reduces government spending to levels that cannot sustain the needs of its citizens.

Saudi Arabia: In Saudi Arabia, government spending soared in the wake of the oil crises of the 1970s, which resulted in a massive increase in oil export revenues, filling government coffers and allowing Riyadh to embark on some of the most lavish public spending programs of any country over the past 50 years. While public spending growth slowed in the first part of the 21st century, it nevertheless expanded by nearly 400% between the years of 2000 and 2014.

However, when oil prices collapsed in 2014, Saudi Arabia's government was deprived of its main source of income. This forced the Saudi government to enact a series of major public spending cuts in the following years, reducing government spending by 25% between 2014 and 2017. This was a shock for a country where government spending had been rising more or less steadily for a number of decades and gave a greater impetus to the Saudi government's efforts to reduce the country's dependency on the oil and gas industry through attempts at diversifying the country' economy. This effort at diversification is continuing, but history has shown us that carrying out a successful diversification strategy has proven quite difficult for economies that have long been dependent upon a single commodity for much of its growth. If these efforts don't succeed, Saudi Arabia could witness more cuts in public spending in the years ahead.

The implications are clear. Without more economic growth in the future, public spending levels will have to come down, in some cases, quite significantly. This has big implications for any number of public spending programs. For example, defense spending, long one of the most important components of government expenditures, will have to be reduced in those countries where economic growth fails to materialize. We have already seen how this can work, as China's defense spending has soared on the back of its rapid economic growth, while Japan, a country that was for a long period the dominant military power in East Asia, has seen defense spending stagnate due to that country's moribund economy since the early 1990s.

Should the global security situation deteriorate, governments will find it hard to make more cuts to defense spending and this would, in turn, force even greater reductions in spending for other public programs.

One such program is infrastructure. As we have seen, this is one component of public spending that has been cut in the wake of previous economic downturns, so there is a real possibility that, should economic growth stagnate in the years ahead, this sector could see some of the largest reductions in government spending. Education is another sector at risk. On one hand, many of the world's slowest growing economies also have student-age populations that are already in decline.

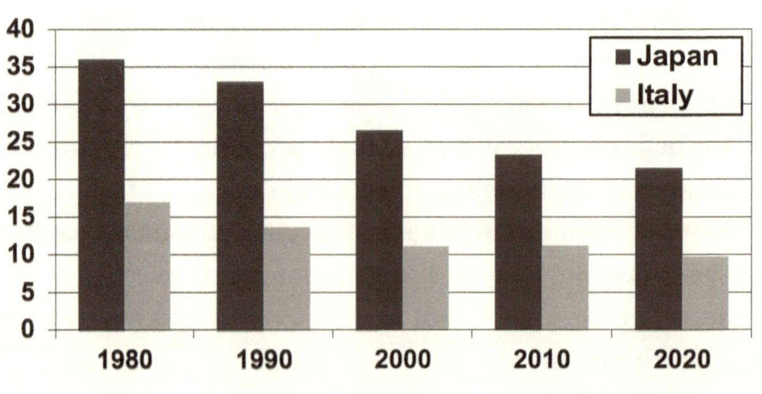

Source: UN

The big question surrounding government spending in the future involves the ever-expanding costs of financing public healthcare and pensions. As the world grows older, the cost of financing these elaborate programs will only grow at a more rapid pace. However, as we have seen, governments either already lack the means to finance these giant programs, or they will soon face such this prospect without a dramatic improvement in their countries' ability to generate economic growth and government revenues. It makes sense for governments to plan to cut back on spending in these areas, but few governments are willing to do so. In democracies, governments that cut healthcare and pension spending are rarely re-elected, while in totalitarian regimes, fear of the public's response to such cuts makes them quite unlikely. Therefore, the spending continues, even as the ability to finance this spending is stretched ever more thinly.

Overall, without long-term economic growth, long-term declines in living standards would be all but unavoidable. In fact, it would be almost inevitable that long-term living standards would erode without a higher level of economic growth, for once an economy enters into a long-term decline, history has shown us that it is very difficult for that economy to return to sustained growth.

There are many examples of this littered throughout our history. For example, the tremendous rise in living standards that were achieved during the glory years of the Roman Empire eventually disappeared as the Dark Ages emerged in Europe, leading to a period of more than 1,000 years in which living standards across much of Europe were significantly lower than they were during the height of the Roman period. China is a more recent example. The gradual decline in living standards that took place in China beginning in the 16th and 17th centuries left most of China destitute by the 19th and early 20th centuries, a situation that has only changed since the economic reforms that were undertaken in that country in the 1980s. Today, there are some concerns that countries such as Argentina, where living standards were among the highest in the world just a century ago, are now headed for a similar long-term decline unless those countries can reverse the downwards trajectories of their economies.

One of the reasons why we would see a decline in long-term living standards without sustained economic growth is that technological advancements would become significantly fewer and farther between without the funding that drives most advancements in technology. With less economic growth, governments and businesses would have less funding available for research and development. Instead, a greater percentage of government revenues would go towards spending on programs that were focused more on sustenance rather than advancements and technological breakthroughs, while businesses would be forced to concentrate on maintaining their revenues and downsizing their labor forces and other cost centers, rather than spending on the "next big thing". In turn, this would lead to lower levels of productivity growth. The scary thing is, this may already be happening, at least in some parts of the world and in some major sectors of the economy. The decline in productivity growth that has bedeviled most of the world's largest economies in recent decades could well be connected to the fact that economic growth in most of these economies has also been trending downwards for more than 40 years. Without higher levels of economic growth, productivity growth will continue to fall. In turn, without higher levels of productivity growth, economic growth will be increasingly hard to achieve.

In an era of ever-declining rates of economic growth, not to mention outright long-term economic decline, life as we know it would become much more basic. Instead of focusing on how to spend free-time or to engage in creative endeavors, survival would be much more in focus. Just look at the collapse of both art and technology in much of the post-Roman world in Europe in order to see how the need to focus on survival trumps all other aspects of life in a world where economic growth is absent. Sustenance would be the key in such a world, with the provision of food, shelter and security becoming the sole focus of economic activity, while trade and investment would collapse as economies became more localized, if not feudal. If one looks at the levels of trade, investment, spending, and research and development, spending on infrastructure or the arts, or any other aspect of spending that is not solely tied to sustenance activities in modern countries where economic growth has been lacking, one can see this pattern already emerging.

THREATS TO STABILITY AND SECURITY

It is widely understood that economic causes are often the root of conflict. Internally and externally, economic issues can fuel discontent or lead to competition that spills from a purely economic arena to one that involves violence and conflict. In some cases, economic rivalry remains just that, a competition between states that remains purely a race for economic supremacy. However, too often has economic rivalry turned into military rivalry, with some of the most devastating conflicts of the modern world having resulted from what had been, at least in part, disputes over economic issues.

Internally, economic issues can often lead to major divisions within a particular country or region. For example, wealth disparities can emerge when the economic growth generated by a country is not dispersed evenly among its citizens. We see this today in many parts of the world where growth has been concentrated among a smaller number of industries, or among a small segment of the population. This has led to a widening of wealth disparities in most of the world's leading economies, including the United States and China. At the same time, economic crises can exacerbate other internal divisions, leading to tensions between different ethnic or religious groups, or different social groups. We have seen over and over again how, in times of economic crisis, internal divisions can be magnified, leading to heightened levels of internal political and societal risk for any country that finds itself in a longer-term economic crisis.

Not only are internal tensions elevated when economic growth is not generated, but so too are external tensions and, as we have seen many times in history, it is these tensions between countries that can lead to some the most traumatic upheavals for the world as a whole. Trade disputes are just one of the many manifestations of these external tensions. For example, 1929's stock market collapse in the United States led to the Smoot-Hawley Tariff Act that essentially led to a worldwide trade war whose end was only brought about by the Second World War. In modern times, the relatively sluggish economic recovery from the Global Financial Crisis in the United States was one of the catalysts for the trade war between the US and China that began in the late 2010s. Another form of external dispute that can arise from a lack of economic growth is a competition to gain access to the vital resources needed to fuel economic growth. Think of Japan's desperate need for Southeast Asia's oil and gas reserves in the early 1940's, or of Russia's efforts to gain a stronger position in Europe's oil and gas export market in modern times. In fact, access to resources has been one of the leading sources of tensions between rival clans. tribes, cities, countries and empires throughout human history, and while the modern world's economy is far more diversified than any economy in history, the need to maintain and control access to the resources needed to both sustain life and to support an expanding economy are as important today as they ever were.

If one were to make a list of the most important wars and conflicts in history, it would quickly become apparent that, for a large majority of these conflicts, there were economic factors at the heart of nearly all of these conflicts. Sure, there are enough examples in history of other factors such as ethnic rivalries, religious tensions and territorial disputes being the root causes of many of these conflicts, been in the end, no factor has been more impactful in terms of leading to military conflict than issues and disputes in the economic realm. In fact, even in those conflicts where the primary causes have been a non-economic factor such as a border dispute, there is often a crucial economic element to the decision to go to war. Sometimes these economic factors will be the actual trigger of the conflict, while at other times, these economic factors could accelerate the start of this conflict. Furthermore, economic factors almost always have a major influence on decision-making during the conflict, as many wars come down to a test of economic strength among the various warring parties.

There are many examples of how economic factors can both lead to war and force difficult decisions upon states when making decisions involving going to war, or decisions taken during a conflict. The Venetian Empire is one such example. Venice, despite its relatively small size, emerged as one of Europe's leading economic powers, and by the 15th century, had gained control of an empire that controlled a large area of the eastern Mediterranean region. This empire's foundation was the economic power of Venice, which was amassed by its ability to dominate trade in the eastern Mediterranean, filling a void left by the declining Byzantine and Muslim empires in the first few centuries of the last millennium. However, when a new power arose threatening to cut off Venice's crucial trade routes, and thus undermine its economic power, Venice was forced to engage in a long series of wars with this new rising power. Unfortunately for Venice, the Ottoman Empire would prove too strong for the Venetians, and this led to both a loss of territory in the eastern Mediterranean and to a gradual decline of Venice itself, culminating in its fall at the hands of Napoleon in 1797. Today, this decline is still evident as the city of Venice has a population that is continuing to decline, while the historical city is engaged in a constant struggle to remain above the waves of the rising Adriatic Sea.

World War One is another example of a conflict that was greatly influenced by economic factors. Prior to the outbreak of war in 1914, there were many experts claiming that war in Europe had become an impossibility due to the growing interdependence of the region's leading economies on one another due to soaring levels of the trade and investment that was flowing between the states of Europe. This belief was exemplified by The Hague Conventions that took place in 1899 and 1907 which attempted to establish guidelines for how conflicts should be fought, but more importantly, focused on the need for peaceful resolutions to disputes between rival states. However, economic concerns helped to lead to what would be the largest conflict ever seen by the world up to that point in history. One of these economic concerns was the rapid expansion of Germany's economic power. Prior to the unification of Germany in 1871, the United Kingdom had been Europe's dominant economic power, while France, despite not being as developed economically as Britain, was still the leading economic power on the continent of Europe. However, the unification of Germany resulted in the creation of a new state that was not only far more economically-advanced than France, but one that was challenging the United Kingdom's role as the leading industrial power in Europe.

At the same time, Russia, a country with a relatively under-developed economy, but one with a good deal of potential for growth, was slowly beginning to industrialize and modernize, raising fears in Germany of the rising economic power on its eastern border. Altogether, by the early 1910s there was a situation in which all of Europe's leading powers were concerned about their economic position in the region, with the United Kingdom con-cerned about the growing threat of German economic power, with Germany

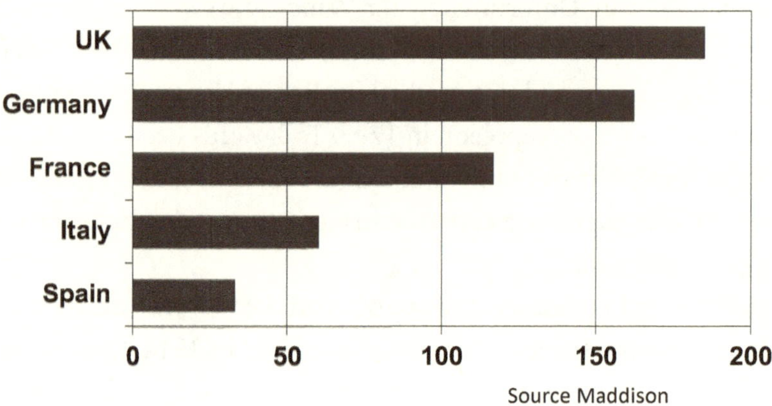

concerned about the threat from Russia's vast economic potential, and with France fearing that its economy was being dwarfed by those of both Britain and Germany. These factors, while not triggering the actual conflict itself, played a key role in convincing many of the political leaders of that time that conflict was both inevitable and desirable, so that their state could both ensure its continued economic growth and restore its rightful place within Europe's economic hierarchy.

The global conflict that followed the First World War by just two decades, the Second World War, was also heavily influenced by economic factors and trends. The Great Depression that began in late 1929 and spanned much of the 1930s was the fuel that lit the fire of right-wing and left-wing fanaticism that gave rise to radical governments in Germany, Japan and elsewhere. At the same time, the economic devastation caused by the Great Depression sapped the confidence of great powers such as the United States, the United Kingdom and France and distracted them from the threats emerging in Germany, Italy and Japan. At the same time, the United States, whose economic power at the end of the First World War was greater than it had ever been before, suffered some of the greatest economic losses of any country in the 1930s.

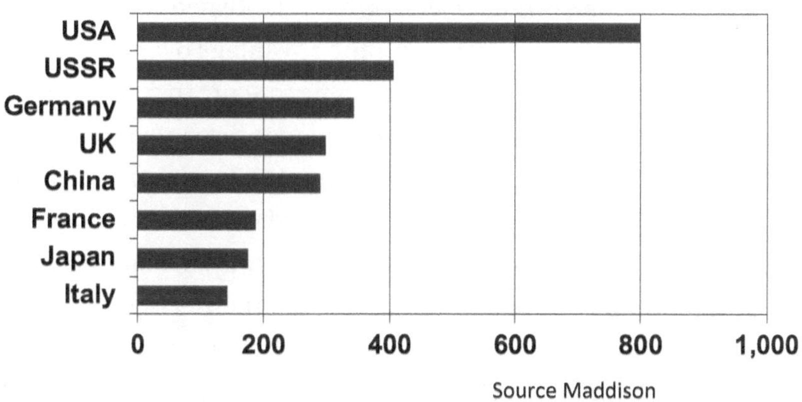

While the United States was focusing on rebuilding its economy by the second half of the 1930s, Germany, under the leadership of Adolf Hitler, was embarking on massive rearmament and infrastructure projects that, while reviving the German economy, threatened to lead to a dangerous overheating of the country's economy. This factor would play an under-appreciated role in Germany's decision to go to war in September 1939. Meanwhile, to Germany's east, the Soviet Union suffered massive economic dislocations in the 1920s and early 1930s, but by the late 1930s had embarked on a massive industrialization program, knowing that the country's industrial base would be the key to its ability to fight a war at that point in history.

In Asia, Japan too would find itself faced with difficult strategic decisions that were in large part based on the health of that country's economy. Most importantly, its loss of access to oil from the Dutch East Indies (today's Indonesia), threatened to bring Japan's economy to a crashing halt and to prevent it from being able to maintain its war efforts in China, or to fight a prolonged war against the United States and its allies such as the United Kingdom and Australia. Furthermore, many of Japan's leading political and economic policy makers were all too aware of the massive disparities in terms of economic and industrial power between their country and the United States. This is why they believed that their only chance to win a war against the United States would be to win such overwhelming victories in the first phase of the war that Washington would deem it too costly to engage Japan in a long war in the Pacific.

By the time that the eventual sides were established in late 1941, it was clear that the Allies had a massive economic advantage over their Axis rivals. Early in the war, Germany and Japan were able to score incredibly impressive victories due to their longer preparation for this conflict and their understanding of how modern warfare was fought in the 1940s. However, the massive economic advantages held by the Allies, thanks largely to the vast economic scale and sophistication of the United States economy, meant that victory for the US and its allies was all-but-assured. By 1943, these economic advantages were already turning the tide of the conflict and by the second half that year, the outcome of the conflict was truly no longer in doubt.

Since the Second World War, there have not been any major armed conflicts between two or more major economies. Sure, there was the Cold War between the United States and the Soviet Union, not to mention the 1962 border conflict between China and India, but neither of these was a full-blown conflict between two major economic powers at that point in time. There were many conflicts involving a single major economic power, especially the series of post-colonial conflicts that raged from the 1950s to the 1970s, but these were never a major threat to the well-being of the global economy.

As we look ahead, one cannot help but wonder if this threat of long-term economic stagnation and decline will not be the catalyst for major conflicts in the future. For one, such economic troubles could fuel political radicalism, as it did in the 1920s and 1930s. At the same time, rising levels of protectionism and nationalism could lead to far worse trade disputes than we have seen in recent years, something that could also turn an economic dispute into a military conflict. Finally, the battle for control of strategic resources such as oil, water, land or rare-earth elements could intensify as economic growth slows, resulting in conflicts over the control of these resources.

There are many examples of potential conflicts between large economic powers that could erupt in the years and decades ahead, particularly if economic growth continues to slow over the longer-term. For example, tensions between the world's two superpowers, the United States and China, have risen steadily in recent years, due in part to US concerns about China's rising economic and military power. As there are a large number of flashpoints that could bring these two giant powers into conflict (Taiwan, North Korea, South China Sea, etc.), the likelihood of a superpower conflict is now greater than it has been at any time since the early 1980s.

This is not the only potential great power conflict that the world faces today. For example, tensions between the United States and Russia have also been rising as the latter seeks to regain some of the geopolitical importance and influence that it lost in the wake of the dissolution of the Soviet Union. The growing rivalry between China and India is another flashpoint that has the potential to erupt into a conflict between two major economic powers, particularly in light of the numerous border disputes between those two Asian giants. In fact, there are a number of potential conflicts involving two or more major economies that could erupt in the near-future, any of which would not only be influenced by economic factors, but would also have a major impact on the economics of the combatants, as well as on the global economy as a whole.

THE NEED FOR GROWTH AMONG THE WORLD'S POOREST SOCIETIES

For much of this book, we have looked at how global economic growth has transformed the world, largely through developments that have occurred among the world's leading economies. However, one aspect of the need to generate global economic growth that should not be overlooked is the fact that this is the surest means to offer hope for the world's poorest countries and regions. In fact, without comprehensive economic growth on a global scale, there is little or no chance that the world's poorest societies will be able to reduce poverty and improve living standards. In fact, the global economic growth generated in recent decades has done a great deal to reduce poverty in some areas of the world, while dramatically raising living standards for billions of people.

The best and most recent examples of how global economic growth can reduce poverty and improve living standards can be found in Asia. In fact, East Asia's three largest economies each serve as an excellent example of how a country can reduce poverty and raise living standards. The country that established this so-called Asian Model is Japan. Following the Meiji Restoration that began in 1868, Japan undertook a series of efforts aimed at implementing and adopting Western technologies and economic processes to transform the Japanese economy from a feudal and relatively-backwards system to a modern and industrialized system. The fact that Japan was able to achieve this in such a short period of time was truly remarkable and this allowed Japan to make an audacious bid to dominate Asia, culminating in its defeat in 1945. Following the war, Japan, which already had the economic foundations laid by the Meiji Restoration, quickly developed a new, modern industrial and technological base. This time, thanks to the post-war trade and investment system put in place by the United States, Japanese manufacturers now found themselves with access to wealthy foreign markets, particularly the United States, and this allowed Japan to record remarkable rates of economic growth in the decades following the Second World War.

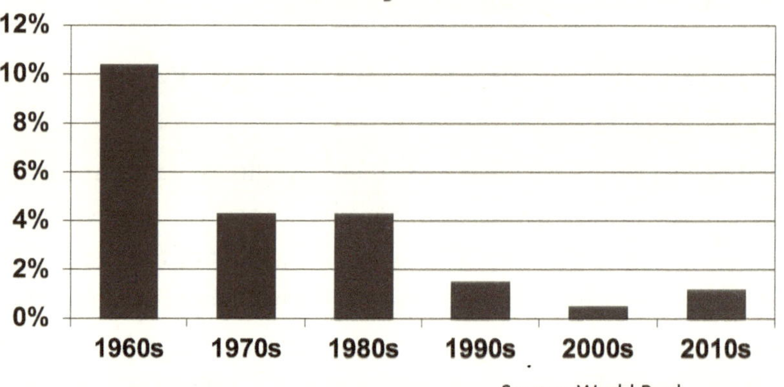

Overall, Japan went from trailing far behind Western powers in terms of economic output and wealth to overtaking nearly all of them in the span of just one century, truly a remarkable feat.

One country the emulated Japan's post-war economic success was South Korea. As we have discussed, poverty was widespread in South Korea following the Korean War, with South Korea trailing behind many Sub-Saharan African countries in terms of wealth and per capita GDP as late as the early 1960s. However, like Japan, South Korea established a system where local industries were both protected against foreign competition and encouraged to export to wealthy foreign markets. South Korea was therefore able to emulate the economic success of Japan, resulting in South Korea recorded extremely high rates of economic growth, while dramatically raising wealth levels and living standards in that country. In fact, while Japan's economy has recorded relatively little growth over the past 30 years, South Korea's economy continues to grow at a relatively fast pace. This has allowed South Korea to overtake Japan in terms of per capita GDP, something that would have seemed impossible just a couple of decades ago.

Finally, China, the giant of East Asia, also learned the lessons of the Japanese and South Korean economic models. Since the 1980s, it too has protected local industries from foreign competition, while encouraging exports to wealthier markets around the world. Remember, in the 1970s, China was one of the world's poorest and most isolated economies, with wealth levels that trailed even behind India by a significant margin. As we know, since the 1980s, China's economy has grown faster than any other in the world. As such, hundreds of millions of people in China have been lifted out of poverty, while living standards that country have improved significantly during these four decades of unprecedented economic growth.

Looking outside of Asia, Central and East Europe is another region that has experienced a tremendous increase in wealth generation and a major decline in poverty thanks to a long period of strong economic growth. Prior to the Second World War and the imposition of Communism on this region in the wake of this conflict, most areas of Central and East Europe were relatively poor, with only a few pockets of wealth such as the modern-day Czech Republic and Slovenia. By the 1980s, the failings of the Communist system had resulted in countries in this region falling further behind most of their neighbors to the west and by the time Communism collapsed in the late 1980s and early 1990s, most countries in this region trailed behind their counterparts in the West by as much as 80% in terms of per capita GDP. In the 1990s, painful economic reforms were introduced in many countries in this region. While these reforms caused massive disruptions to many sectors of these countries' economies, and left many people in this region destitute, they were successful in transforming and modernizing the economies of this region. In turn, this led to a flood of foreign investment into many Central and East European countries, primarily in their manufacturing sectors as their cheaper labor forces and proximity to the wealthy markets of West Europe made them attractive locations for a variety of manufacturing operations.

Since these reforms, the economies of most of Central and East Europe's leading countries have grown much faster than their western counterparts, enabling these countries to dramatically close the wealth gap with West Europe. In fact, when measured using purchasing power parity (PPP), countries such as the Czech Republic, Poland and Hungary are nearing the wealth levels of countries in West Europe such as Italy and Spain. Furthermore, at current economic growth projections, some of these Central and East European countries will overtake a number of West European countries in terms of per capita GDP by the end of the 2020s. None of this would have been possible without the dramatic (and sometimes painful) economic reforms that were enacted in the 1990s. For proof of this, one only needs to look at the situation in countries such as Ukraine and Serbia, where such reforms were not enacted, to see how their economies have fallen far behind their more successful neighbors in this region.

Today, the poorest countries in the world hold up these examples from East Asia and Central Europe as an example of how they can increase wealth generation and reduce poverty in their countries. The lessons they have learned are clear. First, they need to create a climate that is conducive to attracting foreign investment. To do this, these countries such to enact economic reforms, increase their level of political and economic stability, improve their infrastructures and gain access to important export markets. Second, they need to develop manufacturing sectors that are focused on exporting to wealthier markets, just as countries such as South Korea and the Czech Republic were able to do. While some countries have managed to develop export-oriented manufacturing industries on their own, most, particularly lesser-developed countries, have relied on foreign investment, at least to kick-start these industries. In fact, today's poorest countries almost certainly will require a major influx of foreign investment in order to establish major export-oriented manufacturing facilities, given the lack of manufacturing expertise in most of these countries. For those countries that are able to follow this path, the prospects for wealth generation, job creation and poverty reduction will be far greater than for those countries that fail to develop such manufacturing sectors.

Chapter Sixteen

CAN LONG-TERM ECONOMIC GROWTH BE REVIVED?

EVEN WITH THE BOUNCE-BACK of the global economy in the wake of the huge losses suffered in 2020 at the height of the Covid-19 pandemic, the overall trend for most major economies so far in the 21st century has been one of gradually declining levels of economic growth. Worse, as this book has shown, a series of key trends all point to a continued slowdown in terms of economic growth for the foreseeable future. Therefore, it is prudent that we ask ourselves if indeed it is possible to reverse this trend and return the global economy to higher rates of growth before it is too late, for, as we have seen, the consequences of long-term sluggish economic growth are quite dire. Worse, the consequences of no growth are even worse. To do so, we will take one last look at the three primary drivers of global economic growth (demographics, trade and investment, and productivity) to determine whether or not it is within our powers to reverse the downwards trends in growth for each of these factors.

CAN DEMOGRAPHIC DECLINE BE REVERSED?

Of all of the factors that contribute to long-term global economic growth, the one that is perhaps the most difficult to change is demographics. History has shown us that reversing demographic trends is extremely difficult to achieve, and even when it can be reversed, it is a long and drawn-out process, and one whose impact on the economy is often not realized for a long time into the future. In fact, creating or manipulating demographic changes over the near-term is all but impossible, and even when taking a long-term approach towards demographic change, it still can prove to be a very challenging endeavor. In fact, few countries have ever managed to reverse their demographic trends, particularly when it comes to raising population levels.

Despite the fact that demographic change is hard to enact, there are some examples of countries and regions that have, at least for a while, managed to reverse detrimental demographic factors. For example, Europe in the years following the Second World War is a region that managed to overcome some dramatic demographic difficulties. In the 1920s and the 1930s, Europe's population grew relatively quickly, driven by a number of factors that boosted birth rates in the wake of the First World War and the Spanish Flu pandemic.

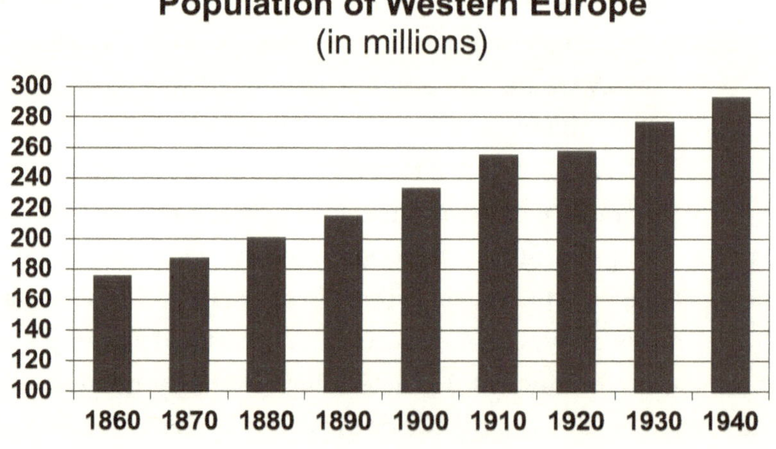

Source: Maddison

However, the Second World War would have a devastating impact on the demographic situation in many areas of Europe, resulting in a sharp decline in the populations of many areas of Europe, particularly among younger working-age males. Had this demographic trend not been reversed in the decades that immediately followed this conflict, Europe would have never been in a position to recover economically from the devastation caused by the Second World War. However, a combination of rising birth rates and an influx of immigration to areas of Europe where labor shortages were the greatest enabled Europe to enjoy 30 years of rapid economic growth following the war.

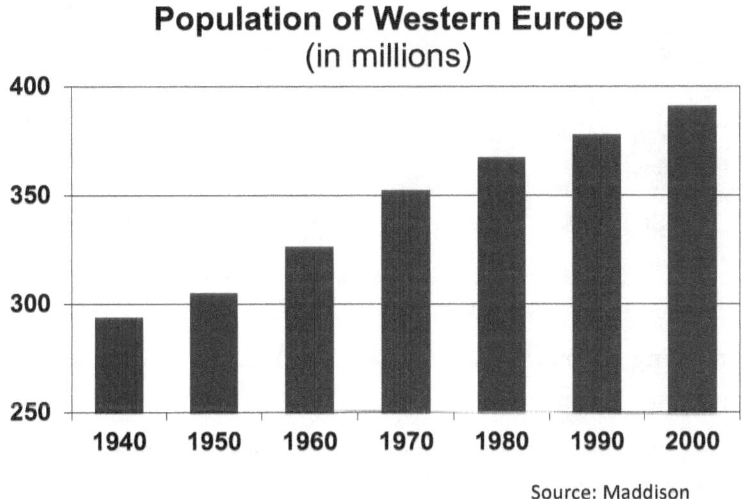

The United States is another example of how much demographics can influence the economic potential of a country. It is no secret that much of the US' economic success has been based upon its ability to attract immigrants from all over the world, many of whom are often highly-skilled and highly-motivated. However, this immigration has been anything but steady, with there being periods in US history where immigration has been discouraged, it not outright halted.

The best example of this is the period preceding and following the Great Depression, when anti-immigration sentiment led to the Emergency Quota Act of 1921 and the Immigration Act of 1924. These acts led to a dramatic decline in immigration into the United States and had a lingering impact on immigration numbers into the US for decades to come. In fact, it was only in the 1990s when immigration in the US returned to the levels reached in the first part of the 20th century. In the past, immigration was a key to the United States' ability to avoid the types of labor shortages that could have hampered its rapid economic growth in the 19th and early 20th centuries. Today, with the US

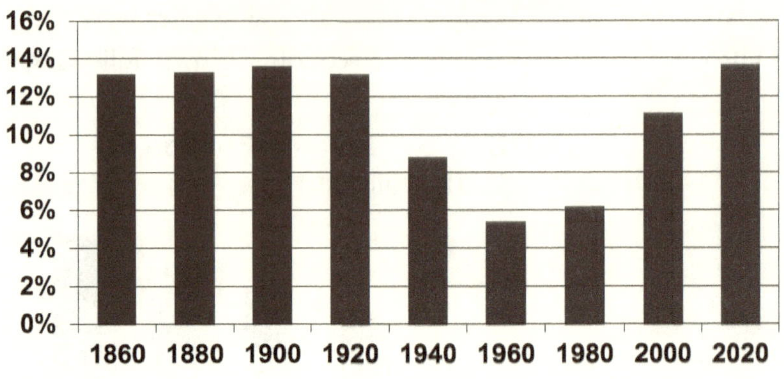

once again facing serious labor shortages, the question of immigration is once again coming to the fore.

In the 21st century, there are very few examples of countries who have managed to reverse, or at least halt, negative demographic trends. One such example is Russia. Between 1987 and 1999, Russia's birth rate fell from 2.22 (above the 2.1 replacement rate) to just 1.16, an almost unprecedented decline in the modern world. This led to dire predictions of a collapse in the population of Russia, particularly for its working-age population. Add to this the fact that Russian men had some of the shortest life expectancies of any country in Europe, and it was clear that Russia would not be able to recover from the economic and geopolitical losses that it suffered in the 1980s and 1990s without addressing this demographic disaster. To his credit, Russian President Vladimir Putin recognized the importance of Russia's demographic situation and took concrete steps to both raise the birth rate in Russia (it rose to 1.78 by the year 2015) and to reduce alcoholism (the leading cause of death for many Russian men). As a result, Russia's demographic situation, while still not ideal, recovered for a short time. However, Russia's invasion of Ukraine led to an exodus of young people from Russia, as well as tens of thousands of deaths on the battlefields of Ukraine.

Another example, while less dramatic than that of Russia, is France. Like most European countries, France was facing a serious threat to its economic future from its declining birth rate. By the mid-1990s, France's birth rate had fallen to 1.73, well below the 2.1 replacement rate. However, a series of French governments took steps to raise birth rates, including efforts to expand childcare availability, and this led to an increase in France's birth rate to 2.03 by the year 2010. As a result, while most European countries are facing looming demographic declines, France's situation in this area has stabilized. Unfortunately, there are not too many other examples of countries or regions that have been able to reverse the downwards demographic trends that have taken hold around the world in recent decades.

Overall, there has been no single method or strategy that has proven successful in raising birth rates around the world. A strategy that has worked for one country is just as likely to have failed in a host of others. In fact, it appears that strategies to raise birth rates are going to have to be tailored to individual countries, making it even more difficult to raise global birth rates. Nevertheless, if a government is convinced that the only way it can promote long-term economic growth within its borders is to reverse the demographic decline that has been in place already for a long period of time, then the effort to raise birth rates, no matter how challenging, will be worth the time and resources that it requires.

Unfortunately, the simple fact today is that it is, for the most part, more difficult to have children than it was in the past. Therefore, if a government is determined to raise its country's birth rate, it must start by easing the burden on parents that is brought about by having children. For example, one of the main reasons why birth rates in the modern world are falling is that parents, particularly mothers, do not have the same amount of time to raise children that they had in the past. This is due primarily to the fact that an increasing number of women are now active in the work force and are either unable to find the time to raise a large family, or are unwilling to sacrifice their careers, to raising children. Therefore, governments that are determined to boost birth rates must take more of the child-rearing burden off of families. One way to do this would be to dramatically expand the amount of childcare available to younger families, while making sure that this childcare does not become an undue financial burden upon these young families. This ties in with another factor that has driven down birth rates in recent decades, the dramatic increase in the expenses involved in having larger numbers of children. In the pre-industrial age, children were viewed as a financial asset, as they could be put to work for the family at a relatively young age, at a time when a family's economic output was largely determined by the number of active workers it had in the family. Today, children are a large financial burden on their families, often well into their 20s.

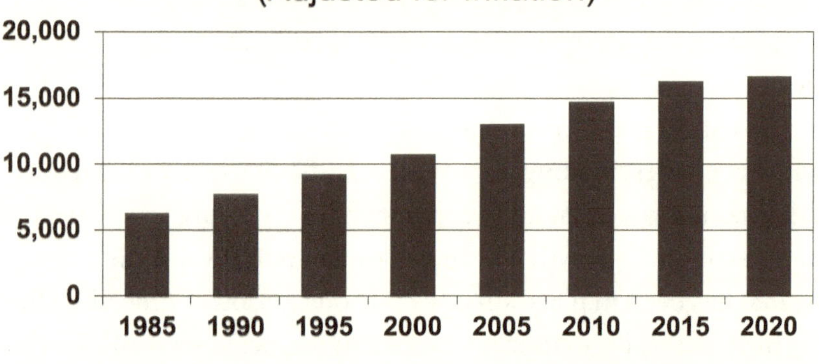

This is due in large part to the dramatic increase in the cost of education and extracurricular activities in recent decades. Therefore, if a government wants to set policies that reverse decades of declining birth rates, making education and extracurricular activities more affordable is another good place to start.

For some countries, space is another constraint that has contributed to falling birth rates. For example, those people living in countries and regions with high population densities find it increasingly difficult to raise larger families due to the lack of available living space, or a lack of agricultural land, that has resulted from the dramatic population increases that we have seen over the past century. Imagine trying to raise a very large family today in crowded areas such as China's Pearl River Delta or Europe's Low Countries. In these cases, space is a major constraint on population growth, one that is likely to prove difficult to overcome. Therefore, governments that want to boost their country's birth rates will have to develop policies that either favor moving populations to less-crowded areas, or develop policies that make it easier for larger families to live in high-population-density areas.

Of these constraints, it is the financial burden on young families that governments are likely to have the most influence over, and the one that governments should be able to help alleviate. There are many tools at a government's disposal. For example, governments can (and many already do) offer substantial tax breaks for families that have children. Larger tax breaks for families that have more than two children, for example, could encourage more people to have larger families, although there are concerns that such a strategy could result in families that lack the financial means of having larger numbers of children doing so only in order to reap the tax benefits of such a policy. Outright cash benefits for larger families are another tool that governments can use to promote larger families, and we have seen during the Covid-19 pandemic how direct cash handouts from governments can help to stimulate an economy. For some governments, this could be a means of promoting higher birth rates. Reducing the cost of childcare, if not offering free childcare outright, is another way in which governments can attempt to reduce decades of falling birth rates. Many young families rule out having larger numbers of children, either due to the career aspirations of both parents and due to the rising costs of raising children in the modern world. By providing free or reduced-cost childcare, governments can help offset these concerns and maybe convince enough young couples to have more children.

Finally, when it proves too difficult to raise birth rates within a country's borders (and this has been the case in most countries in recent years), there is still the option of raising the level of immigration into a country. In fact, for many of the most successful economies of recent years, it has been immigration that has been a key catalyst for this growth by providing the workers needed to offset the threat of labor shortages that has arisen as a result of decades of low birth rates. What is important for a government to consider when formulating its immigration policies is that the immigrants that flow into a country should match the needs of that country's economy. For example, some countries are suffering from massive shortages of skilled workers in the IT field. For these countries, immigration policies should be focused on attracting skilled IT immigrants, as this will not only benefit the economy, but it will also help to avoid anti-immigration backlash as immigration is being focused on a sector of the economy where there are clear labor shortages. We have seen all too often how a severe backlash against immigration occurs when it is perceived by the domestic population that immigrants are coming to take their jobs, or to lower wages, in a field that is already saturated with workers. Fortunately, with education levels rising in many of the world's poorest countries, the pool of skilled immigrant labor is likely to rise in the coming decades, something that could help labor-poor countries reduce the drag on their economies caused by labor shortages, particularly in more skilled sectors of the workforce. Therefore, the ability to compete for, and attract, skilled immigration is likely to be one of the most important factors in a country's or a region's economic success in the decades ahead.

IS POPULATION GROWTH DESIRABLE?

For many people in the modern world, the idea that population growth is a positive for the planet and the human race is an absurd one. In fact, a growing number of people, including many people who are very well educated on this subject, have made strong arguments in support of an eventual decline in the number of people living on our planet. This is not a new idea. At many points in history have influential thinkers argued in favor of a smaller human population. In some cases, this notion was driven by a fear that the planet's resources were insufficient to deal with its rising human population. In other cases, the dramatic growth in the population of the world's leading cities, and their attendant squalor and filth, was enough to convince them that population growth had to be brought to an end. In any case, this idea has been thought before. However, it is unlikely that it has ever been as pervasive as it is today. In fact, this idea has become so pervasive that it is now having a direct impact on demographic trends, particularly birth rates, in many parts of the world.

Simply put, many people now believe that the smaller the human population, the healthier our planet will be. This is a powerful argument when one takes a close look at the state of the planet. For example, our rising population and its soaring levels of consumption, is rapidly depleting many of the planet's most essential resources. For example, the amount of land available for cultivation is proving insufficient for modern-day human food consumption, either leading to food shortages in areas where no other land is available, or to deforestation in areas where forested lands are all that is left when it comes to finding available land for agriculture. Pollution is another area where arguments for smaller human populations gain a great deal of credence. Where population growth has been the fastest, and where consumption levels have risen the sharpest, can be found the parts of the world where pollution and greenhouse gas emissions have risen the fastest. One need only look at pictures of the air above 19th century London, or 20th century Pittsburgh to see the impact on the air that the combination of rising populations and industrialization have had. Today, the air above Beijing or Delhi resembles these dreadful photos from 19th and early 20th century Europe and North America. For many people today, rapid population growth is synonymous with worsening air quality and the fear is, with population growth and urbanization at their highest in poor emerging markets, this problem will worsen in the coming decades without a dramatic decline in population growth. Finally, the worsening lack of space in many areas of the world is yet another argument in favor of a decline in the human population. For them, the extreme overcrowding in areas of the world such as the Ganges River Valley, Nigeria and even Europe's Low Countries is an example of what can go wrong when population growth is allowed to continue for too long and at too fast of a pace. In short, the less people on the planet, the more space people will have.

Unfortunately, many supporters of the idea that the human population on the planet must decline ignore the impact that a shrinking population will have on the global economy, and the subsequent impact that the economic dislocations caused by a shrinking population will have on many other important areas, including stability, security and living standards. The fact is, the modern world and all of its systems such as social welfare, infrastructure and education on built upon the premise that economic growth will continue at some rate for the foreseeable future. This economic growth, in turn, is driven in no small part by the continued growth of the numbers of workers and consumers that drive increases in both supply and demand. In fact, it is hard to envision how the world can maintain high rates of economic growth without any growth in the population, particularly the working-age population. Sure, a handful of countries can continue to record economic growth without population growth (look at South Korea or Germany as examples), but they can only do so through exporting, especially to other parts of the world where the number of consumers is continuing to rise. If the entire planet's population was to decline, these export-dependent economies would find themselves facing a long-term decline that would prove to be almost impossible to pull out of.

The answer therefore is that we need to find a way in which we can continue to record manageable levels of population growth, but in a way that has a much smaller impact on our environment than population growth has had in the past. We must generate economic growth to continue to improve living standards and to maintain the systems that characterize much of what is positive about the modern world. However, we must also do much more to reduce the impact that population growth has on the planet, as well as reducing the environmental footprint that the current population of the planet already has on the environment. There are many reasons to be skeptical, none more so than the examples of history and all of the damage that we have done to the environment since we have become this planet's dominant species. Nevertheless, we must try, for we have no other alternative. The best way to move forward is to promote more sustainable population growth, and to do so in a manner that does far less harm to the environment than the population growth that has taken place since the Industrial Revolution.

THE PROMISE OF TECHNOLOGY

For many, technology is the great hope for the future of the global economy. It is believed that as global population growth slows, and as the global population eventually begins to decline, that technology will help humanity to overcome some of the losses caused by this demographic decline. In fact, technology has become in many ways that last best hope for the global economy, a sort of last gasp throw of the dice that promises to snatch victory from the jaws of impending defeat. However, if we look closely at the impact that technological advancements have had on the global economy in recent decades, we can see that, for all of the transformative technological advancements that have been made, they have done little to truly help the world to generate higher rates of economic growth. As such, if technology is going to save the day and offset the impact of demographic decline and other drags on the global economy, it is going to have to be much of effective at helping to generate higher rates of economic growth than it has of late.

Automation is one example of a technological advancement that many believe can revolutionize the global economy and lead it into a future of long-term sustained (and sustainable) growth. For example, since demographic decline seems inevitable and the shrinkage of working-age populations in so many of the world's leading economies appears to be guaranteed, then it is possible that the loss of potential workers in these economies can be partially, if not completely, offset by a major increase in the use of automation to do the tasks that these missing workers once did. Perhaps automation can result in these tasks being done in a much more efficient way, helping to reverse the long-term declines in productivity growth that have plagued many economies in recent decades. Clearly, automation is a potential answer to some of the supply-side problems that demographic decline can bring about. However, automation will do little to offset the loss of consumers that would result from population decline, and this is likely to have just as great of an impact on the ability of the global economy to generate growth as will the potential loss of workers.

Artificial intelligence is another example of a technological development that holds much promise for the future of the global economy. In fact, great hopes are being placed in artificial intelligence. First and foremost, many economists are hopeful that AI will be the answer to the productivity conundrum that has plagued the global economy in recent decades. This would be the result of significant improvements in areas such as time management and resource allocation, which would allow for long-term productivity growth to accelerate for the first time in decades. Second, artificial intelligence would also help to solve the problems caused by shrinking labor forces. This would be done through something known as "intelligent automation", a process that would enable machines to not only be able to solve problems on their own, but to also be self-learning. Finally, it is hoped that the expansion of artificial intelligence would lead to a burst of innovation across all industries and regions, resulting in the creation of new sectors of the economy that are capable of generating far higher rates of growth than the ones that current dominate the global economy. Certainly, artificial intelligence has the ability to transform the economy and improve living standards. However, many questions remain as artificial intelligence is presently only in its infancy. Whether or not artificial intelligence will meet the lofty expectations that have been placed upon it by so many clearly remains to be seen.

A simpler answer to some of the challenges posed by demographic and productivity issues would be to extend the productive lives of the people living on the planet. The fact is that too many people in the modern world are no longer productive members of society, as this book has shown. In some parts of the world, most notably Europe, people are retiring at relatively young ages and then living for decades thereafter, contributing very little to the economies of the countries where they live. In fact, their generous retirement benefits are becoming an ever-greater drag on their countries' finances and threatening to lead to Ponzi-scheme-like scenario where the money eventually runs out, leaving the next generation in the lurch.

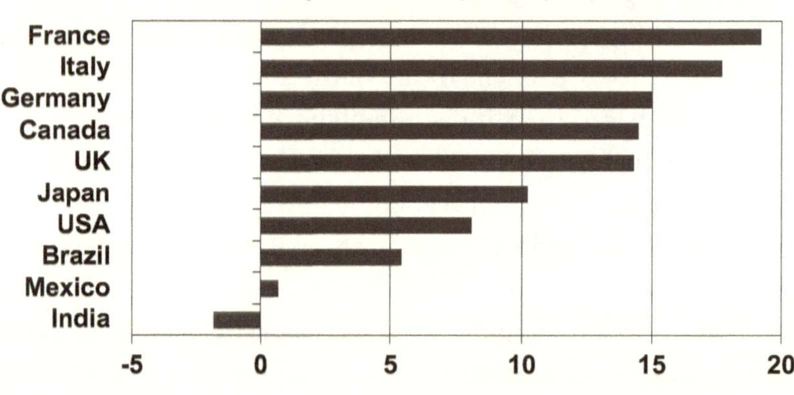

For some, this is a sign of the increasing levels of laziness or lethargy in society. For others, a long post-productive life is a birthright, earned through decades of work. Often, early retirement becomes fixed in place as a result of systems that were implemented decades ago, turning such early retirements into a sort of cultural norm, or expectation.

The fact is, we need to make older segments of our population more productive than they are now. With life expectancies rising in most parts of the world, the share of people above their countries' retirement age will continue to rise to dangerous levels in the decades ahead.

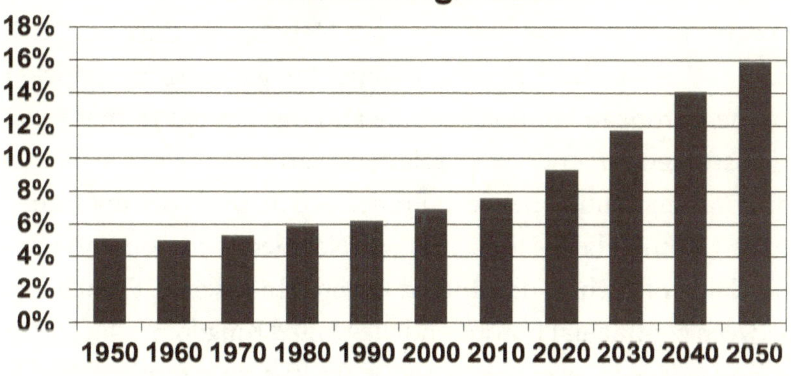

This will place a great burden on public finances and the economy in the future as the cost of sustaining such a large a growing non-productive segment of the population will simply prove too much to bear for most economies. Instead, ways must be found that allow older people to remain productive members of society. As most economies are no longer dependent upon manual labor in the agricultural or industrial fields, making older people more productive is surely possible. However, it is likely to be a major challenge to find the political and popular will to make this happen.

How to Revive Trade and Investment

In the past, most peaks in international trade and investment were followed by subsequent sharp declines in trade and investment. Often, these declines led to a long-term decline in economic output and in living standards, such as in post-Roman Europe or in the later Ming Dynasty in China. However, sometimes these downturns could be reversed, and an economic recovery followed. For example, many economies recovered from the dislocations to trade and investment caused by the Great Depression and World War Two to generate very high rates of economic growth in the following decades on the back of a surge in export revenues. Furthermore, since the Industrial Revolution, the long-term trend for global trade and investment has been upwards, even if it has been interspersed with shorter periods of decline.

Let's look at three such revivals in trade and investment that followed downturns along the lines of the one that we have been living through in recent years. The first took place in post-Napoleonic Europe. During the Napoleonic Wars in which France attempted to gain hegemony over a large share of the European landmass, trade and investment in that region was severely disrupted for a period that lasted nearly twenty years. Not only did the near-constant fighting between France and its rivals disrupt trade, but so too did the Continental System. This was Napoleon's response to the British naval blockade of French-dominated Europe. In essence, France barred all trade between continental Europe and the United Kingdom, which at the time was the most-advanced economy in the world. The main result of this blockade was a major decline in trade and investment in Europe, one that lasted until the final defeat of France in 1815. What followed was a massive increase in trade and investment in Europe and between European countries and their colonies (and former colonies). By the 1820s, global trade and investment was soaring at a level rarely seen before, characterized by massive investments being made by the world's leading economies (especially the United Kingdom) around the world.

Another period that witnessed a massive revival in global trade and investment following a severe downturn was the period that followed the Second World War. As we have discussed, the Great Depression witnessed the erection of devastating barriers to trade and investment that led to a collapse of both in the 1930s. Soon thereafter, the Second World War which saw nearly all of the world's leading economies engaged in a life-and-death struggle, led to a further decline in trade and investment, with the notable exception in the trade of arms. Finally, the devastation caused by the war and the political changes that followed the war added to the downwards pressure on trade and investment in the immediate aftermath of the conflict. In fact, many of the world's most powerful economies (Japan, Germany, France, China and more) were completely devastated by the war, with economic output having collapsed in many of these countries. However, for many of these economies, a period characterized by a remarkably quick recovery in economic output followed. In fact, many of the economies that were most devastated by the Second World War were among those that recorded the highest rates of economic growth in the decades after the conflict ended. At the same time, the country whose economy came to dominate the world after World War Two, the United States, led this recovery, providing funding for devastated economies and creating an international trading system that allowed many of the world's devastated economies to export their way back to prosperity in the 1950s and 1960s.

One final period to consider is the 1980s and 1990s, the era in which globalization fueled unprecedented increases in international trade and investment. As we have seen, the 1970s were a turbulent decade for trade and investment, highlighted by the impact that the decade's oil crises had on many of the world's most important economies. However, the difficulties many exporters and investors faced in the 1970s and early 1980s were followed by a period of remarkable growth, driven by the rise of new markets in East Asia, East Europe and elsewhere. With the United States continuing to champion the spread of the market economy and of the international trading system that it had established after the Second World War, a truly globalized economy emerged by the early 1990s. This time, it was emerging markets that played a key role in the revival of global trade and investment, and by the early 21st century, emerging markets were accounting for a significant share of global trade and investment, a trend that has continued to this day.

There are a number of patterns that we can observe when it comes to these periods of revival for international trade and investment. For example, these revivals often were preceded by major disruptions to global trade, typically caused by wars or economic crises. Typically, these disruptions were a major shock to the global economic system, threatening to usher in a period of significant economic decline. Due to the severity of these shocks, there was usually a renewed commitment by many or all of the world's leading economies to establish a framework in which trade and investment could be revived. Often, this commitment was led by the dominant economic power of the period in question. For example, in the wake of the Napoleonic Wars, it was the United Kingdom (the world's most industrialized country at that time) that championed the revival of trade and investment in Europe and further abroad. After the two World Wars and the 1970s oil crises, it was the United States that played the dominant role in establishing systems designed to boost global trade and investment. Fortunately for the world of the past two centuries, the leading military and economic powers were both pro-trade and pro-investment (for the most part) and this allowed for global trade and investment to rebound following such crises. Remember, it was the United States' brief period of protectionism in the early 1930s that turned a severe financial crisis into the Great Depression, so the impact that the world's most powerful economy can have on the direction of global trade and investment should not be underestimated. As we look at current trends and look to the future, there is no guarantee that the leading economic powers will be as pro-trade and pro-investment as the 19th century United Kingdom or the 20th century United States. In fact, prior to their championing of trade and investment, both the UK and the US had experienced prolonged periods of isolationism, tendencies that remain in place among some segments of each of these countries' societies today.

International trade and investment face a very uncertain future. In fact, it appears as if we are in the midst of a prolonged downturn for trade and investment, with the data for the latter in recent years being particularly concerning. While events such as the Global Financial Crisis and the Covid-19 pandemic would appear to be the causes for this downturn, the fact is that no single issue or event is solely responsible for the slowdown in international trade and investment in recent years.

Meanwhile, if there is to be a revival in global trade and investment in the future, the big question is, who will lead this revival? As the world's largest and wealthiest economy, the United States would seem to be the country best-placed to lead such a revival. After all, the post-war system of trade and investment was largely created by the United States, and this system has provided for the tremendous increase in wealth and economic output that has occurred since the Second World War. However, the US has also witnessed a major increase in support for policies promoting protectionism, from both the political right and the political left in the US. Moreover, it is uncertain if such support will diminish in the coming years, or if these recent trends are the start of an even bigger push for protectionist policies within the US.

The next obvious answer to the question of who will lead a revival in global trade and investment is China. In fact, as support for international trade and investment has weakened in the United States, it has been China that has picked up the baton and attempted to ensure that trade and investment growth returns. This should be no surprise, as China's remarkable transformation into the world's dominant manufacturing center has allowed it to become the world's leading exporter of manufactured goods. In fact, while other major exporting countries saw their export revenues decline during the economic crises of the 21st century, China's export revenues continued to climb, allowing it to secure a remarkable share of global manufactured exports.

Share of Global Manufactured Exports

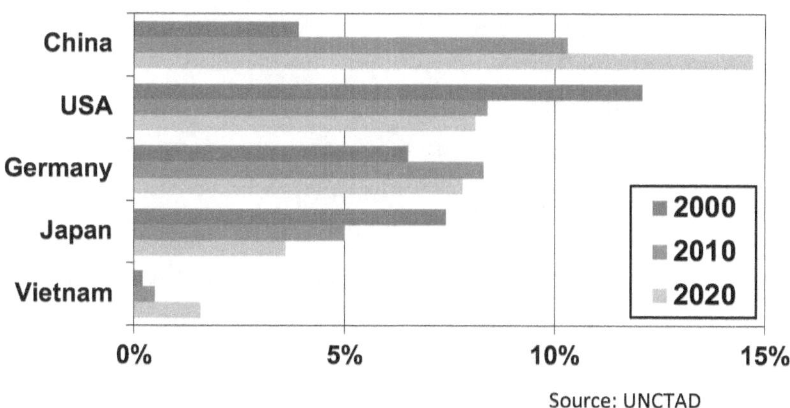

Source: UNCTAD

At the same time, China has become the leading source of foreign investment for much of the world, as evidenced by China's ambitious Belt and Road project. This has enabled China to gain a remarkable degree of economic leverage over dozens of countries all around the world. As a result, Beijing views the maintaining of the open system of global trade and investment as being vital to its longer-term economic interests and the prospects for the future growth and stability of the Chinese economy.

Apart from the United States and China, there are a number of other countries or blocs that would be keen to ensure that global trade and investment growth returns to its previous levels. For example, the European Union, the world's third-largest economy, needs trade and investment growth to generate its own economic growth, as most EU member states are highly dependent upon exports and foreign investment to grow. India too needs trade and investment to generate the rates of economic growth that are needed to lift hundreds of millions of people out of poverty, much as trade and investment did in China in the late 20th and early 21st centuries. Meanwhile, other major economies such as Japan, South Korea, Australia and others are dependent upon export growth to ensure that their economies can generate growth in the future.

DO WE WANT TRADE AND INVESTMENT TO GROW?

While there are many economic arguments for wanting trade and investment growth to accelerate, there are other arguments that suggest that a slowdown in global trade and investment growth could have a positive impact for our world. This has led to increasing support for policies that help to reduce trade and investment growth. For example, support for localization, or reshoring, has risen rapidly in recent years. At the same time, there has been a growing backlash against globalization, with an increasing number of people now believing that the benefits of globalization are now outweighed by the drawbacks that it creates. The job front is another battleground in which globalization has suffered setbacks in recent years, as politicians on both the right and the left are increasingly calling for jobs that may have gone overseas to be brought back home. The same holds true with investment, with pressure mounting on businesses, investors and governments to focus more of their investment activities on their home markets, rather than outside of their countries' borders.

One of the most persuasive arguments against international trade and investment growth is centered around the environmental impact of the flow of trade and investment around the world. For example, it is widely believed that the overall level of global pollution, whether it is air, sea or land pollution, is significantly higher as a result of the shift in manufacturing activities from developed economies where environmental legislation is rigidly enforced to emerging markets, where such legislation is either weak to begin with, or is too loosely enforced. With global temperatures rising, it is believed that a dramatic reduction in international trade and its corresponding reduction in the use of large container ships, cargo planes and other such modes of transportation will help the world to reduce its greenhouse gas emissions. Likewise, it is believed by many that lower levels of trade and investment will also help to reduce the rate of resource degradation around the world.

Not all of the arguments against higher levels of trade and investment are focused on environmental issues. In fact, some of these arguments are economic in nature. For example, there is a strong economic argument that, for some countries, a smaller dependence upon international trade and investment helps these countries to be shielded from external threats and to experience a smaller number of external disruptions to their economies. A good example of this is the United States, which generates a smaller amount of its economic output from exports than any other large economy in the world. According to this argument, this lesser dependence upon trade and investment has helped the United States to withstand the impacts of the economic crises in the 21st century better than most other developed economies. Certainly it can be argued that it will be emerging markets that suffer a disproportionate share of the hardships should global trade and investment levels continue to trend downwards, as we have seen how the most successful emerging markets of the post-war era have used trade and investment to lift their citizens out of poverty and to generate extremely high rates of economic growth and job creation.

For me, while these arguments have merit, they do not hold up to the big picture. The fact that we are in the midst of a period of demographic and productivity decline means that we need to continue to support policies that allow global trade and investment to thrive. In fact, without a return to growth for international trade and investment, it is hard to see how the world will be able to generate higher levels of economic growth. At the same time, we must remember that a large share of the world's population still lives in relative poverty, and for these people, their best hope remains the model that was perfected by the most successful countries in regions such as East Asia or Central Europe, where exports resulted in a prolonged period of economic growth that led to hundreds of millions of people being lifted out of poverty.

Without a return to global trade and investment growth, too many people around the world will lose out and this will have massive impact on the future of our planet.

Higher levels of trade and investment can also help to promote cooperation and cohesiveness among the world's most powerful countries. When leading powers trade with one another and invest in each other's economies, they have developed a higher degree of inter-dependence and inter-connectivity. This results in these countries having more to lose should they take steps to reduce trade and investment with one another. In the modern world, many major powers are highly dependent upon export markets and foreign investment inflows to generate domestic economic growth, and these powers have largely become the leading promoters of trade and investment in recent years. However, other major powers that are less dependent upon international trade and investment, most notably the United States, have turned against trade and investment to some degree. This means that some countries have more to lose when trade and investment declines and this forces these countries to work more closely together to promote policies that encourage more trade and investment.

Trade and investment growth also can go hand-in-hand with technological innovation. With investment flowing to more innovative parts of the world, these areas have the funding and the labor to develop new technologies. At the same time, ideas that would otherwise be limited to a single country can now be shared around the world, speeding the pace of innovation and allowing advancements to spread more rapidly to all parts of the world. Skilled workers can also move more easily during periods when trade and investment is more open, and this allows high-tech and high-growth sectors of the economy to avoid labor shortages that would otherwise stifle their ability to innovate and to bring these innovations to the economy at-large. When trade and investment is limited, or blocked, the spread of innovation is likely to be much slower, holding back overall levels of economic growth for the world.

Overall, it is clear that the benefits derived from international trade and investment vastly outweigh the drawbacks. Furthermore, there is ample evidence that limited international trade and investment can be a direct cause for a global economic downturn, or can turn what would be a relatively minor economic downturn into a full-blown economic crisis. At the same time, economic and political risk levels rise in conjunction with declines in trade and investment, resulting in elevated conflict risk. Altogether, high levels of growth in international trade and investment play a major role in increasing the level of prosperity for a larger number of the world's population, while helping to lift large numbers of people out of poverty. Finally, prolonged trade and investment growth can prolong periods of economic growth, helping to reduce the number of economic downturns, as well as the severity of such downturns.

HOW TO BOOST PRODUCTIVITY

When one takes the long view of human history, we find that there have been many periods in which productivity growth has declined over a long period of time. Worse, there are ample examples of periods of history where long-term productivity actually declined, sometimes precipitously. Furthermore, we have seen how these periods of long-term productivity stagnation or decline have impacted the economies of those regions impacted by these trends, and have impacted the living standards of the people unfortunate enough to live in such periods. In this book, we have analyzed why productivity growth has trended downwards in the past, and why it has done so in recent years. We have also looked at the impact of such long-term productivity declines. What we need to do before the book is over is to look more at those periods in our history when declines in productivity growth were reversed and analyze how and why productivity growth returned after a long period of decline. As such, let's briefly look at three periods of time when long-term productivity declines were reversed, leading to long periods of productivity growth that were the catalysts for three periods of extraordinary economic growth.

The first such period took place during the Song Dynasty in China that lasted from 960 to 1279. Coming on the heels of a series of short-lived dynasties during the Five Dynasties and Ten Kingdoms period that was characterized by economic and political upheaval across much of China, the Song Dynasty was a period in which innovation, trade and economic integration led to a dramatic increase in productivity. In terms of innovation, the Song Dynasty ushered in what can be described as the first modern economic era thanks to the first use of banknotes, moveable print, gunpowder and many more innovations that derived from this period of Chinese history. Furthermore, improvements in iron- and steel-making, the use of coal for energy and a host of other such innovations spurred dramatic increases in productivity that allowed China to overtake the rest of the world in terms of economic output and wealth for the first time in centuries. At the same time, the unification of most of China's main economic centers during this period resulted in a dramatic increase in trade and investment throughout China, while sensible economic policies from the government encouraged trade and investment, instead of stifling it. Finally, China also began trading goods with economic centers much further afield, something that would continue until well after the Song Dynasty had come to an end. Altogether, the combination of technological and process innovations, the expansion of trade and investment and the integration of China's main economic centers all combined to revive productivity in China, leading to a period of unprecedented economic growth.

Another period of history that witnessed a major increase in productivity growth was found in Renaissance Europe, a period that gradually began in the 14th century and lasted until the 17th century. Remember, most of post-Roman Europe was an economic backwater from the 5th century until the Renaissance, a period lasting nearly an entire millennium. Unlike the Song Dynasty that saw productivity and economic growth soar in the early days of the period, the productivity and economic growth recorded during the Renaissance was far more gradual and patchy. This was due in large part to the fact that, while China under the Song Dynasty was largely unified, Renaissance Europe consisted of a patchwork of small- and medium-sized states whose economies were relatively independent of one another. Nevertheless, advancements in terms of banking and manufacturing processes helped to significantly boost what had been for centuries stagnant productivity levels across most of Europe. Furthermore, trade and investment levels increased in most areas of Europe during this period, raising trade and investment to their highest levels in the region since the glory days of the Roman Empire. Finally, the Renaissance saw a significant expansion in the size of European cities, most of which had been quite small at the beginning of this period. This led to increasing levels of specialization, another factor that contributed to the higher levels of productivity growth in Europe at that time.

Finally, a more modern example exists in postwar-Japan, where technological and process innovations led to a dramatic increase in productivity following Japan's crushing defeat in the Second World War. Japan used the manufacturing skills that it had learned in the decades following the Meiji Restoration to become a world-beater when it came to productivity growth, recording some of the highest rates of productivity growth in the world for an extended period of time. Of course, this productivity advantage would come to an end, particularly as new rivals emerged in Asia. These rivals often mimicked the factors that drove Japan's post-war productivity miracle, and in the process, outstripped Japanese productivity growth, a situation that persists to this day.

So what are the factors that have driven productivity growth in the past, and could potentially lead to a revival in productivity growth in the future. For me, there are for key factors:

- A single power in control of a region's or the world's economic infrastructure
- A government that is focused on productivity improvements
- Access to markets and investment
- Technological breakthroughs

Undoubtedly, a single power that is in control over a region's economic infrastructure has the capacity to improve its level of productivity growth. In fact, this might be the single-most-important factor in determining how productive an economy may be. On a global basis, this means that the dominant actor is in control of global trade and investment lanes. As we have discussed, the ability of the Roman Empire to control the trade and investment lanes throughout its vast empire allowed for massive productivity gains to be realized throughout the empire. In fact, it is safe to say that Rome's vast interconnected economic system allowed Rome to record some of the most impressive productivity gains in the ancient world. This too was evident at times when China's economic centers and infrastructure were united as a single state, for it was during these periods that China achieved its most-impressive productivity gains. The British Empire provided something similar, for its vast market enhanced the productivity gains that were the result of the innovations during the Industrial Revolution. Finally, many of the productivity gains that were achieved in the wake of the Second World War were partially the result of the United States' control of global trade and investment.

Now, with China's power on the rise and isolationism raising its head in the United States and other parts of the West, there are fears that a single power will no longer control global trade and investment in the future, potentially fragmenting the global economy and leading to more difficulties for trade and investment to flow around the world. Should this occur, the productivity declines that have occurred in recent decades could continue, or worse, become even deeper.

Another key factor in the direction of productivity growth is whether or not a government actively supports productivity improvements and provides the means for businesses, universities, research institutions and other organizations to work towards developing technologies and processes that allow for productivity growth to accelerate. In fact, there are almost no examples in history of when government support, either direct or indirect, did not play a major factor in contributing to improvements in productivity. Whether it is government-financed technological development projects or an economic system in which governments allow small businesses to flourish, productivity growth can be linked to a government's willingness to allow productivity to grow. Conversely, a government's policies can also have a very detrimental effect on productivity growth, stifling potential growth through a variety of factors that result in lower levels of productivity.

An economies' access to markets and investment can also play an important role in driving productivity growth. For large economies such as the United States or China, there are built-in markets and sources of investment that can help to drive productivity growth by providing access to both sizeable consumer bases and financial resources. This can enable a technological or process improvement to have a nearly-immediate impact upon productivity growth. For smaller economies, it becomes imperative that they gain access to these larger markets or sources of investment. Good examples of these can be found in South Korea or Central Europe, where smaller domestic consumer markets and financial sectors have not prevented those regions from outstripping their neighbors in terms of productivity growth in recent years, Instead, businesses in South Korea and Central Europe have been able to access markets all around the world, while attracting investment from many corners. Much of this investment has gone into enhancing their manufacturing resources, enabling them to use their new-found productivity gains to drive economic growth. Unfortunately, as we have seen, this access to global markets and sources of investment is being jeopardized by rising levels of nationalism and protectionism, potentially threatening to reduce the opportunities to generate higher levels of productivity growth for many economies around the world.

Finally, technology is a critical factor when it comes to determining productivity growth, with technological breakthroughs fueling many of the world's most-notable periods of high-level productivity growth. Given the outlook for some of the other key factors in determining productivity growth, technology may in fact be the last great hope for productivity growth in the future. In many cases, technology has been one of the most important factors in the rise and fall of the world's leading economies. However, we have witnessed many impressive technological advancements in recent decades, but these have done little to boost overall levels of productivity growth for most of the world's leading economies during this period. Nevertheless, there are hopes that new technologies such as artificial intelligence and 3-D printing will finally lead to the productivity breakthrough that the world has been searching for. If not, it is hard to see how we will be able to achieve significantly higher rates of productivity growth in the future, given the outlook for the other factors that play a key role in determining productivity levels.

While the need for higher rates of productivity growth seems apparent, there are nevertheless many people who question the drive for higher rates of productivity. For some, higher rates of productivity growth are associated with harm to the environment, even as the world is in the process of moving towards a post-industrial age. At the same time, there is still a widespread and general fear of technology among many segments of the population and as modern technology becomes more complex, these sorts of fears might continue to grow. Finally, there is a definite sense that, for much of the world, people are working too much, with an increasing share of the population looking to spend less time working and more time engaged in leisure or personal activities. Whether or not one sees these views as laudable or dangerous, it is clear that the drive for a return to higher rates of productivity growth will be neither easy nor straightforward and the fact is, productivity growth rates might not just keep falling, but productivity itself might begin to move into negative territory.

Whether we like it or not, the key to our future economic growth and development lies in our ability to generate higher levels of productivity growth. This is because we know that, for at least the foreseeable future, population growth is not going to rebound. For some economies, this demographic decline has already begun, while for others, it is beginning or will soon begin. The United States, the world's largest economy, is seeing its rate of domestically-generated population growth slow to some of its lowest-ever levels, while China, the world's second-largest economy, is facing an immense demographic decline after decades of a One-Child Policy that has given that country some of the lowest birth rates of any country in the world. As such, we must accept that demographics will no longer be a driver of economic growth for nearly all of the world's largest economies.

As for trade and investment, these factors face a very uncertain future. Remember, not that long ago, we were expecting trade and investment to be major catalysts for future economic growth. However, much has changed in recent years. For one, the champion of the modern system of global trade and investment, the United States, has turned inwards, with nationalist and protectionist sentiment in the world's largest economy growing significantly in recent years. China has moved to step in to the US' role, but few countries trust China and there are serious questions about Chinese intentions. As such, there is a real possibility that the major slowdown in trade and investment growth that has occurred over the past decade will continue. Furthermore, there is a real possibility that the global economy could fragment into regional blocs, something that could dramatically reduce overall levels of international trade and investment.

Add to these aforementioned issues other factors such as climate change, geopolitical tensions and a host of other issues, and it becomes clear that productivity holds the key to our planet's economic future. However, there are serious questions about whether or not wholesale productivity growth can be revived. For some, the temporary increase in productivity rates following the outbreak of the Covid-19 pandemic raised hopes that long-term productivity growth could be revived. However, for others, the fact that so many major economies continue to record little or no productivity growth is a sign that generating higher rates of productivity growth over the long-term could prove to be a bridge too far for the global economy. Whatever the outcome of the productivity question, it will likely hold the key for the future of the global economy.

The Future of the Planet is at Stake

While the need to generate economic growth seems obvious, in recent years there has been a focus on many other topics and issues. In fact, even among many economists that focus has shifted away from growth-related topics to a range of other economic and non-economic issues.

For example, there is an increasing focus on how the global economy impacts the environmental health and balance of our plant. In this case, it is hard to argue with the need to increase the focus on the environment as issues such as climate change and pollution threaten our very existence on this planet. Already, we have seen how the increasing focus on climate change is changing the global economy, with dramatic increases in investment and resources aimed at mitigating the economy's impact on the climate. At the same time, pollution and resource-depletion are issues that will be increasingly in focus as we move forward in the 21st century and these will force massive changes upon the global economy. For some, this means that we have to lessen our focus on economic growth and increase our focus on economic sustainability. For me, this means instead that we have to find a way to promote economic growth in a way that is both sustainable and less-harmful to our planet. There is no other way.

Another issue in focus at the time of the writing of this book is wealth inequality. Much like in the early 20th century, the world's leading economies are dealing with rising levels of wealth inequality and the impact that this having upon global security, society and those who are marginalized by changes to the global economy in the modern world. In fact, wealth has become increasingly concentrated, sometimes among a small group of countries, businesses or individuals, and this has had a detrimental impact on many aspects of society today. Not only has the United States famously felt the impact of rising levels of wealth inequality, but so too have economies that have attempted to prevent their levels of wealth inequality from rising too far, such as Europe and China. However, reducing wealth inequality does not have to be done in a way that reduces the ability of an economy to grow.

Political extremism is another issue that has taken center stage in recent years and has distracted much of the planet from tackling those issues that need to be dealt with in an urgent manner. As we have discussed, extremist or radical political views have taken hold among large segments of our planet's population and have been driven by a wide range of issues, including the aforementioned wealth inequality, resource scarcity, global migration and other. On the political right, extremism has manifested itself in rising levels of support for political parties and leaders that oppose immigration, support the "status quo" and champion a range of socially conservative causes. On the political left, extremism is evident in rising support for policies calling for a radical redistribution of wealth and an overturning of the existing social order. While support for radical right-wing and left-wing policies grows, those leaders and voters who claim to occupy the middle ground of politics are finding both their numbers dwindling and their voices being shouted down from both sides of the political divide. For most major economies, this is a serious threat to their ability to generate long-term growth, as the policies proposed by both the radical-right and the radical-left would cause major harm to a country's economy and its economic competitiveness, particularly over the long-term.

ECONOMIC GROWTH IS NEEDED TO TACKLE THE COMING CHALLENGES

Without sustainable and long-term economic growth, the world will find its ability to deal with future challenges even more daunting than they may appear now. As we have seen, governments will find it impossible to fund the social systems that have been put in place in many parts of the world in recent decades. In fact, even with economic growth, these social systems will struggle to remain solvent, but without economic growth, their collapse is all but assured. Infrastructure is another area that requires constant and long-term economic growth. Much of the world's advanced infrastructure was built during times of growth and maintaining and expanding this infrastructure will require continued economic growth. We have already witnessed how periods of economic stagnation and decline can lead to dramatic reductions in infrastructure expenditures, resulting in what can best be described as a crumbling infrastructure.

Security is another aspect that is often overlooked when it comes to economic projections. Simply put, the more an economy grows, the more a state can spend on defense and security without bankrupting the state or destroying its economy. Time and time again we have seen how former great powers were eventually unable to maintain their global ambitions or even provide for the security of their own territories as a result of the deterioration of their economic position in the world that resulted from lower long-term economic growth rates than their strategic competitors.

Should long-term economic growth falter, as it already has for a number of the world's largest economies, political and economic tensions will inevitably rise, raising conflict risk to levels that are much higher than they are today. Another potential consequence is the increasing concentration of economic growth in all but a small number of countries or regions, something that would likely exacerbate what is already a daunting wealth inequality challenge. Finally, combatting the environment crises that appear inevitable will be far more challenging without a sufficient amount of economic growth that will enable the funding of the technologies and processes that will be needed to both react to the planet's changing environment and to actively move to improve the health and sustainability of the environment.

Steady long-term economic growth needs to be the goal for the planet as a whole, for such growth can provide the world with the resources needed to tackle all of these aforementioned challenges. Look at the examples of Italy and South Korea that we have analyzed in this book. In Italy, where economic growth has been minimal at best since the start of the 21st century, spending on infrastructure, environmental programs, defense and much else has either stagnated or been slashed dramatically. As a result, Italy's ability to defend itself against foreign aggressors, climate change or any other of a number of such challenges has been weakened significantly, while its ability to maintain and expand social welfare programs for its rapidly-aging population has been greatly diminished. In contrast, South Korea, which has been one of the world's fastest-growing developed economies in the 21st century, has made dramatic improvements in many of these areas. While Italy has been forced to cut back spending on all sorts of public programs, South Korea has been able to dramatically boost spending on such programs within its borders, including massive improvements in the country's infrastructure and an expansion of many of its social welfare programs, even as South Korea faces a demographic decline nearly as severe as that of Italy. Recent crises, such as the Global Financial Crisis and the Covid-19 pandemic, have exposed these differences.

Altogether, history has repeatedly shown us how important long-term economic growth is for the well-being of the world's population. We have seen how the Roman Empire flourished thanks to centuries of relatively uninterrupted economic expansion, and how it collapsed when its economic foundations began to crumble. Similar scenes have played out throughout Chinese history, with China reaching its highest levels of civilization and living standards during periods of prolonged economic growth. The British Empire also flourished thanks to the United Kingdom's ability to generate long-term rates of economic growth that were significantly higher than those of its European rivals, due in large part to the Industrial Revolution and the expansion of British trade and investment to nearly all corners of the world. The United States is today's leading power due in no small part to the fact that, despite many crises, the US economy has outgrown most of its rivals for much of its history. Finally, China today is considered a rival to the US in terms of global hegemony, something that would not have been possible without the Chinese economic miracle that brought four decades of incredibly-high rates of economic growth to that country.

Of course, as this book has outlined, there are many questions surrounding the long-term outlook for the global economy. In fact, there is a growing sense of pessimism concerning the ability of the global economy to continue to generate significant amounts of economic growth over the long-term. In fact, most long-term trends point to a deceleration of the global economy in the years and decades ahead. As we have discussed, such a deceleration has been taking place already for decades in developed economies and most signs point to this deceleration continuing, at least in most developed economies. For emerging markets, the previous decades had been one of rapid growth, at least for those that were able to boost their competitiveness and connect themselves to the wider global economy. For those emerging markets that are competitive internationally and have diversified economies, there is hope that long-term economic growth can continue for some time to come. However, recent history suggests that less-competitive and less-diversified emerging markets will struggle to generate significant economic growth over the longer-term. This is a worrying sign, as a large share of the world's population lives in such emerging markets, a share of the world's population that is set to increase in the future, unlike the populations of most of the world's leading economies.

AN UNCERTAIN FUTURE

Unfortunately, this book has described why there are many dangerous trends that are jeopardizing the world's ability to generate economic growth. For example, this book has detailed how a combination of falling birth rates and opposition to immigration are threatening to undermine the demographic component of economic growth that has proven to be a major factor in the expansion of the world's economy over the past 200 years. In fact, not only is population growth stalling in many of the world's largest economies, but it is also on the verge of declining in some of these places. Worse, as birth rates fall and people live longer, the working-age, or productive-age, populations of many of these key economies are already shrinking, sometimes at a dramatic pace. It is hard to understate the impact that this demographic decline will have upon the global economy, particularly in those parts of the world where this demographic decline is either most pronounced or is not accompanied by an offsetting increase in trade, investment or productivity growth. Nevertheless, given the sentiment around the world towards raising birth rates and increasing immigration inflows, it is also clear that much of the world's population is unaware, or is ignoring, the impact that population growth has on their economy.

At the same time, it is all-too apparent that large shares of the global population are also unaware of the impact the slowing trade and investment growth, or outright declines in trade and investment, are having on their economy. This is evident in the wave of protectionism that has swept over many of the world's largest countries, resulting in a serious blowback against the process of globalization that has been in place since the latter decades of the 20th century. Sure, we have seen such waves of protectionism in the past, and many of them had passed, leading to new surges in trade and investment. However, the most significant waves of protectionism, such as those in China in the 15th century and around the world during the Great Depression, caused massive damage to the economies involved, weakening them significantly, and in China's case, for centuries. Other times, only a massive upheaval, such as the Second World War which followed the Great Depression, brought an end to a particular wave of protectionism.

Finally, we have noted that productivity growth in many of the world's most important economies has trended downwards over the past 40 to 50 years, even as massive technological and process breakthroughs have been made during this period. Given these breakthroughs and the impact on productivity that they were expected to have, this decline in productivity growth was not expected. In fact, productivity was expected to be the leading driver of economic growth in the modern world, but with a few exceptions, this has not been the case. Worse, the fact that this productivity decline has been so long lasting and has continued despite so many positive developments in terms of technology or processes suggests that it will be increasingly difficult to raise productivity rates in the future without even greater technological or process breakthroughs. Given the importance of productivity in generating future economic growth, it is easy to see why so many economists are concerned about productivity's impact on the global economy in a future where demographic decline becomes more entrenched and where resistance to higher levels of trade and investment continues to grow.

Hopefully, this book has conveyed to its readers that fact that we have no choice but to pursue economic and political policies that promote economic growth, albeit in a sustainable manner. We simply have no other choice but to find ways to continue generating economic growth for the well-being of our planet and our species. The fact is, our modern world and all of the systems that we have put in place depend entirely upon a continuation of the long-term economic growth that has been in place for most areas of the world for decades, if not centuries. Without this long-term economic growth, our world and our civilization faces the likely prospect of long-term decline.

We need policies, systems, technologies and processes that put the global economy in a position to continue growing despite the many factors that threaten this growth. We need to increase individual productivity, given the slowdown in population growth and the aging of the world's population that we are witnessing today. In fact, we need to generate higher rates of productivity growth overall if we are going to maintain economic growth later in the 21st century. This will require more investment in research and development and will likely take both top-down and bottom-up support. At the same time, we need sensible policies that help to revive global trade and investment in the face of growing popular opposition to such trade and investment. Demographic growth is not likely to return anytime soon, but we can still control our economic destiny through productivity, trade and investment growth.

It is no exaggeration to say that the future of humanity is at stake. The threat of long-term decline is real and has happened before to societies that assumed that their growth and prosperity would last forever. The Ancient Romans believed that their city and their empire was eternal, but demographic decline and collapses in trade, investment and productivity led to the empire's collapse and brought about hundreds of years of poverty, misery and conflict that are aptly described as the Dark Ages. Many Chinese dynasties experienced such declines as well, with China pulling out of one such decline only in recent decades. Even modern societies such as Argentina and Italy are warnings as to what can happen if a society fails to generate economic growth over a longer period of time. Simply put, long-term decline is in no one's interest.

The history lessons are clear. Economic growth is a necessity if the world wants to live in peace and prosperity. We need to heed these lessons from our past, for the well-being of our planet, and the planet that our children will inherit, is at stake.

INDEX